NEW SUNDAY
AND HOLY DAY
LITURGIES

YEAR A

Flor McCarthy is a Salesian priest who has worked as a catechist in second level schools and has extensive parish experience in Ireland and the USA. His other books include *Funeral Liturgies* and *Wedding Liturgies*.

Patrick Pye, painter, stained glass artist and etcher, whose work is reproduced on pages 9, 35, 65, 101, 151, 161 and 355, is one of Ireland's most distinguished artists, and is widely recognised as the country's foremost religious artist. His paintings include the Stations of the Cross at the Church of the Resurrection, Killarney, a sanctuary panel in St Saviour's Church, Dominick Street, Dublin, and a five-panel cycle at Fossa Church, Killarney. Among the venues where his stained glass can be seen are Glenstal Abbey Church, Murroe, Co. Limerick, the Convent of Mercy, Cookstown, Co. Tyrone, and the oratory at St Patrick's College, Drumcondra, Dublin.

New
Sunday and Holy Day
Liturgies

YEAR A

Flor McCarthy

DOMINICAN PUBLICATIONS

First published (1998) by
Dominican Publications
42 Parnell Square
Dublin 1

ISBN 1-871552-66-4

British Library Cataloguing in Publications Data.
A catalogue record for this book is available
from the British Library.

Cover design by David Cooke

This reprint (2004) by
The Leinster Leader Ltd
Naas
Co. Kildare

Contents

Introduction

Fifteen years have passed since the original *Sunday and Holy Day Liturgies* came out. Much to my surprise they proved very successful. Since then I have done a lot of preaching, reflecting and reading. As a result I have accumulated a lot of new material. The new series gives me the opportunity to share this material with others.

Now there are three homilies for each occasion, and sometimes additional material besides. The vast bulk of this material is new. Wherever old material is retained, I have tried to improve it. In general, the homilies are shorter and more focused than in the original series. And once again I rely heavily on stories.

Every part of a liturgy should speak. For this reason I have put a lot of care into the Introduction to the Mass, the Headings for Readings, the Prayer of the Faithful, and the Reflection. The main thing here is to be brief and to the point. We must guard against turning the Mass into a series of mini-homilies.

Even though I have worked and reworked these homilies, they are not put forward as the complete thing. They are put forward as approximations in the hope that someone else may take them up, develop them, refine them, improve them. In this way they can be kept alive. They are sentenced to death once they are judged definitive.

The book contains one new feature. On most occasions I have added a brief Scripture Note which highlights the theme of the readings or the theological meaning of a particular feast. In compiling these notes I am indebted to the works of two Scripture scholars in particular, Wilfrid Harrington and Raymond Brown.

My thanks to Frs Austin Flannery and Bernard Treacy and to all the staff at Dominican Publications for their help and encouragement. My thanks also to the many people who have assured me how helpful they found the original series.

Flor McCarthy

ADVENT

'The Annunciaiton on the Stair'

PATRICK PYE

First Sunday of Advent
WAKE-UP CALL

INTRODUCTION AND CONFITEOR

Today, as we begin a new liturgical year, the liturgy invites us to come to the house of God, so that God may teach us his ways and help us to walk in his light. As we gather in this house of God, let us reflect on how much we need God's guidance and help. [Pause]

Lord, you teach us your ways. Lord, have mercy.

You give us your light so that we may walk in your paths. Christ, have mercy.

You guide our feet into the way of peace. Lord, have mercy.

HEADINGS FOR READINGS

First Reading (Is 2:1-5). This vision of a world at peace under God challenges Christians to work for this new world which was inaugurated by Christ.

Second Reading (Rom 13:11-14). This contains a wake-up call, and urges us to turn away from the darkness of evil, and to walk in the light of Christ.

Gospel (Mt 24:37-44). This Gospel urges us to stay awake because we do not know the day or the hour when Christ will return.

SCRIPTURE NOTE

The chief function of the season of Advent is to prepare us for Christmas. However, to understand Christmas we have to start at the beginning – with the history of salvation.

God's plan of salvation is centred in Christ and realised through him. Advent looks back at the promise of his first coming, when that plan was announced. And it looks forward to his second coming, when that plan will reach its complete fulfilment. And, of course, it celebrates his actual coming in time.

The First Readings of the Advent Sundays (from Isaiah) are concerned with the Messiah and the messianic times. Isaiah kept the hopes of the people alive in very dark times. In today's reading we have the theme of universal peace and salvation. The Gospel and the Second Reading deal with the Lord's second coming, which the first Christians believed was imminent. Both readings convey a sense of urgency through phrases such as, 'Wake up', 'Stay awake', 'Stand ready'.

HOMILY 1   **A wake-up call**

Today's liturgy addresses a wake-up call to us: 'The time has come, you must wake up now' (Second Reading). St Paul tells us that we must wake up now. But there is more at stake than just being awake. We could be awake and yet be only half alive, because we have no awareness, no understanding, no vision. It may take a shock or at least a jolt of some kind to wake us up.

Each day summons us to awake from sleep. Sometimes we can't wait for the morning to come. We wake up in joyful anticipation. We feel good to be alive. We are thankful to God for the gift of a new day. It is a chance to carry on some task we have started, or to begin something we have been postponing, or to repair some damage or neglect in our lives.

Other times we are apathetic about waking up. We greet the new day without enthusiasm. Life may be monotonous or empty for us. Perhaps we are unemployed or retired, and there is nothing to look forward to.

And most of us know or have known days, hopefully not too many, when we dread the approach of morning. We wake up fearfully, and get up reluctantly. Life is dark and burdensome for us. Perhaps we are old or sickly or alone.

How we greet each morning is very important. If we greet the day with joy and thankfulness, we will bring energy and enthusiasm to its tasks. But if we greet it with apathy or dread, we will face its tasks in a half-hearted manner, which means we are going into the day with a very severe handicapped.

No one has a perfect life. All of us have to face difficulties. It is what we make of these difficulties that matters. Difficulties can be challenges. If we don't like something we should try to change it. If we can't change it, then we should try to change the way we think about it. Complaining won't do us any good. Circumstances are beyond our control but our conduct is in our own power. What makes the difference is how we respond to our particular situation.

Advent issues a spiritual wake-up call to us, and has an awakening power. Unless we are spiritually awake we are only half living. In this respect some people are little better than sleepwalkers. They have eyes but do not see, and ears but do not hear. Their minds are narrow and closed. Their hearts have become hardened. To be awake spiritually means to be open and receptive, vigilant and active.

Spirituality is about waking up. It is about understanding things, seeing things, hearing things. It is necessary to reflect, to have the will, and to be wide awake. Not to while away the time in drowsiness. To be spiritually awake means to be attentive to God and to others. It means to be living in love.

We have two options: we can be a watcher or a sleeper. It is easy to be a sleeper. But sleepers waste their lives. It's harder but very much more rewarding to be a watcher. To watch means to be awake, to be alert, to be concerned, to be active, to be interested, to care. In a word, to be a watcher is to be responsible.

Jesus urges us to stay awake, to be on our guard, to be on the watch. We have nothing to fear and everything to gain from answering Advent's wake-up call.

This is the first Sunday of a new liturgical year. Another year has come and gone. Time is passing. Life is short, so we need to get on with our work. We must seize the day. We shall pass through this world but once. Therefore, any good that we can do, to any human being, let us do it now; let us not defer it or neglect it; for we shall not pass this way again.

HOMILY 2 **The night is over**

The theme of light figures prominently in today's readings. St Paul says to us, 'The night is almost over, it will be daylight soon.' He goes on to urge us to turn away from darkness and to live in the light. And Isaiah urges us to 'walk in the light of the Lord.'

But what in practice does this entail?

One day a wise and learned rabbi turned to his pupils and asked: 'How can you tell when the night is passed and the day is on its way back again?'

'When you see an animal in the distance, and you can tell whether it is a sheep or a goat,' one replied.

'When you see a tree in the distance, and you can tell whether it is a fig tree or a peach tree,' another replied.

'When you can see a person in the distance, and you can tell whether it is a friend or an enemy,' yet another replied.

There was a number of other answers. But the rabbi was not impressed. Then his pupils pleaded with him, 'Tell us what your answer is, rabbi.'

And he replied as follows: 'It is when you can look at the face of any human being, and see there the face of a brother or sister, because if you cannot do this, then no matter what time it is, for you it is still night.'

We are a people on whom the light of Christ has shone and still shines. We must, therefore, strive to walk in the light – the light of truth and life, the light of holiness and grace, the light of justice, love and peace.

Nevertheless, darkness still has power over us. Darkness can take many forms. Any kind of hatred, enmity, lack of forgiveness, lack of reconcilia-tion, injustice done to another, immoral behaviour, drunkenness, addic-tion – all of these are forms of darkness. A little reflection will help each of us to identify what form or forms the darkness takes for us. Let us pause for a moment of reflection. (*Homilist sits down for a while*).

The first thing we have to do is recognise the darkness in our lives. That takes courage. But it takes even more courage to take responsibility for that darkness, and to decide to do something about it. There is no joy in living in darkness. Quite the opposite. But with the grace of Christ we can free ourselves of the darkness. We can walk in the light. To walk in the light means to walk in joy and freedom.

Isaiah says to us: 'Come, let us walk in the light of the Lord.' Advent is a wonderful opportunity to respond to these words.

St Paul tells us that God is near. God is always near, but somehow in Advent God seems to be nearer than usual. To have a sense of God's nearness is a very great blessing.

It would be wonderful if at the end of this Advent I could truthfully say that, with God's help, I had left some form of darkness behind me. That I had allowed the light to shine into some area of my life where hitherto darkness reigned. Then I would be more ready to meet the Lord, the Lord of light, the Lord in whose presence no form of darkness can exist.

HOMILY 3   **Towards the mountain**

Alan Paton was a South African writer. Among the books he wrote was the haunting story, *Cry the Beloved Country,* which so poignantly described the situation in South Africa under apartheid. Paton had a dream. He dreamt of a new day for his beloved South Africa, a day in which there would be justice and equality for all. For this reason he entered politics, and fought to end the iniquitous system of apartheid. For decades he followed his dream, and worked generously and courageously to make it a reality. It was a dream that many said would never be realised. Yet it was. Unfortunately Paton didn't live to see it. He died before the dawn.

The prophet Isaiah had an even bolder dream, a dream of universal peace. He dreamt of a time in which people from all nations would stream to the Lord's mountain (Mount Sion on which the temple was built). People would no longer hurt or harm one another. There would be no more war or preparing for war. People would be filled with the knowledge of the Lord, and would walk in his ways.

Isaiah's vision was a splendid one. Some believed that it would be realised at the first coming of Christ. Others believe that it will be realised only at his second coming. Still others dismiss the dream of the holy mountain as mere day-dreaming. But there are some who believe in it and who pursue it.

There is a story about a hunter who set out to capture a particular bird. Large and dazzlingly white, it was the most beautiful bird on earth. He followed it relentlessly but caught only an occasional and fleeting glimpse of it in the distance. One day he found one of its feathers. He died without ever catching the bird itself.

The hunter's search for the great white bird is a symbol of the human search for peace. Isaiah's dream of universal peace may be unrealistic,

First Sunday of Advent

but it is not mere day-dreaming. This is the mountain towards which we spend our lives travelling in hope. However, we must not sit back and expect it to fall from the sky. We have to work towards it, and believe that we are making progress, however slowly.

Even though it is a vision which, in all probability, will never be realised fully on earth, nevertheless the dreaming of it shapes our lives. The important thing is not to give up the quest or the search. The important thing is the goal. Often that goal is enough.

Humanity today is at a cross-roads. Technology has given us great power and brought material progress. It has enabled us to do practically anything, except to bring people together in love and thus make our world a happier and more peaceful place.

When the cold war ended, the world took a gigantic step towards peace. Even so, wherever we go we see divisions among people, in families, communities, cities, countries. God sent his Son into the world to reconcile people with him and with one another. Each of us can play a part in the breaking down of barriers and in the making of peace.

We can do this by being welcoming towards others, especially outsiders, as well as by seeking reconciliation with anyone with whom we have quarrelled or fallen out. The work of reconciliation begins with a simple gesture. It demands that those who do not normally speak to one another should begin to do so. Practising any kind of apartheid, keeping one's distance, only exacerbates differences.

We can't do it without God. We can only achieve it by walking in the ways of God. God has not left us alone. He sent his Son to inaugurate the new world (the Kingdom of God), and to accompany us on our journey towards the mountain of God, which in the last analysis means eternal life.

ANOTHER STORY

God's wake-up call can come to people in many different ways, and will mean different things to different people. In Mexico, in the diocese of Bishop Samuel Ruiz almost 80% of the population of his diocese is indigenous. The bishop has become known as the 'defender of the Indians'. But it wasn't always like that. In a talk given in Westminster Cathedral in Lent, 1996, Bishop Ruiz said: 'For twenty years I was like a sleeping fish. I had my eyes open but saw nothing. I was just proud to be in a diocese where the churches were crowded. Then one day I saw an Indian tied to a tree and being whipped by his boss, because he had refused to work an extra eight hours.'

That incident opened the bishop's eyes and he began to look. What he saw being done to his people spurred him into action. He got involved in negotiations between the Zapatista rebels and the Mexican government.

One of the phrases we often us is 'it dawned on me'. In this way we recognise that it is not enough to be physically awake. We need to be awake socially, morally and spiritually.

PRAYER OF THE FAITHFUL

President: God is the hope and joy of people in every age. With confidence let us make our needs known to him.

Response: Lord, hear us in your love.

Reader(s): For all Christians: that through the practice of prayer and charity they may be effective witnesses to Christ in the world. [Pause] We pray in faith.

For world leaders: that they may continue the search for a just and peaceful world. [Pause] We pray in faith.

For those who are living in the darkness of evil: that they may see the light. [Pause] We pray in faith.

For those who are living in the darkness of unbelief: that the light of faith may shine on them. [Pause] We pray in faith.

For ourselves: that we may awaken our faith from the sleep of routine and habit. [Pause] We pray in faith.

For our own special needs. [Longer pause] We pray in faith.

President: God of love and mercy, listen to our prayers. May your Son at his coming dispel the darkness of our hearts, and enable us to live as children of the light. We ask this through the same Christ our Lord.

SIGN OF PEACE

The prophet Isaiah said: 'They will hammer their swords into ploughshares, and their spears into sickles. Nation will not lift sword against nation, and there will be no more war or training for war'. Lord, grant that the world may put away the weapons of war, so that all of God's children may enjoy the peace and unity of your kingdom where you live for ever and ever.

PRAYER / REFLECTION   **Encircling prayer**

In today's second reading, we heard St Paul say: 'Let your armour be the Lord.' Hence, we might pray as follows:

Circle me, Lord.
   Keep protection near; keep danger afar.
Circle me, Lord.
   Keep hope within; keep doubt without.
Circle me, Lord.
   Keep light near; keep darkness afar.
Circle me, Lord.

Keep peace within; keep strife without.
Circle me, Lord.
Keep love within; keep hate without. Amen.

Second Sunday of Advent
PREPARING A WAY FOR THE LORD

INTRODUCTION AND CONFITEOR

In today's liturgy we hear again the lonely voice of John the Baptist ex-horting us to prepare a way for the Lord. Let us create a space in our minds and hearts so that the Lord can come to us in this Eucharist. [Pause]

John began his mission with a call to repentance. We begin the Mass with the same call.

Lord Jesus, you came to heal the contrite. Lord, have mercy.

You came to call sinners to repentance. Christ, have mercy.

You plead for us at the right hand of the Father. Lord, have mercy.

HEADINGS FOR READINGS

First Reading (Is 11:1-10). We hear about the coming of the Messiah, and the kind of justice and peace he would bring.

Second Reading (Rom 15:4-9). This talks about the importance of hope, and how we should treat others in the same friendly way Christ has treated us.

Gospel (Mt 3:1-12). We hear once again the voice of John the Baptist, saying to us what he said to his contemporaries: 'Repent, for the King-dom of Heaven is close at hand.'

SCRIPTURE NOTE

Isaiah foretells that even though the family tree of Jesse (David's father) has been reduced to a mere stump, nevertheless from that stump a new shoot will spring – a true king filled with the Spirit and endowed with all the virtues of his ancestors. The new king (the Messiah) will be a cham-pion of the poor and will restore paradisal peace.

Matthew introduces John the Baptist as the herald, foretold by Isaiah, of the long-awaited Messiah, and the one who prepared the people to receive him. Matthew sees Jesus as fulfilling the Old Testament promises.

Paul also sees Jesus as the one through whom God fulfilled his prom-ises, and at the same time the reading from Roman continues the theme of peace and harmony of the First Reading.

HOMILY 1   **Vision of a new world**

The astronauts were the first human beings to see the earth from outside. As they gazed down on the earth from space, they realised as never before that we are one family, with spaceship Earth as our common home. One of them said later: 'The first day in space, we all pointed to our own countries. The second day, we pointed to our continents. By the third day, we were aware of only one Earth.'

The prophets had the same kind of high and wide vision, a vision of how things could be. But how real is that vision? When one reads a history book, or even just the daily newspaper, at times one is ashamed to be human. What is history? Wars, wars, and more wars. So many dead. So many tears. So many fears. The world is drenched in blood. Should not all hope be abandoned?

As for the wolf and the lamb living together, often two neighbours, or even two members of the same family, have a falling out and refuse to talk to one another.

Are not these great visions of peace and harmony among all peoples just an utopian fairy tale? No, they are not. They correspond to the deepest longings of the human heart, and point to God's ultimate goal for us. These visions nurture our souls and our hearts. They offer us hope when we are close to despair, and courage when we are tempted to give up on life. These visions fuel our deepest aspirations, and give us the energy to overcome great obstacles and painful setbacks.

The prophets lived in the real world, and were just as dismayed by its horrors and injustices as we are. Yet they had a dream of a new world, a world free from injustice and war. Through faith in God they were able to rise above their dismay. What saved them from despair was their messianic vision and their sense of our capacity for repentance. History is not a blind alley. There is always a way out – through repentance, through turning to God.

The marvellous vision of the peaceable Kingdom, in which all violence has been overcome and all people live in loving unity with nature, calls for its realisation in our daily lives. Instead of being an escapist dream, it challenges us to anticipate what it promises. Every time we forgive a neighbour, every time we make a child smile, every time we show compassion to a suffering person, take care of animals, prevent pollution, and work for peace and justice among peoples and nations, we are making the vision come true.

We need to keep the vision before us. Then it will give us new energy to live it out, right where we are. Instead of encouraging us to escape from real life, this beautiful vision summons us to get involved.

We must open our hearts to the dream which the prophets cherished of a world rid of evil by human effort and the grace of God. Jesus had a word for the new world. He called it 'The Kingdom of God.' He inaugurated that Kingdom. He wants his followers to dedicate themselves to the building of that kingdom.

Ordinary people help to spread that Kingdom by being kind, truthful, honest, just, and so on. Even though it is a struggle that we will never win completely, the struggle is good for us. It awakens everything that is best and precious within us.

Isaiah's vision lives on in our midst as a task for today and a promise for tomorrow.

HOMILY 2   **God's promises**

The Advent readings glitter with bright promises – promises of the wonderful things that would accompany the coming of the Messiah. Mountains would be levelled out, valleys filled in, winding roads made straight, the desert would bloom, the poor would see justice done, the weak would no longer be exploited, war would be banished from the face of the earth.

Christ has come, yet little seems to have changed. So we might well ask: What has become of the great promises? Were they mere mirages? Look at the state of the world. Famine still plagues humankind, the poor are still exploited, and world-wide peace is still an elusive dream.

The Bible shows us that God's people are led forward by promises. Promises play a big part in our lives. When you want a child to behave or to do something, you promise the child something. The child is motivated to work or to behave. In adult life promises are still very important. Married people promise lasting fidelity to one another. They build their lives on that promise.

A promise gives people hope. It gives them a goal to aim at. It motivates and energises them. It makes them struggle for something. This is a good thing. People who have no goal are aimless. It is when people are satisfied that they stagnate. The settled, satisfied person fails to develop further.

The central theme of Advent is that of the faithfulness of God. In spite of the infidelities of his people, God did not forget the covenant he made with their father, Abraham. The Advent liturgy makes us aware of God's faithful love for us, and the wonderful gift he has made to us in Jesus.

The wonderful promises of the prophets are not just promises. They are judgements too. Hence, Advent is not so much about the past as about the present. It awakens us to the presence among us of the Saviour. It reveals his true identity and the nature of his mission, which is to establish the Kingdom of God on earth. We have a vital part to play in making this Kingdom a reality. Advent provides us with a great opportunity to commit ourselves anew to Jesus and his Kingdom.

The new world (the Kingdom of God) was established first of all in

Christ himself. He is the new creation. Here we have humanity restored to the true image of God. Then, through his words and deeds, Christ inaugurated the Kingdom in the world. Through his Church he continues this work. Christians must not sit around waiting for these promises to fall from the sky. They are a blueprint of what humankind could achieve by the grace of God, given so lavishly in Christ.

The world is crying out for salvation. Christians must not be afraid to speak out fearlessly against things such as the arms race and the hoarding of surplus food. Isaiah's vision lives on in our midst as a task for today and a promise for tomorrow.

HOMILY 3   **A place called hope**

One of the images Isaiah uses to describe the messianic age is that of a lamb lying down with a wolf and having nothing to fear. It is a picture of a time of universal peace – the strong would no longer prey on the weak, or the cunning on the innocent.

Advent, with its wonderful promises of a new world, takes us on a trip to a place called hope. If things and people were perfect, hope would not be needed. Hope is required precisely because we live in an imperfect world. We invest our hopes in flawed politicians. So why not in God?

Hope it a vital part of life. We spend a great deal of our lives longing, waiting, hoping for one thing or another. It is impossible to live when one is completely without hope. Hope is as important for our spirit as bread is for our body.

Hope doesn't mean sitting back waiting for things to happen. Hope spurs us into action. It is precisely because we have hope that we work so hard. We believe our efforts are worthwhile, and that they do make a difference. Our strength, our commitment, depends to a great extent on the degree and quality of our hope.

> I am neither an optimist nor a pessimist. I just carry hope in my heart. Hope is not a feeling of certainty that everything ends well. Hope is just a feeling that life and work have a meaning. (Vaclav Havel)

Cynicism is the enemy of hope. Many refuse to accept hope into their hearts. They say: 'Things will never change. It's no good.'

Cynicism comes easy. It requires nothing from us – no trust, no effort, no love.

Hope is not the same thing as optimism. In fact, hope and optimism are radically different. Optimism is the expectation that things will get better, whatever the situation. Hope is the trust that God will fulfil his promises in his way and in his time. The person of hope lives in the present moment, with the knowledge and trust that all of life is in God's hands.

Hope springs from faith that God will fulfil the promises he has made to us. He has given us his word in Jesus. That word is the basis on which our hope rests. And that hope is an anchor of our lives.

All great leaders were people of hope. They felt no need to know what the future would look like. They just tried to do what was right in the present, and trusted that God would take care of the future. It was enough for them to know that God is a faithful God.

What the world needs is new people. Hence, the relevance for us of John's call to repentance. To repent means to change our understanding of what is important in life, and to change our lives accordingly. Changed people will bring about a changed world.

But what in practice can we do? St Paul brings it down to everyday realities. He says, 'Treat each other in the same friendly ways that Christ has treated you.' That would make a difference. It's easy to be critical, to be over-hasty in making judgements, to be intolerant of the faults of others. If we did as Paul suggests we would make the world, or at least the corner of it that we inhabit, a more hopeful place.

It is the task of Christians to keep hope alive, and to set an example. However, we must not depend on results, but only on the rightness and truth of the work itself. We thank God for his blessings in the past, and ask his help for what we must yet achieve.

When all is said and done, this world will never fulfil our deepest hopes. Only God can do that. Meanwhile, we live in a place called hope. This hope enables us to keep one foot in the world as it is, and the other in the world as it should be.

PRAYER OF THE FAITHFUL

President: Let us pray for the coming of a new age of justice and peace for all peoples.

Reader(s): For the followers of Christ: that they may be effective witnesses to the values of the Gospel. [Pause] Lord, hear us.

For world leaders: that through goodwill and co-operation they may strive to put an end to war and oppression. [Pause] Lord, hear us.

For those who are finding life burdensome: that God may be their strength and their hope. [Pause] Lord, hear us.

For the members of this community: that we may be steadfast in faith, joyful in hope, and untiring in love. [Pause] Lord, hear us.

For our own special needs. [Longer pause] Lord, hear us.

President: Heavenly Father, clear a pathway in our hearts and in our world so that your Son can come to us, and the Good News may be heard by everyone. We ask this through the same Christ our Lord.

SIGN OF PEACE

Isaiah said: 'In those days, the wolf will live with the lamb, calf and lion cub will feed together. They will do no hurt, no harm, on all my holy mountain, for the country will be filled with the knowledge of the Lord.' Lord, look not on our sins but on the faith of your Church, and grant that all of God's children may enjoy the peace and unity of your kingdom where you live for ever and ever.

REFLECTION   **The bird of hope**

Hope is the thing with feathers
That perches in the soul,
And sings the tune without the words,
And never stops at all.
And sweetest in the gale is heard;
And sore must be the storm
That could abash the little bird
That kept so many warm.
I've heard it in the chillest land,
And on the strangest sea;
Yet, never, in extremity,
It asked a crumb of me. (*Emily Dickinson*)

Third Sunday of Advent

INTRODUCTION AND CONFITEOR

In today's Gospel we see Jesus at work: enabling the blind to see, the deaf to hear, the lame to walk. It is a marvellous display of compassion for suffering humanity. In this Eucharist we encounter the same compassionate Jesus. Let us not be afraid to let him see our wounds and handicaps. [Pause]

Lord, you open our eyes to see the signs of your presence in the world. Lord, have mercy.

You open our ears to hear your word. Christ, have mercy.

You open our hearts to show compassion towards those who suffer. Lord, have mercy.

HEADINGS FOR READINGS

First Reading (Is 35:1-6.10). God is the hope of his people who are crushed by misfortune.

Second Reading (Jam 5:7-10). St James urges us to be patient with one another, and patient regarding the Lord's final coming.

Gospel (Mt 11:2-11). We see Jesus at work, and hear his words of praise for his imprisoned cousin, John.

SCRIPTURE NOTE

Isaiah uses the image of the desert, made fertile by rain, to portray the confident hope that God would restore his people, crushed by misfortune. Their most crippling disabilities – blindness, deafness and lameness – will be relieved when God sends salvation to his people.

John the Baptist's image of the Messiah was that of a stern judge who would execute a fiery judgement. But Jesus did not fit this image. Hence, John's doubts about him. Jesus dispelled John's doubts by showing that he was doing precisely the kind of things that had been predicted for the messianic times (by prophets such as Isaiah). Once again, Matthew sees Jesus as the one who fulfils the messianic prophecies.

James is talking about the Second Coming of Jesus. He urges the kind of patience and hope farmers show in waiting for the harvest, and which the prophets of old showed as they waited for the promises to be fulfilled.

HOMILY 1   **Not losing faith**

All three readings of today's Mass have comforting words. In the first reading Isaiah says: 'Courage, do not be afraid.' In the second reading St James says: 'Be patient! Do not lose heart.' And in the Gospel we have the lovely words of Jesus to his cousin, John: 'Happy the person who does not lose faith in me.'

John's situation was a grim one. He was locked up in a dark dungeon with the threat of death hanging over him. His faith was being severely tested. He needed reassurance and comforting. No doubt Jesus' words were a source of comfort and strength to John.

The comforting words of today's readings are addressed to us now. And we need to drink them in, because at times we too can find ourselves in dark situations.

We might be going along nicely but then a storm suddenly hits us: unemployment, a serious illness, a suicide in the family ... These kinds of things shatter our faith in the right order of things and even in God. At times like these may we hear the words of Isaiah: 'Courage! Do not be afraid.'

John the Baptist was a holy, God-fearing man, yet he ended up in a dungeon under sentence of death. We can do our best, but things may still go wrong. We feel let down by God. We doubt his love for us and perhaps even his existence. At times like these may we hear the words of Jesus: 'Blessed is the person who does not lose faith in me.'

Modern life is becomingly increasingly stressful. Christmas brings added work and more stress. Some people can feel overwhelmed, and wonder if they will be able to cope. In times like these may we hear the words of Isaiah: 'Courage! Do not be afraid.'

Death constitutes the severest test of all for our faith. We live our lives in the shadow of death. That all of us, but especially those who have recently lost a loved one, and who stand in darkness and in the shadow of death, may hear the words of Jesus: 'Blessed is the person who does not lose faith in me.'

We all want a lasting peace in the world. Some people are working to bring that peace about. These have every reason to grow weary and give up, because of the apparent lack of progress. May the peacemakers hear the words of St James: 'Be patient! Do not lose heart.'

At times we are bewildered by some of the things that are happening in our world: tragedies, wars, famines, genocide ... We feel numbed and powerless, and we wonder where God is, and why he doesn't intervene. In the midst of our bewilderment may we hear the words of Jesus: 'Blessed is the person who does not lose faith in me.'

Some parents have seen their children give up the practice of the faith, in spite of having given them encouragement and good example. For them it's a great pain, and a great sadness. May these parents hear the words of St James: 'Be patient! Do not lose heart.'

Members of our Church have been scandalised and deeply hurt by the revelation of the grave sins committed by some members of the clergy against the little ones. Their faith has taken a severe knock. May they hear the words of Jesus: 'Blessed is the person who does not lose faith in me.'

Alcoholism is a terrible affliction. So too is drug addiction. They cause misery to the sufferer and to those who have to live with him or her. The alcoholic and the addict have to seek help. It takes courage to admit one's need and to ask for help. May such people hear the words of Isaiah: 'Courage! Do not be afraid.'

Thousands of men and women, many of them young and poor, are locked up in our jails. Many of them have very little hope for their futures, either on this earth or in the next life. May all prisoners hear the words of Jesus: 'Blessed is the person who does not lose faith in me.'

Each of us knows the kind of situations that cause us to be fearful and doubtful. We can't stop ourselves from feeling afraid. But we must not allow our fears to cripple us. Courage is not never feeling afraid; it is feeling afraid and going on in spite of it.

Faith is a fragile thing. We mustn't be surprised when doubts arise within us. God will understand our doubts in a world like this. But blessed are we if we do not lose faith in Jesus. And twice blessed are we if, like Jesus, we are able to show forth our faith in deeds of love and mercy.

HOMILY 2   **Are you the one?**

John had prepared the people for the coming of the Messiah. He believed that Jesus was that Messiah. But now, locked up in a dark dungeon with the threat of death hanging over him, it seems that he began to have doubts about Jesus.

John's idea of the Messiah was that of a stern, uncompromising judge who would execute a fiery judgement. But Jesus wasn't living up to that image. Instead of acting like a judge, he was acting like a saviour. His radiant friendliness contrasted sharply with the severity of John. John was an ascetic, who lived apart from the people. But Jesus mixed with the people, eating and drinking with sinners. John prophesied the judgement of God; Jesus prophesied the salvation of God.

Knowing that his life was ending, John wanted to know for sure, so he sent two of his disciples to question Jesus. When the two asked Jesus, 'Are you the one who is to come?' Jesus might have replied with a straight-forward, 'Yes, I am.' But he didn't.

There is a well-known saying: Actions speak louder than words. So, instead of trying to convince John's messengers with words, Jesus pointed to the works he was doing. Those works were exactly the kind Isaiah had predicted for the messianic times (see First Reading). He was quite happy to let his deeds speak for him. And they spoke eloquently.

Yes, Jesus was 'the one who was to come'. But where can people find him today?

Once a group of salesmen were attending a sales convention. They had assured their families that they would be home in time for dinner. But the meeting ran overtime so they had to run for the train. Tickets in hand, they dashed along the platform. One of them knocked over a table supporting a basket of apples. But neither he nor any of his companions stopped to help the young boy who staffed the apple stand.

All reached the train and boarded it with a sigh of relief. But then one of them felt a twinge of compassion for the boy whose apple stand had been overturned. He immediately decided to do something about it. Say-ing good-bye to his companions, he returned to the scene of the accident. He was glad he did so. The discovered that the boy was blind.

The salesman began to gather up the apples. As he did so he noticed that some of them were bruised. He took out his wallet and handing the boy some money he said, 'Here, take this for the damage we did. I hope we didn't spoil your day.' As he started to walk away, the bewildered boy called after him, 'Are you Jesus?'

Are you Jesus? In a sense, he was. Because he acted like Jesus. So where is Jesus to be found today? In his disciples. Blessed are we if we do not lose faith in Jesus. And twice blessed are we if, like Jesus, we are able to show forth our faith in deeds of love and mercy. People will encounter Jesus in us.

HOMILY 3 **Dying in darkness**

The great astronomer, Galileo, was born near Florence, in the year 1564. He confirmed what Copernicus had said, namely, that it is the earth that goes round the sun, and not *vice versa*. His discoveries greatly enlarged our knowledge of the universe. Yet he spent his last years in darkness. When summoned before the Inquisition he wrote:

> Alas, poor Galileo, your devoted servant, has been for a month totally and incurably blind; so that this heaven, this earth, this universe, which by my observations and demonstrations, I have enlarged a thousand fold beyond their previous limits, are now shrivelled for me into such a narrow compass as is filled by my own bodily sensations.

Galileo reminds us of John the Baptist. Like Galileo, John the Baptist ushered in a new age – the age of Jesus. And like Galileo he died in darkness.

John was the last and greatest of the long line of prophets who prepared the people for the coming of the Messiah. He was one of those selfless and courageous people who kept alive the hopes of the people during the long night of expectation, when it seemed that the dawn would never come.

And Jesus paid a great tribute to him. He said that John was no reed swaying in the wind. In other words, he wasn't easily influenced by prevailing trends and opinions. He was his own man – a strong personality and a man of principle.

John didn't go in for a life of comfort and ease. No fancy clothes for him. He lived not in a palace but in the desert – a place of sand, thorn bushes, heat, cold, hunger, thirst, and loneliness.

He devoted himself totally to the mission God gave him, which was to prepare the way for Jesus. When his task was done, he moved aside to make way for Jesus. That took greatness.

He was a true prophet (spokesperson for God). His lifestyle, as well as his personal integrity, lent credence to his words. He was a living example of what he preached. No wonder people flocked to see and hear him.

Yet Jesus pointed out that, great as John was, he missed out on the greatest thing of all. He did not see the coming of the Kingdom of God. And now, instead of the bright, wide-open spaces of the desert, he found himself in a dark, narrow dungeon, awaiting death.

There, he was troubled by doubts. He wondered if Jesus really was the one who was to come. So he dispatched two of his disciples to find out. The truth of his life depended on a positive answer. A negative answer would mean he had wasted his time, and his life would lose all its meaning.

The answer came back: 'Tell John that the blind see, the lame walk … ' In other words, look at the evidence, and draw the conclusion for yourself. The news must have been a great comfort to John. He could now face death. His life had not been in vain. But knowing of his bleak situation, Jesus sent him a personal message: 'Blessed is the man who does not lose faith in me.'

We all have our own struggles. Life can become very dark at times. We do our best but things turn out badly. Hence, we all have our doubts. This is why we too need to hear the comforting words Jesus spoke to John: 'Blessed is the person who does not lose faith in me.'

We should draw inspiration from John, who is a wonderful example of unselfish love. But it is in Jesus that our hope lies. He is the one who gives meaning to all our work and suffering, to our living and dying. He alone can fulfil our deepest longings.

Blessed are we if we do not lose faith in Jesus. And twice blessed are we if we show forth our faith in deeds of love and mercy.

PRAYER OF THE FAITHFUL

President: With confidence, let us pray to the Lord who keeps faith for ever.

Response: Lord, hear our prayer.

Reader(s): For the Pope, the bishops, and all who minister in the Church: that they may give an example of selfless and joyful service. [Pause] Let us pray to the Lord.

For those who hold public office: that God may enlighten their minds and guide their hearts. [Pause] Let us pray to the Lord.

For those who are working for the relief of suffering in others: that they may know comfort themselves. [Pause] Let us pray to the Lord.

For prisoners: that they may not lose hope. [Pause] Let us pray to the Lord.

For this community: that God may strengthen our faith in the midst of uncertainty and doubt. [Pause] Let us pray to the Lord.

For our own particular needs we pray in the presence of God. [Longer pause] Let us pray to the Lord.

President: God of mercy, take pity on our weakness. May the coming of your Son confirm our faith, strengthen our hope, and deepen our love. We ask this through Christ our Lord.

REFLECTION   **A reed in the wind**

John the Baptist was no reed swaying in the wind.
A reed swaying in the wind is a symbol
of those who are easily influenced,
who go along with whatever is popular,
and who have no convictions of their own.
But the humble reed can teach us something.
The fact that it is light means that it is
at the mercy of every wind that blows.
But it has great strength too.
The greatest storm cannot uproot it.
Even when giant oaks come crashing down,
the slender reed still stands secure.
Lord, teach us that there is strength
in weakness and suppleness,
and give us the wisdom to know
when to bend and when to stand firm.

Fourth Sunday of Advent
PREPARING FOR CHRISTMAS

INTRODUCTION AND CONFITEOR

As we approach Christmas, the pace of things speeds up, so that the spiritual side tends to get lost. Let us pause to make room in our minds and hearts so that Christ may come to us during this Eucharist. [Pause]

Lord Jesus, you come into our darkness. Lord, have mercy.
Lord Jesus, you come into our doubting. Christ, have mercy.
Lord Jesus, you come into our fears. Lord, have mercy.

HEADINGS FOR READINGS

First Reading (Is 7:10-14). This reading foretells the birth of a very special child – a child who will be called Emmanuel, that is, God-with-us.

Second Reading (Rom 1:1-7). These opening lines from Paul's letter to the Romans draw attention to the human and divine 'roots' of Jesus.

Gospel (Mt 1:18-25). This shows how the prophecy of Isaiah was fulfilled in Jesus.

SCRIPTURE NOTE

All three readings deal with the identity of 'the One who was to come'.

The identity of the child was vaguely glimpsed in the Old Testament. Isaiah talked about the coming of a very special child (First Reading). But there is no reason to believe that he knew just how special that child would be. No prophecy is fully understood until after its fulfilment.

Matthew shows that Isaiah's prophecy was fulfilled in Jesus, and in a far greater way that the prophet could ever have imagined. The New Testament reveals the true identity of this special Child (Jesus). The Second Reading and the Gospel make it clear that Jesus was the Son of David. This was so because Joseph, his legal father, was descended from the line of David. But he is more than that. He is also the Son of God.

HOMILY 1   **Debating Christmas**

What follows is a debate among Christians, some of whom think that the modern Christmas has nothing to do with the birth of Christ and should therefore be abandoned, and others who are of the opposite persuasion. The purpose of the exercise is to stimulate thought and discussion. (Two voices should be used.)

Against   Let's face it, Christmas is nothing but a big spending spree – for those who can afford it, that is. Think of the gifts, decorations, food, drink, and so on, that we are forced to buy. It's all a money racket. The only people to benefit are the traders who laugh all the way to the bank.

For   No one forces us to buy anything. In any case, most of the things people buy are given to others. However, having said that, I agree that things have got somewhat out of hand. This aspect of Christmas is disturbing to all those who cherish its real meaning. But abuses are inevitable. If you open the window to let in fresh air, the flies will come in too.

Against   Christmas encourages excessive eating. As for drinking – some people wouldn't think it was Christmas if they were still steady on their feet at the end of the day.

For   Christmas is not an excuse for getting drunk. But neither is it a time for long faces. Christmas is a time for joy and celebration. The song of the angels, 'Glory to God in the highest, and peace to his people on earth', is the sweetest music ever heard on earth.

Against   But Christmas brings out the worst in people. More people are killed on our roads at this time than at any other. And it encourages selfishness in our children. We spoil them by buying them all kinds of expensive toys which they neither need nor appreciate.

For   I don't agree that it brings out the worst in people. I think that, by and large, it brings out the best in people. It encourages generosity. It touches our hearts. We feel drawn to think of the needs of the poor and the lonely.

As regards children, the birth of the Christ-Child makes us realise that all children are precious, and come to us as gifts from God. Hence, it is only right that we should fuss over them at Christmas. Besides, they are only young once.

Against You mentioned the poor and the lonely. The fact is that these are little better than onlookers at the feast. Yet the approach of Christmas raises false hopes among them. They look forward to it with heightened excitement, as if expecting something extraordinary to happen. But when it's all over, they feel poorer and lonelier than ever.

For I don't agree that the poor and the lonely are left out of it. More is done for them at this time than during all the rest of the year. As regards expectations, those who pin their hopes on the worldly side of Christmas will always be disappointed. But those who pin their hopes on the spiritual side of it will never be disappointed.

Against Christmas is supposed to be a time of peace and goodwill. But it doesn't really break down any barriers between us and other people, because we share our goodwill only with our friends. Enemies are never guests at the Christmas banquet.

And even where our friends and neighbours are concerned, the picture isn't much better. Oh yes, on Christmas morning we reach out our hand to them, but we quickly dash back into our shells. Alas, Christmas goodwill is like a flower that blooms and dies the same day.

For Christmas causes an outpouring of goodwill. No one can deny that. And barriers do fall down. A lot of togetherness results. Neighbours reach across fences to greet one another. People we have forgotten during the rest of the year are fondly remembered. Scattered families are reunited.

Even if it doesn't last as long as it might, at least it shows us the way we ought to go. Surely it's better to get a glimpse of the light than to live in perpetual darkness?

Against I believe that it does a disservice to our religion. It lets loose a tidal wave of materialism. The spiritual hasn't a chance. Some people make a brave effort. But to little avail. It's like trying to swim against a powerful tide.

For I don't agree that it is devoid of religious meaning. I think it acts as a spiritual tonic to many people. The churches are overflowing. Many prodigals come back to God at this time. It still prepares a way for the Lord to come to us.

Against Far from preparing a way for the Lord, all it does is prepare a way for the vultures of commercialism. What I find most objectionable is the mingling of God and Mammon, something which Christ utterly condemned.

    For I know that commercialism is rampant at this time. But this shouldn't surprise us. If you light a fire you must expect smoke to rise up. That smoke will catch in your throat and bring tears to your eyes. But you willingly put up with these discomforts because a fire has been lit.

        Since the coming of Christ a bright fire has been burning on our earth. At this fire we experience the warmth of God's love, and the glow of human fellowship. We shouldn't be afraid to come in from the cold and warm ourselves at this fire.

Against I still say that Christmas has become a pagan feast. The headlines are dominated, not by the birth of Christ, but by threatened strikes, the price of turkeys, and the coming glut of television shows. Christ hardly gets a look in. Yet to celebrate Christmas without Christ is like celebrating a wedding without the bride and groom.

    For You say there is no room for Christ in our Christmas. But there was no room for him either the first time he came. The inn-keeper refused to take him in. But he still came to those who were waiting for him.

        So, even if our world has little room for him, he still comes. He comes to all those who, like Mary, Joseph, and the shepherds, are ready to welcome him. He will come to us too. All we have to do is make room for him in the manger of our hearts.

Against Christmas is one mad, frantic rush, which leaves people exhausted and frustrated. It's such a terrible waste of time, effort, and money. It's a poor shop window for our religion. In my opinion the shop should be closed down. It's an embarrassment to true followers of Christ. Christ would have nothing to do with it. Neither should we.

    For When all is said and done, Christmas recalls the greatest event in history, namely, the Incarnation, when God's Son came down on earth to confer on us the dignity of children of God.

The world today is in danger of drowning in bad news. It is crying out for good news. Let us not then deprive it of the good news brought by the angels to the shepherds: 'Behold I bring you good news of a great joy for all the people. This day a Saviour is born to you. He is Christ the Lord.'

HOMILY 2   **Double identity.**

The prophet Isaiah talked about the coming of a very special child (First Reading). But there is no reason to believe that he knew just how special that child would be. Every king of David's line was an embodiment of God's promise to be 'with us'. But Christians believe that Isaiah's prophecy only found its complete fulfilment in Jesus. The Second Reading and the Gospel reveal to us the true identity, in fact, the double identity, of this special Child (Jesus). No prophecy is fully understood until after its fulfilment.

Both St Paul and St Matthew make it clear that, in the first place, Jesus was the Son of David. This was so because Joseph, his legal father, was descended from the line of David. David is one of the greatest figures in the Old Testament. He succeeded Saul as King of Israel. It was he who united the scattered tribes and formed them into a nation. Even though he sinned, he repented. Many times in the Gospel Jesus is referred to as 'Son of David'.

To say that Jesus came from the line of David was already a great thing. But he is more than that. He has another, and infinitely greater, identity. He is 'Emmanuel', which means 'God is with us.' He is not just the Son of David but also the Son of God. Hence he is able to save his people from their sins.

The second identity of Jesus was something which was only gradually revealed and gradually understood. In fact, it was only after he had been raised from the dead that he was accepted as 'the Lord' (see Second Reading). He himself said this identity could not be recognised unless it was revealed by the Father. It is a matter of faith, which is a gift of God.

We believe then in the double identity of Jesus. He is Son of David and Son of God. But we too have a double identity. As children of our parents we are human beings, which means we have a human dignity. That in itself is a great thing. But through Jesus we have become children of God, which means we also have a divine dignity. However, our divine dignity, like that of Jesus, is a matter of faith.

Christmas is a wonderful time. It recalls the greatest event in history, namely, the Incarnation, when God's Son came down on earth to confer on us the dignity of children of God. It's not true that Christmas is just about children. It's about us all. We may consider ourselves very ordinary. But nobody is ordinary any longer, not since Christ came on earth.

The world today is in danger of drowning in bad news. It is crying out for good news. But the best news of all is the news brought by the angels to the shepherds: 'Behold I bring you good news of a great joy for all the people. This day a Saviour is born to you. He is Christ the Lord.'

Let us open our hearts to receive the good news.

HOMILY 3   **Fear at Christmas**

There are people who fear, maybe even dread, the approach of Christmas. It's not Christmas itself that causes this fear – I mean the religious side of it. The source of this fear lies elsewhere.

For some it's the hassle and the extra work that makes them fearful. For others it's the strain put on their already overstretched finances by the Christmas splurge. For others it's fear of the conflicts that sometimes occur in families at Christmas time. And for others it is the fact that Christmas reawakens painful memories – the memory of a death or a tragedy that occurred around this time.

Also where there has been a loss during the year, that loss is felt again, intensely, at Christmas. The sight of others surrounded by loved ones re-opens a wound that perhaps was beginning to heal. The result is an intense loneliness. Finally, one's fears may result from advancing age, with the infirmities and sense of mortality this brings with it.

But those who fear the approach of Christmas can take heart and hope from the story of the first Christmas. There was plenty of fear present in it too. In fact, all of the main characters in it were afraid at one time or another.

Joseph was afraid when he found that Mary was expecting a child even though they hadn't yet lived together. But an angel appeared to him in a dream and said to him, 'Joseph, do not be afraid to take Mary home as your wife, because she has conceived what is in her by the Holy Spirit' – words we hear in today's Gospel. Joseph, the just man, trusted God, and so overcame his fear and did what was right.

Mary was afraid on hearing the greeting of the angel Gabriel. But the angel said to her, 'Mary, do not be afraid; you have won God's favour.' The angel went on to tell her that she was to conceive and bear a son by the power of the Holy Spirit, and she must name him Jesus. Mary trusted God, and so overcame her fear and said 'Yes' to what he was asking of her.

And the shepherds were afraid. The Gospel says that when the angel of the Lord appeared to them, and the glory of the Lord shone around them, they were terrified. But the angel said, 'Do not be afraid. Listen, I bring you news of a great joy ... Today a saviour has been born to you; he is Christ the Lord.' And they trusted God, went to Bethlehem, saw the Child, and returned to their flocks glorifying and praising God.

All of us are touched by fear. But we must not allow our fears to cripple us. What we have to do is move from fear to faith. Trust is the thing that enables us to turn fear into faith. And here is where Christmas can be a great help. Somehow it's easier to trust in God at Christmas than at any other time, because we feel that God is very close to us and very loving towards us at this time. In Jesus, God comes to us in the form of a child.

[32]

And surely no one can be afraid of a child?

Christmas challenges us to enter into an intimate relationship with God, trusting that we will receive love, and always more love.

By all means, let us do whatever we can to improve our situation. But having done that, let us leave what is outside our control in the hands of God. We must take courage. Fear can be an opportunity, even a grace. It can force us to trust in God rather than in ourselves.

Loneliness too can be a grace. So, if we should feel lonely at Christmas, let us not be alarmed. Our hearts are always longing for something more, or rather, for Someone else. In every human heart there is an empty chamber waiting for a guest. That guest is God.

Christmas awakens our deepest longings, longings which only God can fulfil. We must not allow our fears to prevent us from opening our hearts to the 'great joy' announced to the shepherds by the angel.

PRAYER OF THE FAITHFUL

President: Let us pray that the whole world may be flooded with the grace of the Lord's coming.

Response: Come, Lord Jesus.

Reader(s): For all Christians: that they may celebrate the birth of Christ with the faith and joy of Mary, Joseph, and the shepherds. [Pause] Let us pray to the Lord.

For all temporal leaders: that in their administration of justice they may ensure that the poor and vulnerable members of society are not left out. [Pause] Let us pray to the Lord.

For those for whom Christmas may be a time of loneliness and sadness: that they may experience the warmth of Christ's presence. [Pause] Let us pray to the Lord.

For husbands and wives: that they may find comfort in time of sorrow, strength in time of trial, and be blessed with an enduring love for one another. [Pause] Let us pray to the Lord.

For all those who are travelling this Christmas: that they may reach their destinations safely. [Pause] Let us pray to the Lord.

For our own special needs and hopes for this Christmas. [Longer pause] Let us pray to the Lord.

President: O God, Father of every family, against whom no door can be shut, convert our hearts and our homes into fit dwelling places for Christ your Son. We ask this through the same Christ our Lord.

REFLECTION   **Christmas expectations**

As Christmas approaches, people's hopes soar.

However, the substance of these hopes

is often dictated by commercial interests.
Little wonder, then, that when
the sun goes down on Christmas Day,
many feel disappointed.
Those who pin their hopes on what the merchants promise
will always be disappointed,
not because they promise too little,
but too much – of the wrong thing.
What our hearts long for is a taste of what
the angels announced to the shepherds:
'Behold, I bring news of a great joy;
today a saviour has been born to you.'
This joy is the real hope of Christmas.
Let us open our hearts to receive it.

CHRISTMASTIDE

'Adoration of the Child Jesus'

PATRICK PYE

Christmas

'Behold, I bring you news of great joy. This day a saviour has been born to you; he is Christ the Lord' – the message given by the angels to the shepherds. Tonight (today), through the voice of the Church, this marvellous message is announced to us too. Let us open our minds and hearts to receive the 'great joy'. [Pause]

Christ is the 'great joy'. We receive the great joy when we receive him.

Lord Jesus, you reveal to us the mystery of the God's unconditional love for us. Lord, have mercy.

Lord Jesus, you reveal to us the mystery of our dignity as children of God. Christ, have mercy.

Lord Jesus, you reveal to us the splendour of our eternal destiny. Lord, have mercy.

HEADINGS FOR READINGS

Midnight Mass

First Reading (Is 9:1-7). This prophecy, about the coming of a Saviour-child who will rescue his people from oppression, is fulfilled in Jesus.

Second Reading (Tit 2:11- 14). St Paul reminds us of what is expected of us if we are to enjoy the salvation won for us by Christ.

Gospel (Lk 2:1-14). This tells about the birth of Jesus, and how the news of his birth was brought by angels to shepherds.

Dawn Mass

First Reading (Is 62:11-12). The joy of the exiles returning from Babylon is a foretaste of the joy Christians experience at the birth of Jesus.

Second Reading (Tit 3:4-7)). We did nothing to merit the birth of Jesus; rather, God sent his Son out of compassion for us.

Gospel (Lk 2:15-20). With Mary we are invited to ponder on the deeper meaning of the birth of Jesus so that, with the shepherds, we may be moved to glorify and praise God.

Day Mass

First Reading (Is 52:7-10). This great hymn of exultation at the return of the exiles from Babylon is also a poem of joy for our redemption.

Second Reading (Heb 1:1-6). The whole history of God's dealings with his people in the past was a preparation for the coming of his Son at a particular moment in history.

Gospel (Jn 1:1-18). This is a great hymn to the Word of God, the source of all life, whose coming among us makes us children of God.

SCRIPTURE NOTE

There is a tendency for preachers to go on about the absence of Christ in Christmas, and about how pagan Christmas has become – as if the first Christmas was ideal. We forget that Jesus came into a pagan world. Far better to stress the presence of Christ in Christmas, and help people to find him.

HOMILY 1   **The Incarnation**

Christmas is all about the Incarnation. The Incarnation means that God's Son came down on earth, took on our human nature in order to confer on us the dignity of children of God. The mystery of the Incarnation is a mystery of love. It constitutes the very heart of the Christian faith. No wonder Christmas is such an important feast.

There is a story about a good and upright man who had a problem with the Incarnation. He couldn't believe that God's Son became one of us, and was too honest to pretend. So on Christmas Eve, when his wife and children went to church, he stayed at home.

Shortly after his family left, it began to snow. He went to the window to watch it fall. 'If we must have Christmas,' he thought, 'then let it be a white Christmas.' A short while later he heard a thudding sound. It was quickly followed by another, then another. It sounded as if someone was throwing snowballs at the window of the living room.

He went to the front door to investigate. There he found a flock of birds huddled miserably in the snow. They had been caught in the storm, and in their desperate search for shelter, had seen the light and flew into the window.

'I can't let these little creatures lie there and freeze to death,' he thought. 'But how can I help them?'

Then he remembered the barn. It would provide a nice warm shelter for them. He put on his coat and made his way through the snow to the barn. There he put on the light, but the birds wouldn't come.

'Food will bring them,' he thought. So he scattered a trail of bread crumbs all the way into the barn. But the birds still wouldn't come. Then he tried to shoo them into the barn by walking around them and waving his arms at them. But they took alarm and scattered in all directions.

Then he said to himself, 'They find me a strange and terrifying creature. If only there was some way I could get them to trust me.'

Just at that moment the church bells began to ring. He stood silently as they rang out the glad tidings of Christmas: 'The Word was made flesh, and dwelt among us' Then he sank to his knees in the snow and said, 'Lord, now I understand why you had to become one of us.'

If you want to really understand and be in touch with ordinary people, you have to go where nobody recognises you. You have to see what they see, hear what they hear, live what they live. Understanding it in an abstract way is different from feeling it with your whole being.

In Jesus, God drew near to us in person. He became one of us. He lived among us. Jesus is the gift of Christmas. This was no loving 'from a distance'. This was loving at close quarters.

God meets us where we are. He took our humanity on himself. This means we don't have to deny or reject our humanity in order to know God. He showed us how to live out the fullness of our humanity. Religion and holiness have become very real. They are not merely concerned with the spirit and with heaven, but with the body and the earth.

By becoming a child, completely dependent on human care, God took away the distance between the divine and the human. We are not afraid of a little child.

Jesus has become a Brother to us. What would we do without him? Abstract talk about God can leave us empty. We need God made flesh, human like us, walking our streets, even in our shoes, teaching us the way of God. And that is precisely what we are celebrating this night (day).

The Son of God comes to us not as a judge but as a saviour. He comes to reveal to us our divine dignity as God's children, and the glory of our eternal destiny in heaven. This is the good news. This is the great joy which the angels announced to the shepherds, and which is announced to us tonight (today). Let us open our hearts to receive it.

HOMILY 2   **The shepherds**

It is sometimes said that religion is an escape from the harsh realities of life. But this is a complete misunderstanding; nothing could be further from the truth.

Consider the story of the shepherds. At the time of Jesus, the status of shepherds was a lowly one – it still is in many countries. Although they performed an important task, their state was an obscure and unrecognised one. The world passed them by. Yet it was to such as these that the good news of Jesus' birth was announced, and it was just such as these who welcomed the news of that birth.

We can picture them in the quiet countryside, keeping watch over their sheep. They were poor and in darkness. But this only meant that they were ripe for the Good News. God comes especially to those who are poor, and who are not afraid to admit it. Material poverty is the most obvious kind of poverty. But there a worse kind – spiritual poverty.

It was while the shepherds were engaged in their lowly task that the great news came to them: 'Today in the town of Bethlehem a saviour has been born to you; he is Christ the Lord.' God came to them in the midst of life – as they were watching over their flocks. Religion is about finding

God, not outside of our lives, but within them. Finding God where we live, in the midst of our daily occupations – in our homes, workshops, offices ...

Having received the message of the angels, the shepherds did not sit back. The message demanded action from them. It demanded that they go and search for the child. So they made the journey to Bethlehem, and found that it was as the angels said. With their outward eyes all they saw was a child 'wrapped in swaddling clothes and lying a manger'. But with their inward eyes, the eyes of faith, they recognised this child as the Saviour sent by God.

Still, when the excitement died down, and the brightness faded, they had to face back to the dark and the cold. But the Gospel tells us that they went back 'glorifying and praising God for all they had seen and heard.' They went back to their flocks. They returned to the same lowly work, the same obscure life. Nothing had changed, and yet everything had changed. Life went on as before but with one major difference: now their hearts were filled with wonder.

They now had a new vision, a new hope, a new sense of the love of God for them and of his presence with them. Their lives, which a short while ago were dim, now glowed with meaning. The old world had become like a new country where everything glistened with marvel.

Even though we haven't seen the angels, we have heard the message of the angels. And tonight (today) we have come to see the Child. Like the shepherds, we must try to see him with the eyes of faith. In this way, we don't just see a tiny baby. We see our Saviour, Christ the Lord. We see God's gift to us. God's love made flesh for us. We see Emmanuel, God with us.

And, again like the shepherds, we have to go back to our homes and get on with our ordinary lives. But let us hope that we will go back glorifying and praising God for his goodness to us. Yes, we go back to our work, to our commitments, to all the small and sometimes dreary tasks that go to make up our daily lives. But we see them differently. Because we see ourselves differently. In the divine Child, we see our own divinity.

Religion is not an escape from life. Rather, it leads to a deeper commitment to life. We have to learn how close we can be to God, and how close God can be to us, in the midst of our sometimes painful and sometimes joyful lives. In the birth of Jesus we see that God has immersed himself in our messy world and confused lives.

Religion is not an escape from life. Religion addresses our deepest longings. It extends human life, adding a dimension that fuels the life deep inside us, that fleeting but precarious life that we are called upon to live and live to the full.

May we experience some of the great joy announced to the shepherds.

This joy springs from a sense of God's presence with us and love for us. Joy is one of the greatest signs of the presence of God. Somebody is watching over us, somebody is watching out for us. Somebody is with us. God is with us in his Son, Jesus. And if God is with us who can be against us?

HOMILY 3   **Christmas: feast of the heart**

In his autobiography, *An Only Child*, the Irish writer, Frank O'Connor, tells how one Christmas Santa Claus brought him a toy engine. On Christmas afternoon his mother took him to visit the local convent. As the engine was the only present he had received, he took it with him to show it to the nuns.

While he was in the convent one of the nuns brought him to visit the crib in the chapel. As he looked into the crib he noticed something which upset him very much. What upset him was the fact that the Child Jesus was lying there in the manger without a single present. He knew exactly how that child felt – the utter despondency of realising that he had been forgotten, and that nobody had brought him anything. Turning to the nun, he asked why the Holy Child hadn't got any toys, and she replied, 'His mother is too poor to afford them.'

That settled it. His mother was poor too, but at Christmas she had always managed to buy him something, even if it was only a box of crayons. In a burst of reckless generosity, he took the toy engine, climbed into the crib, and put it between the outstretched arms of the Child. And he showed him how to wind it as well, because a little baby would not be clever enough to know a thing like that.

This story shows us the power of Christmas. Through Christmas God gives us an opportunity to show what we are capable of. Of course, he set the example himself. He began by making us a gift of his most precious possession – his only Son.

God's Son could have come in power and wealth. Had he come in power, we would have bowed down in fear before him. Thus he would have made us feel small and weak and insignificant. If he had come in wealth, he would have made us aware of our own poverty. Thus he would have evoked a feeling of envy in us, and done serious damage to our hearts.

But he didn't come in power and wealth. He came in weakness and poverty. By coming in weakness, he made us aware of our own power. By coming in poverty, he made us aware of our own riches. His poverty evoked in us a feeling of compassion, thereby bringing our hearts to life.

It was the poverty of the Child Jesus that evoked that reckless act of generosity in the young Frank O'Connor. It was the poverty of Jesus that caused the Magi to 'open their treasures' and lay them before him. The poverty of Jesus is a challenge to us too. It gives us an opportunity to open our hearts. Jesus no longer needs our gifts. But other people may. He wants us to share ourselves with one another.

Christmas is a feast of the heart. It reveals to us what the heart of God is like. At the same time it reveals to us what the human heart is capable of. Christmas causes us to open our hearts. And to open our hearts is to begin to live. What makes us human is not so much our ability to think as our ability to love.

To the extent to which we open our hearts to God and to one another, we will experience something of the 'great joy' the angels announced to the shepherds. Joy is the fruit of love. Joy is an overflowing heart. May the great joy be yours tonight (today).

PRAYER OF THE FAITHFUL

President: With Christ's light shining on us, let us pray to God our Father for the needs of the Church and the world.

Response: Lord, hear our prayer.

Reader(s): For all who believe in Christ: that their faith may be strengthened. [Pause] Let us pray to the Lord.

For all people of good will: that this day may light afresh in their hearts the lamp of hope. [Pause] Let us pray to the Lord.

For all rulers: that Christ, the Prince of peace, may turn their minds and hearts to thoughts of peace. [Pause] Let us pray to the Lord.

For the sick and the lonely: that Christ, who shared our humanity, may give them hope and strength. [Pause] Let us pray to the Lord.

For those who are away from home this Christmas: that Christ may give them a taste of that peace which the world cannot give. [Pause] Let us pray to the Lord.

For prisoners: that Christ may enlighten their darkness. [Pause] Let us pray to the Lord.

For all the dead, especially our relatives and friends: that Christ may bring them into that light which no darkness can quench. [Pause] Let us pray to the Lord.

For our own special needs this Christmas night (day). [Longer pause] Let us pray to the Lord.

President: God of love, may the coming of your Son dispel the darkness of our lives, and bring us safely through the shadows of this world to your kingdom of everlasting light. We ask this through the same Christ our Lord.

SIGN OF PEACE

Lord Jesus Christ, at your birth the angels sang: 'Glory to God in the highest, and peace to his people on earth.' Grant that we who have heard the message of the angels may enjoy the peace and unity of your kingdom where you live for ever and ever.

REFLECTION   **A fire has been lit**

In our times Christmas has become
very commercialised and very pagan.
Many people are lured into overspending
and excessive eating and drinking.
However, these abuses must not blind us
to the true meaning of Christmas.
When thick smoke rises up,
catches in your throat, and brings tears to your eyes,
it is because a fire has been lit.
Ever since the coming of Christ
a bright fire has been burning on our earth,
a fire that will never die.
At this fire we experience the warmth of God's love,
and the glow of human fellowship.
Let us not be afraid to come in out of the cold
and warm ourselves at this fire.
So Happy Christmas, everyone!

Feast of the Holy Family

INTRODUCTION AND CONFITEOR

We gather on the feast of the Holy Family. We have come from our own families into a wider family – the family of the Christian community. Here we are reminded that we have a common Father, God, and that we are brothers and sisters in Christ. Let us reflect for a moment on the quality of our ties with our own family and with this community. [Pause]

It is our sinfulness that makes us want to go our own way, thus weakening our bonds with others. Let us confess our sins to God, and to one another.

HEADINGS FOR READINGS

First Reading (Ecclesus 3:2-6.12-14). This reading is a brief commentary on the commandment: Honour your father and your mother.

Second Reading (Col 3:12-21). This describes the atmosphere which should reign in a Christian community and in a Christian household.

Gospel (Mt 2:13-15.19-23). Matthew casts the Holy Family as displaced persons and homeless refugees.

SCRIPTURE NOTE

Matthew sees Jesus as reliving the history of his people. The Gospel story is coloured by the story of Moses in Egypt. Just as Moses had to be rescued from Pharaoh, Jesus had to be rescued from Herod. The story also contains echoes of the Exodus. Even though the evangelist's intentions are theological, he does show Jesus, Mary and Joseph as homeless refugees.

HOMILY 1   **Reflecting on the Scripture Readings**

This homily comments on the Scripture readings for the feast, and points to their relevance for family life today.

First Reading: This is a commentary on the fourth commandment: 'Honour your father and your mother.' Too often we think of the fourth commandment solely in terms of the obligation of younger children to obey their parents. That is part of it. But there is another essential part of it: the obligation of grown children to ensure that their aged parents are able to live out their final years in comfort and dignity.

It is this second element which is the focus of the reading. This has great relevance today. Because of the pace of modern life, the elderly tend to be pushed to the margins, if not out of the picture altogether. In our strength it is easy to forget those who are weak and perhaps a little senile. Under God, we owe everything to our parents. The author of Ecclesiasticus asserts that kindness to parents is especially pleasing to God, who accepts it as atonement for one's sins.

Second Reading: Fraternal love is the hallmark of Christian community. This love begins in the home. Every family is a small community. St Paul talks about the harmonious atmosphere that should reign in a Christian household – something that depends not just on the obedience of the children, but on harmonious relations among all its members.

This harmony can be achieved only by the practice of virtues such as kindness, humility, gentleness, patience, mutual forgiveness, and, above all, love. All these virtues refer to interpersonal relationships, and build and foster community. They are not easy to practise. But when they are practised with consistency, the rewards are great in terms of peace and harmony in the home. The parents should set an example: the love they show one another is the best gift they can give their children.

Gospel: The First Reading dealt with the obligation of grown children to look after their aged parents. In the Gospel we see exemplified the primary obligation of parents, which is to love and care for their children.

Here we see what Mary and Joseph did in order to ensure the safety of the Child Jesus. As soon as they learned that his life was in danger, they uprooted themselves and went into exile. And when the danger passed, they uprooted themselves again and returned to their native country.

The Holy Family didn't have it easy. As homeless refugees, the Holy Family shared the fate of the many uprooted and dispossessed families in our world today. But because of their deep faith in God, and love for one another, they stayed together and came through it.

They settled in Nazareth. Nazareth was the place of the hidden life, of ordinary life, of family life, of prayer, work, obscurity, silent virtues, practised with no witnesses other than God, and their friends and neighbours. Nazareth was the place where Jesus lived thirty years of his short life, and is where many people live their entire lives.

When Jesus finally left Nazareth and began his public ministry, it can't have been easy for Mary. And later she suffered what for parents is the greatest suffering of all – she saw her child die before herself, and die a terrible death.

The family is very fragile today. For instance, in Britain today three out of ten children are born out of marriage. One in five is brought up in a one-parent family. Almost four in ten marriages end in divorce. It is not that we no longer value the family. Rather, it may be that we have forgotten the disciplines that make it work. The family is built on bonds of commitment, fidelity and self-sacrifice.

Nevertheless, many parents today make enormous sacrifices for their children. Included among those are many single parents. All such parents can draw inspiration from the example of Mary and Joseph.

HOMILY 2 **The role of the family**

If you plant a tree in an exposed place it becomes very vulnerable. It is at the mercy of every wind that blows. If it survives at all, it will be in a twisted and stunted form, a poor specimen of what it could be. If you want a tree to grow to its full potential, you must plant it in a more sheltered place. And you must not plant it on its own. You must plant some other trees with it.

It is of vital importance to get the space between those trees right. They must be close enough to be able to provide shelter and protection for one another. Yet they must not be so close that they will stifle one another. They must be planted far enough apart to ensure that they each has room to grow to its full potential.

It's not good for a tree to be alone. Nor is it good for us to be alone. For our wholeness, and for our mental health, we need ties of love and friendship with other human beings. God made us not for isolation but for community. We are not complete in ourselves. We need other people in order to become what God intended us to be.

This is where the family comes in. Trees planted in the form of a little grove is a good image of the family. In the ideal family there is both closeness and space. The closeness means the members are able to provide support for one another. The space ensures that they do not stifle one another. Each member has the closeness, intimacy, and warmth that he/she needs, yet also has the space to grow to his/her full potential. This is a great challenge: how to achieve closeness without stifling or dominating one another.

In the family we learn to form relationships with others, something that is vitally important for us. Inability to relate is a great handicap and a great sadness. Without close relationships we are at the mercy of the cold winds of anguish and loneliness.

In the little community of the family we learn to bond with others. Here we make room for others in our lives. Here we learn to share with one another, and become responsible to and for one another.

It is within the family that a child learns to use the word 'we' for the first time. Without the word 'we' there would be no community, no sharing, no togetherness.

Of course, being so close involves risk. We have the possibility of helping and healing one another. But we also have the possibility of hindering and hurting one another. Sometimes people keep their best behaviour for outside the home and their worst for inside the home. They are 'angels' outside it and 'devils' inside it.

Harmony in the family can be achieved only by the practice of the virtues St Paul talks about: kindness, humility, gentleness, patience, mutual forgiveness, and above all, love (see Second Reading). These are the virtues which build and foster community. But they are not easy virtues to practise with consistency.

In our society the family is under a lot of pressure. It is not that we no longer value the family. It is that we are not prepared for the disciplines that make it work. The family is built on bonds of commitment, fidelity and self-sacrifice. It was by living in a small community of love with Mary and Joseph at Nazareth that Jesus was able to grow in wisdom and in favour with God and people.

In the little community of family we have a place, we have bonds, we have an identity, we have roots. Even if the family knows hardship this is not necessarily a bad thing. Hardship can be a grace. Trees that grow on hard ground have firmer roots, and thus are better equipped to meet the inevitable storms.

HOMILY 3   **Parents and children**

The First Reading is a commentary on the fourth commandment: 'Honour your father and your mother.' Unfortunately, this commandment tends to be seen in a very narrow way. There are three essential elements in it.

First of all, there is the primary obligation of parents to love and care for their children. We see a beautiful example of this in today's Gospel. There we see what Mary and Joseph did in order to ensure the safety of the Child Jesus. As soon as they learned that his life was in danger, they uprooted themselves and went into exile. And when the danger passed, they uprooted themselves again, returned to their native country and settled in Nazareth. In their home in Nazareth they provided the kind of environment in which, as the Gospel tells us, Jesus was able to grow in wisdom, in stature, and in favour with God and with people.

Secondly, there is the obligation of children to obey their parents. At Nazareth Jesus was subject to Mary and Joseph. Mary was a woman of faith, who loved God with all her heart and soul. And Joseph is described in the Gospel as being *a just man,* that is, a man who made the Law of God the guiding rule of his life. It was to these two dear people that Jesus subjected himself. And it was these two who taught, nourished, and formed him.

At Nazareth Jesus was able to grow quietly in the shadows. Those first thirty years were of crucial importance to him. During those years he was growing, maturing, and ripening. Of all the influences upon us, the family is by far the most powerful. Its effects stay with us for a lifetime.

Thirdly, there is the obligation of grown children to ensure that their aged parents are able to live out their final years in comfort and dignity. It is this element which is the focus of today's First Reading.

This has particular relevance for our times when the elderly tend to be pushed to the margins. In our strength it is easy to forget those who are weak and perhaps a little senile. There is a saying: 'One mother can take care of ten children, but ten children can't take care of one mother.' Under God, we owe everything to our parents. The author of Ecclesiasticus asserts that kindness to parents is especially pleasing to God who accepts it as atonement for one's sins.

Here again the Holy Family serves as a model. As Jesus was dying on the cross he thought of his mother, and entrusted her to the care of his disciple, John. (According to tradition Joseph had already died.)

Caring for one's own kin is no easy task. In no circumstances do greater difficulties present themselves than in nursing one's own. Nobody is more demanding than one's own. Nevertheless, our first and holiest duty is kindness towards our own kin. God is served when we give them a cup of water in his name.

PRAYER OF THE FAITHFUL

President: Let us pray to God who is both Father and Mother to each of us and to the whole human family.

Response: Lord, hear us in your love.

Reader(s): For the Christian community: that it may set an example of unity and peace for a fragmented and troubled world. [Pause] We pray to the Lord.

For the government of our country: that is may support the family as the basic unit of society. [Pause] We pray to the Lord.

For families that are scattered by conflict or war. [Pause] We pray to the Lord.

For single parent families. [Pause] We pray to the Lord.

For the deceased members of our families: that God may bring to a place of refreshment, light and peace. [Pause] We pray to the Lord.

For the particular needs of our own families. [Longer pause] We pray to the Lord.

President: Lord, grant that we may praise rather than criticise, sympathise rather than condemn, give rather than receive, so that our homes may become places where love and peace reign. We ask through Christ our Lord.

REFLECTION   **Children learn what they live**

If children live with criticism, they learn to condemn.
If they live with hostility, they learn to fight.
If they live with ridicule, they learn to be shy.
If they live with shame, they learn to feel guilty.
If they live with tolerance, they learn to be patient.
If they live with encouragement, they learn to have confidence.
If they live with praise, they learn to appreciate.
If they live with fairness, they learn what justice is.
If they live with security, they learn to trust.
If they live with approval, they learn to like themselves.
If they live with acceptance and friendship,
they learn to find love and God in the world. (*Anon.*)

Second Sunday after Christmas

INTRODUCTION AND CONFITEOR

The lights of Christmas are beginning to fade. But the mystery of Christ's presence among us remains. Today's Gospel reminds us of this: 'The Word was made flesh, and dwelt among us ... From his fullness we have all received.' Let us draw close to Christ so that he may enrich us from his abundance. [Pause]

Lord Jesus, you are the light of the world. Lord, have mercy.

Lord Jesus, you are the Word made flesh and splendour of the Father. Christ, have mercy.

Lord Jesus, you are full of grace and truth. Lord, have mercy.

HEADINGS FOR READINGS

First Reading (Ecclesus 24:1-2.8-12). This is a poem in praise of divine wisdom, a wisdom that has made her dwelling among God's people.

Second Reading (Eph 1:3-6.15-18). This reading introduces the theme of God's plan of salvation, a plan which is centred in Christ and realised through him.

Gospel (Jn 1:!-18). This is a great hymn to the Word of God, the source of all life, whose coming among us makes us children of God.

HOMILY 1 **He lived among us**

In an audience Pope Paul VI told how one day, when he was Archbishop of Milan, he went out on parish visitation. During the course of the visitation, he found an old woman living on her own.

'How are you?' he asked her.

'Not bad,' she answered. 'I have enough food, and I'm not suffering from the cold.'

'You must be reasonably happy then?' he said.

'No, I'm not', she said as she started to cry. 'You see, my son and daughter-in-law never come to see me. I'm dying of loneliness.'

Afterwards he was haunted by the phrase 'I'm dying of loneliness'. And the Pope concluded: 'Food and warmth are not enough in themselves. People need something more. They need our presence, our time, our love. They need to be touched, to be reassured that they are not forgotten.'

This is a simple, yet profound truth. There is nothing as important as presence to those we love. Gifts, letters and phone calls are good, but they cannot take the place of presence. Presence brings comfort. Presence brings peace. Time is the best gift we can offer to another person, time just to sit and share.

In today's liturgy we celebrate the Good News of God's presence with his people: 'He lived among us'. In Jesus, God is truly present among us. Before starting his public ministry Jesus proved his love by simple presence among the people. He didn't drop in, say 'hello' and disappear again.

He came and lived among the people.

In Jesus, God has drawn near to us in person. He has become one of us. This is no loving 'from a distance'. This is loving at close quarters. It shows us how close God is to us, and how close we can be to God in the midst of our sometimes painful and sometimes joyful lives.

When people allow themselves to get disconnected from God an enormous loss occurs, and a huge vacuum results. Life is unintelligible and unbearable without God. On the other hand, a sense of God's presence with us, and of his love for us, is the only riches worth having. This is the special gift of Christmas. We feel that God is very close to us and very loving towards us at this time.

We also must try to be present to one another, especially to those we love. By being present, we make God's presence real for people.

HOMILY 2   **Receiving from his fullness**

'He lived among us ... full of grace and truth ... From his fullness all of us have received.' We find these lovely words in today's Gospel.

Some people have lots of possessions yet have an inner emptiness which nothing is able to fill. But there are others who have very little and they are perfectly content.

One day a man and his wife, both staunch Christians, went to an art gallery to see an exhibition of paintings by a highly promising young artist. On the way into the exhibition they passed a beggar sitting on the steps of the building. The wife gave him a little money, but the husband scolded her, saying, 'I never give anything to his kind, because they only go off and drink it.'

Inside, he admired several of the paintings, but one in particular caught his eye. It was a painting of an old beggar man. 'It's so realistic,' he exclaimed enthusiastically to his wife. 'Look at the patches on the beggar's coat. See the dirt on his hands, the sadness in his eyes, the indifference of the passers-by. It's wonderful.' He bought it for a tidy sum of money.

As they made their way out of the museum the beggar man was still sitting there, only this time the husband didn't even see him, so excited was he because of the painting he had bought. He failed to notice that the beggar man in the painting was the same beggar man who was sitting on the steps.

The man in the story was a wealthy man. It wouldn't have cost him much to give a little help to the beggar. But he refused to do so on the pretext that if he fed him, he might feed his vices too. If God used the same logic in dealing with us, where would we be?

St John says of Jesus, 'From his fullness we have all received.' Jesus was like an overflowing fountain. From him life flowed to others. He gave healing, hope and life to people. But he didn't give them mere hand-

[49]

outs. He gave them life, and then told them to go and live that life to the full.

But in order to enrich us he had to begin by emptying himself. He became as we are, like us in everything and every way except sin. By assuming our human nature, and triumphing over evil in it, he opened up new possibilities of being for us. He shows us what our human nature is capable of.

Sadly, most people use only a fraction of their potential. In the words of Solzhenitsyn: 'People exhaust themselves in the senseless pursuit of material things and die without realising their spiritual greatness.'

The greatest good we can do for other people is not to give them of our own wealth, but to show them their own. If Jesus gives to us it is in order to help us to discover our own riches. He yearns to liberate the deepest energies within us. Most cults appeal to people's weaknesses. Jesus appeals to our strengths. He threw down a new challenge to us – to be the best that we can.

All of us have great potential as human beings and children of God. We have riches to share with others. But first of all we have to discover these riches and then develop them. From Jesus we receive mercy, compassion, love, truth and life. But the aim is, not to make us dependent, but to bring us to life so that we in our turn can bring life to others.

HOMILY 3   **The Word was made flesh**

Words are very important. They can give perspective, insight, understanding, and vision. They can bring consolation, comfort, encouragement, and hope. Words can take away fear, isolation, shame and guilt. Words can bring peace and joy, freedom and gratitude. Words can be messengers of love.

Nevertheless, words are a poor substitute for deeds. Deeds make words redundant. One small deed of the heart is worth a thousand words.

Antoine de Saint-Exupery, author of *The Little Prince*, was a pioneer airman. His name is synonymous with the golden age of aviation when pilots flew through desert sandstorms and over high mountain ranges in open cockpits carrying mail. By the time the Second World War broke out he had become a famous writer as well.

He had a great love for his native country, France, which was occupied by Germany. Determined to help his country in its hour of need, he volunteered for active service. However, believing that he was more valuable to his country as a writer than a flier, his friends secured a safe job for him – doing government research. But he refused to take the job, insisting that he be allowed to fly combat missions.

'But what about your writing?' they said.

'If I did not resist with my life, I would not be able to write,' he replied.

Then he added, 'The word must become flesh.'

Eventually a compromise was reached. He was allowed to fly reconnaissance missions. It was during one such mission in 1944 that he disappeared without a trace. His small plane is believed to have been shot down over the sea by a German fighter.

We can only marvel at Saint-Exupery's courage and spirit of self-sacrifice. But what exactly did he mean when he said, 'The word must become flesh.' Words are abstractions. They have to be made concrete. You could talk forever to a starving person about food. But if you really care about him you must one day put a loaf of bread in his hand. That day your word becomes flesh.

Saint-Exupery could have written volumes about patriotism, but what he did spoke louder than anything he might have written. His example helps us to understand today's Gospel. In that Gospel St John calls Jesus the Word of God. In his love for us, God spoke many words to us through creation, through the prophets, and so on. But finally the Word became flesh, in the person of his Son. This is the ultimate proof of his love.

Jesus was not passing through like a tourist. No, he pitched his tent among us. He became one of us. He joined the human family and lived among us. He knows what it is like to be human, what makes us weep, what makes us fall and stumble and somehow rise and go on again.

He assumed our nature, made of the same fragile, perishable material as ours, in order to show us the greatness of our humanity, to show us what it is capable of.

In him God is with us. He is very close to us, and very friendly towards us. God is present to us in a way that we can relate to, for Jesus in like us in all things but sin. He is a brother to us. He has made us children of God. From his fullness we have all received.

In us too the words of Jesus can and must become flesh.

PRAYER OF THE FAITHFUL

President: Let us pray to Christ our Brother, who assumed our human nature, with all its strengths and weaknesses, to show what we can become.

Response: Lord, save us through your coming.

Reader(s): For the people of God: that they may die to sin and live to holiness. [Pause] We pray to the Lord.

For our leaders: that they may show special concern for the weak and vulnerable members of society. [Pause] We pray the Lord.

For all those who are labouring under any kind of burden. [Pause] We pray to the Lord.

For grace to accept the love of Christ and grow in the freedom of the children of God. [Pause] We pray to the Lord.

For our own special needs. [Longer pause] We pray to the Lord.

President: Father, our source of life, you know our weakness. May we reach out with joy to grasp your hand, and walk more readily in your ways. We ask this through Christ our Lord.

REFLECTION   **Prayer at the start of the year**

Lord, I sometimes wonder where I'm going
and what is the meaning of my life.
I wonder especially
what the new year holds for me.
Will it bring joy or sorrow,
success or failure, life or death?
But then I remember that you came on earth;
and that you still travel the road of life with me.
And so I say to my soul:
'Go out into the darkness,
and put your hand in the hand of Christ, your Brother;
that will be better than a light,
and safer than a known path.'

Epiphany
A LIGHT FOR THE GENTILES

INTRODUCTION AND CONFITEOR

Today we hear again the story of the wise men who, guided by the light of a star, came to Bethlehem to honour the Christ-child. We too are on a journey, a journey to that heavenly Bethlehem where we hope to meet the Lord face to face. We are guided, not by the light of a star, but by the light of faith. Let us ask the Lord to strengthen our faith. [Pause]

Lord Jesus, you are the light the world. Lord, have mercy.

Lord Jesus, those who follow you will always have the light of life. Christ, have mercy.

Lord Jesus, you lead us through the darkness of this world to the radiant joy of our eternal home. Lord, have mercy.

HEADINGS FOR READINGS

First Reading (Is 60:1-6). The prophet cheers the returned exiles with a vision of a restored city which will become a beacon of light for all the nations.

Second Reading (Eph 3:2-3.5-6). This reading expresses the theological meaning of today's feast: God invites Jew and Gentile to share on an equal footing the benefits of the salvation brought by Christ.

Gospel (Mt 2:1-12). Three Gentiles came from a far country to pay homage to the Christ-child, while the Jewish leaders rejected him.

SCRIPTURE NOTE

For Matthew, the story of the Magi becomes an anticipation of the fate of the Good News of salvation, a fate that he knew in the aftermath of the resurrection. God revealed himself to the Jews through the Scriptures, and to the Gentiles through nature. Hence, Matthew shows the Magi (who were Gentiles) receiving a revelation through astrology. The story highlights the paradox: the Jews who have the Scriptures reject Jesus, while Gentiles come and, with the help of the Scriptures, find and adore him.

There is nothing to be gained by speculating where the Magi came from and what exactly the star was. The star was only the means by which a great mystery was revealed – the revelation of Christ as the Saviour of the Gentiles too.

The Second Reading expresses the theological meaning of today's feast: God invites Jew and Gentile to share on an equal footing the benefits of the salvation brought by Christ.

HOMILY 1   **A revolutionary feast**

The word *Epiphany* means a manifestation or revelation. Literally, a 'drawing back of the veil.' On this day the veil is drawn back on a great mystery, namely, that Christ is the Saviour not only of the Jews but also of the Gentiles.

It is God's will that all people should be saved and come to the knowledge of the truth. This is the theological meaning of the feast. God invites all, Jew and Gentile, to share on an equal footing the benefits of the salvation won by Christ. It stresses the perfect equality of all men and women (see Second Reading in particular). In Christ all have become part of the one body.

We should not put too much emphasis on the star, otherwise this revolutionary feast will become a very narrow and tame one. Whatever the star was, it was only the means by which a great mystery was revealed – the revelation of Christ as the Saviour of the Gentiles too. In fact, of the whole human race.

In the Old Testament the Jews are portrayed as God's Chosen People. But this idea was interpreted in a way that involved second-class status for all other peoples. This feast shows that election by God is not a privilege for some but a hope for all. It puts an end to every kind of exclusivism.

We are dealing with a universalist feast.

The feast of the Epiphany tore down the barrier between Jews and Gentiles. For the most part Jesus' own mission was restricted to his own people. Nevertheless, he also reached out to Samaritans, Canaanites, foreigners, and all kinds of social outcasts. He angered the Jewish leaders by telling them that the Kingdom of God was open to everyone. The news that the Gentiles would be accepted on equal terms as themselves caused shock and bewilderment to the Jews. And in his final commissioning of the apostles he said to them, 'Go out into the whole world and make disciples of all nations.'

This great and wonderful truth was revealed in embryo when the Magi, three Gentiles, came to honour Christ as their Saviour. The Magi are the first fruits of the Gentile world coming to share in the messianic blessings.

This is a happy feast. It is an inclusive feast. We who were outsiders are now insiders. We who were once aliens are now part of God's family.

HOMILY 2   **Journeying in faith**

The great native American leader, Black Elk, said a very wise thing: 'It is hard to follow one great vision in this world of darkness and changing shadows. Among those shadows people get lost.' Yet this is exactly what the Magi did – they set out in pursuit of a great vision and followed that vision to the end.

Theirs was a bold, courageous, and imaginative journey. Yet to many it must have appeared foolish, even a little crazy. It can't have been an easy journey. No doubt they encountered many difficulties, and knew moments of doubt and danger in the course of their journey. Every time the star disappeared (under clouds or under the light of day) they would have lost their bearings temporarily.

There must have been moments when they asked themselves if they were not wasting their time. And the thought must have occurred to them: What will people think of us? Yet, in spite of doubts, difficulties, and dangers they persevered in their quest, and were rewarded when they finally found Christ.

Though the Magi were guided by a heavenly light, a star, they did not know where the star would lead them. Hence, their journey was very much a journey of faith. And even when they saw the Child, they still had to make an act of faith. Seeing is not necessarily believing.

The story of the Magi has great relevance for us because we too are on a journey – the journey of life. We too are following a vision. As the Magi were guided by the light of a star, we are guided by the light of faith. Their journey can serve as a model for our journey of faith.

However, we have one great advantage over them. We already know

Christ, and have encountered him in faith. Christ, the light of the world, is the 'star' we are following. Nevertheless, the fact that we haven't seen him face to face means we haven't yet arrived at our final destination. The fact that we have faith doesn't mean we know all the answers. We are still searching, still travelling onwards.

We must not be surprised if we have doubts, and if we encounter difficulties. Faith doesn't guarantee an easy journey, only a meaningful one. The Magi's journey was one of searching and questioning, of pain and joy, of fear and hope. The faith journey contains elements of all of these.

The Magi did not journey as individuals. They had each other. They formed a little community of believers. We too have a community to support us in our faith journey.

May the lamp of faith never fail us. May its light see us through the darkness of this world, until we reach the heavenly Bethlehem where we shall see Christ in glory.

HOMILY 3   **Blessed are those who believe**

The Jews were very privileged. God revealed himself to them in a very special way, namely through the Scriptures. The Gentiles didn't have the Scriptures. It was through nature that God revealed himself to them, and so Matthew shows the Magi (who were Gentiles) receiving a revelation through astrology. This was an imperfect revelation; for while it told them of the birth of the 'King of the Jews', it did not tell them where they could find him. The ultimate secret of his whereabouts was locked in the special revelation of God to Israel, namely, in the Scriptures.

But Matthew contrasts the faith of these pagan visitors and the unbelief of the Jewish leaders (civil and religious). The pagans have answered the call to faith in Christ, whereas the chosen people have for the most part rejected it. Matthew highlights the paradox: those who have the Scriptures reject Jesus, while Gentiles come and, with the help of the very same Scriptures, find and adore him.

In this story we see the two main responses to Jesus: belief and unbelief. Here we have the essential gospel story in miniature. The story of the Magi and the star becomes for Matthew the anticipation of the fate of the Good News of salvation, a fate that he knew in the aftermath of the resurrection.

The essence of the Good News is this: God made himself present to us in the life of one who walked on this earth, indeed so truly present that this one, Jesus, was his Son. This revelation was an offence and contradiction to some, but salvation to those who had eyes to see and hearts to believe. The Magi are the forerunners of all those who would come to worship the risen Jesus proclaimed by the apostles.

The story shows us the great benefits of faith. Herod and many in Jerusalem are troubled because of their unbelief. Their fear contrasts with the great joy the Magi felt as they followed the star on the road to Bethlehem. Their joy is the fruit of their faith.

The theme of the happiness, the blessedness of those who believe runs right through the Gospel. Wonderful things happen for those who believe. You could say that the central theme of the Gospel is the blessedness of those who believe. All of Jesus' preaching had as its aim to elicit faith in people's hearts.

However, it was not simply a matter of believing, but of believing and acting on that belief, or living according to it. It was a question of hearing the word and doing it – taking risks on it, and making sacrifices because of it (as the Magi did). We too will be blessed if we hear the word of God and act on it.

PRAYER OF THE FAITHFUL

President: God appointed Christ as the light of the nations. Let us now pray to him in faith for all our needs.

Response: Lord, hear us in your love.

Reader(s): For the Church: that it may make Christ known to all nations. [Pause] We pray in faith.

For temporal rulers: that they may work to bring about a society in which the rights of all citizens are respected. [Pause] We pray in faith.

For missionaries, who are working to spread the Gospel. [Pause] We pray in faith.

For all those who are searching for meaning in life and who still haven't found what they are looking for. [Pause] We pray in faith.

For ourselves: that our lives may bear witness to the hope we carry in our hearts. [Pause] We pray in faith.

For our own special needs. [Longer pause] We pray in faith.

President: God of love and mercy, let the light of your Son bring us safely through the darkness of this world to the radiant glory of your kingdom. We ask this through the same Christ our Lord.

REFLECTION   **A star is born**

The Magi were led to Christ by the light of a star.
But they saw the star only because
they were not afraid to travel in the dark.
The fact is, we cannot see the stars
in the bright light of day,
but only in the darkness of night;
and the darker the night,
the brighter they shine.

In a sense, all of us are night-time travellers.
However, we need no longer fear the darkness,
because with the coming of Christ
a light has come into the world,
a light that shines in the dark,
a light that no darkness can overpower.

Baptism of the Lord

INTRODUCTION AND CONFITEOR

Today we celebrate the Baptism of Jesus. Jesus, the Sinless One, joined the queue of sinners, and was baptised by his cousin, John, in the waters of the Jordan. He did so in order that he might free us from the power of sin. Let us pause to call to mind our sins, and our need for purification and liberation. [Pause]

Lord, you were sent to heal the contrite of heart. Lord, have mercy.

Lord, you came to call sinners to repentance. Christ, have mercy.

Lord, you plead for us at the right hand of the Father. Lord, have mercy.

ALTERNATIVE OPENING RITE   **Blessing and sprinkling with holy water**

Today we celebrate the feast of the baptism of the Lord. It was an event of great significance for Jesus. It marked the beginning of his public ministry. In celebrating it we recall our own baptism and its importance for us.

Jesus stepped into the Jordan and had water poured over him by John the Baptist. On the day of our baptism we had blessed water poured over us. In baptism we are given a share in the undying life of God. We become brothers and sisters of the Lord. And we are given the gift of the Holy Spirit.

Even though we are a baptised people, we know that we have not yet fully lived the life of Christians. Now we will bless some water and sprinkle it over ourselves. It will remind us of the life-giving waters of baptism, and will help us to renew the grace of baptism within us.

Prayer over the water

Almighty God, your Spirit descended on Jesus at his baptism, revealing him as your servant, sent to bring to the poor the good news of salvation. Grant that the same Spirit may descend on us, and accompany us on our journey in the footsteps of Jesus. Bless ✠ this water. May it wash away our sins and bring us to eternal life. We ask this through Christ our Lord.

The priest now sprinkles all present with the blessed water.

HEADINGS FOR READINGS

First Reading (Is 42:1-4.6-7). Here we are given a portrait of a true serv-ant of God. It is something realised perfectly in Christ, and something to which his followers ought to aspire.

Second Reading (Acts 10:34-38). This contains a reference to Jesus' bap-tism, and is an example of the early Christian preaching to non-Jews.

Gospel (Mt 3:13-17). At his baptism, Jesus' true identity was revealed, and he was given power for the mission he was about to begin.

SCRIPTURE NOTE

The story of Jesus' baptism is an epiphany story: Jesus is revealed as the Son of God. This is Matthew's main emphasis. John's baptism was a bap-tism of repentance for the forgiveness of sins' (Mk 1:4). The fact that Jesus should undergo such a baptism was a source of embarrassment for the early Christians. Why did he undergo it? To give an example of humility, to raise John's baptism to a new level, to show solidarity with sinners, and to inaugurate his mission to sinners – a mission which is beautifully described by Isaiah (First Reading). Matthew also probably wanted to show what baptism means for Christians.

HOMILY 1   **Identifying with sinners**

When leprosy broke out among the people of the Hawaiian Islands in the middle of the last century, the authorities responded by establishing a leper colony on the remote island of Molokai. The victims were snatched by force from their families and sent to this island to perish.

However, moved by their terrible plight, a young Belgian priest, Damien De Veuster, asked to be allowed to minister to them. Straighta-way he realised that there was only one effective way to do this: that was to go and live among them.

Having got permission, he went to Molokai. At first, he tried to minis-ter to them while maintaining a certain distance. But he soon realised that he had to live among them in order to gain their trust. As a result he contracted leprosy himself.

The reaction of the lepers was immediate and wholehearted. They embraced him and took him to their hearts. He was now one of them. There was no need, no point any more in keeping his distance. The lepers now had someone who could talk with authority about leprosy, about brokenness, about rejection and public shame.

The baptism of Jesus was a source of embarrassment to the early Chris-tians. Even John the Baptist himself found it incongruous and, as we saw in the Gospel, tried to prevent it. Why was this? It was because John's baptism was a summons to repentance. It was for sinners who were conscious of their sinfulness. Now of one thing the early Christians were certain – Jesus was no sinner. He did not stand in need of repentance. What relevance could John's baptism have for him, and why did he submit himself to it?

It was a symbolic act. He wanted to show solidarity with the people he had come to help. For this reason it was important that he was baptised, and baptised publicly. In this way he was identifying with sinners. When he stepped into the waters of the Jordan he was in effect saying to them, 'I'm on your side.'

On the day of his baptism, Jesus joined the ranks of sinners. The Father approved of what he was doing, and set his seal on it by sending the Holy Spirit to anoint him with the oil of compassion for his mission.

What Jesus did that day at the Jordan was to serve as a model for his public ministry. He would not keep himself apart from sinners. He would not wait for them to come to him. He would seek them out and go among them. He would befriend them. He would welcome them.

Jesus didn't stand apart or put himself above the sinners he came to save. He placed himself among them. He joined them where they were. So much so that he was accused of being a sinner, and was treated as a sinner. In fact, he was treated as a criminal, and suffered the fate of the condemned criminal.

Though completely sinless, Jesus took our sinful condition on himself. He doesn't stand apart from us, but has placed himself beside us as an older Brother. He reveals to us that we are God's precious children. He wants to leads us out from our wretched condition of sin and death. He wants us to have life here and hereafter.

In this way he shows his love for us. And he also shows us what we have to do if we want to help those who are down.

HOMILY 2 **The call to service**

Nelson Mandela will go down as one of the greatest leaders of this century. He was instrumental in ending apartheid and bringing about a multiracial society in South Africa. Mandela belongs to the Xhosa people, and grew up in the Transkei. But how did he come to play such a crucial role in the history of his country?

In his autobiography, *Long Walk to Freedom* (1994, Little, Brown and Company), he tells us that all the currents of his life were taking him away from the Transkei. Yet he had no epiphany, no singular revelation, no moment of truth. He says:

A steady accumulation of insights helped me to see that my duty was to the people as a whole, not just to a particular section of it. The memory of a thousand indignities produced in me an anger, a rebelliousness, a desire to fight the system that imprisoned my people. There was no particular day on which I said, Henceforth I will devote myself to the liberation of my people; instead I simply found myself doing so, and could not do otherwise.

Jesus was thirty years old when he began his public ministry. How did he come to that decision and why did he wait so long to begin the real work of his life? The simple answer is: prior to this he wasn't ready. Jesus was a teacher, not of a subject such as history which can be learnt out of books, but of religion, or better, spirituality. Spirituality has to be lived before it can be taught effectively. This is why time is important. Before the age of about thirty, what experience has a person to draw on?

In Nazareth he was able to grow quietly in the shadows. There were no pressures. No burden of expectations. There was no hurry – many things are ruined by haste. The main influences in his life would have been home, school, and synagogue.

The first thirty years he spent at Nazareth were not a waste of valuable time. They were of crucial importance to him. During those years he was growing, maturing, and ripening. The day he was baptised by John he didn't suddenly became a different person. 'No single event can awaken in us a stranger completely unknown to us.' (Antoine de Saint Exupery). On that day he begin to reap the harvest from what had been growing within him. On that day he answered another call.

The desire to give himself to serving his brothers and sisters of the wider community did not come to him suddenly. It had been sounding inside him during his years in his homeland of Nazareth. Nevertheless, baptism was a very special moment in his life. This was the moment when he decided to commit himself to it and begin it.

There is a great lesson for us in all of this. We must not write off any part of our lives as useless, or any experience as a waste. Everything gives us an opportunity to grow. Life calls for a lot of patient waiting. But we must not wait for something great to happen. We must live the present moment to the full. The future is contained in the present. The future will be the blossoming of the present.

We too are called to grow in wisdom and grace. It took Jesus thirty years to reach maturity and to acquire wisdom. It will take us a lifetime to grow, to mature, and to ripen as human beings and children of God.

The feast of the baptism of Jesus reminds us of our own baptism, and provides us with an opportunity to commit ourselves once again to the Christian life, which is essentially a life of service.

We are not called to save the world, or to solve all its problems. Nevertheless, each of us has our own unique call, in our families, in our work, in our world. We need God's help to be able to be faithful to that call. Faithfulness to small, everyday tasks is our way of responding to the problems of our time and participating in the work of Jesus.

HOMILY 3   **Moment of revelation and confirmation**

Times of change (e.g. change of one's career, change of one's way of life) are times of risk and uncertainty. At such times people become very vulnerable. What they need most is someone to give them support and encouragement.

When the American writer, Maya Angelou, was growing up she didn't see her mother very much. She was brought up in great part by her grandmother, a wonderful and saintly woman. She tells how when she was twenty years old, she took a trip to San Francisco to visit her mother. It was a particularly important yet vulnerable moment in Maya's life: she was struggling to make her way in life and groping her way towards becoming a writer.

She had quite a good meeting with her mother. When it was time to leave, her mother walked her down the hill to the waiting bus. As they parted, her mother said, 'You know, I think you are the greatest woman I have ever met.'

Years later Maya could still recall that moment vividly. She said, 'Waiting for the bus, I sat there thinking: Just suppose she's right. Suppose I really am somebody. It was one of those moments when the sky rolled back. At times like that, it's almost as if the whole earth holds its breath.'

Maya went on to become a highly successful and respected writer and poet. She composed and delivered an inspiring poem at the inauguration of President Clinton.

Prior to his baptism Jesus had lived for thirty years at Nazareth. It had been an uneventful life (as far as we can tell). Nevertheless, during those years he had begun to hear another call – a call away from Nazareth, a call to the service of his brothers and sisters in the wider community. So finally he left Nazareth.

When he appeared before John to be baptised, he had reached a crossroads in his life. He had left behind him the comparatively quiet life of Nazareth, and was about to embark on his public mission. No doubt he came to that moment after a lot of prayer and reflection. Nevertheless, it can't have been easy for him. He must have experienced some uncertainty and anxiety. He needed affirmation.

During his baptism Jesus received that affirmation. He heard the wonderful words: 'You are my beloved son; with you I am well pleased.' These words also set the seal of divine approval on the mission he was about to begin, the mission to bring sinners back to God.

The heavenly Father's words of affirmation put wind in his sails. Not only did he receive approval from on high for his mission, but he also received power from on high for it. This is signified by the descent of the Holy Spirit. The Spirit was not just given for that moment; the Spirit remained with him throughout his public ministry.

This feast in which we recall the baptism of Jesus reminds us of our own baptism, and renews its grace within us. From a spiritual point of view, baptism is the greatest thing that can happen to us. What happened at the baptism of Jesus happens at our baptism too. God calls us by name. He says to each of us, 'You are my beloved son,' or 'You are my beloved daughter.' And the Spirit descends on us, because we too are given a mission: to participate in the work of Jesus.

We are not called to save the world, or to solve all its problems. Nevertheless, each of us has our own unique call, in our families, in our work, in our world. Faithfulness to small, everyday tasks is our way of responding to the problems of our time and of participating in the work of Jesus.

PRAYER OF THE FAITHFUL

President: Let us pray through Christ our Brother that the Holy Spirit may inspire and strengthen us to model our lives on his.

Response: Lord, graciously hear us.

Reader(s): For all the baptised: that they may grow in wisdom and grace. [Pause] Lord, hear us.

For all political leaders: that they may work to build a world free from poverty and oppression. [Pause] Lord, hear us.

For all those who are out of work. [Pause] Lord, hear us.

For grace to be patient with ourselves and with others. [Pause] Lord, hear us.

For our own particular needs. [Longer pause] Lord, hear us.

President: Father, we thank you for the grace of Baptism which made us your children. Help us to live it out in our daily lives by showing you the trust of a child, and by becoming envoys of your love and peace to others. We ask this through Christ our Lord.

REFLECTION   **Baptism**

Baptism was not over and done with
the day we were taken to the font.
W are baptised by all that happens to us in life.
We are baptised by hardship; in its turbulent waters
we are purified of all that is false and useless.
We are baptised by suffering; in its murky waters
we grow in humility and compassion.

We are baptised by joy: in its gurgling waters
we experience the goodness of life.
We are baptised by love: in its singing waters
we blossom like flowers in the sun.
Baptism is like the planting of a seed.
It will take a lifetime for this seed to grow and ripen.

LENT & PASSION (PALM) SUNDAY

'Before Pilate'

PATRICK PYE

First Sunday of Lent

Lent recalls the forty days Jesus spent in the desert, during which time he was tempted by the devil. But through prayer, fasting, and fidelity to the word of God he overcame the tempter. We too have to face temptation. Let us reflect for a moment on our temptations and how much we need God's help to resist them. [Pause]

Lent provides us with a great opportunity to follow more closely the footsteps of Jesus.

Lord, you call us to repentance. Lord, have mercy.

Lord, you call us to self-denial. Christ, have mercy.

Lord, you call us to prayer and works of charity. Lord, have mercy.

HEADINGS FOR READINGS

First Reading (Gen 2:7-9;3:1-7). Adam and Eve succumb to temptation and cause a rift between themselves and God.

Second Reading (Rom 5:12-19). By his obedience to God, Christ won back for us the gifts lost through the disobedience of Adam.

Gospel (Mt 4:1-11). Jesus was tempted by the devil, but unlike Adam and Eve, he did not succumb.

SCRIPTURE NOTE

In the First Reading we have the story of the tempting of Adam and Eve, and in the Gospel the story of the tempting of Jesus. They are two very sophisticated stories, and are not meant to be taken literally.

Jesus is the new Adam, who by his obedience restores for us the gifts lost by the disobedience of the first Adam (see Second Reading). He is also the new Israel. Like the first Israel he too was tested in the desert. But whereas the first Israel was found wanting, Jesus remained faithful to God.

HOMILY 1   **Paradise lost and found again**

The story of the fall of Adam and Eve, and the story of the tempting of Jesus, are two very sophisticated stories. They are essentially about making choices.

Before the fall, Adam and Eve had no choice. It was as if they were programmed to do the will of God. They had no sense of being responsible for their actions and choices. They knew no such thing as remorse or regret. But then they had no sense of well-being at doing the right thing either. They were no better than the animals, who live not by choice but by instinct.

But then God gave them the freedom to choose. In so doing he made it possible for them to be moral, that is, to choose freely to do what is right. Now they had the opportunity to live by choice, to live consciously. They had the freedom to say 'yes' or 'no' to God. Unfortunately they abused that freedom. To choose evil is to abuse freedom.

All our achievements, all our discoveries, all our wars, all the heights to which we have risen, and the depths to which we have sunk, have been about using or abusing the freedom of choice which God gave us.

In the desert Jesus was faced with the same choice as that which faced Adam and Eve: to do his own will or to do the will of God. Unlike Adam and Eve he made an irrevocable decision to do God's will rather than his own.

But we might say, 'Ah, it was easy for Jesus!' It wasn't easy for him. He too had to struggle to do the will of God. He was wholly human. This doesn't mean that he was merely human. The fact that he was 'without sin' did not imply any lack of humanness. Sin is not an intrinsic ingredient of humanness.

Every day we are faced with choices: to do good or to do evil, to choose for or against God. It's clear that we have in us a strain of rebelliousness, of self-centredness, of short-sightedness, which causes us to make the wrong choices, and leads to self-destructive behaviour.

The fact that Jesus won an important victory in the desert didn't mean the war was over. There would be other attacks. Every choice in life must be remade, perhaps many times. However, every right choice makes the next right choice easier. If we do the right thing often enough, eventually it becomes second nature to us. The real punishment for a sin is that is makes it more likely that we will commit the same sin the next time.

Adam and Eve lost their original innocence. So did we: we lost our childhood innocence. However, we can regain it. But this recovered innocence is different from the first. The first innocence was immature, not responsible, unacquainted with sorrow and evil; the second innocence is transfigured through responsibility and acquaintance with sorrow and evil. The first does not know how to sin; the second rises above sin. The first is harmless through weakness; the second is innocent through virtue. The first is incapable of committing sin; the second is unwilling to commit sin.

There is in every human heart a longing for the lost Eden and the lost Paradise. Jesus recalls us to our lost childhood. He recalls us to the source of our beginning. No matter how old we may be, he makes it possible for us to be reborn in innocence of character.

HOMILY 2   **Effective penance**

We have just begun Lent. And when we think of Lent we think of penance. Most people undertake some penance for Lent. This is a good and worthwhile practice. However, penance is not an end in itself.

Once upon a time a very earnest young man visited a famous rabbi. He told the rabbi that he wanted to become a rabbi and asked for his advice. It was winter time. The rabbi stood at the window looking out into the yard while the rabbinical candidate gave him a glowing account of his piety and learning.

The young man said, 'You see, Rabbi, I always dress in spotless white like the sages of old. I never drink any alcoholic beverages; only water ever passes my lips. I perform numerous penances. For instance, I always carry sharp-edged nails inside my shoes to mortify me. Even in the coldest weather, I lie naked in the snow to punish my flesh. And to complete my penance, I take a dozen lashes every day on my bare back.'

As the young man spoke, a stable boy led a white horse into the yard and took him to the water trough. The horse drank his fill of water, and having done so, rolled in the snow, as horses sometimes do.

'Just look!' cried the rabbi. 'That animal, too, is dressed in white. It also drinks nothing but water, has nails in its shoes and rolls naked in the snow. Also, rest assured, it gets its daily ration of lashes on the rump from its master. Now, I ask you, is it a saint, or is it a horse?'

The point the rabbi was making was that penance is not an end in itself. What is the purpose of penance? It is not meant to undo the past – the past is done. Nor is it meant to persuade God to erase our sins and forgo the punishment we deserve for them.

The first thing we are doing when we undertake penance is acknowledging that we are sinners. The second thing we are doing is expressing the desire to change our lives. The whole object of penance is to reform a sinful *way of life*.

Penance is an exercise in saying 'no' to ourselves. It is intended to show that we are capable of better things, and that we sincerely want those things. We want to reform our lives, but we know we cannot do so without the grace of God. Its purpose is to acquaint us with our better side – 'I'm not a bad person; I can do better.' It means taking a step in the right direction.

When people prune a fruit tree, they are not doing it to punish the tree, but to make it more fruitful. So our penances have as their goal to lead us to a new and better life.

It is a lot easier to undertake penances, even severe ones, than to try to change sinful attitudes or habits. For our penance to bear fruit it must result in a sincere effort to change our lives.

Lent provides us with a window of opportunity to look at ourselves to see how we can become better followers of Christ. The example of the sinless Jesus battling with Satan acts as a spur to us. The victorious One will help us to be victorious in our struggles with sin and evil.

HOMILY 3 **Struggle against temptation**

The first thing that needs to be said about the temptations of Jesus is that they were real. This was no play-acting. But the question arises: Can a good person be tempted like the rest of us? The truth is: the good person who resists temptation knows more about its power than the weakling who submits at the very onset of temptation. The following story illustrates the truth of this.

Once upon a time there were three shepherds who each was responsible for a flock of sheep. One winter's night all three were awakened by the howling of a wolf.

The first was about to get out of bed when he heard the rain beating against his bedroom window. He had second thoughts, turned over in bed, and went back to sleep.

The second got out of bed, dressed, and went to the front door. However, on opening it he was hit by a squall of sleety rain. He went back inside and returned to his warm bed.

The third got up, dressed, and went outside. There he had to contend with rain, wind, darkness and cold. But he stuck to his task until he had seen that his sheep were secure. When he got back indoors he was wet through and got a nasty cold as a result of his efforts.

Now which of the three shepherds knew most about the rain, the wind and the dark? The third of course.

Those who give in easily to temptation know little about the struggle involved. Those who struggle with temptation and overcome it, know it best. If you want to know what victory over temptation costs, don't ask a sinner; ask a saint.

It is because Jesus struggled with temptation and was victorious over it that he can help us in our struggles with temptation. If you want to give up cigarettes or drink, you don't look for help from someone who has tried and failed. You look for help from someone who has tried and succeeded.

What did temptation mean for Jesus? It meant the same as it meant for Adam and Eve, and as it means for us. It meant choosing between good and evil, between doing God's will and one's own will.

And his tempting was not a once-off event. He was tempted right throughout his life. His victory in the desert was not the winning of the war, but merely the winning of a battle.

Since even Jesus and the saints were tempted we can't hope to escape it. The struggle is between the passions of the flesh and the longings of the spirit. This struggle, with its almost inevitable falls, is not something to be ashamed of. Ours is not never to fall, but to fall, to rise, and go on in spite of everything.

And temptation is not necessarily a bad thing. By forcing us to choose good over evil it makes us strong. Every time one is tempted to do evil but makes a decision to do good, that makes one stronger. Suffering and struggle make us stronger.

Furthermore, how could we prove our fidelity if there was no temptation? There wouldn't be any particular credit in remaining virtuous through lack of temptation. Virtue would become meaningless if there was no evil, no struggle.

Virtue involves a choice between good and evil. That choice can sometimes be very difficult, and there is no definitive victory. The battle against evil is never over as long as we are on this earth. However, each right choice makes the next right choice more likely and easier.

But we might say, 'It was easy for Jesus!' It wasn't easy for him. He too had to struggle to do the will of God. His victory was no easy one. It was achieved through prayer, fasting, and reflection on and obedience to the word of God. The Holy Spirit was with Jesus during his struggle. And he is with us too in our struggles. It is a great consolation to know that God is not outside our struggle but is with us during it.

PRAYER OF THE FAITHFUL

President: Jesus was tempted in every way that we are, though he is without sin. Let us with confidence, then, approach him in our many needs.

Response: Create a new spirit within us, O Lord.

Reader(s): For the followers of Christ: that they may take the path of self-denial and renewal this Lent. [Pause] Let us pray to the Lord.

For those who hold public office: that they may not seek their own interests and glory, but to serve others humbly and faithfully. [Pause] Let us pray to the Lord.

For all those who have no time for the things of the spirit. [Pause] Let us pray to the Lord.

For ourselves: that we may have the courage and strength to try to overcome our temptations. [Pause] Let us pray to the Lord.

For our own special needs. [Longer pause] Let us pray to the Lord.

President: Heavenly Father, in your gentle mercy guide our efforts at renewing our lives this Lent, for we know that, left to ourselves, we cannot do your will. We ask this through Christ our Lord.

REFLECTION   **Pruning time**

Pruning time is a painful time for a fruit tree.
The pruner rids it of all those suckers

which use up a lot of energy but produce no fruit.
However, the aim of this surgery is not to inflict pain,
but to help the tree produce more and better fruit.
Lent is a kind of spiritual pruning time.
There is much that is useless
and perhaps harmful in our lives,
which saps our energy,
and diminishes our spiritual fruitfulness.
Of what shall we prune ourselves this Lent
so that we may become more fruitful branches
of Christ, the true Vine?

Second Sunday of Lent
THE TRANSFIGURATION

INTRODUCTION AND CONFITEOR

Each year on the second Sunday of Lent the Church puts before us the transfiguration of Jesus. His face shone and his clothes became dazzlingly white. We too can experience transfiguration. Virtue transfigures us. But sin disfigures us. Let us turn to the Lord for the help we need so that we can transfigure our lives by the practice of virtue. [Pause]

Lord, you help us to change hatred into love. Lord, have mercy.

Lord, you help us to change bitterness into forgiveness. Christ, have mercy.

Lord, you help us to change sorrow into joy. Lord, have mercy.

HEADINGS FOR READINGS

First Reading (Gen 12:1-4). This tells of the call of Abraham. Thanks to his faith in God the whole human race has been blessed.

Second Reading (2 Tim 1:8-10). The power of God and the vision of immortality enable the Christian to face the sufferings which faithfulness to the Gospel inevitably brings.

Gospel (Mt 17:1-9). On Mount Tabor the three disciples get a glimpse of the glory of Jesus.

SCRIPTURE NOTE

Like the story of Jesus' baptism, the transfiguration is an epiphany story. Both stories are manifestations of Jesus as he is, or as he will be. In both there is a voice, and the voice says the same words. A mountain is a place of divine manifestation. The cloud is a sign of the presence of God. Moses and Elijah stand for the Law and the Prophets.

It is no longer possible to say what happened on the mountain. Was it a vision? Was it a profound religious experience? There has been a tendency to see the Transfiguration simply as a stage in the education of the apostles. But its first and chief significance was for Jesus himself. It was meant to confirm him in the course he had taken.

But of course it also benefited the apostles. And it's this that Matthew emphasises. In the transfigured Jesus they got a glimpse of the glory of the risen Lord. Even so, they would not understand until Jesus had risen from the dead.

In the First Reading we see the obedience of Abraham, an obedience which brought blessings to many. It also points to the obedience of Jesus (an obedience which took him to death on a cross) and to the blessings that would flow to the world as a result.

HOMILY 1   **A peak experience**

Experiences influence us much more profoundly than talks and lectures. Even though we may not be able to analyse them, we know they affect us (for good or ill), and continue to do so for years afterwards.

The experience on Mount Tabor had great significance, first of all for Jesus himself. It came at a crucial moment in his public life – at the start of his journey to Jerusalem. He knew that the same fate awaited him there as befell all the prophets, namely, a violent death. Naturally he recoiled from such a fate. In order to reflect on it and pray about it, he climbed to the top of Mount Tabor, taking Peter, James and John with him.

As soon as they reached the top, Jesus began to pray. During his prayer, Moses and Elijah appeared to him and spoke to him about his forthcoming passion. More important, he experienced the presence of God. And he heard again the wonderful words of affirmation he had heard at his baptism: 'You are my beloved son; I am pleased with you.'

On Mount Tabor Jesus felt himself comforted, reassured, affirmed and strengthened for the ordeal ahead. It wasn't that everything became rosy. In fact, nothing changed. He still had to face a dark and threatening future. But he knew that somehow it was what God wanted from him, and that God would give him the strength to face it.

But the experience was also of great importance for the three apostles who were with him on the mountain. It confirmed their faith in Jesus and helped them to face that dark future with him.

The Tabor experience could be called 'a peak experience'. We too can have peak experiences or moments of transfiguration. We can have intense experiences of light, peace, unity, joy, exhilaration, meaning … and of the presence of God. These are true moments of grace which can be triggered off not only by prayer, but by poetry, music, nature … But they are more likely to be the fruit of suffering and painful struggle.

In his love for us, God allows us to taste on earth the joys of the world to come. He gives us glimpses of the promised land towards which we are travelling in faith.

Though these experiences are very beautiful, they should not become a preoccupation, for then religion would degenerate into a search for 'highs'. Too much emphasis on peak experiences, which are by definition rare and unpredictable, narrows the scope of God's influence in our lives, and renders the rest of life religiously unimportant. The religious dimension is always present. And in a strange way, the low moments may be just as enriching as the high ones. 'Was it not necessary that the Christ should suffer and so enter into his glory.'

After that wonderful experience on the mountain Jesus and the apostles had to go back down and resume the journey to Jerusalem. After a peak experience we too have to come down from the 'mountain' and return to the plain or valley, where life goes on in the darkness of faith. True religion does not encourage escape from life, but helps us to commit ourselves more deeply to it. This has been expressed beautifully by Emily Dickinson in a short poem which goes as follows:

> Exhilaration is the breeze
> that lifts us from the ground,
> and leaves us in another place
> whose statement is not found;
> Returns us not, but after time
> we soberly descend,
> a little newer for the term
> upon enchanted ground.

HOMILY 2   **Life: a journey of faith**

The Bible presents Abraham as the great model of faith. In one of the Eucharistic Prayers we refer to him as 'our father in faith'. At the word of God he left all the usual securities of life – home, family, country – and set out for a land he had never seen. It's easy to romanticise his journey. God alone knows the difficulties he encountered. The only compass he had was faith in God's promise.

Abraham touches us with his boldness and vulnerability. Even though he didn't know where he would end up, he trusted that God would be with him. From this he derived great strength. God blessed him and rewarded his faith by making him the father of a great people. It was from his descendants that Christ came.

We can identify with Abraham because too are on a journey – the great journey of life. And most of us have at some point also left our home, and embarked on a journey into the world. But even for those who have never left their own home, life is still a journey.

The truth is, we are involved not on one but on two journeys. The first is the outward journey we make through involvement in the world around us and finding our role there. The second is the inward journey. The inward journey is a search, a search for oneself, and ultimately a search for God.

Life's journey is truly a journey of faith because we don't know where it will take us. Faith begins with a call from God in some shape or form. It is a call to embark on a journey. God calls us forward, away from idols, out of where we are now, not necessarily into a new location, but into a new vision, new values, a new way of living. We draw inspiration from the example of those who have gone before us in faith.

That life is a journey is a powerful metaphor. But we must not understand it in too linear a fashion. It's not that simple. Every stage of the road is different. Even with the best faith in the world, we may still end up on dark roads we never imagined or wanted for ourselves. To have faith is not to have all the answers. It is to have bearings. There will be times in each of our lives when we will have to go forward armed only with our courage and our faith.

Even for Jesus life was a journey of faith. On Tabor he had a wonderful experience of the closeness of God his Father. This strengthened him for the journey on which he was about to embark – the journey to Jerusalem where a violent death awaited him.

We too can experience rare moments of light and joy. We get glimpses of the promised land towards which we are travelling in faith. In his love for us, God allows us to taste on earth the joys of the world to come. These moments are given to us so that we can remember them when God seems far away and everything appears dark and empty.

However, for the most part, like Abraham, we travel in the darkness of faith.

HOMILY 3   **Disfiguration and transfiguration**

Picture an old oil lamp covered with layers of dust and dirt. How wretched and useless it looks. Then someone comes along, cleans off the layers of dirt, polishes it until it begins to sparkle, and then lights it. Suddenly the lamp is transformed. It positively glows, radiating light and beauty to every corner of the room. Whereas prior to this it was disfigured with dust and dirt, now it is transfigured with beauty. Yet it is the same lamp. When an object (or a person) is loved and cared for, it is redeemed, and rendered brighter and worthier.

As Jesus went about Galilee his divinity was cloaked by his humanity. But on Mount Tabor God's light burst forth from the body of Jesus, and he was transfigured. The three apostles got a glimpse of his divinity, hidden in the depths of his humanity. They were overcome with the beauty and brilliance of it. It was not a surface thing, but an inner essence shining through. God was in Jesus.

There are two potentialities within us – the potentiality for evil and the potentiality for good. Take the potential for evil. We are capable of such things as hatred, bitterness, cruelty, greed, envy, lust … These are ugly things and bring out the worst in us. They corrupt the heart. And corruption of heart coarsens the face and darkens the eyes. Evil disfigures us.

Take our potential for good. We are capable of such things as love, joy, peace, patience, kindness, mercy, compassion … These are beautiful things and bring out the best in us. They purify the heart. And purity of heart softens the face and causes the eyes to shine. Goodness transfigures us.

Basically, we are transfigured by what we love, what excites us, what moves us, what rouses our spirit, what causes us to be awake and alive. What shows us at our brightest and best.

Van Gogh was not noted for his physical beauty. In fact, his face was described by some as being repulsive. Yet as soon as he began to speak about art, his melancholy expression would disappear, his eyes would sparkle, and his features would make a deep impression on those around him. It wasn't his own face any longer; it had become beautiful. It seemed that he was breathing in beauty.

At times all of us can feel down, a prey to feelings of failure and worthlessness. But then suddenly something nice happens to us – a friend calls, or we get a letter with some good news in it – and suddenly everything is changed. The truth, of course, is that nothing has changed. It's just that a spark of joy or hope or love has been kindled in our hearts, and we see ourselves and our lives in a new and better light.

We are made in the image of God; we carry the splendour of divinity within us. However, sin tarnishes that image and so disfigures us. But virtue causes that image to shine and so transfigures us. We are at our best when we are good.

Like the apostles on Mount Tabor, we too can experience rare moments of light and joy. We get glimpses of the promised land towards which we are travelling in faith. In his love for us, God allows us to taste on earth the joys of the world to come. In between, like Abraham, we travel in the darkness of faith.

PRAYER OF THE FAITHFUL

President: Let us pray that we may not grow faint on our journey but that we may have the courage to persevere.

Response: Lord, hear us in your love.

Reader(s): For all followers of Christ: that they may listen to his teachings and practise them in their lives. [Pause] We pray in faith.

For the Pope and the bishops: that they may lead the people of God with courage and faith. [Pause] We pray in faith.

For government leaders: that they may be wise and just in exercising their authority. [Pause] We pray in faith.

For those whose lives are disfigured by poverty, hunger, and suffering. [Pause] We pray in faith.

For grace to treasure moments of light which give meaning and hope to our lives. [Pause] We pray in faith.

For grace to bear witness to the hope we carry in our hearts. [Pause] We pray in faith.

For our own personal needs. [Longer pause] We pray in faith.

President: Lord God, may the radiance of your glory light up our hearts, and bring us safely through the shadows of this world until we reach our homeland of everlasting light. We ask this through Christ our Lord.

REFLECTION   **Time for adoration**

The Gospels show clearly that Peter was a man of action;
he always needed to be doing something.
So on Mount Tabor, instead of contemplating
in silence and wonder the glory of his Lord,
he wanted to build three tents.
There is a time for stillness,
for contemplation, for wonder,
for adoration in the presence of God.
A time to heed the words of the psalmist:
'Be still, and know that I am God.'
Sometimes we are too busy.
We would be better to be silent,
to be listening, to be wondering,
to be adoring in the presence of God.

Third Sunday of Lent
LIVING WATER

INTRODUCTION AND CONFITEOR

In today's Gospel we read about the moving encounter between Jesus and the Samaritan woman. During it Jesus told her about the gift God wanted to give her – the gift he called 'living water'. Here we encounter Jesus and he offers us the same gift. Let us dispose ourselves to receive the 'gift of God.' [Pause]

Like a deer that yearns for running streams, so our souls are yearning for you, O Lord. Lord, have mercy.

You preserve us for our happiness lies in you alone. Christ, have mercy.

Near restful waters you lead us, to revive our drooping spirits. Lord, have mercy.

HEADINGS FOR READINGS

First Reading (Ex 17:3-7). Despite their ingratitude, God shows his care for his people by providing water for them in the desert.

Second Reading (Rom 5:1-2.5-8). God has proved his extraordinary love for us by the fact that Christ died for us while we were still sinners.

Gospel (Jn 4:5-42). This tells the story of Jesus' touching encounter with a Samaritan woman. *(Three readers could be used.)*

SCRIPTURE NOTE

As the Israelites journeyed through the desert, Moses provided them with the life-saving gift of ordinary water. Jesus, the new Moses, gives the people something infinitely better – 'living water', a share in the very life of God.

HOMILY 1   **Loved in our sins**

One theme runs through all three of today's readings. It is a very important and comforting theme. You could say that it is the heart of the Good News. That theme is: we are loved in our sins.

We see this in the First Reading: in spite of the ingratitude and grumblings of the people, God doesn't write off his people, but shows his love for them by providing water for them in the desert. The message is explicitly stated in the Second Reading: Paul says, 'What proves that God loves us is that Christ died for us while we were still sinners.' And we see the message in action in the Gospel.

Jesus' approach to this outcast woman was ever so gentle. He didn't force himself into her life. Had he done so she would have immediately closed up. There is a world of difference between asking people for the key to their house, and battering the door down.

In fact, he began from a position of weakness. He began with a request for a drink of water. In this way he disposed her to receive the gift he wanted to give her. His heart was already open to her. Now she opened her heart to him. A wonderful dialogue ensued, and a marvellous exchange took place.

He treated her with great respect. Not a hint of judgement or condemnation. The holier a person is the less he is inclined to judge others. Right from the start he was looking into her heart, yet he did not make her feel bad. She didn't feel judged. Rather, she felt accepted and understood.

No one ever paid such close and loving attention to her before. Jesus explained her life to her more sympathetically than she'd been able to explain it to herself. Before she realised it, she had shared with him the whole story of her sad and confused life.

How could someone as pure as Jesus understand a woman like her? Kahlil Gibran says, 'Only the pure of heart forgive the thirst that leads to dead waters.'

Jesus was able to see into her secret being, into that part of her which longed for true love, which was pure and innocent, thirsting to be seen as a person and not as an object. She was a deeply wounded woman, wounded by a series of broken relationships, something that is becoming quite common today.

Christ meets us where we are. He says to us what he said to that lost woman: 'If you only knew the gift God wants to give you.'

We find it very difficult to admit our poverty, weakness, and sins. Hence we are unable to receive the 'gift of God' Jesus wishes to give us.

It doesn't do us much good to be loved for being perfect. We need to be accepted and loved precisely as sinners. Only the person who has experienced this kind of love can know what it is.

Being loved like that gives one surprising courage and energy.

It puts us in touch with our true nature, and to touch our true nature is a kind of home-coming.

HOMILY 2   **The giver who began by asking**

One day a poor man sat by the side of the road begging. But at the end of the morning he had nothing to show for his efforts. Weary and dejected, he continued to sit there in the hot noon sun. By his side lay a sack which contained a handful of wheat – just enough for one last cake of bread.

Suddenly he saw the king's carriage coming towards him, and hope flared up inside him. 'The king is a kind man,' he said to himself. 'He will give me something.'

He got to his feet, his heart beating with excitement. To his delight he noticed that the royal carriage was slowing down. It came to a halt opposite the spot where he stood with his hand stretched out in a begging attitude.

Down came the window, and the king appeared at it. The beggar man bowed low and was about to say, 'Good day, your Majesty. Could you spare a little money for me, your most unworthy servant?' But the king got in the first words. Reaching out his hand he said, 'Friend, could you spare a little corn for your king?'

The beggar man was completely taken aback at this turn of events. But he soon recovered and said, 'Certainly, your Majesty.' With that he opened the sack, took a quick look inside, picked out the smallest grain he could find, and gave it to the king, saying, 'I'm sorry it's so small, your Majesty, but it's all I can afford.'

The king thanked him, and the carriage moved off, leaving the beggar man feeling terribly disappointed and empty. All day long he sat there by the roadside begging but got nothing. When evening came on he made his way home, sad, tired and hungry. Once home, he took a pan and emptied the last of the wheat from the sack into it. As he inspected the meagre heap of grains, he made a startling discovery – the smallest of them had turned into a grain of pure gold.

He bitterly regretted that he had been so miserly with his king. If only he had known what gift the king wanted to give him, he would have given him all the wheat he had. Then he would never have to beg again. The moral of this little parable is simple: it is by giving that we receive, it is by sharing that we are enriched.

The story reminds us of the story in today's Gospel. A poor woman came to a well to draw water. She was an unhappy woman, an outcast in her community. She knew there was something missing in her life. Married five times, she still hadn't found what she was looking for.

At the well she met Jesus. Even though she didn't yet know it, he was the one person who could give her what she was looking for. Clearly she was the one in greatest need. Jesus was thirsting for ordinary water. But she had a deeper thirst – a thirst of the heart. But like the king in the story, he began as the one in need. He began by asking something from her, something very small – a drink of water. She gave him that drink., and a wonderful dialogue ensued.

The woman went away greatly enriched as a result of her encounter with Jesus. Yet he didn't give her anything. On the contrary, he asked something from her. In doing so he awakened her to her own riches, to the 'gift of God' within her. He conveyed to her a sense of her own worth and dignity. As a result, she underwent an extraordinary inner transformation.

In the heart of all people there is an indestructible core of goodness – the image of God. It is on this that the future has to be built. This wayward woman possessed this core too. Jesus was able to put her in touch with that in herself.

The greatest good we can do for other people is not to give them of our own wealth, but to show them their own.

Christ meets us where we are. He knows our deeper thirst – the thirst of the heart, which ultimately only God can quench. For this deeper thirst we need another kind of 'water', water Jesus said he could give and wanted to give. What is this water? It is the life of God bubbling up inside us, yes, bubbling up into eternal life.

What one would not give for a drop of that 'water' which Jesus gave to the Samaritan woman.

HOMILY 3 **Finding our own well**

We know how pathetic it is when people become dependent on material hand-outs. There is no development, no growth. There is only stagnation, and in all probability regression too. Dependency has a corrosive effect – it erodes pride and self-respect. What people need is not a hand-out but a hand-up. People can become spiritually dependent also, and that too is pathetic.

Once there was a woman who had to make a daily trip of a mile to draw water from a public well. Over the years she grew weary of the journey. No matter how much water she brought home, she always ended up with an empty container.

Then one day she was doing some work in her own garden when in a remote corner she came upon a large flagstone lying on the ground. The flagstone was completely covered with moss. Her curiosity flared up. She cleared away the moss, then removed the flagstone to discover a lovely well. She was thrilled. Never again would she have to make that tiresome journey to the public well. She now had an unfailing source of water of her own.

Most of us have been through years of education and spiritual formation of one kind or another. During those years we have had many teachers and spiritual guides. These worked hard at providing us with the waters of knowledge, waters drawn from their own or other people's wells. But we still thirsted. If only our teachers had helped us to find our own well, how much further on we would now be. Surely that should have been their chief concern.

It seems to me that this is what Jesus did for the Samaritan woman. She had been searching for love and happiness but always outside herself. Jesus directed her search inwards.

Ever so gently, he showed her that up to now she had been looking for the right thing (love), but in the wrong places. Then he told her that he could give her the 'water' that would quench her thirst for love and meaning in life. Where was this water to come from? Surprisingly, it was to come from inside herself. The spring was already there. It was just that up to now it had been hidden and blocked off.

Many spiritual teachers fill others from their own abundance. This is good up to a point. It can show people the riches that are available. But it can easily result in making people dependent on the teacher, so that they are content to live on spiritual hand-outs.

This approach makes people painfully aware of their own emptiness.

Sadly, many are content to live like that.

Christ made people aware of their own emptiness, but didn't leave it at that. He showed them how to begin to fill this emptiness, not from without, but from within.

Oh, that we may find the inner well, the well that lies hidden under the moss in our hearts. Then we won't have to be running here, there and everywhere in search of spiritual nourishment. We will have an unfailing source inside us. We must believe that this well is really there.

What is this inner spring? It is the life of God bubbling up inside us. The discovery of God is like a spring within us. A spring from which we can drink and refresh ourselves. A spring which bubbles up into eternal life.

PRAYER OF THE FAITHFUL

President: Let us pray with confidence to God who alone can quench our deepest thirst.

Response: Lord, hear our prayer.

Reader(s): For the followers of Christ: that they may turn away from the murky waters of sin, and seek instead the clear waters of grace. [Pause] We pray to the Lord.

For people everywhere: that they may realise that God alone can quench the thirst in the human heart. [Pause] We pray to the Lord.

For those who are lonely or rejected: that they may find in Christians people who are willing to listen to them. [Pause] We pray to the Lord.

For each other: that through prayer and the sacraments, we may grow in friendship and intimacy with Christ. [Pause] We pray to the Lord.

For ourselves: that our own special needs may have a place within the presence of God. [Longer pause] We pray to the Lord.

President: Heavenly Father, you sent your Son into our world to quench our thirst with the living water of your grace. Help us to accept his gift with eager hearts. We ask this through the Christ our Lord.

REFLECTION **The further thirst**

There is a thirst in every human heart.
Each of us is like that lonely Samaritan woman.
We are thirsting for something,
something that will satisfy all our longings.
But often we search in the wrong places.
We draw water from many wells:
the water of praise to quench our thirst for self-esteem;
the water of success to quench our thirst for importance;
the water of pleasure to quench our thirst for joy ...

But we still get thirsty.
Only God can give us what we are looking for.
He alone can cause a spring to well up inside us.
The water from this spring will sustain us
in our journey to the Promised Land of eternal life.

Fourth Sunday of Lent
CHRIST, THE LIGHT OF THE WORLD

INTRODUCTION AND CONFITEOR

There is a frightening amount of darkness in the world today. But the Gospel of today's Mass contains the wonderful words of Christ: 'I am the light of the world.' Christ is indeed the light of the world and of our lives. Let us reflect for a moment on how much we need his light for our own lives and for the world. [Pause] Let us turn to Christ whose light is shining on us now.

Lord Jesus, you help us to walk in the light of faith. Lord, have mercy.
Lord Jesus, you help us to walk in the light of hope. Christ, have mercy.
Lord Jesus, you help us to walk in the light of love. Lord, have mercy.

HEADINGS FOR READINGS

First Reading (1 Sam 16:1. 6-7.10-13). God chose David, the least of Jesse's sons, to be king of Israel. While people look at appearances, God looks at the heart.

Second Reading (Eph 5:8-14). Paul tells the Ephesians that now that Christ has enlightened them, they must adopt a lifestyle in keeping with their new state.

Gospel (Jn 9:1-41). Jesus, the light of the world, not only gives sight to the physically blind, but the light of faith to the spiritually blind. *(Three readers could be used.)*

SCRIPTURE NOTE

The Gospel story is a lesson on growth in faith. The climax of the story comes when the man makes a profession of faith in Jesus, 'Lord, I believe.' His journey from blindness to sight symbolises the journey from unbelief to faith, which is a journey from darkness to light. St Paul says, 'Once you were in darkness, but now you are light in the Lord' (Second Reading). Sadly, while the blind man opens more and more to the light, the Pharisees, who are physically sighted, become more and more spiritually blind. In giving sight to a blind man Jesus shows that he is 'the light of the world'.

The First Reading talks about the depth of God's seeing. While people look at appearances, God looks at the heart.

HOMILY 1   **The gift of sight**

In the Gospel story Jesus gives the gift of sight to a blind man. But since we are not blind, we might think that the Gospel story has no relevance for us. It is precisely because we can see that it has relevance for us. The question is: how well do we see?

The blind man in the Gospel story saw more than the religious leaders, in the sense that he had more faith in Jesus than they had. The Pharisees had perfect eyesight, yet they had no faith in Jesus.

To see well, good eyesight alone is not sufficient. We must not think that blindness is an illness that affects the eyes only. There are many forms of blindness besides physical blindness. In some ways these are just as crippling. Some examples:

Selfishness blinds us to the needs of others.

Insensitivity blinds us to the hurt we're causing to others.

Snobbery blinds us to the equal dignity of others.

Pride blinds us to our own faults.

Prejudice blinds us to the truth.

Hurry blinds us to the beauty of the world around.

Materialism blinds us to spiritual values.

Superficiality blinds us to a person's true worth and causes us to judge by appearances.

It is not with the eyes only that we see. We also 'see' with the mind, the heart, and the imagination. A narrow mind, a small heart, an impoverished imagination – all of these lead to loss of vision, darken our lives, and shrink our world.

It has been said that the greatest tragedy is not to be born blind, but to have eyes and yet fail to see. But there is an even worse situation: to have eyes and refuse to see. The latter was the situation of the Pharisees.

The most important eyes of all are the eyes of faith. The smallest child with faith sees more than the smartest scientist who had no faith. The Gospel story is essentially a faith story – the story of a man who came to faith in Jesus. The climax of the story is where the man makes a profession of faith: 'Lord, I believe.'

While the blind man opened more and more to the light of faith, the Pharisess, though physically sighted, became progressively more spiritually blind. Their blindness was caused by sin. Theirs was a wilful blindness – the refusal to see.

The man's journey from blindness to sight symbolises the journey from unbelief to faith, which is a journey from darkness to light. Physical sight is a wonderful gift which we should never take for granted. But faith is a deeper and more wonderful kind of seeing.

Paul says to the Ephesians, 'Once you were in darkness, but now you are light in the Lord.' Without faith we are in deep night and do not know where we are going.

Those who have been enlightened by Christ can never again see themselves and their lives in the same light as before. Everything is lit up with an inner radiance. Faith helps us to find our way through the chaos, confusion and darkness of the modern world.

The real voyage of discovery consists not in seeking new landscapes but in having new eyes.

HOMILY 2   **It's the heart that matters**

Israel needed a king. The first king of Israel, Saul, on whom such great hopes and expectations had been placed, had proved a failure and had been rejected by God. The prophet Samuel was commissioned by God to look for a new king.

As Samuel set out he pondered on the sort of qualities he should look for in the new king. His search led him to Bethlehem and the household of Jesse. There, one by one, he was introduced to seven of Jesse's sons. All of them possessed outstanding physical attributes. They were tall, strong, good-looking. They created a very good image. Samuel was impressed and was tempted to settle for one of them. Yet he wasn't quite satisfied. Something told him to continue his search.

He was looking for something else, something not so obvious but which he felt he would recognise if and when he saw it. Then, almost as an afterthought David was introduced to him. A mere youth, he was still physically underdeveloped. Judged by appearances, he didn't have much going for him. He didn't cut a good image.

Today the image has become more important than the reality, the appearance than the substance. Because we look only at appearances, we judge by appearances. And to judge by appearances is to judge superficially. Appearances can be very deceptive and very misleading. Everything that makes up the kernel of a person's life, is hidden from us. In the memorable words of the Little Prince, 'What is essential is invisible.'

Now while David didn't cut a good image, he did have something going for him. Samuel, a wise and perceptive man, noticed it at once. We are told that he had 'fine eyes and a pleasant bearing'. This tells us that there was another side to young David – an inner side. Though this other side was largely invisible, there were some outward manifestations of it. It showed itself in his pleasant personality. But above all it showed itself in his eyes. His clear and bright eyes pointed to a good heart.

As soon as Samuel saw David he knew that his search for a successor

to Saul was over. David made a good king and is one of the most important figures in the Old Testament. This doesn't mean that he was perfect.
He sinned and sinned grievously. But he always repented. Another sign
of his greatness was his ability to forgive his enemies. Several times in the
Gospel Jesus is called 'Son of David'. It was meant as a compliment.

David's heart was good. When all is said and done it is the heart that
matters. Darkness of heart is the blackest night of all. Emptiness of heart
is the greatest poverty of all. A heavy heart is the most wearisome burden
of all. A broken heart is the most painful wound of all.

In the Gospel story we see that the hearts of the Pharisees were in darkness. And not even Jesus, 'The light of the world', was able to bring light
to them. As for the poor blind man, not only his eyes became bright, but
his heart was filled with light as a result of his encounter with Jesus.

While we tend to look at appearances, God looks at the heart. God sees
what is in the heart. That is why only God can truly judge people.

HOMILY 3   **Work while you have the light**

The question of human suffering was a big problem in biblical times. It
still is a big problem.

An Old Testament view saw a connection between suffering and sin.
Suffering was seen as God's punishment for sin. Every time they saw
suffering served as a stark reminder to them of this side of God. But this
left them with a very negative image of God. It made God out to be spite-
ful and vindictive. And, by and large, this was the view that prevailed.

Hence, when the apostles saw the blind man they immediately concluded that his blindness was the result of sin. But there still remained
the problem: for whose sin was he suffering – his own or his parents'? So,
hoping that Jesus would solve the problem for them, they asked him,
'Why was this man born blind? Who sinned? Was it the man himself or
his parents?'

Jesus said, 'Neither this man nor his parents, but in order that the works
of God might be displayed in him.' Thus he rejected the connection between suffering and sin. The man's blindness was not a punishment from
God. God does not do evil. God does good.

We are no wiser as to the actual cause of the man's blindness. It might
have been the result of a genetic flaw, or the poor health practices in Palestine at that time, or just a random thing. We simply don't know. And it
really doesn't matter.

Jesus went on to say, 'This an opportunity for me to show you what
the works of God are really like.' Then he proceeded to heal the man. So
the man's blindness did reveal something about what God is like. It shows
God's compassion in the face of human suffering. The disciples may not
have found Jesus' answer fully satisfying. But it was the perfect answer

to the blind man. Talking about a problem will never solve it. Only action will.

Evil is a reality. The best response to it is good. What this man needed was not a lecture on the origins of evil but healing. Thus, what was a problem for the apostles became an opportunity for Jesus – an opportunity do the work of God, to show what God is really like.

Jesus went on the say that for himself time was running out. The day of his earthly life was drawing to a close; the night of death was fast approaching. The time for works of love and mercy was limited. 'As long as the day lasts I must carry out the work of the one who sent me.'

The suffering of others is an opportunity for us too – an opportunity to show care. The night is coming for us too. We do not know how much of life's day remains to us. Hence, we must try to make use of every opportunity that comes our way to do good.

We shall pass through this world but once. Any good, therefore, that we can do, or any kindness that we can show, to any human being, let us do it now; let us not defer it or neglect it, for we shall not pass this way again.

PRAYER OF THE FAITHFUL

President: Once we were darkness, but now we are light in the Lord. So let us pray as children of the light.

Response: Lord, that we may see.

Reader(s): For all Christians: that the light of faith may grow stronger in their lives. [Pause] Let us pray to the Lord.

For all those in positions of authority: that they may be able to judge wisely and act justly. [Pause] Let us pray to the Lord.

For all those who are in the darkness of doubt or unbelief: that Christ may enlighten them. [Pause] Let us pray to the Lord.

For all gathered here: that we may be saved from the calamity of having eyes, yet failing to see. [Pause] Let us pray to the Lord.

For our particular needs. [Longer pause] Let us pray to the Lord.

President: Heavenly Father, in this life we see as in a glass darkly. Open our eyes that we may walk with confidence along the road which leads to your Kingdom, where we shall see as we are seen. We ask this through Christ our Lord.

REFLECTION   **Blind to the usual**

One night a few years ago
there was a total eclipse of the moon.
Everybody was talking about it.
Many stayed up till the small hours

[86]

in the hope of witnessing it.
I asked myself:
'Why all this interest in the moon,
simply because it is disappearing?'
I was convinced that most of those people
wouldn't see a full moon in the sky,
much less stop to admire it.
It brought to mind the words of Emerson:
'The fool wonders at the unusual;
the wise person wonders at the usual.'

Fifth Sunday of Lent

CHRIST, THE RESURRECTION AND THE LIFE.

INTRODUCTION AND CONFITEOR

In today's Gospel we see a scene with which all of us are familiar, namely, people weeping over the death of a loved one. Jesus is at the centre of that scene. He is the one who gives hope to those who are surrounded by the shadows of death. [Pause]

Lord Jesus, you raise the dead to life in the Spirit. Lord, have mercy.

Lord Jesus, you bring pardon and peace to the sinner. Christ, have mercy.

Lord Jesus, you bring light to those who live in darkness and in the shadow of death. Lord, have mercy.

HEADINGS FOR READINGS

First Reading (Ezek 37:12-14). The exile of the people to Babylon is described in terms of death. And their return home is described in terms of resurrection and spiritual renewal.

Second Reading (Rom 8:8-11). It was the Spirit who raised Jesus from the dead. Now this same Spirit lives in us.

Gospel (Jn 11:1-45). By raising Lazarus from the dead, Jesus shows that he is Lord of life and death. *(Three readers could be used.)*

SCRIPTURE NOTE

John's main aim is to elicit faith in Jesus and to show the effects of faith in him. 'Lazarus is dead; and for your sake I am glad I was not there because now you will believe.' And the story ends with the words: 'Many of the Jews who had come to visit Mary and had seen what he did believed in him.' Martha is presented as a model of faith. In defiance of the evidence, she makes a wonderful profession of faith: 'I believe that you are the Christ, the Son of God, the one who was to come into the world.'

Jesus in the source of life, not just physical life, but the undying life of God. This new life is not a mere future hope but a present reality which physical death, despite appearances, does not negate. The key words in the story are: 'I am the resurrection and the life.' The delay in coming to Martha and Mary, and the fact that Lazarus has been dead for four days, serve to underline the point the evangelist is making, namely, that Jesus is the Master of life and death.

HOMILY 1   **We are not alone**

Everybody needs friends – even Jesus. In the village of Bethany Jesus had three very special friends – the sisters, Martha and Mary, and their brother, Lazarus. Their house remained open to him when many other houses were being closed against him.

When Lazarus got sick, it was only natural that the first one the two sisters should turn to for help was Jesus. They sent an urgent message to him, couched in language calculated to appeal to his heart. It said simply, 'Lord, the man you love is ill.' Their hope was that he would drop everything and come and cure him.

But surprisingly Jesus did not drop everything and rush to the bedside of his dying friend. Instead he stayed on where he was for two whole days. We don't know why. His delay in coming must have been heartbreaking for the sisters. Right in front of their eyes their brother's life was ebbing away. And the one they believed could do something about it wasn't there.

Well, Lazarus died. The Gospel shows the desolation his death caused to Martha and Mary. Of the two, Mary seems to have been the worst affected. She wouldn't even leave the house. While they had sympathetic people around them, the one they most wanted to be with them was not there. Jesus, their friend and the friend of Lazarus, was absent. And when he finally came, they suggested that he could have prevented this death 'Lord, if you had been here, our brother would not have died.'

The desolation experienced by Martha and Mary is one many of us have experienced. And when something bad happens to us or to a loved one, we can't help thinking that if God really cared about us, if he really loved us, then he wouldn't have allowed this thing to happen. We feel abandoned by God. We feel he has left us alone.

So what can we do? We must try to imitate Martha. The story presents her as a model of faith. In her hour of grief, she ran to the Lord and poured out her sorrow to him. And when he challenged her to believe, she made a wonderful profession of faith: 'I believe that you are the Christ, the Son of God, the one who was to come into the world.'

What we have to do then is to turn to God. We have to go on praying, to go on believing in God. Neither a good life, nor a close relationship with God, will necessarily save a person from a tragic death. In the face of our pain all we can do is commend ourselves to God, and abandon ourselves to his care.

When we suffer it seems as though God is absent. But when we pray we come to realise that God is not absent, but is present in our suffering. God is with us as our hope in adversity, and our strength in weakness.

The story shows Jesus as a faithful friend. It shows that even in death we are not beyond the reach of his help. He didn't leave Martha and Mary to grieve alone. He came to them at the height of their grief, shared their sorrow, and gave them hope by announcing eternal life to those who believe in him.

He does not leave us alone either. He surrounds us with the love and support of the community. And he challenges us to have faith in himself: 'I am the resurrection and the life. Anyone who believes in me will never die [eternally].' To believe doesn't mean that we know all the answers.

Jesus understands the anguish caused by death. He experienced it himself. He overcame death, not by avoiding it, but by undergoing it and overcoming it. Thus he has become a pathfinder and a beacon of hope for us.

HOMILY 2   **The therapy of tears**

One of the most surprising parts of the story of the raising of Lazarus is the part where Jesus breaks down and cries. Why should this be so?

Perhaps it is the sight of a man weeping in public that surprises us. In general, men are not good at showing emotions. A man is supposed to take the knocks. Some people build a wall behind which they hide what is fragile in themselves: their deepest feelings about life and other people. The Stoics of old were proud of their ability to conceal their feelings. They hid their anger, their sadness, and even their joy.

Our own culture is not comfortable with tears. Tears tend to be seen as a sign of weakness. But what is so natural, right, and healthy as tears when we lose a loved one? Besides, tears have a great therapeutic value, provided of course they are genuine, and not merely sentimental.

Jesus did not conceal his feelings. The Gospel makes this clear. He was moved with pity on seeing the plight of the ordinary people. He wept over the city of Jerusalem because he saw that it was heading for destruction. And he wept on the way to the tomb of Lazarus.

There are times when a leader shows sorrow in public, and it does not diminish him in the eyes of the people. Rather, the reverse. His vulnerability makes him more attractive. This is true of Jesus. The very fact that he broke down tells us more about his heartfelt sympathy for Martha and

Mary, and his solidarity with them, than a thousand words.

The story also shows the anguish of Martha and Mary at the death of their brother. But they were not afraid to express their grief, though they did so in contrasting ways. In spite of everything, Martha somehow continued to function, forcing herself to go on with life. Mary, on the other hand, retreated into her shell. We must help the process. We must try to help ourselves. We must allow others to help us.

Grief is one of the strongest emotions we are ever likely to experience. Some are embarrassed about expressing their grief in public. Believing that they are expected to bear up, they suppress their grief. It is now generally accepted that to suppress grief is not only bad but dangerous, and may lead to serious emotional problems later on.

The way to deal with grief is not to run away from it, or pretend it isn't there, but to face it and work through it with as much honesty and love as one can. Shed tears are bitter, but unshed tears are even more bitter.

Jesus accompanied Martha and Mary and shared their grief. At the same time he challenged them to believe: 'I am the resurrection and the life. Anyone who believes in me will never die [eternally]. Do you believe this?' And Martha said: 'I believe that you are the Christ, the Son of God, the one who was to come into the world.'

Faith is our great ally in facing death. It doesn't mean we have all the answers. And it doesn't dispense us from the painful work of grieving. But it does add a vital element to our grieving. That element is hope. We grieve as people who believe that death doesn't have the last word.

Faith also helps us to come to terms with our own mortality. We see the agony that weighs on the lives of many people today because death has been banished from their thoughts and their awareness. We have to find a way of thinking about death that integrates it into life instead of excluding it.

To become reconciled to death is a very great grace. A deeper and more human life results, as well as a falling away of fear.

In one of his books, the late Bryan McMahon tells how he once visited an old man who was close to death.

'Are you afraid of dying?' he asked the man.

'I'm not,' the man replied. 'The Almighty God put a blanket around me coming into the world and I don't remember being born. He'll put another blanket around me going out of it, and I won't remember dying but as little.'

HOMILY 3   **An invincible spring**

The Gospel story presents us with a scene which, alas, is all too familiar to us – people weeping over the death of a loved one. Of all the causes of tears, death is the chief culprit.

Death is like winter – only worse. In nature's winter, despite appearances to the contrary, life doesn't cease. It merely goes underground. The outward dies, but not the core. But in the winter of death, life seems to cease altogether. Death seems to rob us of everything.

When the winter of death came for Lazarus, his sisters, Martha and Mary, were plunged into grief. It is natural, right, and healthy that people should grieve when death robs them of a friend or family member. But Jesus didn't leave them alone in their grief. He came to them and shared their grief. He was so overcome with sorrow that he broke down. The very act of breaking down tells us more about his heartfelt sympathy and solidarity than a thousand words.

But he didn't leave it at that. He challenged them to have faith in himself. He said to them, 'I am the resurrection and the life. Those who believe in me, even though they die [to this life], will live. Do you believe this?' And Martha said, 'I believe that you are the Christ, the Son of God, the one who was to come into the world.'

It can't have been easy for them to believe as all the evidence was against them. Nevertheless, they believed. Faith isn't easy for us either. Death constitutes the severe test for our faith.

'I am the resurrection and the life.' This is one of the greatest statements in the Gospel. It means that Jesus holds the key to life and death. Though he himself experienced the winter of death, by rising from the dead in our mortal humanity, he broke the power of death forever. He entered the dark kingdom of death, and emerged victorious. Thus he has become a pathfinder for us. He has caused a new and invincible spring to dawn on all who believe in him.

We feel sad at the onset of winter. And it's hard to believe in spring when we see snow on the hills and feel a bitter wind in our faces. However, we are not too despondent because we know that spring will eventually renew everything again. In the same way, we are sad when the winter of death claims the life of a loved one, and when we think of our own death. Nevertheless, we are not overwhelmed. What sustains us is our faith in Jesus, the resurrection and the life.

Just as the expectation of spring takes the sting out of winter, so the resurrection of Jesus takes the sting out of death for us.

Eternal life is not something that begins when we die. It begins the moment we hear the voice of Jesus and believe in him. Thus, even in the midst of winter, we know that spring is already quietly at work, though its full blossoming is still in the future.

ANOTHER APPROACH.

Lazarus got his life back. Many people have a somewhat similar experience: e.g. those who have come out of a coma or who have recovered from a serious illness or accident. Such people have their life given back to them. (It might be possible to tell the story of one such case).

How precious life appears to such as these. All seems a grace, a blessing, a miracle. They know what Lazarus felt like. Against all the odds, they wake, come round and start to recognise the place and their loved ones. It's like being reborn.

However, the Gospel story speaks not just to these but to us all. Each morning we wake from the little death of sleep to find that our life has been given back to us. Life is such a precious thing. But, alas, we tend to take it for granted. What we must try to do is to receive it daily as a gift from God. Then we will not cease to be amazed at the wonder and mystery of life.

But there is much more at stake in the story of the raising of Lazarus than adding a few extra years to one's earthly life. What is really at stake is eternal life. Jesus in the source of eternal life for all who believe in him. He came that we might have life and have it to the full, here and hereafter.

PRAYER OF THE FAITHFUL

President: With confidence we raise up our prayers to the God with whom is mercy and fullness of redemption.

Response: Lord, hear us in your love.

Reader(s): For the Church: that it may proclaim to all the good news of eternal life won for us by Jesus Christ. [Pause] We pray in faith.

For political leaders: that they may facilitate the work of those engaged in caring for and in preserving life. [Pause] We pray in faith.

For those who care for the sick and the dying. [Pause] We pray in faith.

For all those who are grieving because of the death of a dear one. [Pause] We pray in faith.

For ourselves: that we may treasure the beautiful but fragile gift of life. [Pause] We pray in faith.

For our departed relatives and friends. [Pause] We pray in faith.

For our own special needs. [Longer pause] We pray in faith.

President: Lord God, through the resurrection of your Son, you have kindled in our hearts the hope of eternal life. Guard this hope with your grace, and bring it to fulfilment in the kingdom of heaven. We ask this through Christ our Lord.

REFLECTION   **I believe in death**

I believe in death.
I believe that it is part of life.
I believe that we are born to die,

to die that we may live more fully;
born to die a little each day
to selfishness, to pretence, and to sin.
I believe that every time we pass
from one stage of life to another,
something in us dies and something new is born.
I believe we taste death in moments of loneliness,
rejection, sorrow, disappointment, and failure.
I believe that we are dying before our time
when we live in bitterness, in hatred, and in isolation.
I believe that each day we are creating our own death
by the way we live.
For those with faith, death is not extinguishing the light;
it is putting out the lamp because the dawn has come. (*Anon.*)

REFLECTION   **Seeds of consolation**

What can I say to you, my friend,
in your hour of grief?
Just a word from my heart.
In the midst of your sorrow seeds are being sown –
seeds of consolation, hope, resignation, and even gratitude.
This winter will pass,
and spring will again visit the garden of your heart.
You will see these seeds grow, blossom, and bear fruit.
Then your sorrow will turn into joy,
a joy no one will be able to take from you.

Passion (Palm) Sunday

INTRODUCTION

The solemn procession with palms is the traditional start of this, the first liturgy of Holy Week, the most solemn week in the Church's year. When the procession reaches the church, Mass begins with the Collect.

HEADINGS FOR READINGS

Gospel for procession (Mt 21:1-11). Jesus enters Jerusalem, not as an all-conquering warrior, but as a gentle, humble bearer of Good News.

First Reading (Is 50:4-7). The prophet suffers in carrying out his mission, but is sustained by the firm belief that God will not abandon him.

Second Reading (Phil 2:6-11). Because Jesus took on himself our human condition, and accepted death on a cross, the Father has raised him up and made him Lord of heaven and earth.

Gospel (Matthew 26:14–27:66). St Matthew shows the passion as fulfilling the prophecies of Scripture, and portrays Jesus, because of his foreknowledge and free decision, as being in complete control of the situation.

HOMILY 1   **Those who put Christ to death**

At the end of World War II an international military tribunal was set up at Nuremberg to try the leading members of the Nazi regime, who were charged with crimes against humanity. These were the men who had made the whole of Europe shiver with fright. Yet they weren't devils incarnate. They were just human beings making evil choices. One observer, on being asked what the accused looked like, replied, 'They looked so ordinary, like men who had sat up all night in a third-class railway carriage.'

The people who put Christ to death were not a uniquely evil bunch of people, acting from the vilest possible motives. They were ordinary people. They belonged to the same human family as we do. In each we glimpse something of ourselves, of our failings, and the need of grace. This may be a troubling kinship but we cannot reject it.

Let us look briefly at the main characters in the Passion Story and the motives out of which they acted.

The Pharisees: These were austere, religious men, who devoted all their energy to doing good and the study of God's Law. But they were convinced of their own rightness, and history shows that such people are capable of the most appalling evil. Examples: the unconverted Paul; the Crusades; the Inquisition; the torture of suspects by governments, the atrocities of guerrillas …

Caiphas: He was perhaps thinking mainly about religious orthodoxy and how easily people get led astray by false messiahs. The Church condemned heretics to burn at the stake, thinking it was doing a service to God.

Pilate: He was thinking about his high office and the preservation of law and order at a time of great unrest. He knew that Jesus was innocent, but he feared that trouble would ensue if he did not give the religious leaders what they wanted. No doubt he was also thinking about his own job. Most people know what is right, but they don't always have the courage to do it.

Judas: Most likely he was a disillusioned man. But even he came to recognise and condemn the evil he had done. He could not live with the killing of an innocent man. Plenty of people today seem to have no such problem. Think of executioners, abortionists, terrorists, death squads. At times we all betray our ideals, if not our friends.

Peter: Here we have a man who was simply weak and cowardly. Any one of us would probably have denied Jesus in the same circumstances. Peter at least shed tears over his denials. How many of us shed tears over our denials?

The soldiers: They were simply carrying out orders. The Nazi leaders made the same excuse. At the Nuremberg trials they tried to convince their accusers that they really were men of good character whose only crime was loyalty. We too are rather good at blaming others for our sins. We refuse to accept responsibility for our cowardly acts and evasions.

The crowd: It was a highly emotional occasion. They simply got carried away. They didn't really know what was happening. Do we not often take refuge in the crowd? 'Everybody is doing it,' we protest.

But we must not lose sight of the central character in this sordid story, namely, Jesus himself. He shows us that the only way to overcome evil is by good. He loved us to the point of dying for us.

Dark evil sleeps in us all. Holy Week provides us with an opportunity to look at this. Christ will help us to confront the evil that is in ourselves and overcome it. But that's only the negative bit. There is a positive side. He will help us to become instruments of truth, justice, peace, and love in the world.

HOMILY 2   **The tracks we leave behind**

It's a winter's afternoon and the fields are covered with soft, clean snow. The snow is full of tracks made by birds and animals. On looking closely at those tracks it is possible to identify some of these birds and animals, and even to tell what they are up to.

Most of what you see there is harmless – the tracks of little creatures trying to stay alive in a hostile climate. For instance, you see the scratchings of sparrows in their quest for a worm, and the rootings of rabbits looking for a blade of grass. But then you see a spatter of blood on the snow where a fox or a bird of prey has made a kill.

On a normal day you could cross and re-cross these fields, and you would see nothing of the doings of the birds and animals. Everything would be covered up. But on this day their cover is blown and all is revealed. Everything is written there in the snow – innocence, fun, resourcefulness, pain, cunning, and red murder.

Something like this can happen in the world of humans. Something happens in the community or in the work-place, and people are forced to take a stand. Suddenly their cover is blown and they appear in their true colours. Some come out well, but others are shown in a very poor light.

The trial and execution of Christ was one of those events which revealed the minds and the hearts of people. Christ was such a transparently innocent person that when he was put on trial, the snow of his innocence fell from heaven and covered the earth. All those who were abroad on that day left clear tracks behind them. All had their cover blown.

It wasn't Christ who was judged on that day. It was his disciples, and especially his accusers and executioners. But it wasn't he who judged them. They judged themselves – by the tracks they left behind. Looking at those tracks even a child could tell who was for Christ and who was against him on that day.

When we look at those tracks what do we see? We see some ugly things. We see the hatred and fanaticism of Caiphas and the religious leaders who plotted his death. We see the cold, calculating evil of Judas who betrayed him. We see the weakness of Peter who disowned him. We see the cruelty of Herod who mocked him. We see the cowardice of Pilate who, though he knew he was innocent, signed his death warrant. We see the unthinking hostility of the mob who shouted: 'Crucify him! Crucify him!' We see the dutiful obedience of the soldiers who carried out the execution.

But we also see some lovely things. We see the compassion of Veronica who wiped his face. The courage of Simon of Cyrene who helped him carry the cross. The sympathy of the women of Jerusalem who wept for him. And the steadfast loyalty of a little group of friends who stayed with him to the end, among these were his mother and the disciple John.

All of us leave tracks behind us. This week gives us an opportunity to put down our bags and look back at the tracks we are leaving behind us. Are they the tracks of a coward, or a hypocrite, or someone who lives only for himself/herself? Or are they the tracks of a courageous, generous person, who is not ashamed to call himself/herself a disciple of Jesus.

We will see whether or not we are on the side of Christ in so far as we are on the side of our brothers and sisters, or whether we are against him because we are against our brothers and sisters.

The extent of our virtue is determined, not by what we do in extraordinary circumstances, but by our normal behaviour. It is modest, everyday incidents rather than extraordinary ones that most reveal and shape our characters.

However, we must not lose sight of the central character in the Passion Story, namely, Jesus himself. He shows us that the only way to overcome evil is by good. He forgave those who killed him.

And from the depths of his own pain he reached out to others. He sympathised with the women of Jerusalem. He brought hope to the repentant thief. He thought about his mother and asked John to take care of her. Some people are like sugar cane: even when crushed in the mill, completely squashed, reduced to pulp, all they yield is sweetness.

HOMILY 3   **The long silence**

I had a dream that it was the end of time. Billions and billions of people were assembled on a great plain before the throne of God, waiting to be judged. Some were fearful but others were angry.

A woman said, 'How can God judge us? What does He know about suffering? We endured terror, beatings, torture, death.' Then she pulled up her sleeve to show a tattooed number from a Nazi concentration camp on her arm.

Then a black man lowered his collar to show an ugly rope burn around his neck. 'What about this?' he asked. 'Lynched for no crime but being black. We have suffocated in slave ships, been wrenched from loved ones, toiled till only death gave us release.'

Next a girl with the word 'illegitimate' stamped on her forehead said, 'To endure my stigma was beyond, beyond … ' and her voice trailed off to be taken up by others.

All had a complaint against God for the evil and suffering he had permitted during their lives on earth. How lucky God was to live in heaven where all was sweetness and light, where there was no weeping, no fear, no hunger, no hatred. What did God know about human suffering?

They decided that God should be sentenced to live on earth – as a man. But because he was God, they would set certain safeguards to be sure he could not use his divine powers to help himself.

Let him be born a Jew. Let the legitimacy of his birth be doubted so that none will know who is really his father. Give him a work so difficult that even his family will think he is out of his mind when he tries to do it.

Let him be betrayed by his dearest friends. Let him be indicted on false charges, tried before a prejudiced jury, convicted by a cowardly judge.

At last, let him see what it means to be terribly alone, completely abandoned by every living thing. Let him be tortured and mocked. Then let him die. Let him die so that there can be no doubt he died. Let there be a great host of witnesses to verify it.

As each portion of the sentence was announced, loud murmurs of approval went up from the great throng of people assembled. When they had finished pronouncing sentence, a long silence ensued. No one uttered a word. No one moved. For suddenly all knew. God had already served his sentence.

Our God came to live among us. Put God on trial if you will. Shake your fist at him, spit in his face, scourge him and finally crucify him. What does it matter? It's already been done to him.

It is a great comfort to us to know that Christ, the innocent and sinless One, has gone down the road of suffering before us, and gone down it to the end. On the cross he gathered up all human pain and made it his own.

[97]

Though the road of suffering is narrow and difficult, it is not the same since Christ travelled it. A bright light illuminates it. And even though it leads to Calvary, it doesn't end there. It ends at Easter.

Those who link their sufferings to those of Christ become a source of blessings for others, and will share Christ's Easter glory.

PRAYER OF THE FAITHFUL

President: As we begin the week in which Christ suffered, let us pray for our needs to God.

Response: Lord, hear our prayer.

Reader(s): For Christians: that they may respond with compassion to the sufferings of those around them. [Pause] Let us pray to the Lord.

For judges and government leaders: that they may strive to see that justice is done in all cases. [Pause] Let us pray to the Lord.

For all who suffer unjustly. [Pause] Let us pray to the Lord.

For those in pain of any kind. [Pause] Let us pray to the Lord.

For each other: that we may be able to unite our sufferings to those of Christ, and so know his power in our weakness. [Pause] Let us pray to the Lord.

For grace in our own sufferings and those of our loved ones. [Longer pause] Let us pray to the Lord.

President: Father, help us to follow Christ your Son along the road to Calvary so that we may share in his Easter victory. We make this prayer through the same Christ our Lord.

SIGN OF PEACE

Lord Jesus Christ, you looked with love on the holy city of Jerusalem, and with tears in your eyes you said, 'If only you understood the message of peace. But, alas, it is hidden from your eyes.' Look with pity on our world, torn asunder by war and strife, and grant that all of God's children may enjoy the peace and unity of your kingdom, where you live for ever and ever.

REFLECTION   **Prayer for forgiveness**

Lord, remember not only people of good will
but also people of ill will.
Do not remember only the sufferings
that have been inflicted on us,
but remember too the fruit we have bought
as a result of this suffering:
the comradeship and loyalty,
the humility and courage,

the generosity and greatness of heart
that has grown out of it.
And when they come to judgement,
let all the fruits that we have borne be their forgiveness.
(Prayer found in Auschwitz).

EASTERTIDE

'The Resurrection'

PATRICK PYE

Easter Sunday

This is a day for celebration. This is the day Christ our Brother broke the chains of death and rose in triumph from the grave. He did this, not just for himself, but for all of us. He wants us to share in his great victory over sin and death. Let us pause to reflect on this. [Pause]

Our sharing in the resurrection begins now.

Lord Jesus, through your resurrection you free us from our sins. Lord, have mercy.

Lord Jesus, through your resurrection you free us from the power of death. Christ, have mercy.

Lord Jesus, through your resurrection you enable us to live in the freedom of the children of God. Lord, have mercy.

HEADINGS FOR READINGS

First Reading (Acts 10:34.37-43). This is part of an early sermon preached by St Peter in which he proclaims the risen Jesus to be the Saviour of those who believe in him, and Judge of the living and the dead.

Second Reading (Col 3:1-4). Through our Baptism we already share in the risen life of Christ, though in a hidden and mysterious way.

Gospel (Jn 20:1-9). On their finding Jesus' tomb empty, the truth of his resurrection begins to dawn on his disciples.

HOMILY 1   **Renewal of baptismal promises**

Each member of the congregation should have a candle lit from the Paschal Candle.

Priest: My dear sisters and brothers, we were once in darkness, but in his great love for us, God has called us out of darkness into the wonderful light of his Son. We must live as children of the light. The effects of the light are seen in goodness, right living and truth.

Now that we have completed our Lenten exercises, and the light of Easter has dawned for us, let us renew our belief in the light of Christ, and commit ourselves to follow it more faithfully. This, after all, is what we promised at baptism when this precious light was first kindled in our hearts.

Response: I do.

Do you believe in God the Father, source of all light, and in his love for you?

Do you reject the many false gods the world offers for your adoration?

Do you reject Satan, the prince of darkness?

Do you reject the works of darkness, namely, sin?

Do you reject the false lights by which Satan seeks to lure you from the path of the Gospel: greed for material things, lust for pleasure, craving for power and popularity?

Do you believe in Christ, the light of the world?

Do you believe that Christ has entrusted his light to us, and that he now depends on us to let the light of goodness shine in the world today?

Do you believe that by rising from the dead Christ has overcome the darkness of death, and that we can do the same if we have faith in him?

Do you believe in the Holy Spirit who dwells within us, consoling us in times of sorrow, strengthening us in times of difficulty, and binding us together in the love of Christ?

Do you believe in the Church, the community of believers in the light, brothers and sisters in the Lord?

Do you believe that Mary, the Mother of Jesus, is also our Mother, and the Mother of the entire Christian community?

And now, my sisters and brothers, I say to you in the name of Christ: Hold up your heads. Never be ashamed of this light. Then Christ will not be ashamed of you before his Father in heaven.

May the Lord bless you and keep you faithful.

The priest now blesses the people with holy water, inviting them to pray silently for the grace to be faithful to Christ. As far as possible, he should go all around the church in order to ensure that everybody is sprinkled. If need be, let him get some help.

Let us pray:

God of love and mercy, through the resurrection of your Son, you have kindled in our hearts the hope of eternal life. Guard this hope with your grace, and bring it to fulfilment in the kingdom of heaven. We ask this through Christ our Lord.

HOMILY 2 **Don't look among the dead for one who is alive**

A nun working in England tells the following story.

A few weeks before Easter the father of one of the pupils from the convent school was involved in a horrible accident. While burning some branches in his garden he accidentally set fire to himself, and died as a result of his burns.

Naturally his family went into deep shock, and a pall of grief settled over the house. The fact that the tragedy happened at home made it even worse. His wife was so distraught that she couldn't go out into the garden where the accident happened. Indeed, she found it difficult even to look out the window that faced onto the garden in case it brought the whole thing back to her.

However, the days went by, and Easter came around. On Easter Sunday afternoon the nun visited the family again. She was expecting to find them still grief-stricken. But she got a very pleasant surprise. As soon as she stepped into the house, she sensed that the gloom had lifted, and she got a feeling of peace, even of joy.

'Something has happened here,' she said to the mother. 'I can sense it.'

To which the mother replied, 'This morning my sister and a neighbouring woman came to visit me. They asked me to go out into the garden to get some fresh air. I became almost hysterical at the thought of going into the garden. But convinced that it would help me, they insisted, so eventually I went out with them.

'Slowly we walked down to the place where the fire had happened. As we approached the spot my whole body began to shake. But suddenly, I don't know how or from where, the words of the Gospel came to me: "Why do you look for the living among the dead? He is not here. He is risen." And at that moment it was as if a heavy load was lifted off my back, and I felt a great sense of peace and joy.'

This story brings to mind the women who visited Jesus' tomb on Easter Sunday morning. It can't have been easy for them either to go to the place where they had laid his body. They would have done so with heavy hearts and leaden feet. But they had a job to do – to complete the embalming of his body. They felt sad, terribly sad. Jesus was dead. Jesus was gone. And it seemed for ever. The world felt so empty without him. They couldn't imagine life without him.

However, when they reached the tomb, they found that it was empty. But then they heard the wonderful news: 'Do not look for the living among the dead. He is not here. He has risen.' He is not here in this place of death; he is alive, he is risen. The burial robes were left behind, because they are for the dead, not the living. By God's power, Jesus has escaped from the bonds of death and corruption.

But where and how is he living now? He has not returned to earthly life. He has risen to a new and richer life. A radically new life, where his perishable flesh is now transfigured and radiant with the glory and splendour of divinity. It is the same Jesus, but a new manner of living – like a seed which dies in the ground and comes to new life as a plant. The plant comes from the seed but is barely recognisable as its offshoot. As St Paul puts is: 'What is sown is perishable, what is raised is imperishable.'

And the disciples believed. Perhaps not completely at first. But gradually the Easter message took root in their hearts. Jesus was not dead. He was alive. So they must not waste their time looking for him at the tomb.

Through the Church's Easter liturgy, the same message is announced to us: 'Do not look for the living among the dead. He is not here. He has risen.' Jesus has overcome death, not just for himself, but for all of us. He is the first to rise from the dead, but we are to follow him. For a Christian, then, there is no such thing as death in the sense of final extinction. Our dead are not dead. They share the life of the risen Christ. They are alive. And that's how we should think of them.

What happened at Easter enables us to let go of our loved ones in faith. However, this doesn't mean forgetting them. Easter also helps us to face our own death with courage and hope. Just as the expectation of spring takes the sting out of winter, so the resurrection of Jesus takes the sting out of death for us.

HOMILY 3   **The hope Easter gives**

We can face anything, endure anything, as long as we know or believe it will not last for ever, and that something better will happen.

For instance, people will face a long, painful and dangerous operation if they believe it will make them well again. Prisoners can face a long sentence as long as they believe it will end, and that they will enjoy freedom again. We can face the rigours of a long and miserable winter because we know that spring will come again.

What all this underlines is the importance of hope. Hope is as necessary for the spirit as bread is for the body. It is amazing what the human spirit can endure and overcome provided it is nourished by the bread of hope.

Easter provides an enormous injection of hope for the human spirit. And how much it is needed. There is a lot of tragedy in life. Good things are destroyed. Good people are cut down: Thomas More, Mahatma Gandhi, Martin Luther King, Oscar Romero … And of course Jesus. He too was cut down. But he rose again.

The world didn't take much notice of the resurrection of Jesus. The reason for this lies in the fact that it was a humble, hidden event. Jesus did not appear in triumph in the Temple in Jerusalem, humiliating those who humiliated him. Only those whom he called by name, with whom he broke bread and to whom he spoke words of peace, were aware of what happened. And even they had difficulty in believing. Like us, they were slow to believe. Yet, it was this hidden event that freed humanity from the shackles of death.

Jesus rose as a sign to those who loved him and followed him that God's love is stronger than death. The resurrection of Jesus must not be separated from the resurrection of humanity saved by him. By entering fully into human life, and by experiencing the bitterness of death, Jesus became a Brother and a Saviour to all people. The death of Jesus was part of God's plan. Jesus is the Pioneer and Leader of our salvation: pointing the way and leading the way along the road of obedience and suffering.

At Easter we still feel the pain of the world, the pain in our families and among our friends, and the pain in our own hearts. But a new element has been introduced into our lives. It doesn't remove the pain but it gives it a meaning. It lights it up with hope. All is different because Jesus is alive and speaks his words of peace to us as he spoke them to the apostles.

Faith in the resurrection of Jesus is the basis of our hope of eternal life, a hope which enables us to bear patiently the trials of life. Therefore, there is a quiet joy among us and a deep sense of peace because we know that life is stronger than death, love is stronger than fear, and hope is stronger than despair.

> Had this one day not been, or could it cease to be –
> How smitten, how superfluous were every other day.
> *(Emily Dickinson)*

PRAYER OF THE FAITHFUL

President: Let us pray to God who rescued his beloved Son from the darkness of death and brought him into the light of glory.

Response: Lord, hear us in your love.

Reader(s): For all Christians: that they may experience the joy of Christ's victory over death. [Pause] We pray in faith.

For all government leaders: that Christ's victory over evil may encourage them in their work for justice and peace. [Pause] We pray in faith.

For those who have no faith in an after-life: that the joy of this great day may be felt by them too. [Pause] We pray in faith.

For each other: that we may be able to overcome our fear of death, since Christ underwent it and overcame it for us. [Pause] We pray in faith.

For our deceased relatives and friends, and all the faithful departed: that they may share in the risen life of Christ. [Pause] We pray in faith.

For our own special needs. [Longer pause] We pray in faith.

President: God our Father, the power of this day drives away all evil, washes away all guilt, restores lost innocence, brings joy to those who mourn, casts out hatred, brings peace, and humbles earthly pride. May we experience its power in our lives and in our world. We ask this through Christ our Lord.

SIGN OF PEACE

Lord Jesus Christ, on Easter Sunday evening you appeared to your frightened and disheartened disciples and said to them: 'Peace be with you'. Then you showed them your wounded hands and side, and they were filled with joy. Grant that we who have heard the message of Easter, may enjoy the peace and unity of your kingdom where you live for ever and ever.

REFLECTION   **Death overcome**

As long as the sun comes over the hills,
scatters the darkness, and fills the world with light;
as long as the fields get green again,
and the primroses and violets return;
as long as the trees fill up again with leaves,
there is hope for us and for the world.
So come, let us follow the footsteps of spring,
for the snow has melted,
and life is awakening from its sleep
and wanders through the hills and valleys.
Come, let us ascend the heights
and gaze upon the waving greenness of the plains below.
O come, let us rejoice on this Easter Day,
for death has folded up his tent and gone away.

Second Sunday of Easter
DOUBTING THOMAS

INTRODUCTION AND CONFITEOR

In today's Gospel we meet Doubting Thomas. Each of us has something in common with Doubting Thomas, because at times we too are troubled by doubts. Instead of denying our doubts, let us bring them to the Lord. [Pause]

In his love for us, the Lord helps us to turn our doubts into faith.

Lord Jesus, you help us to believe that your love for us is unchanging and unfailing. Lord, have mercy.

Lord Jesus, you help us to believe that your forgiveness is all-embracing. Christ, have mercy.

Lord Jesus, you help us to believe in your promise of eternal life. Lord, have mercy.

HEADINGS FOR READINGS

First Reading (Acts 2:42-47). The early Christian community was characterised by worship of God and loving service towards one another.

Second Reading (1 Pet 1:3-9). Faith in the resurrection of Jesus is the basis of our hope of eternal life, a hope which enables us to bear patiently the trials of life.

Gospel (Jn 20:19-31). When he touched the wounds of the risen Jesus, Thomas' doubt was turned into faith.

HOMILY 1 **Faith and community**

It seems that after Good Friday Thomas had cut himself off from the other apostles, and walked alone. This was a big mistake. But we must remember that he was in deep grief. People who are grieving have a tendency to isolate themselves. While it is understandable it is not helpful. In cutting himself off from the other apostles, Thomas made things more difficult for himself.

However, it seems that he hadn't cut himself off completely. Whenever he met them, he would have noticed a difference in them. Their fear was largely gone, and had been replaced by joy and peace. It was clear that someone had breathed new life into them. They claimed that they had seen Jesus.

But Thomas refused to take their word for it. He had to be sure. We can sympathise with Thomas. He was merely echoing the human cry for certainty. However, here on earth there is no such thing as absolute certainty about spiritual things. If there was, faith would not be necessary.

But Thomas was being stubborn too. However, he did one good thing. He rejoined the apostles. Now he had the support of the community.

The great power of the community was brought home to me very vividly one Sunday morning a couple of years ago. It was a sunny morning in early April. The snowdrops had handed over the torch of spring to the primroses. On my way into Dublin I passed through a small town. Trickles of people were filtering from every street and forming into little pools. Soon the pools joined up to form streams. Near the church the streams became a river. They came in ones, twos, and larger groups. Every age-group was represented. It was a heartening sight. God's scattered children were being gathered together. God's fragmented family was being reunited.

Suddenly the power of example came home to me. We create a current that makes it easier for one another to go to the house of God. This week my faith may be weak. I may be feeling apathetic. In that case, let me not be ashamed to yield myself to the current, and allow myself to be carried. Next week (Who knows?) my faith may be strong, and I may be feeling enthusiastic. Then I will help to carry someone else.

It was only when he rejoined the community that Thomas encountered the risen Jesus, and so found faith again.

To be a believer, or just a spiritual person, in today's world can be a lonely business. We need support. Here is where the community comes in. It is only with the help of the community that we can resolve our doubts and sustain our faith. We live as members of a community of believers whose common faith strengthens the faith of each individual.

We see the kind of community the first Christians enjoyed. They supported one another by praying and worshipping together, and by a loving service of one another. Our ministry to one another consists not so much in doing things for one another, as in travelling together, listening to and learning from one another.

HOMILY 2   **The true greatness of Jesus**

Christy Brown, the disabled Dublin writer, died in 1981. One day, long before he became famous, he saw a picture of the English novelist, Margaret Foster, on the dust cover of one of her books, and immediately fell in love with her. He wrote her a letter that brimmed with charm and wit. She replied, and thus began a warm friendship.

Christy was very anxious to meet her. However, when she learned that he was severely physically handicapped, she was dead against it. From the kind of letters he wrote, she had formed a beautiful image of him in her mind, and was afraid that if she met him, her fantasy would be destroyed.

However, they did eventually meet. By this time Christy was a well-known writer himself. Sure enough, when she saw Christy's severely crippled body, she couldn't take it. She stopped answering his letters, and their friendship petered out.

Christy could move only the toe of his left foot. With this he somehow learned to type. It was with this toe that he wrote those charming letters and his subsequent books. His greatness lay in the fact that, despite his handicap, he still managed to write those letters. But Margaret was unable to see this. All she could see was a twisted body. Unable to take this, she eased him out of her life.

The death of Jesus had a similar affect on the apostles. They had come to believe, or at least to hope, that Jesus was the long-awaited Messiah. But they had an idealised picture of the Messiah. They pictured him as a great leader and a triumphant conqueror. The idea of a suffering and crucified Messiah was a million miles from their minds. So, when Jesus was killed, all their hopes were shattered. Thomas was the worst affected.

But when Thomas touched the wounds of Jesus, the true greatness of Jesus dawned on him, his doubts vanished, and his faith was re-born. He realised that this was how Jesus had proved his love for them. He didn't just talk about love; he gave an example of it, and had the wounds to prove it.

Many of us probably have an idealised picture of Jesus. If we met the real Jesus, especially the Jesus of the passion, we might not recognise him; we might not even want to know him.

And yet, just as the greatness of Christy Brown lay in the fact that, in spite of his severe handicap, he could write so well, so the greatness of Jesus (speaking in very human terms) lay in the fact that, despite being bruised, beaten, broken in body, he still went on loving. It is here that his true greatness shines out. It was thus that he proved his love for us. And it was in this way that he attained to glory.

And in so doing, he shows us the path to go.

HOMILY 3 **The human need to touch**

When tourists visit a so-called 'beauty spot', they feel the need to take photos, buy cards, and souvenirs. They want to have some tangible memento to take home to show their friends, and which will help to keep alive their memory of the place.

You see this especially with pilgrims to the Holy Land. They want to touch and to kiss things. They buy lots of souvenirs. And they collect lots of little things to take back home with them from the various holy places they visit – a leaf, a wild flower, a pebble, a bottle of water, a little soil … They want to have something tangible to take away to show their friends, and as a visible reminder to themselves of their trip. And here we are talking about people whose faith is sound and sure.

This expresses the universal human need for the visible, the concrete, the tangible. Hence, we can sympathise with Thomas when he declared that he would not believe the Lord was risen unless he actually touched him. He was merely echoing the human cry for certainty. Nevertheless, where faith is concerned we have to go beyond this. Because here on earth there is no such thing as absolute certainty about spiritual things. If there was, faith would not be necessary.

Why did Thomas insist that he had to touch Jesus? Wasn't seeing him enough? He had to touch him in order to be healed. He had seen others healed by touching him. Some of these were healed by touching just the hem of his robe, so strong was their faith. But Thomas' faith was so weak that he had to touch Jesus himself.

In truth, Thomas was the wounded one. His mind was darkened by doubt. His heart was broken with grief. Even though these wounds were invisible, they were very real and very painful. But Jesus was able to see them. It was he who touched Thomas' wounds, and so made him whole and well again.

The human heart is healed only by the presence of another human being who understands human pain. The Lord's wounds help us to recognise our own wounds, and to find healing for them. His wounds were caused by his love. They were the proof of his love. They were the mortal wounds the Good Shepherd suffered for the sake of his sheep.

The story of Doubting Thomas brings home to us just how frail is the human container in which the gift of faith is carried. And it also shows us that Christian faith is essentially faith in a Person who loves us – and has the wounds to prove it. That person is Jesus. At the heart of biblical faith is not only the faith we have in God, but the faith God has in us.

Jesus said to Thomas, 'Thomas, you believe in me because you have seen me and touched me. But blessed are those who have not seen and yet believe.' This was a little dig at Thomas' stubbornness. But it was also meant as an encouragement to us who are asked to believe without being able to see or touch Jesus.

PRAYER OF THE FAITHFUL

President: As people who have not seen and yet believe, we turn in prayer to the God of life.

Response: Lord, hear us in your love.

Reader(s): For Christians: that like Thomas they may acknowledge Jesus as their Lord and God, and show by their lives that their faith is real. [Pause] We pray in faith.

For government leaders: that they may have more faith and trust in one another, and so spread understanding among peoples. [Pause] We pray in faith.

For those who right now are finding it hard to believe. [Pause] We pray in faith.

For those who are grieving the loss of a loved one: that the Lord, may console them and restore them to full fellowship with their friends and the community. [Pause] We pray in faith.

For each other: that we may be able to see Christ in the signs that he left us: giving us life in Baptism, forgiving us in the sacrament of Reconciliation, and nourishing us in the Eucharist. [Pause] We pray in faith.

For ourselves: that we may bring our own special needs to the Lord. [Longer pause] We pray in faith.

President: Lord God, through the resurrection of your Son, you have kindled in our hearts the hope of eternal life. Guard this hope with your grace, and bring it to fulfilment in the kingdom of heaven. We ask this through Christ our Lord.

REFLECTION   **What faith does**

Some people think that if you have enough faith
life will be plain sailing for you. But this is not so.
The fact that we can swim doesn't prevent us
from being knocked about by the waves.
In the same way faith doesn't shield us
from the hard knocks of life or death.
What, then, does faith do?
It gives us bearings and thus enables us
to live in a topsy-turvey world
without getting lost or giving in to despair.

Just as swimmers trust that if they don't panic,
and if they do a few simple things,
then the power of the sea will uphold them,
so believers entrust their lives
to a power greater than themselves,
a power greater than us all.
This power is the power of God,
who brought his Son, Jesus, back from the dead.

Third Sunday of Easter
THE ROAD TO EMMAUS

INTRODUCTION AND CONFITEOR

One of the loveliest stories in the Gospel is the story of how the risen Jesus joined two of his disciples on the road to Emmaus. He explained the Scriptures to them, and revealed himself in the breaking of bread. The same thing happens for us when we celebrate the Eucharist. Jesus speaks to us in the Scriptures and nourishes us in Communion. [Pause]

Lord Jesus, you are our companion on our journey of faith. Lord, have mercy.

Lord Jesus, you speak to us when the Scriptures are read. Christ, have mercy.

Lord Jesus, you nourish us with the bread of the Eucharist. Lord, have mercy.

HEADINGS FOR READINGS

First Reading (Acts 2:14.22-28). On the feast of Pentecost, Peter preaches to the Jews about the resurrection of Jesus.

Second Reading (1 Pet 1:17-21). The benefits we enjoy as Christians were won by Christ through the shedding of his blood. Our response should be a life of holiness.

Gospel (Lk 24:13-35). The risen Jesus joins two of his disciples on their journey, and shows them that it was by dying that he entered into glory.

SCRIPTURE NOTE

The Emmaus story is a sophisticated eucharistic catechesis: a 'liturgy of the Word' is followed by a 'liturgy of the Eucharist'. The expression 'breaking of bread' is a technical term for the Eucharist. Luke deliberately uses eucharistic language: Jesus *took* bread, *blessed*, *broke*, *gave* it to them.

By the time Luke wrote his Gospel half a century had gone by since the

Lord's death and resurrection. So his readers might look back with envy at the people who were fortunate enough to have seen the risen Lord with their own eyes. But in this story Luke makes the point that those who were in that enviable position did not truly know Jesus until the Scriptures were expounded and the bread was broken.

The Christians of Luke's time had those same means of recognising the Lord – the Scriptures and the breaking of the bread. And so have Christians ever since, for the Scriptures and the Eucharist are the essential components of our Sunday service. In the matter of encountering Jesus with faith, a past generation is no more privileged than the present one.

HOMILY 1   **Sharing the story**

They say that all sorrows can be borne if we tell a story about them. Well, those two disciples had a very sad story to tell. The death of Jesus had plunged them into gloom. Their dreams about him being the long-awaited Messiah had been reduced to rubble. As they went along they were talking about his death. They looked at it from every possible angle, and still couldn't make the slightest sense of it. A humiliated, crucified Messiah! It was impossible. It was unthinkable.

Then Jesus joined them. He showed great sensitivity by joining them as a stranger. People often find it easier to talk to a stranger. With a simple, direct question, asked in a kindly manner, he got them to open up. And they began to pour out their sad story to him. When they started to talk, he listened patiently and lovingly so that all that was dammed up in them poured out.

What Jesus did was accompany them. Whatever age we are we need someone to walk with us. Accompaniment is something very gentle. Communion is gradually built up, and mutual trust and a desire for the truth increase over time. Sometimes people do not want to listen to the truth or to look at reality. We have to wait for the right moment to help them accept their reality.

Only when the disciples had finished did Jesus begin to talk. He took up the story where they had left off. He opened their minds to a new way of looking at the Scriptures. He showed them how all the prophets had foretold that the Messiah would suffer and die, and thus enter into glory. No one can attain to glory except through sacrifice and suffering. So the death of Jesus, far from being the end of the dream, was precisely the way in which it had been realised.

However, it was not until it was all over that the two disciples understood what had happened to them on that journey. But isn't this how it always is in real life? We live our lives forward, but understand them backwards. We never know at the time what is happening to us. We have no perspective, no understanding. We have enough to do just to cope from day to day or hour to hour. It's only afterwards, perhaps long afterwards, that our eyes are opened and we begin to understand that experience. Hence the importance of reflecting on our experience.

Eventually we may even be grateful for that sad experience because we are the better for having been through it. And so we begin to understand the message of Jesus' death and resurrection – glory attained through suffering.

We don't expect to find God in pain. We expect to find him in joy. This was the great discovery the two disciples made on the journey to Emmaus. It gave a meaning to suffering. A meaning to our pain doesn't remove it, but it changes our attitude to it.

And it enabled the disciples to turn their lives around. They were going away from Jerusalem. They had lost faith. But after encountering Jesus, they returned to Jerusalem. They resumed their discipleship and their ties with the community. The encounter is not meant to foster evasion of responsibility, but to encourage commitment.

The life of each of us can be looked on as a series of stories which coalesce over time to form one story. However, the sad fact is, all our stories end in death. We do not like stories that end like that. We want our stories to end happily.

Jesus helped the two disciples to share their story so that it mingled with his. He drew it out of them, and then illuminated it with his own story. The resurrection of Christ opens all our stories to the prospect, not just of a good ending, but of a glorious ending. The first and last words in each of our stories belong to God.

HOMILY 2   **Burning hearts**

There is a disturbing little story about a dying Buddhist monk who asked a Catholic priest to instruct him in the truths of the faith. The priest did his best to comply with the monk's wishes.

Afterwards the monk thanked him, but added, 'You filled my mind with beautiful thoughts, but you left my heart empty.'

So his heart was empty – empty of what? What was it that he really wanted? Comfort and reassurance, I suppose. In a word – love. Beautiful thoughts can nourish the mind. But they can't nourish the heart. Only an experience of love can nourish the heart.

The story of the journey to Emmaus is essentially a story about the heart. As the two disciples made their way homewards, they were talking about Jesus. Just as we can't stop talking about a loved one who has just died, so they couldn't stop talking about Jesus. He had filled their lives with meaning, hope and joy. And now that he was dead they were haunted by his absence.

As they set out on that journey their hearts were cold and empty, heavy with sorrow, wounded by disappointment, and numb with grief. They had firmly believed that Jesus was the Messiah. But his death, and in particular the manner of it, had reduced their hopes to rubble. A humiliated, crucified Messiah! It was impossible. It was unthinkable.

But then Jesus joined them and began to open their minds to the idea of a suffering Messiah. With the words of Jesus light and warmth began to filter into their dark, cold hearts. By the time he revealed himself at supper, they were transformed. So much so that they immediately set off back to Jerusalem. Even though the night was dark, their hearts were bright. Even though their feet were heavy, their hearts were light.

What was it that happened to them? What did Jesus do for them? He certainly illuminated their minds – no question about that. But he did something better. He set their hearts on fire. 'Were not our hearts burning within us as he explained the scriptures to us?'

Faith is very much concerned with the mind in so far as it has to do with truths, dogmas, doctrines, creeds, catechisms. But it is even more concerned with the heart. It consists in a relationship of love with the God who first loved us. Without this, faith is like a fireplace without a fire.

> We will never believe with a vigorous and unquestioning faith unless God touches our hearts. It is to the heart that the call of God comes. (Blaise Pascal).

What was the main thing that came across to the two disciples on the road to Emmaus? It was the conviction that Jesus loved them. That is what made their hearts burn. The story shows the goodness of God who makes our deepest dreams come true in the most surprising of ways.

And the story also shows us what ministry is all about. It means to walk with people, to be present to them, to listen – these are the essential 'good works' of today.

HOMILY 3   **The storyteller**

There is a painting by the Dutch painter, Rembrandt, of Jesus sitting at table between the two disciples. The painting tries to capture the rapturous joy on the faces of the disciples at the moment when they recognised Jesus.

Once a guide was showing the picture to some visitors to the museum where it was on display. He began by telling them the story behind the picture, the story we just read in the Gospel.

In the group was a couple, Mr and Mrs Browne, whose only son had recently been killed in a car accident. They were still in a state of shock, and had come to the museum that day merely in the hope that it might take their minds off their sorrow for a little while.

As the guide started the story the Brownes were only half listening. However, he told it in such a way that by the time he had finished, they were completely captivated. Afterwards they approached the guide and said, 'We've heard that story many times, but it never moved us until now. You told it with such feeling and conviction.'

'There was a time when I told it very badly,' the guide replied.

'What happened to change that?' the Brownes asked.

'Three years ago,' the guide began, 'my wife got cancer, and died a slow, agonising death. I could see absolutely no meaning in her terrible suffering and untimely death. She was a good person. She didn't deserve all this. I was heartbroken. It was as if the world had come to an end. Nevertheless, I was persuaded to go back to work here at the museum. So once again I found myself telling the story, only more mechanically than before.

'Then one day something clicked with me, and suddenly I realised that the story was not just about those two forlorn disciples but about me too. Like the two disciples, I was going down a sad and lonely road. Even though I'm a believer, regrettably, up to this Jesus had been little more than a shadowy figure who lived only in the pages of the Gospels. But now he came alive for me. I felt his presence at my side, the presence of a friend who knew all about human suffering.

'It was as if at that moment my eyes were opened and I saw things differently. My heart began to burn within me. As I went on telling the story, a healing process was at work inside me. Even though at times I'm still fragile, I have begun to hope and live again.'

By this time the Brownes were unable to hold back their tears. 'Strange,' they said, 'but as you told the story, we too felt our hearts burn within us.' Then they told him the story of the tragic death of their son. They chatted further over a cup of coffee.

As they parted the Brownes said, 'Thank you for what you did for us. You are a true storyteller.'

We can truly tell a story, or truly hear it, only when we see how it applies to ourselves. Then and only then does it really come alive for us.

Even though we may never have been to the Holy Land, all of us have been on the road to Emmaus. Some people are very familiar with that road. It represents the road of disappointment, failure, sorrow, grief, shattered dreams ...

The risen Jesus is with us on this journey, even though we may not recognise him. He is so close to us that our stories merge with his. It is only his story that makes sense of ours.

It is especially by accepting the dark side of our story that we learn what God's grace and love are all about. However, in the final analysis it is only the Christ Story – glory achieved through suffering and death – that helps us to make sense of our own story. Anything else is simply not adequate. The resurrection of Jesus opens all our stories to the prospect, not just of a good ending, but of a glorious ending.

PRAYER OF THE FAITHFUL

President: As people of faith and hope, we pray God to show us the path of life.

Response: Stay with us, Lord.

Reader(s): For the Pope and the bishops: that they may lead the people of God with courage and love. [Pause] Let us pray to the Lord.

For our political leaders: that they may never take the easy way and so abandon the right way. [Pause] Let us pray to the Lord.

For those who are sad and disillusioned: that Christ may renew their faith and hope. [Pause] Let us pray to the Lord.

For each other: that, especially in dark moments, we may put our trust in God and in his love for us. [Pause] Let us pray to the Lord.

For all our dear ones whom death has taken away from us: that the Lord may bring them to a place of refreshment, light and peace. [Pause] Let us pray to the Lord.

For our own personal needs. [Longer pause] Let us pray to the Lord.

President: All-powerful God, in your mercy inflame our hearts and raise our spirits, so that we may journey towards your kingdom with renewed hope. We ask this through the same Christ our Lord.

REFLECTION 1 **Jesus: life's companion**

All through life's day, you walk with us, Lord.
But often we don't recognise you,
for we are blinded by work and worry,
doubt, confusion and fear,
and so you remain a stranger to us.
Before the day's end we will ask many questions,
experience many sorrows and disappointments.
And then, suddenly, whether we are young, middle-aged, or old,
we will find that night is approaching.
In that moment we pray,
that, like the disciples on the road to Emmaus,
our eyes will be opened, and that we will recognise you.
And you will not vanish from our sight,
but stay with us to guide us to the Father's house.

REFLECTION 2   **How to recognise the Lord**

If you wish to have life,
do what the disciples did.
They offered him hospitality.
The Lord looked set on continuing his journey
but they detained him.
At the end of their journey they said to him:
'Stay with us, for the day is far spent.'
The Lord revealed himself in the breaking of bread.
Hospitality restored to them
what lack of faith had taken away.
So, if you wish to recognise the Saviour,
take in the stranger.
Seek the Lord in the sharing of bread. (*St Augustine.*)

Fourth Sunday of Easter
CHRIST THE GOOD SHEPHERD

INTRODUCTION AND CONFITEOR

This Sunday is known as Good Shepherd Sunday. Christ is our Good Shepherd. Let us pause to reflect on his unfailing love for us, and how he wants us to love one another. [Pause]

Lord, with you as our shepherd, there is nothing we shall want. Lord, have mercy.

Lord, even if we should walk in the valley of darkness, we will fear no evil, because you are with us. Christ, have mercy.

Lord, in your own house we will dwell for ever and ever. Lord, have mercy.

HEADINGS FOR READINGS

First Reading (Acts 2:14.36-41). Here Peter proclaims Jesus as the risen Lord, and urges his hearers to repent and accept baptism.

Second Reading (1 Pet 2:20-25). Addressing slaves, Peter urges them to bear their unjust sufferings with patience as Christ, the Good Shepherd, bore his sufferings for love of us.

Gospel (Jn 10:1-10). Jesus compares his love for his disciples to the love of a shepherd for his sheep.

SCRIPTURE NOTE

In his address to slaves (see Second Reading), Peter urged them to bear their unjust sufferings with patience as Christ, the Good Shepherd, bore his sufferings for love of us. Slavery was a fact of life in New Testament times. The New Testament writers do not, as might have been expected, lead a campaign against it. Even if they had wanted to do so, they must have been aware that such a stance could only be judged subversive and would imperil the tenuous foothold Christianity was gaining in the world of the day. Peter's words have a wider application. He singled out slaves only because their burden of suffering was heavier than that of others.

HOMILY 1   **Living life to the full**

'I came so that you may life and have it to the full.' (Gospel).

Is Jesus talking only about eternal life or also about this life? I have no doubt but that these words are to be applied to our life on earth as much as to our hope of eternal life.

There is a lovely Spanish legend that goes like this. When people arrive at the gate of heaven seeking to enter, St Peter asks them a strange question. He says to each one, 'Tell me this. Have you taken advantage of all the earthly joys which God in his goodness made available to you while you were on earth?'

If a person replies, 'No, I haven't,' Peter shakes his head sadly and says, 'Alas, my friend, I can't let you in – not yet at any rate. How can you expect to be ready for the heavenly joys if you have not prepared yourself for them through the medium of earthly ones? I shall be obliged to send you back down to earth until you learn better.'

In the past the Christian religion tended to be identified with restrictions and prohibitions. Many of us were brought up on a theology of detachment from the world. This present life was viewed as nothing more than a time of trial. This kind of spirituality discouraged enjoyment of life. It led to half-heartedness. It was as if we were always keeping something back. Always living cautiously, fearfully, miserly.

It ought to be possible to enjoy life to the fullest while being devout and religious at the same time. However, to live fully is not the same as to live it up.

Life is a fragile gift. Every moment is utterly unique. This should concentrate our attention on what we are experiencing now. But every moment is also fleeting. How quickly life's stream runs down to the sea. This fleetingness gives life its poignancy and makes it all the more precious. 'For we do not enjoy this world everlastingly, only briefly; our life is like the warming of oneself in the sun.' (Aztec Indians).

The Lord, the Good Shepherd, wants us to have life. Therefore, let us not be so timid and fearful. Let us live whatever presents itself to us, because everything is a gift from God. Life is generous to those who seize it with both hands.

Mere existence is not enough for us. 'What people are looking for is not meaning in life, but the experience of being alive – the rapture of living' (Joseph Campbell). We are meant to live. It is a well-known fact that those who have lived fully and intensely, do not feel cheated at death. 'Fear not that your life will end; rather fear that it may never have begun.' (Thoreau). The poet, Patrick Kavanagh, said:

> Autumn I'd welcome had I
> known love in Summer days.
> I would not weep for flowers that die
> if once they'd bloom for praise.
> I would not cry for any tree
> Leaf lost, a word of misery.
> I would not make lament although
> My harvest were a beggar's woe.

Jesus began his ministry with these words: 'Believe in the Good News.' What is the Good News? The Good News is: 'I came that you may have life and have it to the full.'

HOMILY 2   **Healed by his wounds**

Even though Peter's words were originally addressed to slaves (Second Reading), they have a wider application. He singled out slaves only because their burden of suffering was heavier than that of others.

Referring to the wounds of Christ, Peter said, 'Through his wounds you have been healed.' But we may ask: How could the wounds of another heal our wounds? The following true story shows how it can happen.

Anne's husband died of a heart attack. He was only in his mid-forties. In the weeks and months after the funeral, Anne was consumed by grief. Friends advised her to go on a weekend for the bereaved. Somewhat reluctantly she agreed to go.

She was surprised to find that most of the people on the weekend were not widows but separated people. At a certain stage the participants were divided into groups, and it was Anne's bad luck to find herself the only widow in her group.

She felt she didn't belong in the group. The other members had their husbands. It was their own fault that they had broken up. They could get back together if they really wanted to. But she had lost her husband. He was dead and gone – a good man who didn't smoke or drink, but stayed at home with the family. She felt she had nothing in common with these people. She refused to share with the group. When invited to do so she said, 'I won't be staying.'

Even though she didn't talk she did listen. As she listened, she began to realise that the other people had suffered a great deal. Some of them had put up with a terrible amount of abuse. What especially moved her was the suffering of the children. Gradually her eyes were opened. She had no idea what went on in some homes. She thought that all marriages were like hers. She realised that she had had it very good.

Whereas earlier she had felt no sympathy for the others, now she began to feel very close to them, so much so that when she was given the chance to join another group, she said she wanted to stay where she was. Eventually she began to talk about herself. One woman said to her, 'What I wouldn't give for just one of your days.' The weekend proved to be a turning point for Anne. Her wounds began to heal.

Suffering softens our hardened hearts and enables us to enter a world of suffering where all people live at some time. In reaching out to others, we move out of our isolation into a world of shared suffering. In the simple act of showing sympathy for others there is healing.

Compassion is not learned without suffering. Unless you have suffered and wept you really don't understand what compassion is, nor can you comfort someone who is suffering. Unless you have cried you can't dry the tears of another. Unless you have walked in darkness you can't help wanderers to find their way. But if you have suffered you can become a pathfinder for others.

The wounds of others can help us to cope with and recover from our own wounds. It is by reaching out to others from our own wounds that we ourselves are healed. Shared pain is a bit like shared bread; it brings its participants closer to each other. Intimacy is the fruit that grows from touching each other's wounds.

If we can draw encouragement from the wounds of others, how much more so from the wounds of Christ, the Good Shepherd. His wounds help us to recognise our own. The sacred, the precious wounds of Jesus are a source of consolation, courage and hope to us. Truly, by his wounds we are healed.

HOMILY 3   **The wounded messenger of love**

As we go through life we can't avoid picking up some wounds. But carers are apt to pick up more than others. If you raise children, you have lots of scars. So has anyone who has truly loved another human being, or who has committed himself or herself to a cause. The important thing is how we react to those wounds.

Ellen was in high spirits as she set out to deliver flowers to her friend Mary, and sang as she went along. But, out of the blue, a wasp stung her in the arm, and what had been a sweet journey suddenly turned sour.

Leaving aside the flowers, she sat down by the side of the road to inspect the damage. The spot in which she had been stung felt very sore, had turned red, and was swelling up alarmingly. As she sat there wincing with pain and feeling very sorry for herself, a passer-by came to her aid.

'I know exactly how you feel. I've often been stung myself,' said the passer-by.

The stranger took out a jar of ointment and applied some of it to the wound. The ointment had a soothing effect on the wound, and soon Ellen was on her way again. However, as she went along, she couldn't keep her eyes off the wound. Fortunately the swelling subsided and the pain eased up.

Along the way she met up with other travellers. She insisted on telling them about the wasp sting. With every telling, the wasp got more vicious and the wound more serious. Her confidants could see that she was very bitter about it. All of them tried to help her.

'Ignore the whole thing,' said one.

'Bury it,' said a second.

'Treat it as if it never happened,' said a third.

And so it went on. Though her advisers used different expressions, their advice came to the same thing – forget the sting. This sounded like good advice and she grasped at it.

She tried to forget the sting. However, memory is a strange thing. We forget the things we want to remember, and remember the things we want to forget. No matter how hard she tried, she could not forget. And every time she remembered, she felt a stab of pain.

Eventually she had the good fortune to meet up with an old and wise friend by the name of Sheila. Naturally she opened her heart to her also.

'Forget the whole thing! Why should you forget it?' asked Sheila.

The question surprised Ellen. She hesitated, then replied,

'Everybody I meet tells me that I must forget it.'

'But it happened,' Sheila insisted gently. 'It's part of the story of your journey. Besides, it's not something to be ashamed of.'

'But every time I remember it, I feel the hurt all over again,' said Ellen.

'It's how you remember it that matters,' said Sheila. 'You're on a mission of love, aren't you?'

'Yes.'

'Well then, don't let the sting distract you from that. Above all, don't let its poison diminish your love. Then when you arrive at your friend's house, your gift will be all the more precious because you suffered a wound in delivering it.'

After they parted, Ellen reflected on what her friend had said. Gradually she came to see the sting in a new light. With that, the bitterness left her, and once again she found herself going along with a happy step.

Here we see that the problem is solved, not by removing it, but by giving it a new meaning. Meaning is different from happiness. Our greatest desire, greater even than the desire for happiness, is that our pain should mean something.

Jesus bore the marks of our violent world on his body. He didn't hide his wounds. Nor was he bitter about them. Those wounds were an expression of love and so they had a meaning. They were the mortal wounds the Good Shepherd picked up in caring for his sheep. His wounds help us to recognise our own wounds. Love triumphs over the disfigurations, the wounds, and the scars of life.

PRAYER OF THE FAITHFUL

President: Gathered together in the Lord's house, we trust him to surround with goodness and kindness all for whom we pray.

Response: Lord, hear our prayer.

Reader(s): For all Christian leaders: that they may be true shepherds to the people of God. [Pause] We pray to the Lord.

For those who hold public office: that they may give a generous service to others. [Pause] We pray to the Lord.

For parents, teachers, priests, and other leaders: that they may be true shepherds to those in their care. [Pause) We pray to the Lord.

For each other: that all of us may realise that we can imitate the Good Shepherd by the concern we show for others. [Pause] We pray to the Lord.

For vocations to the priesthood and religious life: that more people may hear the call to become shepherds to the flock of Christ. [Pause] We pray to the Lord.

For our own private needs. [Longer Pause] We pray to the Lord.

President: Father, you sent Christ your Son among us that we might have life, and have it to the full. Help us to listen to his voice, so that he can guide us along the path of eternal life. We ask this through the same Christ our Lord.

REFLECTION   **Compassion and healing**

Compassion is not learned without suffering.
Unless we have suffered and wept,
we really don't understand what compassion is,
nor can we comfort someone who is suffering.
Unless we have walked in darkness,
we can't help wanderers to find their way.
But if we have suffered we become pathfinders for others.
And it is by reaching out to others
that we ourselves are healed.
Jesus bore the marks of our violent world on his body.

Those wounds were the proof of his love.
They were the mortal wounds the Good Shepherd
picked up in caring for his sheep.
The wounds of Jesus are a source of consolation,
courage, and hope to us in our sufferings.
By his wounds we are healed.

Fifth Sunday of Easter
JESUS, THE WAY, THE TRUTH AND THE LIFE.

INTRODUCTION AND CONFITEOR

Everybody needs a home. Jesus assures us that ultimately all of us have a home to go to, namely, the heavenly Father's house. He even promises to prepare a place for us in that house. This is a cause of tremendous hope for us. [Pause]

Our sins cause us to stumble on the road to God's house. Let us confess them, asking forgiveness from God and from one another.

I confess to almighty God ...

HEADINGS FOR READINGS

First Reading (Acts 6:1-7). We see the growth of the first Christian community, and how they sorted out in a peaceful and just manner the problems that inevitably arose.

Second Reading (1 Pet 2:4-9). This describes the responsibility and special dignity of the members of the Christian community.

Gospel (Jn 14:1-12). Jesus consoles his friends who are distressed over his words that he is going away.

HOMILY 1 **Faith in a time of crisis**

There come times in the lives of all believers when things get very dark, and they have to believe what they cannot prove, and to accept even though they cannot understand or make sense of what's happening. It's at such times that we really need strong faith, but its precisely at such times that our faith fails us.

It's easy to convince ourselves that we have a strong faith when things are going well. When a crisis arises we discover what kind of faith we have, or if we have any faith at all. By faith here I mean trust in God.

Of course, there are people who think that if God was with them, and if he really loved them, then no storm would ever hit them. Life should be all plain sailing. So, when a storm does hit them, they experience a deep crisis of faith, thinking that God has abandoned them.

During the Last Supper the apostles were thrown into crisis when Jesus started to talk about his death. On hearing this their hearts were troubled and filled with fear. Knowing that their faith would be severely tested, Jesus tried to prepare them for the ordeal. He said to them, 'Do not let your hearts be troubled. Believe in God, and believe also in me.' Since the apostles already believed, in effect what he was saying to them was, 'You must go on believing in God and in me.'

At a time of crisis people feel that God has abandoned them. But Jesus assured the apostles that, even though he was leaving them, he was not abandoning them. Rather, he was going to prepare a home for them, and would return to take them to that home. Hence, no matter what happened, no matter how difficult things might get (and they would get very difficult), they must go on believing, go on trusting in him and in the Father. That's all they would have to do. Go on believing, go on trusting. Easier said than done.

But at a time of crisis that is the only thing we can do – go on stubbornly trusting in God. Trust is the greatest thing we can give to another person. At that hour we must believe that somehow there is a purpose to it all, and that good will come of it. Then the unbearable becomes bearable, and in the darkness a glimmer of light appears.

What real faith does is assure us that God is with us in the midst of the crisis. It is that feeling, that conviction, that we are not alone, that we are not abandoned, which enables us to get through the crisis.

Life is unintelligible and unendurable without God. That's why faith is so important. When the English singer, Charlie Lansboro, became a Catholic he said, 'I believe completely. I can't imagine my life without my faith. But it took me a long time to get there.'

Those who have faith have a source of comfort and inspiration, especially when trouble strikes. They know that God will be good to them in the end, both in this world and in the next. It is not we who keep the faith; it is the faith that keeps us.

A person with a grain of faith in God never loses hope, because he believes in the ultimate triumph of truth (Gandhi).

So when things are bad, may we hear the gentle words of Jesus: 'Believe in God, and believe also in me.'

HOMILY 2   **Importance of home**

It's impossible to exaggerate the importance of home. I once heard the governor of a prison say: 'If you were to give the prisoners a choice between going home and staying here in a luxury suite, complete with colour TV, a sauna, a cocktail cabinet, and so on, there isn't a single prisoner who wouldn't choose to go home.'

When things fail, when we feel tired and lonely, there is always home to go to. 'Let's go home.' 'I want to go home.' How many times and in how many different circumstances have we heard people say those words, or have said them ourselves. Home is where we are safe. Home is a place of communion. If you know you're going home, the trip is never too long or too difficult. We must go out into the world to know how lovely our own home is. Imagine if we had no home to go to.

Nelson Mandela tells how during the long years of his imprisonment on Robben Island he had a recurring nightmare. He says:

In the dream, I had just been released from prison – only it was not Robben Island but a jail in Johannesburg. I walked outside the gates into the city and found no one to meet me. In fact there was no one there at all, no people, no cars, no taxis. I would then set out on foot towards Soweto. I walked for many hours before arriving in Orlando West, and then turned the corner towards No. 8115. Finally I would see my home, but it turned out to be empty, a ghost house, with all the doors and windows open but no one there at all. (*Long Road to Freedom*, 1994, Little, Brown and Company)

To have a home is not just to have a house. It is to have a set of close ties with people who accept us for what we are, and who give us a feeling of belonging. But in spite of all the buildings we put up and roots we put down, here on earth we do not have a lasting home. All we have, as Paul says, is a kind of tent. At death the tent is folded up.

Hence, it is not only on earth that we need a home. We also need a home to go to when death brings down the curtain on the day of our life. Without such a home life would be a journey to nowhere.

During the Last Supper Jesus began to talk to the apostles about the fact that he was leaving them. On hearing this, they were plunged into sorrow. But he consoled them with these words, which are probably the loveliest words in the Gospel: 'There are many rooms in my Father's house. I am going to prepare a place for you. I shall return to take you with me; so that where I am you may be too.' This means that we have an eternal home to go to, namely, the Father's house.

For a child home is not so much a place as a relationship of love and trust. A child can move around a lot and not feel homeless, as long as its parents are there. It is the same for those who have a close relationship with God.

We spend our lives searching for God, and groping our way towards him. To die is to find him, to meet him, and to see him.

To die is to go to God, and to go to God is to go home.

HOMILY 3   **Returning to God**

Once on a beach about forty miles south-east of Dublin I watched as a
man took a crate of homing pigeons from the boot of his car. Then he
opened the crate and released the pigeons. They flew straight up into the
air. However, instead of heading directly for Dublin which was their home,
they proceeded to fly in circles above us. Round and round they went. To
someone who didn't understand what was going on this seemed silly
and a waste of time. But apparently what the pigeons were doing was
finding their bearings. Once they had found their bearings they would
set off for home.

This homing instinct which many birds possess is an almost miraculous thing. With some it seems to be an in-built thing. But others, such as
pigeons, have to be trained. The basic requirement of training is to keep
them in good health so that they are capable of sustained flight. Fog, snow,
rain and adverse winds are some of the obstacles they have to overcome.

We too have a homing instinct. God, who made us for himself, has not
left us rudderless. He has put a homing instinct in us. This is a very subtle
and fragile thing, since God will never take away our freedom. It takes
the form of an inner restlessness and discontent. This restlessness, this
discontent, this longing, far from being a curse, is a blessing.

Just as the homing instinct doesn't save the birds from the necessity of
having to struggle against the wind and the rain, so faith doesn't shield
us from the hard knocks of life and death. But what it does is give us
bearings. It enables us to live in a topsy-turvey world without getting lost
or giving in to despair. It assures us that we have a home to go to, and
points us in that direction.

During the Last Supper when Jesus told the apostles that he was leaving them, they were deeply distressed. But he consoled them with these
words, which are among the loveliest words in the Gospel: 'There are
many rooms in my Father's house. I am going to prepare a place for you.
I shall return to take you with me; so that where I am you may be too.'

These words mean that we have an eternal home to go to where all our
hopes will be fulfilled. But there remains the question of how to get there.

If you are in a strange city and ask for directions, a person may say, 'Go
straight down until you come a set of traffic lights. Turn right at the lights
… ' Sometimes the instructions are so complicated that you can't remember them. But you may be fortunate enough to meet an exceptionally
kind person who says to you, 'Look, it's a bit difficult to explain. Follow
me and I'll show you the way.'

The way to God has confused and baffled many. Some have got hopelessly confused; others have got lost. When Thomas asked Jesus, 'Show
us the Father.' Jesus didn't give him a lot of complicated directions. Instead he said, 'I am the Way.' What he was saying in effect was: 'Follow

me and I'll show you the way.'

Meanwhile in the Church we have a spiritual home, built on the foundation stone of Christ (see Second Reading). Here we have brothers and sisters who accompany us on our journey to that other home, our heavenly one.

A woman was returning to Ireland with her husband after spending three years in Australia. On reaching England she phoned her mother in Dublin, who had volunteered to meet her at the boat terminal in Dun Laoghaire. She said to her mother, 'You'll easily recognise me. I'll be wearing a bright red coat.' On hearing this her mother said, 'Don't be silly. Do you think I won't recognise my own daughter.'

We are God's precious daughters and sons. Don't you think God will recognise us when we return home to him at the end of life's journey?

'Only those who fly home to God have flown at all.' (Patrick Kavanagh).

ANOTHER STORY

Young Martin was so tense that he had to talk to someone. So he told his story to a complete stranger who was sitting next to him on the train. He told him that he had just been released from prison where he had spent three years for robbery and other offences. While there he had undergone a change of heart. He now felt very bad about having let his family down, and wondered if they wanted him to return home.

All the time he had been away, they had neither written to him nor come to see him. But he was hoping against hope that they had forgiven him and wanted him to come home. However, in order to make it easy for them, he had written to them. If they wanted him back into the family, they were to give him a sign.

Their house was close to the railway line. In the back garden grew an old apple tree. If they wanted him back, they should put up a white ribbon on the apple tree. If they didn't, they were to do nothing. In this case he would stay on the train until it reached the first large city, where he would get lost.

As the train neared his house the suspense became so acute that he was unable to look out the window. So he asked the man to keep a lookout for the apple tree. The man gladly agreed to do so. After a while he touched Martin on the shoulder, and said, 'Son, take a look'.

Martin looked, and there before his eyes stood the old apple tree, covered in ribbons. Tears began to run down his face, and with those tears all the bitterness that had poisoned his young life up to this was washed away. The other man said later, 'I felt I had just witnessed a miracle. I had never realised until that moment what it means for a young lad to have a home to go to.'

Without faith life is like a journey that leads nowhere. To have faith is to believe that we have a lasting home to go to.

PRAYER OF THE FAITHFUL

President: Jesus is the way, the truth, and the life. Let us pray with confidence through him who shared our earthly exile in order to bring us to our heavenly home.

Response: Lead us home, Lord.

Reader(s): For all Christians: that they may support one another in the journey of faith. [Pause] Let us pray to the Lord.

For political leaders: that they may seek and know the guidance and help of God. [Pause] Let us pray to the Lord.

For those who have no faith. [Pause] Let us pray to the Lord.

For the poor and the homeless; for orphans and widows. [Pause] Let us pray to the Lord.

For ourselves: that our lives may bear witness to the hope we carry in our hearts. [Pause] Let us pray to the Lord.

For our deceased relatives and friends: that the Lord may bring them into the light of his presence. [Pause] Let us pray to the Lord.

For our own special needs. [Longer pause] Let us pray to the Lord.

President: Lord, may you support us all day long, till the shadows lengthen, and evening falls, and the busy world is hushed, and the fever of life is over, and our work is done; then, in your mercy, grant us a safe lodging, a holy rest, and peace at last. We ask this through Christ our Lord.

SIGN OF PEACE

Lord Jesus Christ, the night before you died you said to your friends: 'Peace I leave with you; my own peace I give you. A peace which the world cannot give, this is my gift to you. So do not let your hearts be troubled or afraid.' Lord, take pity on our troubled and fearful hearts, and grant us the peace and unity of your kingdom where you live for ever and ever.

REFLECTION   **Going home**

> Going to heaven!
> I don't know when,
> pray do not ask me how.
> Going to heaven!
> How dim it sounds!
> And yet it will be done
> as sure as flocks go home at night
> unto the shepherd's arm.

If you should get there first,
save just a little place for me
close to the two I lost.
The smallest 'robe' will fit me,
and just a bit of 'crown';
for you know we do not mind our dress
when we are going home.   *(Emily Dickinson)*

Sixth Sunday of Easter
KEEPING HIS COMMANDMENTS

INTRODUCTION AND CONFITEOR

Christ says to us what he said to his apostles: 'If you love me, keep my commandments'. We can't truly call ourselves his disciples if we don't listen to his words and make an effort to live by them. We know we fail, and our lives are the poorer for that. We need the Lord's help to do better. [Pause]

Lord, your words are a lamp for our steps and a light for our path. Lord, have mercy.

Lord, those who belong to you listen to your voice. Christ, have mercy.

Lord, you alone have the words of eternal life. Lord, have mercy.

HEADINGS FOR READINGS

First Reading (Acts 8:5-8.14-17). We learn about the joy and enthusiasm with which the Samaritans received the Gospel.

Second Reading (1 Pet 3:15-18). Peter encourages Christians to remain steadfast under pressure in their attachment to Christ.

Gospel (Jn 14:15-21). To love Christ is to listen to his words and, with the help of the Holy Spirit, to put them into practice in our lives.

HOMILY 1   **The leave-taking**

The parting of friends is never easy. But some partings are harder than others. The most painful parting of all happens when someone dies. What makes this parting different from all others is the finality of it.

It was the night before Jesus' death. For some time he had been giving the apostles hints of his death. Now he talked to them openly about it. Except he didn't speak of death in the way we tend to do – in the sense of life ending. He spoke of his death as a going away, 'going to the Father'. But all the apostles heard was the fact that he was leaving them.

He was indeed leaving them. But there are degrees of leaving.

[130]

There is a leaving which implies abandonment. Sadly, now and again we read in the newspapers about babies that are abandoned at birth. To be abandoned is the most painful and damaging thing that can happen to anyone, particularly in the case of the very young and the elderly. In the Gospel we are not dealing with this. Jesus is not abandoning the apostles.

There is a leaving which implies rejection. For instance, a girl had hopes of marriage but her fiancé suddenly leaves her for someone else. The girl feels rejected. This can be extremely painful. Here we are not dealing with that. Jesus is not rejecting the apostles.

There is a leaving which is necessary because it is for the good of the one leaving. For example, a person is leaving to return home or leaving to take up a better job somewhere else. This is certainly true here. Jesus' leaving is for his own good. He is returning to his Father. To return to the Father is to go home. It is to go to honour and glory.

Finally there is a leaving which is for the good not only of the one leaving but also of those left behind. This is the full truth of what is happening here. Jesus' leaving is, or will be, good for the apostles too, because he will send them the Spirit. His departure will not leave them unsupported and unguided as they feared. 'I will not leave you orphans,' he said.

But there was another thing that would have been a great consolation to the apostles at this sad and painful hour. Even as he spoke about leaving them, he spoke about coming back to them. He would come to them through the Spirit, and he would come to them himself. They did encounter him after the resurrection. And even though after the ascension they would see him no more, he assured them that he would still be with them, yes, even to the end of time.

Jesus did not leave his disciples orphaned or desolate. By their faith they were able to 'see' him, and through their obedience to his commandments, they were drawn into a loving communion with him.

Nor does Jesus leave us orphaned. We have the same access to his presence, and to the help of the Holy Spirit as the first Christians had. Jesus is not present as a vague memory of a person who lived long ago, but as a real, life-giving presence that transforms us.

Nowhere do we feel so close to him as when we receive him in the Eucharist. When we receive the Eucharist we are not just in communication with him, but in communion with him – a holy communion. Here he nourishes our hearts with his love. The food of the Eucharist gives us the strength to do his word and to live as his disciples.

HOMILY 2   **Keeping his commandments**

A number of times during the last supper Christ said these or similar words to his apostles: 'If you love me, keep my commandments.' Clearly he was not talking about the Ten Commandments. What commandments then was he talking about? A look at the Gospels will provide some clues as to the answer. There we find certain *Do's* and *Don'ts* he talked about.

However, it's clear that he is talking, not so much about commandments as about guidelines for his followers. What we are really dealing with is a new spirit, new values and attitudes towards God, towards our neighbour, and towards life.

Keeping this in mind, to look at some of the *Do's* and *Don'ts* he talked about is not only helpful, but necessary. Let us imagine that Christ is speaking directly to us.

Don'ts

Do not return evil for evil. Nothing is achieved by retaliation, except to pile darkness upon darkness.

Do not judge your neighbour. No one knows all the facts in any particular case except God. Therefore, leave judgement to God.

Do not condemn your neighbour. This follows from the last. If you are not to pass judgement on your neighbour, neither are you to pass sentence on him.

Do not worry about food, and drink, and clothes, as if these were the most important things in life. Make it your first concern to live a life worthy of a son or a daughter of God, and all the rest will fall into place.

Do not store up treasures for yourselves here on earth – money, property, goods, and so on. These are like chaff in the eyes of God, chaff to be blown away in the first winds of judgement.

Do not look back once you have put your hand to the plough, that is, once you have decided to follow my way. And once you have made what you are sure is a right decision in life, go forward trusting in God.

Do not give up hope when times are rough. Keep on trusting in me and in the Father. Remember that you are worth more than thousands of sparrows.

Do's

Let the light of your goodness shine before people. The light you shed around you will help others to find their way, and the Father will be glorified.

Love your enemies. To be kind to those you don't like, or who may have been unkind to you, is hard. But if you do this, you will be the salt of the earth.

Give generously. The measure you give to others, will be the measure you receive from God.

Forgive those who sin against you. Then you have nothing to fear in regard to your own sins. God has already forgiven them.

Clean the inside of cup and dish, and the outside will become clean too.

See that your minds and hearts are clean. Then all your thoughts, words and deeds will also be clean, like water coming from an unpolluted well.

Take this bread and eat it. Take this cup and drink it. Do this in memory of me. In the Eucharistic Banquet you will find the nourishment you need to live as my disciples.

And love one another, the way I have loved you. Then all will know that you are disciples of mine.

We can't truly call ourselves disciples of Jesus if we don't listen to his words and make an effort to live by them. One wouldn't be much of a Christian if one didn't try to live as Jesus taught.

HOMILY 3   **Love and obedience**

In today's Gospel passage we have part of the farewell discourse of Jesus during the last supper. In these last hours with his apostles he spoke about essentials. Many of the things he said were naturally directed towards the future, at how he wanted them to live when he was gone. One of the things he said to them was: 'If you love me, keep my commandments'.

We are not talking about keeping a specific set of commandments but rather about following his way of life. What is involved here is Christian discipleship. We can't truly call ourselves disciples of Jesus if we don't listen to his words and make an effort to live by them. One wouldn't be much of a Christian if one didn't try to live as Jesus taught.

But we must be clear about one thing. We don't keep his commandments so that he will love us; we keep his commandments because he loves us. During that same supper Jesus said, 'Love one another as I have loved you.' It was he who first loved the apostles, and loved them unconditionally.

The greatest need each one of us has is for real, unconditional love. Yet we find it hard to believe that this is how God loves us. We tend to believe that God will love us only if we are good. God loves us, not because we are good, but because he is good. Our very existence is a sign of God's love. God's unconditional love for us is the Good News. Our response is to try to return that love.

Jesus knew that the Father loved him. He responded by loving the Father. He showed his love for the Father through his obedience, even though that obedience cost him his life. And it is through obedience that we are to show our love for Jesus. What does this mean in practice? It means listening to his word and putting it in action. To love is to obey. And to obey is to love.

There are those who proclaim their love for Jesus in words, but who deny him in their deeds or by their way of life. Real love is shown in deeds. People know us by our acts, not by what we say with our lips.

It's not easy to live as a disciple of Jesus in the modern world. It never was an easy thing. But for that reason Jesus has given us the Holy Spirit. When we are weak we must pray to the Spirit. The Spirit comforts us in times of sorrow, enlightens us in times of darkness, and makes us brave and strong in times of weakness.

The word Jesus used for the Spirit is the word 'Advocate', a legal term for one who supports a defendant at a trial. The Spirit will be the great defender of the disciples in time of trial. And the follower of Jesus can expect to suffer. But, as St Peter says (Second Reading), it is better to suffer for doing the right thing than for doing the wrong thing. Knowing that our cause is right gives us great strength. Besides, we have the example of Christ who, though innocent, suffered and died for our sins.

The apostles knew that Jesus loved them. And we know that Jesus loves us too. There is no mistaking love. You feel it in your heart. It is like a flame that warms your soul, energises your spirit and supplies passion to your life. Love is our connection to God and to each other. Love is the climate in which the Christian lives.

'Love one another as I have loved you.' That sums it all up.

PRAYER OF THE FAITHFUL

President: We rejoice in the God who has called us out of darkness, and we pray that all the world may be bathed in his wonderful light.

Response: Lord, graciously hear us.

Reader(s): For the Pope and the bishops: that they may help the People of God to obey Christ's commandments not out of fear but out of love. [Pause] Lord, hear us.

For government leaders: that they may be guided by the commandments of God. [Pause] Lord, hear us.

For those who are suffering persecution because of their belief in Christ. [Pause] Lord, hear us.

For each other: that we may never lose sight of Christ's great commandment, the commandment to love one another. [Pause] Lord, hear us.

For our own special needs. [Longer pause] Lord, hear us.

President: Father of grace who sent us your Son to be a light for our steps and a lamp for our path, help us to listen to his words, and to let them guide our lives. We ask this through you, Christ our Lord.

REFLECTION   **Learning from the sea-gulls**

It's a chilly day by the seaside,
far too windy for my comfort.

But the gulls don't seem to mind the wind.
In fact, they seem to enjoy it.
I watch them flying about:
they go with it, they go against it,
they soar into the sky, they plunge back to earth.
All the time they are using the wind,
they are availing of its power.
And I reflect on how we, the disciples of Jesus,
are so easily blown off course by the winds of adversity.
Lord, send us the Holy Spirit who will enable us
to turn the hard and easy to our advantage,
so that everything that happens to us
may bear us along the road to your kingdom.

Ascension of the Lord

INTRODUCTION AND CONFITEOR

The ascension of Jesus is the climax of his victory over sin and death. It is a day of joy and hope. Jesus wants us to share in his victory. It's important to realise that he hasn't left us, but is still with us, helping us in our struggles. [Pause]

Lord, you give us strength in times of weakness. Lord, have mercy.
Lord, you give us consolation in times of sorrow. Christ, have mercy.
Lord, you give us light in times of darkness. Lord, have mercy.

HEADINGS FOR READINGS

First Reading (Acts 1:1-11). This describes the Ascension of Jesus into heaven, and his promise to send the Holy Spirit to his disciples.

Second Reading (Eph 1:17-23). Here Paul describes the meaning of the Ascension: God raised Jesus above all earthly powers, and made him Head of the Church and Lord of creation.

Gospel (Mt 28:16-20). Jesus commissions the apostles to preach the Gospel to all nations, and promises to remain with them always.

SCRIPTURE NOTE

The resurrection, the ascension, and the giving of the Spirit are part of the same event. In one action that goes beyond earthly time, Jesus emerges from the tomb, returns to the Father, and gives the Spirit. However, from the viewpoint of the first disciples, who continued to live on within time, these actions are described as having taken place at different times: They found the tomb empty on Sunday morning; the risen Lord appeared to them on that day or subsequently; the termination of the appearances caused them to realise that Jesus was now permanently with God; and they received the Spirit.

The theological meaning of this feast is expressed in the Second Reading: God has glorified Jesus, raising him above all earthly powers, and making him Head of the Church and Lord of creation.

In both the First Reading and the Gospel Jesus gives a mission and makes a promise to his followers.

HOMILY 1   **The meaning of the Ascension**

St Luke gives us what appears to be an eye-witness account of the Ascension of Jesus into heaven. However, we must not take this literally. The Ascension of Jesus is a mystery which is beyond words. Nevertheless, it stands for something real that happened to Jesus. The following illustration may go some way in helping us to understand what we are celebrating on this great feast.

Lech Walesa worked for years as an electrician in the Gdansk shipyards. During those years he and his fellow workers founded the movement which became known as *Solidarity*. Walesa became its leader. This brought them into open conflict with the communist rulers.

Eventually the workers won out. The communist regime collapsed and democracy returned to Poland. Then, on December 9, 1990, something happened which a few years prior to this would have been unthinkable. Walesa, the shipyard worker, was elected first president of a free and democratic Poland.

It was a great honour for Walesa. His fellow workers were delighted. They too felt honoured because of their association with him. However, there was sadness too. They knew that it would change for ever the way they related to him. They knew they were losing him. However, they were hoping that he would not forget them and that he would help them from his new and more influential position. Walesa himself tells us:

> The day after my election as President of the country, I went back to the Gdansk shipyard where I had worked. I emerged from the bullet-proof Volvo that was now my official car, and went directly to my former workshop. I got choked up when I looked at the small metal locker where I used to store my tools. Workers in overalls, looking embarrassed, congratulated me. I was no longer one of them. But I wanted them to understand that I knew how they felt. Shyly, they said, 'We hope you will be able to change our lives, Mr President.'

During the years of his public ministry Jesus ate and drank in the company of the apostles. They experienced his love and care every day. In many ways he was just like one of themselves. Did the Ascension mean that he had left them and ended all this intimacy and familiarity? Yes and no.

Jesus would no longer be physically present to them, but he hadn't left them entirely. He had simply taken on a new role, assumed a new position. After many years of humble labour and dangerous struggle, Walesa achieved the great honour of being elected president of his country. After his years of struggle on earth, Jesus was crowned with glory by his heavenly Father, and became Lord of all creation. (See Second Reading.) For those who have faith, Jesus is closer to them than ever, and in a better position to help them.

The Gospel ends with Jesus' promise to remain with his disciples always, right to the end of time. The Ascension of Jesus is his liberation from all restrictions of time and space. It does not represent his removal from the earth, but his constant presence everywhere on earth. During his earthly ministry he could only be in one place at a time. If he was in Jerusalem he was not in Capernaum; if he was in Capernaum he was not in Jerusalem. But now that he is united with God, he is present wherever God is present; and that is everywhere.

The first Christians understood this very well. They knew that Jesus was still with them, even if not in the same way as before. They believed he still shared their lives, and that death would mean being united with him in glory for ever. In the meantime he was relying on them (and now on us) to make sure that the Gospel was preached and lived.

HOMILY 2   **His witnesses**

There is a story that when Jesus returned to heaven after his death and resurrection, the Archangel Gabriel was surprised to see him back so soon. Thirty three years is not a long time, especially when you think about the importance and proportions of the task he had been given to do.

'Back so soon?' Gabriel said to Jesus.

'Well, I would have stayed longer but they crucified me,' Jesus replied.

'Oh, so they crucified you,' said Gabriel. 'That means you failed.'

'Not necessarily,' said Jesus. 'You see I called together a little group of disciples. They will carry on my work.'

'And what if they should fail?' asked Gabriel.

'I've no other plans,' Jesus answered.

Jesus had preached the Gospel only to Israel. But now he commissioned the apostles to preach the Gospel to all nations. It was a daunting task. But he promised that he would send them the Holy Spirit. He also assured them that he would be with them always: 'I'll be with you always; yes, to the end of time.'

But how could this be? The Ascension of Jesus is his liberation from all restrictions of time and space. It does not represent his removal from the earth, but his constant presence everywhere on earth. During his earthly ministry he could only be in one place at a time. But now that he is united with God, he is present wherever God is present; and that is everywhere.

Other than that promise to be with his apostles, he gave them no assurances. However, that assurance would give them the courage and strength to face whatever difficulties lay ahead.

A sense of the presence of Christ with us doesn't change the world for us, but it can give us the courage to face it. God's closeness shields us against a sense of abandonment and despair.

In spite of the grave failings of his followers, and many terrible persecutions, the Gospel has come down to us across two thousand years. The explanation for this surely lies in the promise of Jesus: 'I will be with you always, to the very end of time.'

Jesus now depends on us. We are his witnesses before the world. It's a daunting task but a great privilege too. When we witness to truth, justice, love and peace we are witnessing to Jesus. The way to witness to truth is to live truthfully. The way to witness to justice is to act justly in all one's dealings with others. The way to witness to love is to act lovingly towards others. And the way to witness to peace is to live in peace with others.

In short, the most effective way to witness to Jesus is to live a Christian life. We can draw encouragement from what Mother Teresa said: 'I don't pray for success; I pray that I may be a faithful witness.'

HOMILY 3   **Jesus leaving**

Jesus is going to the Father, going to glory. But in his going he is not thinking only of himself. His going is connected with the sending of the Spirit. His going was necessary for him and for the apostles.

It was necessary for him because thus he was entering into his glory. It was necessary for the apostles because otherwise the Spirit could not come. 'Unless I go, the Spirit cannot come. But if I go I will send him to you.' Thus, in his going he was not thinking just of himself and his own glory, but of the needs of his friends.

The apostles seemed to understand this because St Luke says that they returned in joy to Jerusalem. However, pain was mingled with their joy. They were glad that Jesus was going to glory, but sad that he was leaving them.

Yet they glimpsed that somehow his going was necessary. There are things people can give us and do for us in their absence which they can't give us or do for us in their presence. In their absence we see their true worth. We get a fuller picture of their characters and a better appreciation of their achievements and of what they have meant to us and done for us.

There is a sense in which they enrich us through their going. By going they make space for us. They give us room and freedom. They give us a chance to assume responsibility. They show confidence in us by the trust they place in us. And we know that they are still interested in us, and still love us. We still enjoy their support.

The leaving of a dear one is a painful thing because we become conscious of his or her absence, and of our own emptiness and aloneness. But this pain has to be faced.

Jesus honoured his apostles (and now honours us) by entrusting them with the task of carrying on his mission. That task was first of all one of preaching. They were to tell the Good News to all those who had never heard it.

Secondly, the task was one of healing. Christianity is concerned not just with the soul but also with the body. Jesus wished his followers to bring health of mind and body to people.

The only assurance he gave them was that he would be with them always: 'I'll be with you always; yes, to the end of time.' However, that assurance would give them the courage and strength to face whatever difficulties lay ahead.

The idea that they could drink a poisoned drink or pick up a dangerous snake and come to no harm must not be taken literally. These are symbols of evil, and Jesus was saying that his power would enable them to triumph over evil.

A sense of the presence of Christ with us doesn't change the world for us, but it can give us the courage to face it. God's closeness shields us against a sense of abandonment and despair.

Jesus now depends on us to be his witnesses before the world. It's a daunting task but a great privilege too. The most effective way to witness to Jesus is by living a Christian life.

PRAYER OF THE FAITHFUL

President: With joy and hope in our hearts because of the victory of Christ, let us pray in the name of him who now sits at the right hand of the Father in glory.

Response: Lord, hear our prayer.

Reader(s): For Christians: that they may be faithful witnesses for Christ before the world. [Pause] Let us pray to the Lord.

For those who hold public office: that they may work for justice and peace. [Pause] Let us pray to the Lord.

For those without hope. [Pause] Let us pray to the Lord

For each other: that our lives bear witness to the hope we carry in our hearts. [Pause] Let us pray to the Lord.

For this community: that we may be rooted in love. [Pause] Let us pray to the Lord.

For our own special needs. [Longer pause] Let us pray to the Lord.

President: Heavenly Father, grant that we may follow your Son faithfully on earth, and come to share his glory in heaven. We ask this through the same Christ our Lord.

REFLECTION   **Returning to God**

We are born in exile and die there too.
As soon as we set sail on the great voyage of life,
we begin our return.
We spend our lives dreaming
of a homeland we have never seen.
Like homing birds that are released in a strange country,
and know no rest until they return home,
so it is with us.
When we die,
we do not so much go to God as return to him.
You have made us for yourself, O Lord,
and our hearts will never rest until they rest in you.

Seventh Sunday of Easter
OUR NEED OF THE SPIRIT

INTRODUCTION AND CONFITEOR

After the Ascension of Jesus, the apostles went back to Jerusalem and 'joined in continuous prayer' as they awaited the coming of the Holy Spirit. We are gathered here to do the same thing. Without the Holy Spirit we cannot live the life of a Christian. [Pause]

Lord, your Spirit is to us what rain is to dry ground. Lord, have mercy.

Lord, your Spirit is to us what wind is to a sail boat. Christ, have mercy.

Lord, your Spirit is to us what warmth is to a cold person. Lord, have mercy.

HEADINGS FOR READINGS

First Reading (Acts 1:12-14). Here we see the disciples gathered in the upper room, waiting in prayer for the coming of the Holy Spirit.

Second Reading (1 Pet 4:13-16). Peter encourages those who suffer because of their faith in Christ.

Gospel (Jn 17:1-11). This is part of Jesus' solemn prayer at the Last Supper. Here he prays for himself and for his disciples.

HOMILY 1   **Our need of the Spirit**

St Paul tells us that no one can say, 'Jesus is Lord' without the help of the Holy Spirit (1 Cor 12:3). In other words, we can't do anything in the spiritual life without the help of the Holy Spirit. We are tempted to protest: 'This can't possibly be true. St Paul was exaggerating. We can do lots of things. All we need is some will-power.' But St Paul was not exaggerating.

All the great artists were painfully aware of their need for inspiration. Van Gogh put it like this: 'In order to do beautiful things, you need a certain dart of inspiration, a ray from on high, things not in ourselves.'

Anyone who has made serious attempts at living a spiritual life will know that without God's grace we are powerless. We need a strength we ourselves do not possess. In this 'do-it-yourself' age, this truth will come as a blow to our pride. It is especially in times of difficulty and crisis that we come face to face with our limitations.

When Christ died the apostles were like sheep without a shepherd. Worse, during the passion they learned some uncomfortable things about themselves. Before it they thought they were brave, strong, and generous. During it they discovered they were cowardly, weak, and selfish.

But Christ had foreseen all this. He knew well they needed strengthening. That was why he told them to do nothing until they received 'power from on high', that is, the Holy Spirit. Only with the help of the Spirit would they be able to go out and preach the Gospel. The experience of their own weakness during the passion disposed them to receive the Spirit.

We all have experiences which make us painfully aware of our own weakness. A sudden illness, or perhaps a brush with death, and we are face to face with our powerlessness and mortality. We find that we are not capable of the simplest prayer. All the saints knew such moments. Far from being moments of damnation, these can become moments of enlightenment and salvation. They convince us of our need of the Spirit.

During the nine days between the Ascension and Pentecost the apostles, with Mary in their midst, assembled in the upper room to prepare for the coming of the Holy Spirit. Their preparation for receiving the Spirit was prayer. This is the oldest and most important novena in the Church. We must try to make these days, days of prayer. Jesus prayed for those he left behind to carry on his work (see Gospel). He prays for us too. Each Pentecost renews the gift of the Holy Spirit in the Church.

HOMILY 2   **What the Spirit means to us**

The death of Jesus left the apostles lost, sad, and wounded in spirit. The resurrection revived their faith in Jesus. But they were not quite courageous and strong enough in spirit to face the world. They needed the Holy Spirit to lift their spirits and to breathe new life into them.

The spirit is extremely important – our own spirit, that is. This is evident from some of the everyday expressions we use that include the word 'spirit'.

For instance, we talk about a person being low in spirits, or being in high spirits

We talk about someone approaching a task in the right spirit or in the wrong spirit.

We talk about a person giving a spirited performance.

We talk about a person having a joyful spirit, or a generous spirit, or a mean spirit, and so on.

We talk about breaking or crushing a person's spirit.

These are but a few examples of the way we acknowledge the importance of the spirit to us. The human spirit is more powerful than any drug. Our spirit is our most precious possession. It is our greatest source of energy. It is to us what wings are to a bird, or roots are to a tree.

However, while the human spirit can be very strong, it can also be very brittle. It can ascend the heights, or plumb the depths.

It can be an oak unmoved in a storm, or a frail reed swaying in the wind. It can be a piece of granite, or a piece of china. The human spirit can be easily broken or crushed. When this happens, terrible harm is done to the person.

The Bush-people of Africa (the Bushmen) were the first inhabitants of the continent. But down the centuries they suffered persecution at the hands of both white people and black people. Today there is only a remnant of them left in Southern Africa, in and around the Kalahari desert. They are used to living in wide open spaces. Most people would find such an environment almost unbearable. Not so the Bush-people. For them it is their element.

Once a Bushman was imprisoned because he had killed a giant bustard, which was a crime, since the bustard is a protected species. Locked up in a small cell, he began to waste away like a candle. He had sufficient food and drink, yet he continued to pine away.

Puzzled and alarmed, the authorities called in a doctor to examine him. The doctor gave him a thorough examination, but could find nothing wrong with him physically. When asked why he was ill all the man could say was, 'I can't live without being able to see the sun go down over the Kalahari desert.'

I don't know how the story ended, but I hope the authorities had the good sense to release him. His problem was not lack of food for his body, but lack of nourishment for his spirit. It was his spirit not his body that was dying.

Because the spirit is easily broken, easily crushed, it needs strengthening and nourishing every bit as much as the body does. If strengthened and nourished it has great powers of recovery.

What are the things that strengthen and nourish the spirit? What is it that enables the spirit to soar, and what is it that causes it to sink?

Sadness weighs it down; joy lifts it up.

Criticism erodes it; praise builds it up.

Failure shrinks it; success enlarges it.

Despair causes it to wilt; hope breathes new life into it.

Rejection wounds it; acceptance heals it.

Hatred poisons it; love purifies it.

Fear cripples it; solitude calms it; prayer strengths it.

The Holy Spirit continually breathes new life into our spirits. So, as we prepare for the feast of Pentecost, we might make our own the prayer: Spirit of the living God, fall afresh on us.

HOMILY 3   **The waiting room**

Before leaving his apostles Jesus told them to wait in Jerusalem for the coming of the Holy Spirit. So they returned from the Mount of Olives to the upper room. There they gathered with Mary the mother of Jesus and other disciples, and waited for the promised Spirit. The upper room became a waiting room.

All of us are familiar with waiting rooms of one kind or another. We have waited for people. We have waited for planes, trains, buses. We have been in the waiting rooms of doctors and dentists and hospitals. No two waiting rooms are the same. In some you feel close to heaven; in others you feel close to hell. There is no comparison between waiting in a comfortable airport lounge for a plane to take you on an exciting trip, and waiting in a hospital room for news of a loved one who is clinging to life by a slender thread.

We are familiar with the peculiar atmosphere that prevails in waiting rooms. An air of uncertainty prevails which makes us feel nervous and apprehensive. In general, the people we meet in waiting rooms are strangers to us. Still, it's better than being alone. But of course it's so much better if you have a friend or friends by your side.

What makes the experience so difficult is precisely the waiting. Waiting is not easy. It means being idle. Idleness can be unbearable, especially for active people. The poor do more waiting than the rich. The latter are able to skip the queue.

But the hardest thing of all about waiting is the sense of powerlessness that usually accompanies it. Things are out of our control. Our destiny is in the hands of someone else. There is nothing we can do but wait. This can be excruciating for capable people who like to take control of things.

We look for some distraction, something to make the time pass more quickly and to keep our minds off the future. In many waiting rooms you will find reading material left there for that purpose. But often you find yourself unable to concentrate on it.

But waiting, though painful, can be a graced thing. The soul is nurtured by want as well as by plenty. Waiting brings home to us how interdependent we are. We need others. Besides, waiting is part of life. The earth has to wait for the rain. The farmer has to wait for the spring. Waiting is necessary for change, growth, and healing to happen.

One psychologist says that people need to be empowered – that is her definition of health. But there are also times when we may need to be weak and powerless, vulnerable and open to experience. Only when a hole appears in the wall are we able to see beyond.

What was it like for the apostles? I'm quite sure that they would have experienced most of our emotions as they waited in that room. They put their trust in the word of Jesus. But that doesn't mean they weren't apprehensive about the future. And as they waited, they became aware of their own powerlessness. But that only served to dispose them to receive the gift of the Spirit.

As they waited they prepared themselves for the coming of the Spirit by prayer. In that way they supported each other.

We must try to make these days, days of prayer. Each Pentecost renews the gift of the Holy Spirit in the Church.

PRAYER OF THE FAITHFUL

President: Let us pray for the coming of the Holy Spirit as Christ urged his disciples to do.

Response: Come, Holy Spirit.

Reader(s): For the Church: that the Holy Spirit may renew the commitment of its members. [Pause] Let us pray.

For all those who guide the destiny of nations: that the Holy Spirit may open their ears to the voice of conscience. [Pause] Let us pray.

For all whose spirits are crushed: that the Holy Spirit may breath new life into them. [Pause] Let us pray.

For each other: that the Holy Spirit may warm our hearts with his love. [Pause] Let us pray.

For our own particular needs. [Longer pause] Let us pray.

President: God of love, open our minds and hearts to the coming of the Holy Spirit, so that we may be able to follow your Son more faithfully. We ask this through Christ our Lord.

REFLECTION   **The human spirit**

Our spirit is our most precious possession.
It is our greatest source of energy.
However, while it can be very strong,
it can also be very brittle.
It can be an oak unmoved in a storm,
or a frail reed swaying in the wind.
It can be a piece of granite or a piece of china.
What is it that enables the spirit to soar,
and what is it that causes it to sink?
Sadness weighs it down; joy lifts it up.
Criticism erodes it; praise builds it up.
Failure shrinks it; success enlarges it.
Despair causes it to wilt; hope breathes new life into it.
Rejection wounds it; acceptance heals it.
Hatred poisons it; love purifies it.
Fear cripples it; solitude calms it; prayer strengths it.
Spirit of the living God, fall afresh on us.

Pentecost Sunday

INTRODUCTION AND CONFITEOR

This is the day when, true to his promise, Jesus sent the Holy Spirit to the apostles. The coming of the Spirit changed the apostles and saw the launching of a new community (the Church).

This day renews the gift of the Spirit in each of us and in the Church as a whole. Let us pause to reflect on our need of the Spirit, and to dispose ourselves to receive him. [Pause]

Lord Jesus, your Spirit enlightens our minds and opens our hearts. Lord, have mercy

Lord Jesus, your Spirit kindles within us the fire of your love. Christ, have mercy.

Lord Jesus, your Spirit heals the wounds of sin and division. Lord, have mercy.

HEADINGS FOR READINGS

First Reading (Acts 2:1-11). Luke describes the descent of the Holy Spirit on the apostles, and the effect it had on them.

Second Reading (1 Cor 12:3-7.12-13). The Holy Spirit gives different gifts to different people, for the good of the Church, the Body of Christ.

Gospel (Jn 20:19-23). The risen Jesus gives the gift of the Holy Spirit to his disciples and inaugurates the mission of the Church.

SCRIPTURE NOTE

St Luke exploits Jewish tradition which saw Pentecost as the feast of the giving of the Law on Mount Sinai. According to the legend a mighty wind turned to fire and a voice proclaimed the Law. In a further refinement, the fire split into seventy tongues of fire corresponding to the seventy nations of the world: the law was proclaimed, not only to Israel, but to all humankind. Luke, too, has the mighty wind and tongues of fire coming upon the group of disciples. But for Luke the universal proclamation was not that of the Law, but of the Good News, a proclamation that has undone the sentence of Babel and re-united the scattered nations.

St John has the giving of the Spirit happening on Easter day. However, we must avoid any impression of a twofold solemn bestowal of the Spirit. John and Luke are both are saying the same thing: the risen Lord gives the gift of the Spirit and inaugurates the mission of the Church. That they differ in their dating is due to theological concerns.

HOMILY 1   **Empowerment**

Prior to the coming of the Holy Spirit the apostles were virtually living in hiding in the upper room. A great task had been entrusted to them, yet they had neither the strength nor the will to begin it. But after the coming of the Holy Spirit they were changed people. They left their hiding place, and set out courageously to preach the Gospel.

What was it that the Spirit did to them?

In promising the Spirit Jesus said to them, 'You will receive power when the Holy Spirit comes on you, and then you will be my witnesses not only in Jerusalem, but … to the ends of the earth.' (Acts 1:8)

I think the key word here is the word 'power'. Power was precisely what they needed. At the moment they felt completely powerless. They were crippled with fear and a sense of inadequacy. They felt totally incapable of carrying out the task of preaching the Gospel and witnessing to Jesus. After all, they had witnessed what happened to Jesus. They needed courage. They needed someone to empower them.

Empowerment is one of the 'in' words nowadays. And with good reason. We have seen individuals or groups of people who initially felt powerless to change their situation, suddenly become able to do so when someone empowered them. We have seen what a good motivator can do for a football team. Players who had been lacking in self-belief, begin to believe in themselves and play away above their normal selves.

What does empowerment mean? In the first place, it means to give or delegate power or authority to someone; to authorise someone. This wouldn't apply to the apostles – they had already been given that by Jesus.

In the second place, it means to give ability to, or to enable someone to do something. This is the usual sense in which the word 'empowerment' is used, and it certainly applies to the apostles at Pentecost.

When people are empowered, they become able and willing to take charge of their situation. They no longer wait for someone else to do it for them. They accept that they and they alone have to do something about it.

The Holy Spirit empowered the apostles. He came down on them in the form of wind and fire. Wind and fire (heat) are symbols of power. Wind has the power to move, to uproot. Fire has the power to refine and transform.

The power they symbolise here is the power of God. Here they symbolise the presence and action of God. The coming of the Spirit provided the apostles with the energy, the momentum, the enthusiasm, the courage, the love and the passion to get on with the task Christ had given them. The Holy Spirit would help them, but he wouldn't do it for them.

However, we mustn't think that the change in them came about in an instant. It had to be a gradual thing. It had to be a growth process. And growth can be slow and painful. We do not easily let go of old ways, old habits and old attitudes.

People change when they are given hope; when someone believes in them and gives them a task to do; when someone takes an interest in them. Above all, they change when they are loved. They come out of their shells, and hidden energies are released in them. The miracle of human change is the only real miracle.

We too need someone to empower us so that we are able to take charge of our lives, and live them responsibly. This means being willing to change what needs to be changed. But we especially need empowerment in order to witness to our Christian faith. The power that changed the apostles is available to us too. The Holy Spirit energises and strengthens our spirits and warms and purifies our hearts.

HOMILY 2   **The miracle of change**

After Pentecost the apostles were changed people. It is a mistake to think that the change came about in an instant. It had to be a gradual thing, a process. It was a growth process, set in motion by the action of the Holy Spirit. And growth happens gradually. Though we are dealing with mystery, that doesn't mean we can't understand anything about it. Let us look at how spring goes about its work of change and renewal.

Each year in Ireland towards the middle of March you will see patches of green begin to appear in the fields and on the hillsides, new patches on an old garment. Day by day the patches get bigger. A month or so later spring will have woven a completely new garment.

Yet spring doesn't make anything happen. It is only a facilitator. It merely creates a climate in which things can grow. The new life comes from within. It cannot be imposed. All these brand-new things that we see, come from within. What spring does is provide living things with the opportunity, gives them the impulse to realise what is already inside them in a germinal state.

Spring's task is to awaken and call forth. This calling forth is a gentle process. Force is out of the question. Persuasion is the only effective weapon. For unless there is a response from within, all spring's efforts will be in vain.

If a tree has no life in it, then all the sunshine of all springs that have visited this earth will not succeed in producing a single bud in it. One good thing about nature – it is incapable of deception. It does not put on an outward show when there is nothing inside.

People too need to renew themselves. This renewal, however, cannot be imposed. If this is attempted it will merely result in an outward show, a dressing up. It will not enrich the person, and will soon fade and eventually wear out like a garment.

Many people have violence done to them. People try to form them, to press them into shape from the outside or squeeze them into a mould, as if they were lumps of clay. These people betray them.

What people need is someone to awaken them to what is inside them, to bid them live, and help them grow. But growth is slow and painful. We do not easily let go of the old garment, woven out of old attitudes, old ways, and old habits.

But we have been given a wonderful Facilitator, namely, the Holy Spirit. The Spirit awakens us to the mysterious power within us, bids us live, and helps us grow. This gives us some understanding of what happened to the apostles at Pentecost, and what can happen to us too.

Alas, too many people are left unawakened, and die without having experienced even one spring.

HOMILY 3   **A new language**

Language is a great tool of communication. If you are in a country where you are unable to speak the language, you feel lost. You have great difficulty in communicating with people. How happy you are when you finally meet someone who understands your language.

For the most part it is by means of words that human beings express their needs, laws, transactions, intentions, thoughts, emotions, longings, hopes, and creeds. Yet words are such elusive symbols. How rarely a simple statement conveys the same meaning to two people.

Language of itself is not enough to bring people together. In fact, as the Little Prince said, 'words are a source of misunderstanding.' Just because we use the same language doesn't mean we are one. There may still not be a meeting of minds and hearts.

But the opposite can happen too. People may speak different languages, they may be strangers to one another, yet a bond can be created among them, so that they become not only comrades, but brothers and sisters. On the day of a great joy, or a great sorrow, or a great danger for a community or a country, differences of language are swept aside. We stand shoulder to shoulder. We find ourselves of one mind and one heart.

There are other ways of communicating besides words. So important are signs and symbols that perhaps only twenty per cent of communication happens through words. In St Luke's account of Pentecost we find two powerful symbols – wind and fire, both symbols of energy.

Still, language is hugely important. We are told that on Pentecost day everyone understood the apostles. It wasn't that they spoke a completely new language. It was one all of us are familiar with but which, alas, we tend to forget or leave unused.

What was this new language? It was the language of peace rather than of war; the language of reconciliation rather than of conflict; the language of co-operation rather than of competition; the language of forgiveness rather than of vengeance; the language of hope rather than of despair; the language of tolerance rather than of bigotry; the language of friendship rather than of hostility; the language of unity rather than of division; the language of love rather than of hate.

This 'new' language gave rise to a new community, the community of those who believed in Jesus – a community of faith and love. According to the Acts of the Apostles, the first followers of Jesus were 'one in mind and heart'.

Through the gift of the Spirit, people of many languages learned to profess the one faith, to the praise and glory of God. That is the real miracle of Pentecost. And it is a miracle which, thankfully, still happens.

NOTE: If we have people of different nationalities in the parish, we could get representatives to make a prayer in their native languages. This would give expression to the fact that the Spirit unites the races and nations in proclaiming in different tongues the one faith.

PRAYER OF THE FAITHFUL

President: As one body in Christ, we offer up our prayers to the Father of grace who sends forth the Holy Spirit to renew the face of the earth.

Response: Send forth your Spirit, O Lord.

Reader(s): For the Church: that the Holy Spirit may bind its members together in a community of faith and love. [Pause] Let us pray.

For world leaders: that the Holy Spirit may guide their feet into the way of peace. [Pause] Let us pray.

For all those who are imprisoned by doubt, fear, inadequacy, depression, or habits of sin: that the Holy Spirit may help them to experience the joy and freedom of the children of God. [Pause] Let us pray.

For each other: that the Holy Spirit may inspire in each of us a desire for holiness. [Pause] Let us pray.

For our own particular needs. [Longer pause] Let us pray

President: God of power and love, on Pentecost Day you sent the Holy Spirit on the apostles, and with hearts on fire, they went forth to preach the Gospel to the world. Grant that we too may experience the power of the Holy Spirit in our lives and in our world. We ask this through Christ our Lord.

REFLECTION   **Love is gentle**

It was late spring and the buds still refused to open.
Tightly wrapped up in themselves, they were as hard as stones.
The wind shook them. The hail beat them.
The frost squeezed them in a fist of iron.
All three shouted, 'Open up! Open up!'
Instead of opening up,
the buds reinforced their shells,
and retreated even more deeply into themselves.
Then along came the sun.
It issued no threats and made no demands.
It just created a more friendly climate.
And what happened?
Almost overnight the buds began to soften and expand.
Then their shells cracked, and they burst out.
If you love, you are gentle.
And there are certain tasks
which only gentleness can accomplish.

SOLEMNITIES OF THE LORD

'The Journey'

PATRICK PYE

Trinity Sunday

Today we celebrate the greatest mystery of our faith, namely, the mystery of the Trinity. God is Father, Son and Spirit. It is not so much something to talk about, as something to celebrate, pray, and live. [Pause]

Lord Jesus, you reveal to us the mystery of the Father, and of his unconditional love for us. Lord, have mercy.

Lord Jesus, you reveal to us the mystery of your own divine sonship, and you share your divine inheritance with us. Christ, have mercy.

Lord Jesus, you reveal to us the mystery of the Holy Spirit who binds us together in unity. Lord, have mercy.

HEADINGS FOR READINGS

First Reading (Ex 34:4-6.8-9). God reveals himself to Moses on Mount Sinai as a God who is faithful to his promises and rich in tenderness and compassion.

Second Reading (2 Cor 13:11-13). Paul encourages the Corinthians to live in peace and love. The reading contains a trinitarian blessing which is used as a greeting at Mass.

Gospel (Jn 3:16-18). God has shown his love for us by sending his Son to save all us. All who believe in him will be saved.

HOMILY 1 **Rublev's icon**

None of us likes to be left out. For instance, a wedding is coming up to which we expect to be invited. However, when the invitations are sent out, we don't receive one. This hurts, sometimes a great deal. We feel excluded. We feel we are not wanted.

Of course, we have to look at ourselves and see how generous we are when it comes to inviting other people in. From time to time people come to our door. Some we dismiss immediately, barely exchanging a word with them. Others we have a polite but brief chat with at the door, without bringing them into the house. Others we bring into the parlour where we talk business, and when that business is concluded we show them to the door. But there are a select few whom we welcome, invite in immediately, and offer them food and drink.

There is a beautiful Russian icon of the Blessed Trinity painted by a monk by the name of Rublev. It depicts the three Divine Persons sitting at a table. A dish of food lies on the table. But the thing that immediately strikes you is the fact that at the front of the table there is a vacant place. The vacant place is meant to convey openness, hospitality, and welcome towards the stranger and outsider.

That vacant place is meant for each of us, and for all the human family. It signifies God's invitation to us to share in the life of the Trinity. God doesn't exclude us. He doesn't talk to us at the doorstep. He invites us to come in and sit at his table. He wants to share his life with us. In the words of the Gospel for this feast: 'God loved the world so much that he gave his only Son ... '

Many are intimidated by the great mystery of the Blessed Trinity. This is a pity. We should see the Father, the Son, and the Holy Spirit as friends to whom we can relate, and to whom we can talk in prayer. Because God's Son, Jesus, befriended us, we are no longer strangers and outsiders. We are God's children. We are part of the family.

He has already given us a place at the banquet of earthly life. But he wants us to have a place at the banquet of eternal life too. Only at God's table can we find the nourishment our hearts are hungering for.

From all this we see that God is a God of love. Our response can only be one of trust in God and love towards one another. What St Paul said to the Corinthians is meant also for us: 'Help one another. Be united; live in peace, and the God of love and peace will be with you.'

HOMILY 2   **Being tuned in**

One day a farmer went into the city. As he was walking down a busy street he suddenly stopped and said to a friend who was with him, 'I can hear a cricket'. His friend was amazed and asked, 'How can you hear a cricket in the midst of all this noise?'

'Because my ears are attuned to his sound,' the farmer replied.

Then he listened even more intently, and following the sound, found the cricket perched on a window ledge. His friend couldn't get over this. But the farmer showed no surprise. Instead he took a few coins out of his pocket and threw them on the pavement. On hearing the jingle of coins, the passers-by stopped in their tracks.

'You see what I mean,' said the farmer. 'None of those people could hear the sound of the cricket, but all of them could hear the sound of the money. People hear what their ears are attuned to hear, and are deaf to all the rest.'

The point being made here is fairly obvious: We could be tuned in to God if we took a little trouble. Voltaire said: 'It is natural to admit the existence of God as soon as one opens one's eyes.' And Abraham Lincoln said, 'I can see how it might be possible for the man to look down upon the earth and be an atheist, but I cannot conceive how he could look up into the heavens and say there is no God.'

At the sight of something or other, a person will know in an instant that these things do not exist through themselves, and that God is. As a house implies a builder, a dress a weaver, a door a carpenter, so the world proclaims God, its Creator.

When you look at a work of art it is impossible not to think of the artist. To look on the created world and not see the Creator is to be blind to the meaning of the whole of creation and of ourselves. Yet sadly many look and see nothing. They listen and hear nothing. Jesus spoke about God as a merciful and forgiving Father. He spoke about himself as the Son of the Father. And he sent the Holy Spirit to us to help us live as his disciples and children of God.

We are dealing with a great mystery. Yet any child can grasp it in such a way as to be able to pray it and live it. We think of God as our Father (and Mother), a Father who loves us deeply. We think of Jesus as our Brother who gave his life for us. And we think of the Holy Spirit as a friend who helps us to live like Jesus, and who binds us together as brothers and sisters in a community of faith and love. As Christians, this is the atmosphere in which we live, and move, and have our being.

HOMILY 3 **A God of love**

One day two learned men were walking along the seashore, discussing the mystery of God. However, they weren't making very much progress. Suddenly they came upon a small boy playing on the beach. He had dug a hole in the sand and kept running down to the sea, dipping his toy bucket in the water, and running back up the beach to empty the water into the hole.

The two men watched him for a while as he ran back and forth filling and emptying his bucket. They found the scene amusing. They went up to the boy and asked him what he was doing. Very seriously he told them he was emptying the ocean into the hole he had dug in the sand.

The two smiled, and walked on, resuming their discussion about God. After a while, one of them stopped and said to the other, 'You know, we were amused just now when that child told us what he was trying to do. Yet what we have been trying to do in our discussion about God is just the same. It is just as impossible for us to understand the mystery of God as it is for that child to put the water of the ocean into that hole. Our minds are but tiny thimbles, whereas the reality of God is as great as the ocean.'

As the story says: it is impossible for us to understand God. God is a mystery. But a mystery is not something we can know nothing about. A mystery is something which is so full of meaning, that no matter how hard to try, we will never get to the bottom of it. Therefore, the story must not be used to justify laziness or superficiality in our efforts to understand something of the mystery of God.

It's possible to know of the existence of God by our own reasoning. At the sight of something or other, a person will know in an instant that these things do not exist through themselves, and that God is.

But we would know very little about God if he hadn't revealed himself to us. It is especially in the Scriptures that we know God. From the Scriptures we learn that God is Father, Son and Spirit.

And from the Scriptures we learn what God is like. For instance today's First Reading says that God is 'a God of tenderness and compassion, slow to anger, rich in kindness and faithfulness.' And the Gospel says: 'God loved the world so much that he gave his only Son ... '

Both readings have the same message: God is a God of love. That is something tremendously important to know about God. God loves us, not because we are good, but because God is good. Our very existence is a sign of God's love. God's unconditional love for us is the Good News.

Our response can only be one of trust in God and love towards one another. What St Paul said to he Corinthians is meant also for us: 'Help one another. Be united; live in peace, and the God of love and peace will be with you.'

PRAYER OF THE FAITHFUL

President: We raise our hearts in prayer to the God of tenderness and compassion, rich in kindness and faithfulness.

Response: Lord, hear us in your love.

Reader(s): For the People of God: that they may worship the Father, the Son, and the Holy Spirit in sincerity and truth. [Pause] We pray in faith.

For the world in which we live: that people may reject false gods and come to know and worship the one true God. [Pause] We pray in faith.

For all those who are sincerely searching for God. [Pause] We pray in faith.

For each other: that the Holy Spirit may help us to live a life in keeping with our dignity as children of God. [Pause] We pray in faith.

For our particular needs. [Longer pause] We pray in faith.

President: Father, our source of life, you know our weakness. May we reach out with joy to grasp your hand and walk more readily in your ways. We ask this through Christ our Lord.

REFLECTION **Reflection in a well**

Once a young boy stood watching a gypsy
as he drank from a well in the town square.
After drinking, the man continued to gaze into the well,
as though looking at someone.
He was a giant of a man but had a friendly face.
So the boy approached him and asked:
'Who lives down there?'

'God does,' answered the gypsy.
'Can I see him?'
'Sure you can,' said the gypsy.
Then taking the boy into his arms he lifted him up
so that he could see down into the well.
All the boy could see, however,
was his own reflection in the water.
'But that's only me,' he cried in disappointment.
'All I see is me.'
'Ah,' replied the gypsy,
'now you know where God lives.
He lives in you.'

The Body and Blood of Christ

INTRODUCTION AND CONFITEOR

In talking about our unity in Christ, St Paul says that we are like grains of wheat that have been brought together to form one loaf. It's a beautiful image. The Eucharist celebrates and strengthens our unity in Christ. [Pause]

Lord Jesus, you are the vine, we are the branches. Lord, have mercy.

Lord Jesus, separated from you and from one another our lives become barren. Christ, have mercy.

Lord Jesus, united with you and with one another our lives become fruitful. Lord, have mercy.

HEADINGS FOR READINGS

First Reading (Deut 8:2-3.14-16). The author exhorts the people to remember that they are God's people who need to nourish themselves on his word.

Second Reading (1 Cor 10:16-17). In the Eucharist we all share the same bread, and so, however many we are, we form one Body in Christ.

Gospel (Jn 6:51-58). As food and drink nourish the body, so Christ nourishes us for this life and eternal life.

HOMILY 1   The bread of life

As human beings we cannot live on bread alone. We suffer from many kinds of hunger. Let us turn to the Gospel to see the various kinds of 'bread' Jesus offered to people, thus satisfying their many hungers.

To the people who followed him into the desert, and who were starving, he offered ordinary bread, and so satisfied their physical hunger.

To the leper whose body was falling apart, he offered the only bread that mattered to him – the bread of physical healing.

To the lonely woman at Jacob's well, he offered the bread of human kindness, and thus satisfied her hunger for acceptance.

To sinners he offered the bread of forgiveness, and thus satisfied their hunger for salvation.

To the rejects and outcasts, by mixing with them and sharing their bread, he offered the bread of companionship, and so satisfied their hunger for self-worth.

To the widow of Nain who was burying her only son, and to Martha and Mary who had just buried their brother Lazarus, he offered the bread of compassion, and showed them that even in death we are not beyond the reach of God's help.

With Zacchaeus, the rich tax collector who had robbed the bread from the tables of the poor, he began by inviting himself to his table. Then, having awakened within him a hunger for a better life, he got him to share his ill-gotten money with the poor.

To the thief who died at his side he offered the bread of reconciliation with God, thus bringing peace to his troubled soul.

But, surprisingly, there were some who refused his offer of bread.

There was the rich young man to whom he offered the bread of discipleship, but who refused it because he was not willing to part with his riches.

There were the Scribes and Pharisees to whom he offered not once, but several times, the bread of conversion, but they refused to eat even a crumb of it.

There were the people of his beloved city of Jerusalem to whom, with tears in his eyes, he offered the bread of peace, but they refused it with the result that their city was destroyed.

There was Pilate to whom he offered the bread of truth, but he had no appetite for it because it meant putting his position at risk.

Jesus shared himself with others in many different ways, and under many different forms, before offering himself to them as food and drink at the Last Supper.

Jesus nourishes us in so many ways, and of course especially in the Eucharist. The presence of Christ in the Eucharist becomes a problem only when we have lost our sense of his presence in all that is. Those who have a deep sense of the presence of God in the whole of creation, will not have great difficulty in believing that He is present in a very special way in the Eucharist.

God alone can satisfy all the longings and hungers of our hearts, because he alone can give us the bread of eternal life. This is the bread we receive in the Eucharist. Without it we would not have the strength to follow Christ.

HOMILY 2 **Not on bread alone**

Ethiopia suffered a terrible famine during the years 1984 to 1986. Cardinal Hume of Westminster tells about an incident that happened when he visited Ethiopia in the middle of the famine. One of the places he visited was a settlement up in the hills where the people were waiting for food which was unlikely to arrive. He was taken there in a helicopter.

As he got out of the helicopter a small boy, aged about ten, came up to him and took his hand. He was wearing nothing but a loincloth round his waist. The whole time the cardinal was there the little child would not let go of his hand.

As they went around he made two gestures: with one hand he pointed to his mouth, and with the other he took the cardinal's hand and rubbed it on his cheek.

Later the cardinal said, 'Here was an orphan boy who was lost and starving. Yet by two simple gestures he indicated our two fundamental needs or hungers. With one gesture he showed me his hunger for food, and with the other his hunger for love.

'I have never forgotten that incident, and to this day I wonder whether that child is still alive. I remember that as I boarded the helicopter he stood and looked at me reproachfully.'

Today's first reading says: 'A human being doesn't live on bread alone but on every word that comes from the mouth of God.' Jesus quoted these words during his temptations in the desert.

We need ordinary bread. That is our first and most basic necessity. But we need more than that. Bread nourishes only half of us – the physical side. But we have a spiritual side. It too cries out for nourishment. Even that starving little child realised that. In the Eucharist we are nourished with the food of God's word, a word which comforts, guides, inspires and challenges us. And in Holy Communion we are nourished with the food of eternal life.

In the eucharistic banquet we have nourishment for our minds, hearts and spirits. Here we experience the abiding presence of Christ with us. He is not present as a vague memory of a person who lived long ago, but as a real, life-giving presence that transforms us. By eating the food of the Eucharist, we are nourished, and like Christ are able to nourish others.

HOMILY 3 **One loaf, one body**

Take this loaf of bread. (*Hold one up for all to see.*) It is a wonderful thing.

Indeed, it is a kind of miracle. It is a gift of God, but like most of God's gifts, it doesn't fall ready-made into our hands.

Many agents contributed to the making of this loaf: the soil, the sun, the rain, the work and intelligence of people. It comes to us not from one hand but from many hands – the hand of the farmer, the hand of the miller, the hand of the baker, the hand of the merchant ... And of course we must not forget God's part in it. Though it is people who bring forth the bread, it is to God that we give thanks. Without God none of this would be possible.

All this is beautifully expressed in the prayer we say over the bread at the Offertory of the Mass: 'Blessed are you, Lord, God of all creation. Through your goodness we have this bread to offer, which earth has given and human hands have made. It will become for us the bread of life.'

Many grains of wheat went into this loaf. These grains were once scattered over the fields. But eventually they were brought together and ground into flour. And from that flour this loaf resulted.

St Paul uses a loaf of bread as a symbol of our unity in Christ (Second Reading). Once we were separated from one another, but now we have been gathered together to form the Body of Christ, the Church. This is an even greater miracle than a loaf of bread. As one body, we become living witnesses of God's desire to bring all peoples and nations together into one family.

During the week we are scattered all over this area, and maybe even further afield. But here we are brought together. Here we are the Body of Christ made visible.

Here we lay down our differences and become one family. Here we are in from the cold and experience the warmth of community. Love is the atmosphere we breathe here. We must try to rise above the things that prevent us from experiencing and expressing our unity – shyness, coldness, and indifference.

The Eucharist is the sign and source of our unity. We form a single body because we all share in the one loaf. We can't be truly in communion with Jesus without being in communion with one another.

Alas, when we leave the church we tend to forget all this. We no longer recognise the ties that exist between us. We go our own ways, ignoring one another, and sadly sometimes turning against one another. When we depart from here we must take out into the world some of the warmth we have experienced here.

PRAYER OF THE FAITHFUL

President: As one body, we pray to the living Father who gives life to the world.

Response: Lord, hear our prayer.

Reader(s): For Christians: that the celebration of the Eucharist may form them into a community of love. [Pause] Let us pray to the Lord.

For all government leaders: that they may spare no efforts to ensure that all of God's children have enough to eat. [Pause] Let us pray to the Lord.

For the lonely, who are hungering for the bread of companionship; and the sick who are hungering for the bread of health. [Pause] Let us pray to the Lord.

For each other: that we may hunger for a life of goodness and holiness. [Pause] Let us pray to the Lord.

For our own special needs. [Longer pause] Let us pray to the Lord.

President: Father, may the food we eat at this banquet make us strong, and bind us together in unity and peace. We ask this through the same Christ your Son our Lord.

PRAYER AFTER HOLY COMMUNION

Heavenly Father, the bread we have eaten was once scattered over the fields, but here was gathered together and became one loaf. So may your Church be gathered together from the ends of the earth into your Kingdom. To you belong power and glory through Jesus Christ, for ever and ever.

REFLECTION   **Blessed are the hungry**

'Blessed are the hungry; they shall get their fill.'
It is in our emptiness that we are filled.
It is in our confusions that we are guided.
It is in our weakness that we are strengthened.
It is in our sins that we are forgiven.
It is in our hunger that we are fed.
We believe that God has a homeland prepared for us
where all our hungers will be satisfied
and all our hopes will be fulfilled.
This conviction makes it possible for us
to travel onwards with an ache in our hearts
and an unquenchable longing in our souls.

SUNDAYS OF THE YEAR

'The Robe of Baptism'
PATRICK PYE

Second Sunday of the Year
JESUS, THE CHOSEN ONE OF GOD

INTRODUCTION AND CONFITEOR

Jesus is the Lamb of God who takes away the sins. Let us begin our celebration by bringing our sins to him and asking for his forgiveness and healing. [Pause].

I confess to almighty God ...

HEADINGS FOR READINGS

First Reading (Is 49:3.5-6). This talks about the servant God has chosen to bring Israel back to him, and not just Israel, but all peoples.

Second Reading (1 Cor 1:1-3). Here Paul reminds the Christians at Corinth of their call to holiness.

Gospel (Jn 1:29-34). Isaiah's prophecy is fulfilled in Jesus. He is God's Chosen Servant who takes away the sins of the people and baptises them with the Holy Spirit.

SCRIPTURE NOTE

Jesus is the Paschal Lamb of the Christian Passover, who by his death delivered the world from sin, as the original paschal lamb's blood delivered the Israelites from the destroying angel. And Jesus is also the Servant of God described in Isaiah as being led without complaint like a lamb before the shearers, a man of sorrows who 'bore the sins of many and made intercession for the transgressors.' Thus at the beginning of his Gospel John outlines a whole Christology: Jesus is the eternally existing One, who is to die as the Paschal Lamb and Suffering Servant for the sins of men and women, and then pour forth the Holy Spirit on a new Israel.

HOMILY 1   **Taking away our sins**

When John the Baptist said of Jesus, 'There is the Lamb of God that takes away the sin of the world ... ' he uttered a great truth about the mission of Jesus. Jesus' mission was directed at sinners. Jesus was that Servant, whose coming was foretold by Isaiah, and whose mission would be to bring sinners back to God. But how was he to do this?

In Old Testament times, on the day of atonement the Jews would choose a goat. The priest made a list of the sins of the people, while at the same time calling on them to repent. Then placing his hands on the goat's head, he pressed down, thereby imposing the sins on the goat, as if he and he alone was guilty. Then, laden with the sins of the people, the goat was sent into the desert.

Is this the kind of thing John the Baptist had in mind? That all we have to do is dump our sins on Jesus and then forget about them. Could it be that simple? That easy?

Jesus does indeed take away our sins in the sense that through him we have forgiveness for our sins, and so are able to put them behind us. When we are forgiven, a very real load, a great burden, is lifted from us, and we are able to go forward freely and joyfully.

But we also have to accept responsibility for our sins. And even when we are forgiven, everything doesn't magically come right for us. We don't suddenly become new people. Our old weaknesses, habits and compulsions are still with us. Which means we still have to struggle.

Sin is not an object that can be removed from us. We are a sinful people – that is the plain truth. Our sinfulness is not the same as our sins. The first is the disease, the second the symptoms. Sin is a condition in which we live, a condition from which we need to be redeemed. Jesus came to redeem us from that condition, and to enable us to live a new life.

How did he get sinners to change their way of life? He did so, not by condemning them and keeping his distance from them, but by befriending them. He put them in touch with that core of goodness which exists in everyone. Through his own luminous goodness he evoked goodness in them.

Jesus befriends us too. And he evokes goodness in us too. That is the only way to go if we wish to overcome sin. Evil can be overcome only by goodness. Here the Sacrament of Reconciliation (Confession) is a great help. It is a place where we can experience the love of Jesus for us in our sins. It is not an impersonal getting rid of sins. Rather, it is a loving encounter with Jesus our Saviour, who calls us away from sin to goodness of life.

Victory over sin comes about as a lifelong struggle. We must not become depressed when we see ourselves making what seems like very little progress. What is important is the struggle for goodness. The purpose of a good life is not to win the battle, but to wage it unceasingly.

Besides personal sin and personal redemption, there is social sin and social redemption. The whole human family is damaged because of sin. Jesus came to bring us back into relationship with God and with one another.

HOMILY 2   **A lesson from John the Baptist**

They say that we see other people not as they are but as we are. The following story illustrates the truth of this.

Once upon a time there was a king who called one of his servants. The same servant was known to be a cruel, mean man, who had no friends. The king said to him, 'I want you to go and travel the length and breadth of my kingdom and find for me a truly good person.'

The man went. In the course of his travels he met and spoke with a great number of people. However, after a long time he came back to the king saying, 'I have searched the whole kingdom as you asked me, but I couldn't find even one truly good person. All of them, without exception, are mean, cruel, deceitful and evil. The good person you seek is nowhere to be found.'

Then the king called another servant. This man was known for his generosity and kindness and was loved by everyone. The king said to him, 'Go and travel the length and breadth of my kingdom and find for me a truly wicked person.'

The man went and travelled far and wide. But after a long time he returned to the king saying, 'I have failed in the task you gave me to do. I found people who are misguided, people who are misled, people who act in blindness or in passion, but nowhere could I find a truly evil person. All of them are good at heart, despite the bad things they have done.'

We see people, not as they are, but as we are. Today's Gospel provides us with another illustration of this truth. Jesus had only recently arrived from Nazareth. As yet he was completely unknown. Hence, he needed someone to introduce him to the public, and so launch him on his public mission. He found that person in John the Baptist.

One day, shortly after he had baptised Jesus, John saw Jesus passing by. Turning to his disciples he said, 'There is the Lamb of God that takes away the sin of the world. This is the one I spoke of when I said: A man is coming after me who ranks before me … ' With these generous words John introduced Jesus to his own disciples and to the public, and thus opened the way for him.

These words tell us a lot about the identity and mission of Jesus. Jesus was that Servant whose coming was foretold by Isaiah, and whose mission was to bring sinners back to God. But these words also tell us a lot about the kind of person John was.

John could have ignored Jesus, or criticised him. But far from doing this, he pointed him out to the people, he built him up before them. He did not see him as a threat, but as a friend and ally. Thus he facilitated the start of his mission. This shows what a good and generous man John was.

There is an important lesson here for us. If we are always finding fault with other people, always putting them down, we should look at ourselves. We may be saying more about ourselves than about other people. Once our hearts are open to others, we discover good in them, even when it is hidden.

Jesus is the supreme example of this. How did he get sinners to change their way of life? He did so, not by condemning them and keeping his distance from them, but by befriending them. He believed in them. He saw goodness in them. He put them in touch with their own goodness.

Through his own luminous goodness he evoked goodness in them.

Jesus befriends us too. He puts us in touch with our own goodness. And once we are in touch with our own goodness, we will find goodness in others and help to bring out that goodness.

HOMILY 3   **Jesus, the Chosen One of God**

When a new prime minister takes up office one of the first things he or she does is to appoint cabinet ministers. Then in an official ceremony the chosen ones get their seal of office. These are not slow in telling the world how pleased they are to have been chosen. You hear them say such things as, 'I feel very privileged,' 'I feel very honoured.' The odd one may say, 'It's a great challenge,' or 'It's a great responsibility.' But I don't think I've ever heard anyone say, 'It's a wonderful opportunity to serve.'

Of course it's an honour to be chosen. But what many of them forget, if indeed they were ever aware of it, is that it is a call to service, to ministry. There is the very human temptation to be attracted by 'the Mercs and perks' that go with the job, as well as the status it bestows on the holder.

We are at the start of St John's Gospel. Jesus has just appeared on the public stage. John the Baptist, who prepared the way for him, now has the further task of introducing him to the people. How does John introduce Jesus? What role does he ascribe to him? He calls Jesus God's Chosen One.

Jesus did not take this role upon himself. He was called by God and sent by God. But once the call came, he made a total gift of himself to it. From now on he will seek, not his own honour, but the honour of his Father. And he knows that he is sent to minister to his brothers and sisters: 'The Son of Man came, not to be served, but to serve.'

John the Baptist also gives us a wonderful example of service. His function was to direct people to Jesus. His task was to draw back the curtain, introduced the main character, and then withdrew into the shadows. In doing this he knew he was inviting his disciples to leave him. Yet there was no jealousy on his part. In this we see his greatness. There is no harder task than to take second place especially when one has enjoyed the first place.

Through our baptism we have been called to be disciples of Jesus. This is a great honour and a great privilege. But we must not forget that it is a call to service. We need the Holy Spirit to touch our hearts. We must learn from John the Baptist not to make ourselves the centre of the world. We must put our gifts at the service of others, not just of ourselves.

In our society our being chosen always implies that others are not chosen. But this is not true for God. God chooses his Son (and the disciples) to reveal to us that we too are chosen. In the Kingdom of God there is no room for competition or rivalry. In the Kingdom each person is precious and unique.

ANOTHER STORY

Once upon a time there was a beautiful porcelain teapot. But it was very frail and delicate. Consequently it was used only on very special occasions, and only for important visitors. But then one day a careless servant dropped it. The lid and spout got broken. The beautiful teapot was now considered to be useless and was thrown out.

For a long time it lay in a refuse dump. Coats of dirt settled on it, blotting out whatever traces of beauty it still possessed. From time to time people came to the dump, hoping to find something of value. On seeing the teapot they would say, 'What a pity it got broken! It must have been beautiful when it was in one piece.'

Then one day a famous flower grower visited the dump. He found the teapot and took it home with him. The first thing he did was clean it up. In spite of its brokenness he found it very beautiful, and he wondered how anyone could have thrown it away. Then he had an inspiration. He would use it as a flower pot.

He filled it with soil, planted a seed in it, and placed it in the front window of his house. Time passed. The seed grew and blossomed into a beautiful flower. Passers-by stopped to admire the flower, and also the handsome pot in which it grew.

Sin is not a physical stain that we can just wash away. Nor can we take it away as if it was a thing. Sin is not a thing. Sin is a condition – a condition of brokenness and woundedness. Each of us is damaged and broken.

Jesus came to redeem us. To be redeemed is to be made whole and well. It is to be restored to our original brightness through the grace of the Holy Spirit. However, this is a lifelong process. We are not things to be repaired. We are people, people to be brought back into relationship with God and with one another.

PRAYER OF THE FAITHFUL

President: Let us pray to Jesus, the Lamb of God, for our own needs, the needs of the Church, and the needs of all the world.

Response: Lord, graciously hear us.

Readers: For the Church: that Christ may heal in it the wounds caused by sin and division. [Pause] Lord, hear us.

For all nations: that they may be bound together by bonds of cooperation and peace. [Pause] Lord, hear us.

For all the sick and the handicapped: that through the love of others they may find health and self-worth. [Pause] Lord, hear us.

For grace, through the Holy Spirit, constantly to seek to overcome our sinfulness. [Pause] Lord, hear us.

For grace to bring our own individual needs before God. [Longer pause] Lord, hear us.

President: Father, we make all our prayers to you, through Christ, the sinless One who takes away our sins, and who now lives and reigns with you and the Holy Spirit, one God, for ever and ever.

INVITATION TO HOLY COMMUNION

We receive Jesus not because we are worthy but because we are sinners who need his help. So we hear again the words of John the Baptist: 'This is the Lamb of God who takes away the sins of the world ... '

REFLECTION   **Healing the wounds of the heart**

All of us are wounded by sin.
The part of us which is most deeply
damaged by sin is the heart.
The heart is so beautiful, so innocent,
but it can be betrayed, scorned, and broken.
Darkness of heart is the blackest night of all.
Emptiness of heart is the greatest poverty of all.
A heavy heart is the most wearisome burden of all.
A broken heart is the most painful wound of all.
Only love can heal the wounds of the heart.
Lord, send your Holy Spirit to us,
to heal the wounds of our hearts
so that we may produce the fruits of love.

Third Sunday of the Year
A LIGHT SHINES IN THE DARK

INTRODUCTION AND CONFITEOR

'The people that lived in darkness have seen a great light.' This is how St Matthew describes the impact of Jesus' ministry. That light shines on us now as we gather in the Lord's name. Let us reflect for a moment on our need of this precious light. [Pause]

Lord Jesus, you cause the light of faith to shine on us. Lord, have mercy.

Lord Jesus, you cause the light of hope to shine on us. Christ, have mercy.

Lord Jesus, you cause the light of love to shine on us. Lord, have mercy.

HEADINGS FOR READINGS

First Reading (Is 8:23-9:3). The prophet predicts future liberation for an oppressed people.

Second Reading (1 Cor 1:10-13.17). Paul launches a passionate appeal for unity in the community at Corinth.

Gospel (Mt 4:12-23). The wonderful prophecy of Isaiah is fulfilled in Jesus. *(Shorter form recommended. The call of the four apostles occurs again on the third Sunday of Ordinary Time, Year B.)*

SCRIPTURE NOTE

The territory occupied by the tribes of Zebulun and Naphtali (later known as Galilee) was the most northerly part of Israel. Because it bordered on pagan territory it would have been associated with darkness. It was the first province of Israel to be conquered by Assyria in 732 BC. Isaiah predicted future liberation for the people of that region. In his Gospel, Matthew sees Isaiah's prophecy as fulfilled in Jesus.

HOMILY 1   **The arrival of the light**

Some Alpine valleys are so deep that the rays of the sun do not reach them at all for days or even weeks in the middle of winter. These days can be very depressing ones for the people who live in those valleys. It's almost as if life was one long night. A priest who ministered in one of these valleys tells the following story.

One day in the depths of winter he was in the classroom of the local school chatting with the children, who hadn't seen the sun for nine days. Then all of a sudden a ray of sunshine shone into the classroom. On seeing it the children climbed onto their desks and cheered and shouted for sheer joy. It shows that even though the sun may not touch the skin it can still warm the soul.

This little incident shows how light is a source of great joy. For sick people the night is usually the hardest time of all. How they welcome those first rays of light which signal the end of the night and the dawning of the day. The coming of electricity to rural Ireland transformed life for those living in the country.

Matthew compares the arrival of Jesus on the scene to the coming of a great light to a people who had been living in deep darkness. He saw Jesus as fulfilling the great prophecy of Isaiah: 'The people that lived in darkness have seen a great light; on those who dwell in the land and shadow of death a light has dawned.' Jesus described his mission in similar terms when he said: 'I am the light of the world.'

History is littered with examples of teachers who brought darkness into the world through their teachings. The teaching of Jesus was truly a source of light to all who accepted him, and of course still is.

He said, 'Love your enemies and pray for those who persecute you.' Thus he rejected the darkness of revenge, and brought the light of forgiveness and reconciliation.

In his parable of the Good Samaritan he rejected the darkness of neglect and indifference, and urged people to care for one another.

In his teaching on authority he rejected the darkness of domination and oppression, and urged those in positions of leadership not to lord it over people, but to serve them in gentleness and humility.

But it was above all through his deeds and encounters with people that his luminous goodness manifested itself. How many people came to him in darkness and went away bathed in light.

Thus he brought sinners out of the darkness of sin into the light of God's grace and love.

He brought outcasts out of the darkness of rejection into the light of acceptance by the community.

He brought the sick and the wounded out of the darkness of pain and illness into the light of wellbeing.

He brought Zacchaeus out of the darkness of greed and selfishness into the light and joy of sharing.

He brought Martha and Mary out of the darkness of grief into the light of hope and life.

He brought the Good Thief out of the darkness of hopelessness into the light of heaven itself.

By rising from the dead he scattered the darkness of death, and promised those who follow him that they will never walk in darkness but will always have the light of life. How dark the world would be if the light of Christ had never shone.

> While we are on earth, we grope in the dark, and, but for the precious image of Christ before us, we would lose our way completely and perish. *(Dostoevsky)*

And yet, though Jesus brought God's light into the world not everybody welcomed it. Sadly, some refused his light and opted to remain in darkness. This is why he began his preaching with a call to repentance: 'Repent, for the kingdom of heaven is close at hand.' To repent means to acknowledge our darkness, and to open ourselves to the light. For those who accepted him, Jesus truly became the light of their lives, and the light of the world.

We still walk in the bright light Jesus brought into our world. By living in it, we become a source of light to others, a lamp for their steps and a light for their paths.

HOMILY 2   **Allowing the light to enter**

'The people who lived in darkness have seen a great light; on those who dwelt in darkness and the shadow of death, a light has dawned.' These beautiful words come from the prophet Isaiah. St Matthew sees them as fulfilled in Jesus. Jesus' coming was like the dawning of a great light. Indeed, this was how Jesus described his own mission when he said: 'I am the light of the world.'

Normally light is something we welcome. However, in certain circumstances we might fear it. Why? Because it shows up everything, things we want to see and things we would prefer to keep hidden from others and perhaps even from ourselves.

A woman invited a priest to bless her house. As he performed the blessing, she escorted him around the house. He noticed that everything was immaculate, banisters polished, beds neatly made, not a thing out of place, not a cobweb or speck of dust in sight.

He sprinkled each room with holy water, and they prayed as they went along. Even the two fat cats asleep on the sofa were not spared. He splashed them with water, and one of them jumped up. So the blessing disturbed something in this neat and orderly house.

They blessed the living room, the 'den', the kitchen, the laundry room, the bathroom, the bedrooms.

As it happened they finished up at the top of the stairs that led down into the basement. Seeing the priest hesitate there the woman said, 'Oh, you wouldn't want to go down there.'

So he left it at that. But afterwards he wondered why she had refused to take him to the part of the house that most needed a blessing. Was it that she didn't want to embarrass him by taking him down there? Or was it that she didn't want to embarrass herself by letting him see all the junk that was piled up down there?

How typical this is. The parts of ourselves and of our society which most need to be redeemed are the parts we tend to hide. For this reason we don't allow the light to shine into the dark areas of our lives and of our society. We don't find it easy to talk about those dark areas. Instead, we try to cover them up and hide them away. Yet the dark areas are the ones which have most need of the light, and which could most benefit from it.

Every house, indeed every person, has such a place, a 'basement' area where old hurts, hates, painful memories and fears are locked away. It enables us to show the world a tidy, even beautiful face while having a real dump somewhere behind the scenes. What can we do about these grubbier parts of ourselves? We could open them to the light of Jesus.

Jesus shed light through his teaching, but more especially through the way he treated people. Many rulers and leaders have brought immense darkness into the lives of others by the harsh and oppressive way they have treated them. Indeed, we ourselves can cause darkness to others in this way. Not so Jesus. How many people came to him in darkness and went away bathed in light.

Still, there were those who refused to acknowledge their need of his light, and so rejected it. We need to acknowledge our darkness and our need of the light. This is why Jesus began his preaching with a call to repentance: 'Repent, for the kingdom of heaven is close at hand.' To repent is to admit our darkness, and to open ourselves to the light.

The light of Christ comes as a friend. His light brings healing not hurt, freedom not oppression, life not death. Those who follow Jesus will always have the light of life. By living in it, we become sources of light to others, a lamp for their paths.

HOMILY 3   **Our need of salvation**

Matthew compares the arrival of Jesus on the scene to the coming of a great light to a people who had been living in deep darkness. He saw Jesus as fulfilling the great prophecy of Isaiah: 'The people that lived in darkness have seen a great light; on those who dwell in the land and shadow of death a light has dawned.'

Mother Teresa gives us a beautiful example of a man who was brought out of darkness into the light. One day in Melbourne, Australia, she visited a poor man whom nobody knew existed. The room in which he was living was in a terrible state of untidiness and neglect. There was no light in the room. The man hardly ever opened the blinds. He hadn't a friend in the world.

She started to clean and tidy the room. At first he protested, saying, 'Leave it alone. It's all right as it is.' But she went ahead anyway. Under a pile of rubbish she found a beautiful oil lamp but it was covered with dust. She cleaned and polished it. Then she asked him, 'How come you never light the lamp?'

'Why should I light it?' he replied. 'No one ever comes to see me. I never see anybody.'

'Will you promise to light it if one of my sisters comes to see you?'

'Yes,' he replied. 'If I hear a human voice I'll light the lamp.'

Two of Mother Teresa's nuns began to visit him on a regular basis. Things gradually improved for him. Then one day he said to the nuns, 'Sisters, I'll be able to manage on my own from now on. But do me a favour. Tell that first sister who came to see me that the light she lit in my life is still burning.'

At first he didn't like the light. He felt threatened by it. It made him uncomfortable. Why? Because it showed up the misery in which he was living; first of all the physical misery, then the misery of spirit. But gradually he came to see it as a friend, which comforted him and brought hope into his dark existence. Thus he slowly turned his life around. The light had saved him. Of course, it wasn't the lamp itself that had done this, but the kindness and goodness it symbolised, first in Mother Teresa, then in her Sisters.

In order to appreciate a light, one must be conscious of one's darkness, and desire to escape from it. One must realise one's need to change, and want to change. Before people seek redemption, things must go badly for them. They must have experienced the darkness of sorrow and disappointment. Then they are ripe for the light of salvation.

This is why Jesus began his preaching with the message: 'Repent, for the kingdom of heaven is close at hand.' To repent is to admit the darkness in which we are living, and to open ourselves to the light. We show our repentance by a new way of living. To be saved is to have come out of darkness into the light.

Each of us has areas of darkness in our lives – fear, illness, pain, sin, guilt, loneliness, and so on. Society too has its dark areas. Hence our need of the light of Christ. Though the light comes as a friend, it also disturbs because it shows up what is wrong.

There still are many people who live in darkness and in the shadow of death. We need the light of Jesus now more than ever. Fortunately the lamp Jesus lit continues to burn, a glowing goodness that illuminates the world. It burns in the lives of some of his followers (like Mother Teresa's Sisters). The light of Jesus did not come to judge us, but to save us, to show us how to live, to show us the way to the Father's Kingdom.

Each of us can be sources of light to a darkened world. Indeed each of us is called to that task. But unless our own lamp is lighting, we won't be able to enlighten anyone else. There is great joy in being in the light. And there is an even greater joy in being a source of light to others.

PRAYER OF THE FAITHFUL

President: With Christ's light shining on us, let us bring our needs into the presence of God.

Response: Lord, hear our prayer.

Reader(s): That all Christians may strive to walk in the light of truth and goodness. [Pause] Let us pray to the Lord.

That the light of Christ may guide the nations of the world into the way of peace. [Pause] Let us pray to the Lord.

That the light of Christ's comfort may shine on those who are in the darkness of grief. [Pause] Let us pray to the Lord.

That the light of Christ's love may shine on the sick and the lonely. [Pause] Let us pray to the Lord.

That our departed relatives and friends may enjoy the light of eternal life. [Pause] Let us pray to the Lord.

That our own needs may be blessed in God's sight. [Longer pause] Let us pray to the Lord.

President: Almighty God, may the radiance of your glory light up our hearts, and bring us safely through the shadows of this world until we reach our homeland of everlasting light. We ask this through Christ our Lord.

PRAYER / REFLECTION   **An instrument of his love**

Lord, make me an instrument of your love.
Where the darkness of loneliness reigns
   let me bring the light of friendship.
Where the darkness of bitterness reigns
   let me bring the light of forgiveness.
Where the darkness of hurt reigns
   let me bring the light of healing.
Where the darkness of discord reigns
   let me bring the light of harmony.
Where the darkness of sadness reigns
   let me bring the light of joy.
Where the darkness of doubt reigns
   let me bring the light of faith.
Where the darkness of despair reigns
   let me bring the light of hope.
And where the darkness of hatred reigns
   let me bring the light of love. Amen.

Fourth Sunday of the Year
THE BEATITUDES

INTRODUCTION AND CONFITEOR

In the beatitudes we see the values a Christian should live by. While they present a great challenge, they also offer great rewards both here and hereafter. Alas, the values we live by often have little to do with the values of the Gospel. [Pause] Christ helps us to live by his values.

Lord Jesus, you help us to put our trust in God. Lord, have mercy.

Lord, you help us to be gentle and merciful in our dealings with one another. Lord, have mercy.

Lord, you help us to see right living as the most important thing in life. Lord, have mercy.

HEADINGS FOR READINGS

First Reading (Zeph 2:3; 3:12-13). The prophet holds out hope of salvation for those who seek God, and who practise integrity and humility.

Second Reading (1 Cor 1:26-31). God chooses the poor, the weak, and the lowly, people who are conscious of their limitations, and who therefore rely on God rather than on themselves.

Gospel (Mt 5:1-12). We see the values Christ preached and lived – values he wishes to see in his followers.

SCRIPTURE NOTE

In these readings it is not starvation and misery that are being blessed – these are evil things. What is being blessed is reliance on God. Those who know their need of God, and who live life as he would have them live it, are truly blessed. They are the most fortunate people in the world. God will give them all they need. Only God can fill our emptiness, only God can satisfy the hunger of our hearts. Those who put their trust in human things will be disappointed. Those who put their trust in God will not be disappointed. God becomes the champion of the poor, the weak, and the lowly, who practise integrity and humility.

HOMILY 1

The Sermon on the Mount contains the essence of Christ's teaching. The Beatitudes are the essence of that essence. They list the qualities Christ wishes to see in his followers, qualities which were exemplified in his own life. A mere glance shows that they are a complete reversal of conventional standards and values. *(Two voices could be used.)*

The world says: Happy are you who are well-off: you can have whatever you want. Be glad and rejoice when the money is coming in fast. Never stop to ask by what means or at whose expense. You will be the envy of all.

Christ says: Happy are you who know your need of God. You who put your trust in God rather than in material things. All that you need will be given to you.

Happy you who realise that it is not the amount of money you possess that makes you rich, but the kind of people you are. You will be rich in God's eyes, and that's what matters.

The world says: Happy you who are tough. You who throw your weight around. You who are ruthless. People will be afraid of you, and you'll get results.

Christ says: Happy you who are gentle and kind. You who refuse to get on by trampling on others. Gentleness is not a form of weakness as many think; it is a form of strength. There are many vital tasks which only gentleness can accomplish.

The world says: Happy are you who live it up. Remember you only live once. So let your hair down. Always strive to keep yourself high on something or other. Life will be great fun.

Christ says: Happy are you who remember that the most valuable things in life have to be bought with pain and sacrifice. You who don't confuse real happiness with cheap and passing thrills. Even though you may sow in sorrow, you will reap in joy.

The world says: Happy are you who hunger for power, status, and fame. Never stop to ask if something is right. Ask only if it benefits you. You will always be in the limelight.

Christ says: Happy are you who have standards and values, and who are prepared to live up to them. You who realise that to live rightly is what life is about. Those who rate this as important as eating and drinking will taste real happiness even here on earth.

The world says: Happy are you who crush your opponent. You who show no mercy or forgiveness to those who make mistakes. You'll be the boss, and everybody will know it.

Christ says: Happy are you who are able to make allowance for the sins of others, and whose greatness lies in your ability to forgive. The sun of God's mercy will shine warmly on you.

The world says: Happy you who have clean teeth and clean skins. You who keep up to date with the latest style in clothes. You will really be with it.

Christ says: Happy are you who have clean hearts. It is from the heart that all our thoughts, words, and deeds flow. If the heart is clean, then all that flows from it will be clean – like water flowing from an unpolluted spring.

The world says: Happy are you troublemakers and war-mongers. People will fear you, and you will get sensational headlines.

Christ says: Blessed are you peacemakers. Happy you who spread understanding among people, who welcome the stranger, and who work for a just society. You are true children of God.

The world says: Blessed are those who steal and cheat, and who get off scot-free.

Christ says: Blessed are you who make a stand for what is right. If you suffer for your stand, the wounds you bear will be honourable wounds, and they will mark you out as a true disciple of mine. You will gain honour on earth and glory in heaven.

Conclusion: The beatitudes are the badges of a disciple of Christ. They make us rich in the sight of God. They open our minds and hearts to a new way of seeing and judging. They give us a whole new set of bearings.

A person who lives according to the beatitudes is already living in the kingdom of heaven. Eternal life will merely be the full blossoming of a plant that is green with life.

HOMILY 2

The beatitudes are at the heart of the Gospel. Yet many regard them as impractical and far too demanding for ordinary human beings.

What follows is an imaginary discussion between a disciple and the Lord. It tries to show that the beatitudes are extremely practical, and are within the reach of human beings – with a little help from above, of course. *(Five or six might be enough to present at one time. The second and the fifth are very similar, as are the fourth and the eight. Two voices should be used).*

1. Happy the poor in spirit: theirs is the kingdom of heaven.

Happy the poor! Surely you mean: Happy the rich, because they can have whatever they want?

But rich people are never satisfied, so how can they be happy?

By 'poor' I take it you don't mean living in a hovel.

Of course not. People need a certain amount of material things in order to be able to live with dignity.

What then do you mean by 'poor in spirit'?

I mean those who put their trust in God rather than in money.

Lord, in our world money is the name of the game. It opens all doors.

All doors but the one that really matters, namely, the door to the kingdom of God.

But everybody wants to be rich.

If only they knew what true riches consisted of.

What riches are you talking about?

It's not the amount of possessions you have, but the kind of person you are, that makes you rich in the sight of God.

2. Happy the gentle: they shall inherit the earth.

Happy the gentle! You must be kidding! If you're gentle, people will walk all over you.

You mean, if you want to get on, you must be hard.

Exactly. In this world gentle people get left behind. Aggressive people get on.

Yet, is it not true that deep down we all pine for gentleness, and we can't open up and grow without it.

That may be so. But people see gentleness as a form of weakness.

Gentleness is not a form of weakness. It is a form of strength, and is one of the most necessary qualities in life. Think of the gentleness required in the hands of a mother or a surgeon.

Are you saying that we should never stand up for ourselves?

No.

Then by 'gentle' you don't mean a timid little person who wouldn't say boo to a goose?

Of course not. It takes a strong, self-confident person to be gentle.

3. Happy those who mourn: they will be comforted.

Happy those who mourn! Are you out of your mind, Lord?

Surely everybody is entitled to get some joy out of life?

Indeed. But joy is not the opposite of suffering. It is the opposite of sadness and bitterness. If you love and are loved, you can be joyful even in the midst of suffering. Sorrow is a part of life, and can make life deeper and richer.

But sorrow usually means tears, and many people are ashamed of tears, especially men.

You mean they see tears as a sign of weakness?

Yes.

Tears are a kind of riches. They show that we have feelings. In short, that we have a heart. Without a heart, a person is no better than a block of marble.

But if you open your heart to others, you're sure to get hurt.

True. But to open your heart is to begin to live. To close it is to begin to die.

4. Happy those who hunger and thirst for what is right: they shall be satisfied.

Lord, the only hunger most people understand is bodily hunger.

I don't agree with you. People hunger for a lot of things besides food.

For example?

People hunger for something to believe in. People hunger for hope. And of course, people hunger for love. One cannot live without love.

So then to nourish human beings is not the same as to fatten cattle?

To live rightly is what life is about. Those who rate that as important as eating and drinking will taste real happiness even here on earth.

5. Happy the merciful: they will have mercy shown them.

Mercy! That makes even less sense than gentleness.

Oh, so we're back to hardness and toughness again.

If you're merciful, people will take advantage of you.

Are you saying that the world doesn't need mercy?

I'm not saying that it doesn't need it, but that it's got no room for it.

Well then, it's got to make room for it, because without mercy the world would be a jungle.

But that's more or less how it is.

The world is crying out for mercy. How many barriers would fall down, how many broken relationships would be mended, if people were prepared to show mercy and forgiveness to one another.

The merciful will receive mercy from God for their own sins.

6. Happy the clean of heart: they shall see God.

People talk about clean teeth, clean skins, and so on. But you never hear anyone talk about a clean heart.

That's because people are more concerned about outer cleanness than inner cleanness.

Inner cleanness? What do you mean?

I mean cleanness of mind and heart, which results in moral living.

Lord, today people are more concerned about hygiene than about morality. See how big an issue pollution is.

People are right in wanting clean rivers, clean air, and so on. But they should be even more concerned about the most dangerous pollution all, namely, evil.

Evil? Could you be more specific?

Pride, anger, hate, lust, greed, envy … all these are dangerous pollutants.

So what must we do?

We have to purify the source. The heart is the source. It is the well-spring from which all our thoughts, words, and deeds flow. If the heart is clean, then all that flows from it will be clean, like water flowing from an unpolluted spring.

What about being able to see God?

Just as you can't see the sun through a murky sky, so you can't see God through a murky heart. But if the heart is clean, we will be able to see God in all that is good and beautiful in the world.

7. Happy the peace-makers: they shall be called the children of God.

It's more like: Happy the trouble-makers.

Why do you say that?

Because the trouble-makers get all the headlines.

But trouble-makers are very unhappy people.

But we have peace. We're not at war with anybody right now.

Peace! People can be almost as cruel to one another in times of peace as in times of war. Some neighbourhoods, some football grounds, and sadly, even some homes, at times resemble battlefields.

You've a point there. How come there's so little peace in the world?

Because there are so few peace-makers. Peace doesn't just happen. It has to be made.

But try reconciling warring factions, and you'll see what a wearisome, dangerous, and thankless business it is.

I couldn't agree more. Peace-making is a tough business. The peace-maker has to be armed, not with the sword or the gun, but with courage, determination, and patience. Still, everyone could do something.

What in practice can one do?

Forgive those who offend you. Welcome the strange. Do not provoke others to anger. Heal what is wounded. Bind up what is broken. And above all, be just in your dealings. Justice is the foundation of peace.

8. Happy those who are persecuted in the cause of right: theirs is the kingdom of heaven.

Some people would say: Happy those who lie, steal, cheat, and who get off scot-free.

No one can escape the eye of God, or the eye of one's own conscience, for that matter.

Lord, some people have no conscience. Their only commandment is the eleventh commandment – Thou shalt not get caught.

But are they happy?

I don't know, but they certainly seem to prosper.

Perhaps. But how dark the world would be if everyone adopted that attitude. Those who stand up for what is right, are the light of the world and the salt of the earth.

But it's not easy to stand up for what is right. It won't bring you any honours in this world. It is much more likely to bring you insults and injuries.

If you pick up wounds in taking a stand for what is right, those wounds are honourable wounds. Besides, it is a wonderful feeling to know that you are living the kind of life God wants you to live. It's a foretaste of heaven.

PRAYER OF THE FAITHFUL

President: Let us pray to our heavenly Father for those qualities Christ wants to see in his followers.

Response : Lord, hear our prayer.

Reader(s): For all Christians: that they may set their hearts on the Kingdom of God, and on its justice. [Pause] We pray to the Lord.

For all in positions of authority: that they may be gentle and merciful in their dealings with those they serve. [Pause] We pray to the Lord.

For those who mourn: that they may be comforted. [Pause] We pray to the Lord.

For those who are working for peace: that their efforts may bear fruit. [Pause] We pray to the Lord.

For those who suffer for doing what is right: that they may be strong. [Pause] We pray to the Lord.

For all here present: that we may hunger for a life of goodness. [Pause] We pray to the Lord.

For our own particular needs. [Longer pause] We pray to the Lord.

President: Heavenly Father, give us the grace to imitate you Son more closely, and to follow him more faithfully, so that we may know the blessedness of belonging to your kingdom. We ask this through the same Christ our Lord.

REFLECTION   **The beatitudes**

> The beatitudes are the badges
> of a true disciple of Christ.
> They are the marks of a child of God.
> They make us rich in the sight of God.
> They open our minds and hearts
> to a new way of seeing and judging.
> They give us a whole new set of bearings.
> The things the beatitudes stand for
> are very beautiful and very precious –
> things such as peace, goodness, joy, love,
> gentleness, compassion, mercy, integrity …
> A person who lives according to the beatitudes
> is already living in the kingdom of heaven.
> Eternal life will merely be the full blossoming
> of a plant that is green with life.

Fifth Sunday of the Year
SALT OF THE EARTH AND LIGHT OF THE WORLD

INTRODUCTION AND CONFITEOR

We are Christ's disciples. As such we are called to be the salt of the earth and the light of the world. This is a wonderful task but a difficult one. Let us reflect on how much we need God's help if we are to be faithful. [Pause]

Lord Jesus, you call us to trust in you and to rely on your strength. Lord, have mercy

You call us to overcome our laziness, selfishness and cowardice. Christ, have mercy.

You call us to be generous, merciful and just in our dealings with others. Lord, have mercy.

HEADINGS FOR READINGS

First Reading (Is 58:7-10). Genuine worship of God is shown forth in the practice of justice and in concern for the poor and the needy.

Second Reading (1 Cor 2:1-5). The success of the Gospel doesn't depend on human cleverness but on the power of God.

Gospel (Mt 5:13-16). Christ's disciples are to be the salt of the earth and the light of the world.

SCRIPTURE NOTE

Matthew has already introduced Jesus as the light of a darkened world (see Third Sunday). Now the function of enlightening and guiding a morally confused humanity is shared with his disciples.

In the ancient world, salt was one of the most important necessities of life, especially for preserving and seasoning food. So too was light for obvious reasons. We shouldn't turn salt and light into allegories. They are just images. Both images are making the same point: Jesus' disciples have a vital role to play in the world through their good deeds. When the disciples stop witnessing through their deeds, they become as useless as salt that has lost its taste or a lamp that doesn't give light.

HOMILY 1   **Salt of the earth, light of the world**

Jesus said to his disciples, 'You are the salt of the earth; you are the light of the world.' In the ancient world, salt was one of the most important necessities of life, especially for preserving and seasoning food. So too was light for obvious reasons. Both are still vitally important today. What was Jesus saying when he used these two images? He was telling his disciples that they have a vital role to play in the world through their good deeds.

When religious practice is divorced from life a vital element is missing. It is like salt that has lost its taste, or a lamp that no longer gives light. But when religious practice leads to deeds, a very effective witness is given.

One day a man visited Mother Teresa's home for the poor and the dying in Calcutta. He arrived just as the Sisters were bringing in some of the dying off the streets. They had picked up a man out of the gutter, and he was covered with dirt and sores. Without knowing that she was being watched, one of the Sisters began to care for the dying man. The visitor kept watching the Sister as she worked. He saw how tenderly she cared for her patient. He noticed how as she washed the man she smiled at him. She did not miss a detail in her attentive care for that dying man.

After carefully watching the Sister the visitor turned to Mother Teresa and said, 'When I came here today I didn't believe in God, and my heart was full of hate. But now I am leaving here believing in God. I have seen the love of God in action. Through the hands of that Sister, through her tenderness, through her gestures which were so full of love for that wretched man, I have seen God's love descend upon him. Now I believe.'

This is surely an example of the kind of thing Jesus had in mind. When he tells us that we must let our light shine, the light he is talking about is the light of our good deeds, especially our deeds of love. People take notice of good deeds. Our good deeds don't have to be as spectacular as the above example. Generally they will be much simpler, much more ordinary. But that doesn't mean they can't give effective witness to the light.

When Jesus tells us to let our light shine before people, he doesn't mean that we should advertise our good deeds, much less crow about them. He is asking us to do them. If we do them they will speak for themselves.

A good life is a strong and effective witness, and in itself is a proclamation of the Gospel. The light will shine when one is a genuine person, when one sees that the truth is told, that justice is done, when one exercises mercy and shows compassion and love.

In order to produce its effect, salt has to be mixed in with the food. And a light has to be put in a high place in order to be able to reach people. So we Christians have to be in the world. But we must not allow ourselves to be absorbed by the world. 'The world today needs Christians who remain Christians' (Albert Camus).

As Christians we have a very positive role to play in the world. We have something to offer, something the world desperately needs, even though it may not always welcome it. We should not be shy or apologetic about our role. A certain boldness and courage are called for.

The task is not one for the individual Christian only but for the Christian community as a whole. It is easier – and more effective – to witness to Christ as a member of a supportive community.

HOMILY 2   **Let your light shine**

Christ asks us, his disciples, to be the salt of the earth and the light of the world. What does this imply? It doesn't mean that we have to leave our jobs, rush out, and get involved in a whirlwind of good works. It means that we are called to practise our Christianity, not just in church, but out in the world in whatever situation we happen to find ourselves. All the more so if, by reason of our position, we happen to be situated on some 'hilltop' where all can see us, and where people look to us for light. Here are some examples.

If I'm a teacher, what do people expect from me? That I teach well, and that I refrain from showing favouritism. If I show favouritism, then I bring light to some and darkness to others. If a Christian teacher should show any kind of favouritism, it should be towards the children who find learning difficult.

If I'm a judge, what do people expect from me? Justice. Justice is the salt of society. Solzhenitsyn says, 'A corrupt court is worse than highway robbery.' A good judge causes the light of justice to shine.

If I'm a politician, what do people expect from me? That I work for the good of the country and not just for my own good. A corrupt politician has a lot to answer for. But then a good politician can bring light into the lives of many.

If I'm a doctor, what do people expect from me? That I would treat all the sick alike. A good doctor brings the light of healing to many.

If I'm a police officer, what do people expect from me? That I would not try to bend the law or break it, but uphold it and enforce it fairly.

If I'm an employer, what do people expect from me? That I pay a fair wage and create decent working conditions for my employees. People who do this shed a lot of light around them.

If I'm a worker, what do people expect from me? That I know my job and do it to the best of my ability.

If I'm a reporter, what do people expect from me? That I deal in facts, not in half-truths and lies. That I write about important issues, and do not go in for trivialities and sensationalism. A good journalist can shine the light of truth into many dark corners.

If I'm in business, what do people expect from me? That I do not over-charge, and that I give value for money.

If I'm a parent, what do my children expect from me? That I be there for them. That I put them before everything else, including my career.

If I'm a priest, what do people expect of me? That I would try to prac-tise what I preach.

We could multiply the examples and still not cover everything. Each of us must look at our own situation and ask ourselves how we can prac-tise our Christianity there. How we can be 'salt' and 'light' among the people we meet every day, and in the humdrum situations that occur. We may not be able to be a beacon. But we can at least be a humble candle which sheds light in its own immediate vicinity.

There is a tendency to take big matters seriously and neglect small ones. Here is where corruption begins. Here is where the light goes out, and the salt loses its savour. There is only one remedy. To set aside for the time being the big things, and to take seriously the small things, to turn one's attention to the task of the moment.

This Gospel is basically about goodness. But goodness can't be a put-on thing. The good deeds I do must be an expression of the kind of per-son I am. The authenticity of their lives is the best witness Christians can give.

OTHER STORIES

Here are two more stories that could be used in much the same way as the Mother Teresa story is used in the first homily. One at a time of course!

1. Often we think we are good simply because we are not conscious of doing any great evil. But what about the good we fail to do?

Alexander Solzhenitsyn recalls, as he says, 'with shame', an incident he witnessed at the front when he was a captain in the Russian army.

'One day I saw a sergeant of the secret police, on horseback, using a whip on a Russian soldier who had been captured serving in a German unit. The man, naked from the waist up, was staggering under the blows, his body covered in blood. Suddenly, he saw me and cried out: "Mister Captain, save me!"

'Any officer in any army in the world should have put a stop to this torture, but I was a coward. I said nothing and I did nothing. This picture has remained in my mind ever since.'

He could have brought light into that dark situation but he didn't. 'Be not simply good,' says Thoreau, 'be good for something.'

2. Once upon a time there was a great biblical scholar who was also noted for his great piety. He spent hours every day secluded in his room studying the Scriptures, and praying and meditating. One day a holy man visited the town in which the scholar lived. On hearing about it, the scholar set out to look for him.

He looked first in the church, but did not find him there. Then he looked in a local shrine, but he wasn't there either. He looked in other likely places but failed to find him. Eventually he found him in the marketplace.

On meeting him he told him who he was, and how he spent hours every day in the study of the Scriptures and in prayer and meditation. Then he said, 'I have come to seek your advice on how I might grow in the service of God.'

The advice he got was simple and direct. Looking at him intently, the holy man said, 'It's easy to be a sage and a saint in your room. You should go out into the marketplace and try to be a saint there.'

We are not told whether or not the scholar had the courage to act on that advice. It is the kind of advice Christ himself would have given. In fact, this is exactly the advice he is giving us in today's Gospel when he says, 'You are the light of the world. No one lights a lamp to put it under a tub; they put it on lamp-stand where it shines for everyone in the house. In the same way your light must shine in the sight of people, so that seeing your good works, they may give praise to your Father in heaven.'

It is easy to let the light shine in the comfort and safety of one's room. But that can be a selfish thing, because it means we are keeping the light to ourselves. It is not so easy to let the light shine in the rough and tumble of the marketplace. But that is where it is most needed.

PRAYER OF THE FAITHFUL

President: Called by Christ to be the salt of the earth and the light of the world, let us pray to the Father for all our needs.

Response: Lord, hear our prayer.

Reader(s): For Christians: that the light of their good deeds may be clear for all to see. [Pause] We pray to the Lord.

For our political and civil leaders: that they may help to keep society good and healthy by promoting truth and justice. [Pause] We pray to the Lord.

For those Christians whose light has gone out. [Pause] We pray to the Lord.

For each one here: that our lives may bear witness to the faith we profess with our lips. [Pause] We pray to the Lord.

For our own needs. [Longer pause] We pray to the Lord.

President: Merciful God, we thank you for the light of grace and love your Son Jesus brought into our world of sadness and shadows. Help us to keep his light burning brightly in our lives. On seeing this light others will find their way, and so you will be glorified. We ask this through the same Christ our Lord.

REFLECTION   **Let your light shine**

The most important thing about each of us
is our capacity for goodness.
We can be a source of light.
We have hands that can care,
eyes that can see,
ears that can hear,
tongues that can speak,
feet that can walk,
and above all hearts that can love.
Unfortunately, through laziness, selfishness,
and cowardice, our light can be dimmed,
so that we become shadows of the people we could be.
Lord, help us to believe in our own goodness,
and to let the light of that goodness shine.
On seeing this light others find their way,
and you will be glorified.

Sixth Sunday of the Year
NEW STANDARDS OF GOODNESS

INTRODUCTION AND CONFITEOR

Jesus says, 'If you are bringing your offering to the altar and there re-member that your brother has something against you, leave your offer-ing there before the altar, go and be reconciled with your brother first, and then come back and present your offering.'

Let us reflect on those words for a moment. [Pause] Now let us confess our sins to God and to one another.

I confess to almighty God ...

HEADINGS FOR READINGS

First Reading (Eccles 15:15-20). God has given us the freedom to choose to do good or evil, to choose life or death.

Second Reading (1 Cor 2:6-10). True wisdom comes from God, and re-veals the wonderful things God has prepared for those who love him.

Gospel (Mt 5:17-37). Jesus proposes new standards of goodness for his disciples. *(Shorter form recommended).*

SCRIPTURE NOTE

Murder and adultery are born in the heart. Jesus reinterprets the fifth commandment so that it embraces those angry feelings and emotions which may lead up to murder. And he reinterprets the sixth command-ment so that it embraces lustful thoughts and desires which may lead to sexual sin and infidelity.

As for oaths: he encourages people to behave in such a way that oaths are superfluous. The disciples are simply to be truthful.

HOMILY 1   **A deeper virtue**

Jesus said, 'If your virtue goes no deeper than that of the Scribes and Pharisees, you will never get into the kingdom of heaven.' That state-ment must have surprised his hearers. And it must have greatly angered the Scribes and Pharisees, who liked to think of themselves as truly virtu-ous people. Jesus shattered their complacent belief in their own goodness and virtue. He declared that their virtue was superficial, their goodness skin-deep. His disciples would have to do better.

But you might think: virtue is virtue. Not so. There is shallow, inauthentic virtue. Virtue is shallow when the motive is not pure – an unworthy motive can spoil even the best deed. Virtue is shallow when it lacks personal conviction, and is practised merely out of convention or conformity or routine. Virtue is inauthentic when the person is not sincere.

But then there is the genuine article. There is deep, true, authentic virtue. It's not a skin-deep thing, but an expression of what one is inside. Above all, it's a revelation of the heart.

Sin and virtue, badness and goodness, are essentially matters of the heart. And it is from the perspective of the heart that a Christian should assess them. Corruption of heart is the worst kind of badness – it is to be bad at the core. Goodness of heart is the best kind of goodness – it is to be good at the core.

Hence, we must not be content merely to look at the surface of our lives – at our words and deeds. We must have the courage to search our hearts. We need to look at what is going on inside us – at our thoughts, intentions, attitudes, and desires.

When considering our sins, we have to consider the sins of the heart – resentments, jealousies, angers, hatreds, lusts. Sins of the heart may be our worst sins, and the root cause of our external sins. They are the kind of things which, if allowed to go unchecked, can lead, as Jesus says, to murder and sexual sin and infidelity.

From a spiritual point of view, one of the worst things we can say about anyone is that he or she has a cold heart or a hard heart. To be cold-hearted is to be unable to show kindness, understanding, sympathy. To be hard-hearted is worse again. It means that one is unable to show pity, mercy, forgiveness.

For all their piety, the Pharisees were both cold-hearted and hard-hearted. If one's heart is cold and hard, how can one be virtuous?

On the other hand, one of the best things we can say about anyone is that he is warm-hearted or soft-hearted. This means he is capable of goodness, kindness, tenderness, pity, compassion, mercy … There are the virtues of the heart. Without a warm, compassionate heart one cannot call oneself a true human being, never mind a truly religious or virtuous person.

When all is said and done it is the heart that matters. It's what's in the heart that matters. The heart is what I am deep down. It is the real me. And what is in the heart will out. The state of the heart will deeply affect how I live.

What we have to strive for is goodness of heart. Then our good deeds will flow from what we are, as naturally as good fruit from a good tree. They will be true and genuine. They will come from the heart. You can't go any deeper than that.

HOMILY 2   **Handling anger**

Today's Gospel talks about anger. All of us have anger in us. Many of us were taught from our earliest years that anger was a sin – in fact, one of the seven deadly sins. Hence, we feel guilty about getting angry. So what do we do? We probably either deny it or repress it.

The first thing that needs to be said is that anger is normal and even healthy. If we love and value ourselves, we will naturally get angry if we are treated badly. We shouldn't deny our anger. Nor should we be afraid to allow ourselves to feel angry. Anger is just a feeling. In itself it is neither good nor bad morally. We may have been told that anger is a bad emotion. It is a dangerous emotion, but that doesn't make it a bad one.

Neither should we repress our anger. Psychologists tell us that repressed anger is very dangerous, and can result in self-hatred, depression, and even bodily ills such as asthma and ulcers. Anger needs to be released, but this must be done in a wholesome way. When given a means of expression, relief follows.

When Jesus says to us, 'Do not get angry with your brother,' he is not condemning anger in itself. After all, he himself got angry when he drove the traders out of the temple. There are times when we ought to be angry. An unjust situation should make us angry. Anger need not give rise to a lessening of love, much less to hate.

It is when anger turns into hostility that it becomes dangerous. Hostility rather than anger is the real deadly sin. It causes us to act out our anger, and leads to deep resentments, negative attitudes, insults, and so on, which are directed at the object of our anger.

If we find ourselves getting angry often, we should look at the cause of our anger. The cause may lie with ourselves. We may be hypersensitive, or over-impatient, or full of hurt that we haven't dealt with. In which case we have to look at ourselves.

But the cause may lie with others. Some people are full of anger, which makes them very difficult to live with. Instead of owning their anger, they direct it on to others. If the cause of our anger lies with another person, we have to look at our relationship with that person.

Finally the cause may lie in some unjust situation. If so, then we should try to put that situation right. Anger can be a good thing – it can spur us to put right something that is wrong. There is an old saying: 'You measure the size of a person's soul by the size of the things that make him angry.'

Nevertheless, anger is a dangerous thing. 'Anger in the heart is like a worm in a plant.' (*Talmud*) Anger is no resting place. If our heart is filled with anger, there is no sleep, no appetite, no smile. We ruin our health, our friendships, in short, everything.

We can't avoid getting angry, but we can avoid acting out our anger.

Jesus tells us that we have to seek to be reconciled.

A small example. A man had a row with his wife before going to work in the morning. Halfway through the morning it was still bothering him, so he rang his wife and apologised for his part in it. Later he said to a friend, 'I didn't want her to carry that all day.'

He didn't do himself any harm either.

HOMILY 3   **Jesus and the Law**

All of us are subject to law. Jesus himself was subject to law, both human and divine. As he grew up he obeyed Joseph and Mary. He obeyed the law of the land. And of course he obeyed the law of God. Here it is Jesus' attitude to the law of God that concerns us.

He found no fault with the law itself. His problem lay with the way it was interpreted and applied by the religious leaders of his day. For them it was the letter of the law that mattered. Once you fulfilled that you were okay. But for Jesus it was the spirit of the law that mattered. The important thing is not how many commandments we obey, but the spirit in which we obey them.

The Pharisees looked only at the outward act. But God sees the heart. So Jesus said we have to look not just at our acts, but at our thoughts and desires, even though they may never actually lead to acts. We may never have killed anyone, but we may have entertained hostile thoughts about them and harboured hostile attitudes towards them. We may never have committed adultery, but we may have entertained lustful thoughts and desires.

Again, Jesus saw that the commandments were interpreted in a very negative way which led to minimalism – doing the bare minimum. He interpreted them in a positive way. For example, the fifth commandment says, 'Thou shalt not kill.' But he said, 'You must love your neighbour.' The seventh commandment says, 'Thou shalt not steal.' But he said, 'You must share your goods with your neighbour when he is in need.'

He also saw that obedience was often rooted in fear. He wanted it rooted in love. His whole relationship with his heavenly Father was based on love. When you love someone, you avoid doing anything to hurt that person. Where there is love, there is really no need of law.

But the most significant thing of all that Jesus did was this: he brought in a new and more exacting law – the law of love. Far from contradicting or abolishing the old law, the new law goes beyond it, and so brings it to perfection. He said that all of God's laws could be reduced to two: love of God and love of neighbour. In truth, there is only one law – the law of love.

ANOTHER STORY

It is terrible to live near an active volcano. What makes it so terrible is the unpredictability of its behaviour. One minute you are peacefully going about your business, and everything is normal. Next minute sparks begin to fly, and the mountain goes up, spewing out deadly lava. It is too late to escape. You have no choice but to bear the full brunt of the eruption.

When the eruption is over, the mountain quickly becomes its benign self once more, offering its slopes to sheep, and providing limpid streams to irrigate the thirsty valleys. It doesn't seem to be any the worse for the eruption. On the contrary, you sense that it has experienced a great relief because it has vented its anger and frustration.

But you will continue to smoulder. For hours, maybe even days, you will still be reeling under the effects. Everything you had built up, all those walls and fences, all those carefully laid paths and bridges, have been swept away. You feel humiliated and worthless. You ask yourself, 'What did I do to cause this eruption?'

The truth is, for you it never really passes. It is always with you. Hence you can never relax. You have to be on your guard all the time. This is a terrible way to live. You end up going around on tip-toe, so as not to cause vibrations which might set the mountain off again. You are constantly trying to humour it. In a nutshell, you are a hostage to the mountain. And meanwhile, unknown to yourself, you become a cauldron of hurt and anger so that other innocents suffer from your eruptions.

I've never been within an ass's roar of a real volcano. How come then I know so much about volcanoes? From time to time over the years I've lived in the shadow of something similar but worse – a human volcano.

Some people have an awful lot of anger in them, which they have never acknowledged or dealt with. They erupt every now and then, making life intolerable for those who are close to them.

PRAYER OF THE FAITHFUL

President: With longing in our hearts for all that God has prepared for those who love him, let us pray.

Response: Lord, hear our prayer.

Reader(s): For all followers of Christ: that they may have the kind of relationship with God which makes obeying his commandments natural and easy. [Pause] We pray to the Lord.

For those who make and enforce our laws: that they may be guided by the wisdom that comes from God. [Pause] We pray to the Lord.

For those who are in the grip of a bad habit, or a compulsion, or an addiction. [Pause] We pray to the Lord.

For ourselves: that our virtue may be true and genuine. [Pause] We pray to the Lord.

For all gathered here: that we may have wisdom to use our anger positively. [Pause] We pray to the Lord.

For our own special needs. [Longer pause] We pray to the Lord.

President: All-powerful God, help us to keep our thoughts clean, our desires pure, our words true, and our deeds kind. We ask this through Christ our Lord.

REFLECTION   **A prayer for the end of the day**

Grant, O Lord, that each day
before we enter the little death of sleep,
we may undergo the little judgement of the past day,
so that every wrong deed may be forgiven
and every unholy thought set right.
Let nothing go down into the depths of our being
which has not been forgiven and sanctified.
Then we shall be ready
for our final birth into eternity,
and look forward with love and hope
to standing before you,
who art both judge and saviour,
holy judge and loving saviour. (*Bishop Appleton*)

Seventh Sunday of the Year
LOVE YOUR ENEMIES

INTRODUCTION AND CONFITEOR

Jesus tells us that God loves all of his children, deserving and undeserving. And he urges us to imitate this all-embracing love of God. We know how difficult love can be, especially in relation to people we don't like. [Pause].

Jesus not only shows us how to love but helps us to love.

Lord, you show us that God cares for all of his children, deserving and undeserving. Lord, have mercy.

Lord, you show us how he lets the sun of his love shine on good people and bad people. Christ, have mercy.

Lord, you show us how he lets the rain of his mercy fall on saints and sinners. Lord, have mercy.

HEADINGS FOR READINGS

First Reading (Lev 19:1-2.17-18). We imitate the holiness of God when we refuse to exact vengeance or bear a grudge against another.

Second Reading (1 Cor 3:16-23). Paul gives us a profound reason why we should respect one another: we are the Temple of God.

Gospel (Mt 5:38-48). What differentiates the disciples of Christ different from others is their willingness to love as God loves.

SCRIPTURE NOTE

Since God is holy, we are to be holy. We are holy when we imitate the generosity of God by not exacting vengeance, or bearing a grudge against another. In Levitcus, the commandment: 'You must love your neighbour as yourself' is restricted to fellow-Israelites. But Jesus broadened it to include everyone, Gentiles as well as Jews, enemies as well as friends. Why? Because this is the way the heavenly Father acts. He shows equal love towards good and bad, not because he is indifferent to morality, but because he loves without limit.

Paul gives us a profound reason why we should respect one another: we are the Temple of God. Individually and collectively the Holy Spirit dwells in us. This is also the basis of our unity.

HOMILY 1   **A better way**

When Jesus says, 'Offer the wicked man no resistance', he is not telling us to be passive in the face of physical danger or abuse. He is rejecting retaliation of any kind. We are not allowed to have hatred in our hearts for anything, even our enemies.

Hatred is a very dangerous thing. It must be handled with great respect. It should be kept for a cause such as intolerance or injustice, not for an individual. This was the key to the success of Nelson Mandela.

Mandela spent over twenty-seven years in South African prisons. When he was finally released, he had every reason to feel bitter, and to come out vowing to get revenge on those who unjustly deprived him of his freedom. Instead, he came out smiling, and seeking reconciliation with the leaders of the regime that had put him in prison. Thus he became the cornerstone of a new South Africa. If he had harboured bitterness, who knows what would have happened?

In his autobiography, *Long Walk to Freedom* (1994), he tells us:

I knew that people expected me to harbour anger against whites. But I had none. In prison, my anger towards whites decreased, but my hatred for the system grew. I wanted South Africa to see that I loved even my enemies while I hated the system that turned us against one another. I saw my mission as one of preaching reconciliation, of healing the old wounds and building a new South Africa.

When we hate we expend far more energy than in any other emotion. We must save our strength for better things. Hate drives out everything else and corrodes and warps the soul.

When Jesus talks about 'the enemy' he is not necessarily referring to an enemy in war. He is talking about someone who is close to me – someone in my family, my community, my neighbourhood, my work-place, who is making life difficult for me. Who are the people whom we seek to avoid at all costs, whom we find hard to forgive, who awaken in us feelings of unease, fear and anger which can easily turn into hatred?

The enemy can arouse hatred in us. When we discover our capacity to hate and harm, it is very humbling. At the same time this can be a good thing. It puts us in touch with our poverty. Then we discover perhaps that the enemy is not outside us but inside us. The problem is not with the other person but in ourselves. It is only when we recognise and look at the world of shadows, the chaos within us, that we can begin to travel towards freedom. Only the truth can set us free.

Our enemies are not those who hate us but those whom we hate.

Jesus' command, 'Love your enemy', is a radical rejection of violence. Returning love for hate is one of the most difficult things in the world. It's a very high ideal, and a very difficult one, but it makes sense.

As Christians, we are on the side of non-violence. However, this is not an option for weakness and passivity. Opting for non-violence means believing more strongly in the power of truth, justice, and love than in the power of war, weapons and hatred. We must try to respond to the worst with the best.

As Christians we must try to imitate the generosity of God in our readiness to forgive, not to exact vengeance, or to bear a grudge against another. Unless Christians seek to imitate the all-embracing love of God, they are no better than others.

Mandela suffered much and suffered unfairly. Yet he achieved the only triumph worth achieving – that of not being soured by his suffering or tempted to the ultimate surrender of dignity by seeking revenge.

HOMILY 2   **Hatred is like poison**

Hate poisons the heart; love purifies it. Jesus says to us, 'Love your enemies.' It is not only for the sake of the enemy that he says this but for our sake too, and because love is more beautiful than hate. The greatest gift we possess is the gift to love. There is one thing that can utterly destroy this gift, and that is hatred.

Two farmers, John and James, were good friends until a dispute arose between them over a piece of land. Unable to settle the issue among themselves, they went to court over it. The court decided in favour of John. James was bitter, and put poison in John's well, not a fatal dose, but enough to give it an obnoxious taste.

John was very angry. His neighbours heard about it. Some refused to get involved. But others were supportive and declared that James should be made to pay for what he had done.

John was about to go by night and poison James' well when a stranger arrived at his house. On hearing the story the stranger agreed that it was a pretty nasty situation, but he wouldn't agree with retaliation. 'Poison is not a thing to play around with,' he declared. 'I've a better idea. I'll show you in the morning.'

His idea was to clean out the well. He offered to help. Reluctantly John agreed. It was a messy business and took them two whole days. Then they ran the fresh water through the well several times. Finally, the stranger took a cup of the water, drank it, and declared that it was clean. John also drank from the well, but insisted that he could still taste the poison. To which the stranger replied,

'Take it from me, the water is perfect. But you will continue to taste the poison until you do one more thing.'

'What's that?' asked John earnestly.

'You must forgive your neighbour. You have got rid of the poison from the well, but not the poison that lodges in your mind and heart. Not until you let go of your bitterness, and forgive your brother, will the water taste right.'

That evening John went over to his neighbour and made peace with him. When he came back he tasted the water again. This time it tasted good.

Hatred is a very dangerous thing. It can destroy us. We consume more energy in hating than in all our other activities. It creates a legacy of bitterness, hostility, and resentment. Christ's way is a better way. It is not a soft way. It's a hard way that calls for great strength and toughness. The person who is truly non-violent, who is incapable of violence, is the person who is fearless.

Chesterton said, 'Christianity has not been tried and found wanting; it has been found hard and left untried'. More than any other, the exhortation to love one's enemies has been left untried.

HOMILY 3   **On not retaliating**

As one reads history, one is absolutely sickened, not by the crimes the wicked have committed, but by the punishments the good have inflicted; and a community is infinitely more brutalised by the habitual employment of punishment than it is by the occasional occurrence of crime. (Oscar Wilde)

If the light becomes darkness, what hope is there for the world?

Oskar Schindler was a German industrialist. During the Second World War he set up a factory in Poland. He saved over a thousand Jews by giving them work in his factory. When the Germans surrendered at the end of the war, Schindler abandoned the factory and escaped westwards to avoid the Russians who were approaching from the east. Meanwhile the liberated workers waited in the factory for the arrival of the Russians.

While they waited, they found a German officer by the name of Amon bunkered inside the factory. Amon had been responsible for several brutal killings. A group of men dragged him out and enthusiastically and mercilessly hanged him. Some inmates tried to intervene, but the executioners were in such a rage that they could not be stopped.

This was the first homicide of the peace. It was an event which would be abhorred forever by those who witnessed it. The hanging of Amon sickened them as profoundly as any of the executions Amon himself had carried out. After all, Amon was a Nazi, and beyond altering. But these hangmen were their own brothers. Instead of reaping satisfaction from it, all it did was sadden and depress them.

Our pain and hurt can so easily turn into rage, with the result that we inflict on others the injuries inflicted to us. Hatred is a very dangerous thing. It burns up a hundred times more energy than love. It drives out everything else and corrodes and warps the soul.

'Love you enemies' – this is one of the most revolutionary things ever said. All the revolutionaries said the enemy must be destroyed.

Love our enemies? Most of us find it hard enough to love our friends. How then can we be expected to love our enemies? All of us have some enemies, or at least some people we positively dislike. Why is that we dislike these particular people? It may be because of something they said or did to us. But there is a deeper reason. It is because they bring out the worst in us.

Enemies expose a side of us which we usually manage to keep hidden from our friends, a dark side of our nature which we would rather not know about. The enemy stirs up ugly things inside us. This is the real reason why we hate him.

To love one's enemy is not in the first place to do him good. Rather it is to allow him to be different, to be himself, and not try to turn him into a copy of ourselves so that we may be able to love him.

We are not expected to feel love for our enemy. Love is not a feeling; it is an act of the will. We can make a decision to love someone even though we do not have feelings of love for that person.

To love an enemy goes clean contrary to human nature. Only God can help us to love in the way Christ asks of us. When Christ asks us to be perfect as our heavenly Father is perfect, the perfection he is talking about is the perfection of love. God loves his children unconditionally. He loves them not because they are good but because he is good.

PRAYER OF THE FAITHFUL

President: We accept that together we are the temple of God, and we make our common prayer to the God who crowns our lives with love and compassion.

Response: Lord, graciously hear us.

Reader(s): For peace and harmony among Christians of different traditions. [Pause] Lord, hear us.

For peace and harmony in countries where the population is made up of different religious and ethnic groups. [Pause] Lord, hear us.

For the healing of relationships that are strained or that have gone sour. [Pause] Lord, hear us.

For those who have hurt us in any way, and whom we find hard to love. [Pause] Lord, hear us.

For our own special needs. [Longer pause] Lord, hear us.

President: Merciful God, fill our hearts with your love. Give us the grace to rise above our human weakness, and keep us faithful in loving you and one another. We make this prayer through Christ our Lord.

SIGN OF PEACE

Lord Jesus Christ, you said to your disciples: 'Love your enemies; pray for those who persecute you. In this way you will show that you are true children of your Father in heaven'. Help us to be merciful and forgiving towards those who make life difficult for us, and thus we will enjoy the peace and unity of your kingdom where you live for ever and ever.

REFLECTION   **Turning enemies into friends**

When Abraham Lincoln was running for president
of the United States there was a man called Stanton,
who never lost an opportunity to vilify him.
Yet when Lincoln won the election
he gave Stanton a post in his cabinet. Why?
Because he considered him the best man for the job.
And Lincoln was proved right.
Stanton gave him loyal service.
Asked why he didn't destroy his enemies, Lincoln replied,
'Do I not destroy my enemies when I make them my friends?'

Eighth Sunday of the Year
TRUSTING GOD

INTRODUCTION AND CONFITEOR

We are gathered in the house of God. Let us come into his presence in a spirit of trust and confidence because we are his precious daughters and sons. Jesus urges us to let go of worry, and to trust in the love and care of God for us. [Pause]

Lord, in you alone our souls are at rest. Lord, have mercy.

Lord, you alone are our rock, our stronghold, our fortress. Christ, have mercy.

Lord, in you we put our trust. Lord, have mercy.

HEADINGS FOR READINGS

First Reading (Is 49:14-15). These words of consolation and hope, first spoken to the exiles in Babylon, are now spoken to us.

Second Reading (1 Cor 4:1-5). God is the only one who can judge rightly, because he alone knows the secrets of the heart.

Gospel (Mt 6:24-34). Jesus urges us to place our lives in the hands of our heavenly Father, to whom we are important and precious.

SCRIPTURE NOTE

God's love for his people is like the steadfast love of a mother for her child – only greater (First Reading). In the Gospel Jesus reminds us that we are God's precious children. The knowledge of this should free us from fretting and worrying. Worry is essentially distrust in God. Such distrust may be understandable in a heathen who believes in a jealous, capricious, unpredictable god; but not in one who has learned to call God by the name of Father. The Christian must put his future in the hands of God and pray only for the modest needs of today.

HOMILY 1   **Can a mother forget her child?**

'Does a woman forget her baby at the breast, or fail to cherish the son of her womb? Yet even if these forget, I will never forget you.' When the prophet Isaiah spoke those lovely words, the people of God had reached a very low ebb. The temple had been destroyed, Jerusalem sacked, and the people taken into exile in Babylon. They felt that God had abandoned them. But Isaiah assured them that God had not abandoned them, no more than a mother could abandon her child.

A poor woman in a Dublin parish had a son who was ruining her life.

He wouldn't work. He spent his time drinking and hanging around with trouble-makers. He robbed everything of value she had in the house. Again and again she pleaded with him to change his life, but he refused to do so. He broke her heart and made her life a misery.

Eventually he ended up in prison. Surely now she would leave him to his fate? Not at all. She visited him without fail every week, carrying cigarettes and other things to him in a little carrier bag. One day one of the priests from the parish met her as she was on her way to the prison.

'This son has ruined your life,' the priest said. 'He'll never change. Why don't you just forget about him?'

'How can I?' she replied. 'I don't like what he's done, but he's still my son.'

You could say that that mother was foolish. Yet she was only doing what any mother worthy of the name can't help doing, that is, loving her child through thick and thin. A mother never gives up. For most of us, the love of a mother is the most reliable kind of human love we will experience. It's no wonder that the Bible uses a mother's love as an image of God's love for us.

If a mother, who after all is a mere human being, is capable of such steadfast love, then how much greater is God's love for us who are his children. Even when we are in sin, God does not cease to love us.

People accumulate money and possessions, because they give the illusion of security. Then when they start to lose some of these, they get anxious and worried. People of faith do not rely on those things but on God, who is everlasting love. God is their security, and their chief concern is to do his will. This gives them a deep trust in life, and enables them to live the present moment free from attachments and worries.

When Jesus says, 'Do not worry about tomorrow', he is not condemning human resourcefulness. We have to plan for tomorrow. What he is condemning is the fretting and worrying that keeps us from lifting up our gaze beyond material values and the cares of this world.

We are in constant danger of becoming immersed in the affairs of the world and of becoming enslaved to material things. Jesus reminds us that we are God's precious children, and that only in God can we find rest. We must put our future in the hands of God and pray only for the modest needs of today.

HOMILY 2   **Dealing with worry**

Worry is something that affects us all. It is part of our daily lives. It is not caused by external circumstances only, but also by internal disposition. Some people are natural worriers and are perpetually anxious. Anxious people are not thankful enough for the good things that have happened to them, and instead are over-anxious about what might happen to them.

A story is told about the people of a certain town who were terrible worriers. So they called a meeting to see what they could do about the problem of worry. Various suggestions were made. One suggested that the town should have a park where people could relax. A second suggested that it should have a golf course. A third suggested that it should have a cinema. And so it went on. Finally a man got up and said, 'I've just thought of a much simpler solution. Why don't we ask David, the town cobbler, to do our worrying for us.'

'Wait a minute,' said David. 'Why pick on me?'

'Because if you agree, we'll make it worth your while. We'll pay you £1,000 a week.'

'Well in that case, why not me?' David exclaimed, beaming all over.

Everybody agreed that the idea was a very good one. However, just as the motion was about to be put to a vote, this fellow got up and said, 'Wait a minute! If David earned £1,000 a week, what would he have to worry about?'

A good question. But since he was a worrier just like the rest of them, I'm sure he would have found something. Worriers always do. According to a survey, the most common worries which people have are: money (45%), other people (39%), personal health (32%), exams (20%), job security (15%).

Worry is not only useless, but is positively injurious to one's health. Worry puts a stoop on the shoulders. Even though it is probably impossible to live a life beyond all fear and anxiety, it is possible to reduce worry's power over us. How can this be done? Jesus tells us to concentrate on what is essential – on doing the will of God. Worry is banished when trust in God and the desire to please him are the dominant elements in one's life.

The other way to defeat it is to live a day at a time. Worry robs us of the present, or at least prevents us from living it fully. We should strive to handle the demands of each day as it comes, without worrying about the unknown future and things which may never happen.

Worry is essentially distrust in God. Such distrust may be understandable in a heathen who believes in a jealous, capricious, unpredictable god; but not in one who has learned to call God by the name of Father. When we put ourselves in God's hands, we open ourselves to enjoy the full grace of God's protection. We resemble the birds of the air and the lilies of the field. And we are able to live life, to celebrate the present moment.

To know that life is full of risk, yet to affirm it; to sense the full insecurity of the human situation, and yet to rejoice: this is the essence of faith. It is not a comforting illusion that all is well. It is rather the courage to celebrate in the midst of uncertainty, and to rejoice in the transitory shelter of the human condition.

Entrust the past to God's mercy, the present to his love, and the future to his providence. *(St Augustine)*

HOMILY 3 **Our relationship with God**

There is an abyss between knowledge about things and immediate perception of things. A child knows practically nothing about its teddy-bear, yet it knows it in a way that most grown-ups can never do.

The same holds true with regard to people. We may have lots of acquaintances but only a few close friends. There is a world of difference between an acquaintance and a friend.

If you ask Mary to describe her father she says: 'He works in an office. He gets up very early. He comes home very late. He drives a car. He's very tall. He's about forty years old … '

If you ask her does she love her father, she replies, 'I don't see very much of him. He's away a lot'. And if you ask her does she trust him she replies, 'It depends on the mood he's in. If he's in a good mood, yes. But if he is in a bad mood, no.'

Sadly, for Mary her father is little better than an acquaintance. She knows some facts about him, but doesn't enjoy a close relationship with him. And this colours her whole attitude to him. She does what is right, but only to please him. She avoids what is wrong, only because she is afraid of punishment. Her life is a kind of bargaining – something given for something received. Her moral growth will be stunted like that of a shrub planted in a cold climate.

Now let's take Katie. She describes her father like this: 'I like my Daddy very much. He makes me happy. He buys me presents, and I buy him presents. He doesn't like it when I'm naughty. He takes me for walks in the woods. Once he saved me from running in front of a car. I'm getting a card for him for Father's Day, but I'm keeping it a surprise … '

Katie is telling us that she loves her father and that he loves her. She is talking about a relationship of love that exists between them. In a climate like this, Katie will grow like a flower in the sun.

We could know facts about God (learned from our religion books) without having a loving relationship with God. There is a vast difference between knowing about God and knowing God. Even the devils believe in God's existence and know certain facts about him. But they do not love him. Faith is trust in God, not just ideas about God.

We might be able to recite the Creed word-perfect, but not have the kind of trust in God that Jesus speaks about in the Gospel. Jesus tells us that the heavenly Father loves us. That we are precious in his eyes. God is not an impersonal God, remote from us and from our world. He is near us, and loves us unconditionally.

We are not grains of sand or specks of dust. We are children of our heavenly Father, and we have a splendid destiny. Sure of his love, and of our own dignity and destiny, why worry? The whole of Christianity can be summed up in the concept of God as our Father, a Father who rejoices in his children.

ANOTHER STORY

Once upon a time a flower-lover by the name of Amadeus took pity on the wild flowers. Having built a large greenhouse, he roamed the fields and hillsides in search of them. On finding a flower, he carefully dug it up and transplanted it to the greenhouse.

When he had them all gathered in he proceeded to lavish attention on them. How they thrived! The greenhouse was transformed. All the colours of the rainbow were visible in it. All the perfumes of Arabia were let loose in it. Amadeus was highly pleased with himself.

However, one day he noticed to his surprise that even though his charges were thriving, they didn't seem happy.

'What's the matter?' he asked.

'We don't want to sound ungrateful, but we really think that our place is not in here but out in the fields and hillsides,' a violet answered.

'I don't understand,' said Amadeus, deeply disappointed.

'It's like this,' a primrose added. 'We believe that we have a God-given task to perform.'

'A task! What task?'

'Our task is to be witnesses to God's care for creation,' the primrose replied. 'Was it not of us that the Lord was speaking when he said, "Look at the flowers of the field. See how beautiful they are. I tell you not even Solomon in all his glory was robed like one of these"?'

Amadeus thought for a while. Then he said, 'You know, you're absolutely right. I never looked at it like that before.'

And being a true lover of flowers, that very day he restored them to their natural habitat.

There they were once again assailed by a relentless wind, became a prey to every kind of bug, and had to make do with the scanty food they managed to scrounge from a thin soil. Nevertheless, they were happy because their lives glowed with meaning.

God grows weary of great kingdoms, but never of little flowers. (Rabindranath Tagore)

PRAYER OF THE FAITHFUL

President: With great confidence and trust let us make our needs known to our heavenly Father.

Response: Father, hear our prayer.

Reader(s): For the Church: that through its ministry people may experience the tender, steadfast love of God. [Pause] Let us pray to the Father:

For all parents: that they may love their children in good times and in bad. [Pause] Let us pray to the Father:

For our own parents, who first gave us an experience of love. [Pause] Let us pray to the Father:

For all those who are burdened with problems and worries: that they may know the strength that comes from trust in God. [Pause] Let us pray to the Father:

For the grace to place our own special needs before God. [Longer pause] Let us pray to the Father:

President: Heavenly Father, grant us in all our tasks your help, in all our doubts your guidance, in all our weaknesses your strength, in all our dangers your protection, and in all our sorrows your consolation. We ask this through Christ our Lord.

SIGN OF PEACE

Lord Jesus Christ, you said to your disciples: 'Do not worry about food or drink or clothes. Set your hearts on the kingdom of God, and your heavenly Father will take care of you'. Help us to live by these words, so that we may enjoy the peace and unity of your kingdom where you live for ever and ever.

REFLECTION   **Out in the fields**

The little cares that fretted me
I lost them yesterday
Among the fields above the sea,
Among the winds at play,
Among the lowing of the herds,
The rustling of the trees,
Among the singing of the birds,
The humming of the bees.
The foolish fears of what may happen,
I cast them all away,
Among the clover-scented grass,
Among the new-mown hay;
Among the husking of the corn
Where drowsy poppies nod,
Where ill thoughts die and good are born,
Out in the fields with God. (*Anon.*)

Ninth Sunday of the Year
BUILDING ON ROCK

INTRODUCTION AND CONFITEOR

God's word provides a rocklike foundation for our lives. But it is not enough to listen to it; we have to do it. We know we haven't always done it, so let us ask God's forgiveness, and the strength to do better in the future. [Pause]

Lord, your words are a lamp for our steps and a light for our path. Lord, have mercy.

Lord, when we build our lives on your word, we are building them on solid rock. Christ, have mercy.

Lord, your words will never pass away. Lord, have mercy.

HEADINGS FOR READINGS

First Reading (Deut 11:18.26-28). Those who obey God's commandments will be blessed.

Second Reading (Rom 3:21-25.28). We are made friends of God, not through our own efforts, but through God's grace.

Gospel (Mt 7:21-27). If we build our lives on the teaching of Christ, we are building them on solid rock.

SCRIPTURE NOTE

The First Reading stresses the blessings that will accrue to God's people provided they obey the words of God. And in the Gospel Jesus says that those who make his teaching the firm basis of their lives will be able to withstand all assaults and temptations. People can pretend to be religious and pious while failing hopelessly to do the will of God.

HOMILY 1   **Building on rock**

Tobias Wolff, a modern American writer, had a difficult childhood. After his father and mother divorced, he accompanied his mother as she wandered across America in search of work. He had an anguished adolescence, and was frequently on the verge of delinquency.

During that time he got a rudimentary education in the faith – his mother was a Catholic but didn't go to church. When she married again, the stepfather was very cruel to him. Somewhere along the line he made up his mind that he would be a writer, though it seemed an impossible dream at the time. After high school, he joined the US army and spent a year in Vietnam, an experience he found 'extremely corrupt and corrupting.' He lost good friends there. After leaving the army he managed to get accepted into Oxford University. All this time he had given up the practice of his faith.

At Oxford he had a strange experience. One night he was doing a translation from old English into modern English. The passage assigned to him was from the West Saxon Gospels. The passage began to sound vaguely familiar to him. It told the story of a wise man who built his house on a rock, and a foolish man who build his house on sand.

This caused him to reflect on his life. He realised that up to now he had known very little security. There had been nothing solid or reliable in his life. Yet now this amazing thing had happened to him: he was a student in a famous university. And indeed it was truly amazing that a boy from his background should end up in a university such as Oxford. The winds that had blown him here could have blown him anywhere, even off the face of the earth.

But he was here. All the other moments of his life had somehow conspired to bring him here. And with this moment came these words of Jesus. And as he copied out his translation in plain English, he thought that, 'yes, I would do well to build my house upon a rock, whatever that meant.'

Gradually he found out what it meant to build one's life on the words of Jesus. How? By observing the lives of some fellow students who were active Catholics. He noticed that while many other students had no solid values, and were blown all over the place, these possessed something. They seemed to know where they were going, and what life was truly about. He wanted what they had. And so it was that he became an active Catholic himself. Notice, he wasn't won over by their arguments (words), but by their lives (deeds).

In comparison with faith, there is nothing sure or lasting in the world. Human opinions are rooted in appearances, and change from day to day, but the words of Christ do no change or pass away. We would do well to build the house of our lives on his precious words.

The people who heard the Sermon on the Mount were enormously impressed. But Jesus told them that it was not enough to listen to his words. They would have to act on them, if they wished to benefit from them.

Jesus said his disciples would be judged, not by their words, but by their deeds. There is only one way in which a person can prove his sincerity, that is, by his practice. Fine words can never take the place of deeds. Sadly, some who confess God with their lips deny him with their lives.

Jesus said that those who listened to his words, but who did not act on them, were building on sand. Time would erase everything from their minds. Nothing would remain, nothing would come of it. On the other hand, those who listened to his words and who did act on them, were building on rock. They would have something to show for their efforts, something that would last.

It's never too late to begin to act on the words of Jesus.

HOMILY 2 **What to build on**

Christ says, 'Everyone who hears these words of mine and acts of them will be like a sensible man who built his house on rock.'

What a wonderful promise. If we build our lives on his words, then we are building them on solid rock. However, there are lots of other voices which, directly or indirectly, tell us to build our lives on very different values. These say something like this:

> If you want to get on in life, if you want to succeed, here are some of the pillars on which you must build.
>
> Look after yourself. If you don't, nobody else will. Follow every path that advances your own interests. Never ask whether something is right, only if it benefits you.
>
> Be ambitious. This means that on occasions you will have to throw your weight around, which means people may get hurt. But don't let that rob you of any sleep. It's all a rat-race anyway.
>
> Get to know the people who matter. You may have to grease a few palms along the way, but it will be worth it. But don't neglect your cronies either. Hopefully they will return the compliment. But do not concede as much as an inch to your opponents.
>
> Try to project the image of a successful person. Even when things are far from well, don't let on.
>
> Do not hesitate to raise your hat to religion and to God if you have to. Keep up the facade of outer observance if it enhances your respectability. But do not let religion rob you of a single one of your comforts or pleasures, or interfere in the slightest way with your standard of living.
>
> These are some of the pillars you should build on. These should suffice to see your fortunes soar, and your house to rise steadily.

What Christ says is very different:

> Remember this: The most important thing in life is to be a person of integrity, and to live rightly. Build on the following pillars.
>
> You are not a rat, so you don't have to behave like a rat. You are a human being and a child of God. The most important thing about you is your capacity for goodness.
>
> If you raise your status, make sure to raise yourself too. What sense does it make if you work hard at advancing your career, but you don't

work at your character? What does it matter for you to be always in the limelight if your soul is in darkness? What does it matter if your bank account is bulging while your heart is empty?

Take care of your conscience, and listen to it. If you live without a conscience, can you still call yourself a human being?

Do not be afraid of sacrifice. If your sole aim is to grab as many pleasures as possible out of life, you are doing a terrible injustice to yourself. Without sacrifice and struggle you can never grow up and discover who you are.

Be faithful to your promises. To live loosely is to discover one day, sooner or later, that you haven't anchored your boat to anything solid. When the storm strikes, you will find that you are alone and adrift. Fidelity is a beautiful thing. It is a precious stone, a true gem.

Do not be ashamed of your beliefs and values. Without beliefs and convictions, you are no better than a ship without rudder or port of destination.

These are some of the pillars on which the Christian ought to build the house of his/her life. The essential thing is to do the will of God. It is not enough merely to listen to the words of Christ. We have to act on them, to live them. Otherwise we are building on sand.

People may think they are religious and pious while failing hopelessly to live by the teachings of Christ. Such people are building on sand. Their house will not last. Those who base their lives on the teachings of Christ are able to withstand all assaults, temptations and crises.

HOMILY 3   **Building on his words**

Some years ago, while Russia was still ruled by the communists, some dissidents were arrested. They were subjected to a thorough body-search. One man was found to have a small ball of paper in his mouth. It contained a few pages from a book.

The man knew that long years in some remote prison camp lay ahead of him, and that it was quite possible he would never return home. What pages was he taking with him to give him the necessary courage and strength to face such a bleak future? The pages contained the Sermon on the Mount, the conclusion of which we have just read.

It is reasonable to assume that he was not turning to the words of Christ merely as a last resort. Rather, he was turning to something that had already filled his life with meaning and hope. Which suggests that he was not only a listener of the word but also a doer of it.

So it was to these marvellous words of Christ that he now fled. He wanted to take with him a lamp that would illuminate the dark path which stretched out unendingly before him. On these words he would build whatever hopes he still had for himself and for his life on earth.

What were some of those words on which he was pinning his hopes? No doubt it was words such as the following:

Blessed are those who are persecuted in the cause of right; theirs is the kingdom of heaven.

Where your treasure is, there will your heart be also.

No one can serve two masters ... You cannot be the slave both of God and of money.

Look at the birds of the air ... If God looks after them, how much more will he look after you, you of little faith.

Set your hearts on his kingdom first, and on his rigtheousness, and all these others things will be given to you as well.

Enter by the narrow gate, since the road that leads to perdition is wide and spacious; but it is a narrow gate and a hard road that leads to life.

Only a house built on a sound foundation can withstand the storm. Only a life build on the words of Jesus will be able to withstand the inevitable assaults, temptations and crises of life.

However, it is not enough to listen to the words of Christ. We have to do them. Only then will they shed light into our lives. To believe in his words, but not to live by them, would be like carrying an unlit lamp.

PRAYER OF THE FAITHFUL

President: We open our hearts in prayer to the God who leads us and guides us.

Response: Lord, hear our prayer.

Reader(s): For the Church: that it may continue to bring the message of Christ to the world. [Pause] Let us pray to the Lord.

For all Christians: that they may live their lives according to the values of the Gospel. [Pause] Let us pray to the Lord.

For world leaders: that they may seek the help and guidance of God in all their undertakings. [Pause] Let us pray to the Lord.

For those who are building their lives on values that are contrary to those of the Gospel. [Pause] Let us pray to the Lord.

For each of us: that we may not just listen to the words of Christ, but put them into practice in our lives. [Pause] Let us pray to the Lord.

For our own special needs. [Longer pause] Let us pray to the Lord.

President: Lord, grant that what we have said with our lips, we may believe with our hearts, and practise with our lives. We ask this through Christ our Lord.

REFLECTION **Building on rock**

There is nothing sure or lasting in this world.
Human opinions change from day to day,
but the words of Christ do no change or pass away.
However, those who listen to his words
but do not act on them, are building on sand.
Time will erase his words from their minds;
nothing will remain, nothing will come of them.
On the other hand, those who listen to his words
and who do act on them, are building on rock;
they will have something to show for their efforts,
something to be proud of,
and something that will last, last eternally.

Tenth Sunday of the Year
JESUS, THE FRIEND OF SINNERS

INTRODUCTION AND CONFITEOR

In today's Gospel we see Jesus eating and drinking with sinners. We are gathered around the Lord's table, not because we think we are better or more deserving than others, but because we know we are sinners, sinners who need the Lord's forgiveness and healing so that we may do better. [Pause]

Lord Jesus, you came to heal the broken-hearted. Lord, have mercy.
Lord, you came to call sinners to repentance. Christ, have mercy.
Lord, you came to seek out and to save the lost. Lord, have mercy.

HEADINGS FOR READINGS

First Reading (Hos 6:3-6). What God wants from his people (and from us) is not sacrifices, but a genuine and faithful love.

Second Reading (Rom 4:18-25). Abraham's faith in God should serve as a model for our faith in Christ.

Gospel (Mt 9:9-13). Jesus shocks the religious leaders by eating and drinking with sinners, and calling one of them to be an apostle.

SCRIPTURE NOTE

Jesus was recognised as a holy man. Yet he accepted sinners. Sinners drew the obvious conclusion: because they were acceptable to him, it meant they were acceptable to God. Jesus distinguished between the sinner and the sin. He condemned the sin but forgave the sinner. His over-riding motive for acting the way he did was one of compassion.

HOMILY 1 **The friend of sinners**

The Pharisees despised sinners, but Jesus befriended sinners. It was not a question of a few kind words, or a gesture or two, on his part. He associated with sinners. He shared their food and drink. He didn't just tolerate them. He welcomed them. In his presence they felt accepted and loved just as they were. It's not surprising then that many of them heeded his message and changed their lives. Matthew is an example of this.

Jesus' attitude to sinners was one of kindness and persuasion rather than condemnation and denunciation. He didn't wait for sinners to repent before becoming their friend. No, he befriended them in their sinfulness. This is what scandalised the religious authorities: that he associated with sinners and rejoiced in their company while they were still sinners. Just as today some people see compassion for the criminal as a betrayal of the victim, so the Pharisees saw Jesus' compassion for the sinner as a betrayal of the virtuous.

Jesus' defence was very straightforward: he said he went where the need was greatest. In associating with sinners he wasn't condoning their situation. Rather, he was trying to show them a new life. But he could not do this without associating with them and being sympathetic towards them. You never improve people by shunning them. In acting the way he did, Jesus revealed the mercy of God towards sinners.

Jesus did not show a lack of moral principles by sitting at table and consorting with sinners. Rather, his humanity was rich and deep enough to make contact, even in them, with that indestructible core of goodness which is found in all, and upon which the future has to be built. He put them in touch with that in themselves. His goodness evoked goodness in them.

It would have been easier, safer, and more popular for him to go among the good. But he wasn't thinking of himself. He was thinking of others, and of the mission given him by his Father. He did not come to call the virtuous but sinners to repentance.

A man lived on the same street as a doctor. Since he enjoyed excellent health, he had no reason to visit the doctor. Hence, he had only a nodding acquaintance with him. The doctor seemed to be a nice man, and he had heard people who had been to his surgery say that he was very compassionate and very kind.

Then the man got sick and immediately went to see the doctor. The doctor welcomed him. He spoke gently to him, and examined him with patience and thoroughness. He diagnosed what his trouble was and prescribed some medication. Within a week the man was well again.

Now the man knew at first hand the kind of man the doctor was. Prior to this he knew him only by hearsay. Now he had experienced his kindness. But this happened only because he got sick. Later he said to a neighbour, 'No one wants to get sick. But if one should get sick, it's nice to know that there is a doctor like him around.'

If we are sinners – and which of us is not a sinner? – then Christ loves us not less but more. It doesn't do us much good to be loved for being perfect. We need to be accepted and loved precisely as sinners.

It is in and through our sins that we experience the goodness and mercy of Christ. If we never sinned, we'd never know his forgiveness. This is not an excuse for sinning. But it's nice to know that this is how Jesus receives sinners.

Saints bear witness to God – that's obvious. But so too do repentant sinners. Theirs is a different kind of witness, but one that is just as true and every bit as necessary. Saints bear witness to God's grace and fidelity. Sinners bear witness to God's love and mercy. Furthermore, Jesus allowed repentant sinners to serve: Mary Magdalen, Peter, Thomas, Matthew …

HOMILY 2   **Matthew: a late vocation**

Today Jean Vanier is known in many parts of the world. At an early stage in his life he had a good, secure, well-paid job – he was a university lecturer. But then he gave it up and decided to devote his life to working with the mentally handicapped. Why? Because the lecturing job didn't satisfy him. There was something missing in his life. He says, 'I wanted more than a job. I wanted something that would give expression to the passion I felt about people, especially people such as the mentally handicapped.'

As Jesus was passing by the customs office he saw a tax collector by the name of Matthew sitting there. He stopped and spoke to him. He made no threat, nor did he offer any reward. He simply said, 'Follow me.' And Matthew got up at once and followed him. How do we account for this? Since the Gospel gives no explanation for Matthew's decision to follow Jesus, we can only guess. What happened to Jean Vanier is very relevant.

At that time tax collectors were very unpopular. It may be that Matthew was not fulfilled in the job. It may be that it had given him all it had to give, and that he was looking for a new challenge. It may be that there was an emptiness in his life. He may have come to that point in life where he found himself thinking, 'There must be more to life than this.'

Or again it may be that he was finding the job soul-destroying. So when Jesus offered him a chance to do something better with his life, he grabbed it immediately, and with both hands. It would seem that he was suffering from an unsatisfied thirst for goodness. The call of Jesus may have caused him to remember the dreams he once had of doing something worth-while with his life.

Whatever the reasons for his response, it can't have been easy for him. Tax-collecting was a secure and lucrative job. Nevertheless, he received more than he gave up. Before his encounter with Jesus he had a career. After that encounter he had a vocation.

A career and a vocation are different though not mutually exclusive. We might express a vocation through a specific career – teacher, nurse, doctor ... But a vocation can never be reduced to these activities. It is something deeper. It involves vision, motivation, dedication. A career usually means furthering oneself. But a vocation means serving others.

The banquet which followed Matthew's call was a banquet of and for sinners. But the presence of Jesus transformed it into an occasion of joy and celebration.

Every Sunday we celebrate the banquet of the Eucharist. Jesus is the host, we sinners are the guests. In this banquet we are nourished with the word of God and the bread of life. And, like Matthew, we are called to something better – not necessarily a new career, but a new way of living.

If someone or something makes us aware of a certain emptiness in our life, we should not despair; rather we should rejoice. It may be the voice of God calling us to something better. The settled, satisfied person fails to develop further. Therefore, pay attention to what you vaguely feel at your heart's core, even if you do not want to feel it.

The call of someone like Matthew shows that Jesus not only saw what a person was, but also what he could be.

HOMILY 3   **What I want is mercy, not sacrifice**

It's tragic to find religious people devoid of the chief human attribute – compassion for others. This was the chief fault of the Pharisees. Grim, earnest men, they practised severe virtues while condemning others who did not measure up to their standards.

Once there was a very holy abbot called Anastasius. In fact, he was considered a saint by his fellow desert monks. One day when a monk by the name of James sinned and was told to leave the community, Anastasius got up and walked out with him, saying: 'I too am a sinner.' James, how-ever, did not reform and fell very low. Years later he came to visit Anastasius as he was saying his evening prayer.

'Forgive me for interrupting your prayer and making you break your Rule,' James said.

'Don't worry,' Anastasius replied. 'My Rule is to receive you with hos-pitality.'

And he gave him food and lodgings for the night. Now Anastasius had an old copy of the Bible which was worth quite a bit of money. Seeing the book, James took it with him when he was leaving next morning. When Anastasius realised that he had stolen the book, he didn't follow him, fearing that he might only make him add the sin of perjury to that of theft. James went to a nearby merchant to sell the book, asking a high price.

'Give me the book for a little while so that I can find out whether it's worth that much,' the merchant said.

He took it to Anastasius. Anastasius took one look at it and said, 'Yes, this is a splendid book. In fact it's worth much more.' The buyer came back and told the thief what Anastasius had said.

He asked, 'Was that all he said? Did he make no other remarks?'

'No,' said the merchant, 'he didn't say another word.'

On hearing this, James was deeply moved, and said, 'I've changed my mind. I don't want to sell the book after all'. And he hastened back to Anastasius, and, with tears in his eyes, gave him back the book and begged his forgiveness. Anastasius received him with the same kindness as before.

He simply said, 'I forgive you. Keep the book. Read a little from it each day, and pray to Christ who received sinners like us, and brought them back to God's love and friendship. Now go in peace.'

His fellow monks were surprised to see him wasting his time on someone like James, but he said, 'Tell me, if your robe is torn, will you throw it away?' And they replied, 'No, we will mend it and put it back on.' Then he said, 'If you take such care of your robe, will not God be merciful to one who bears his image?'

And the kindness of Anastasius paid off. James changed his life. He returned to the life of a monk and became known for his goodness and holiness.

Anastasius placed kindness, hospitality and mercy towards fellow human beings above the practice of penance and the observance of his Rule. He modelled himself on Jesus. Jesus sat down and ate with sinners, which means he became their friend.

When a person combines true religion and deep humanity, you have a powerful combination. It's like well-polished mahogany. Here you have true holiness. Such people are other Christs.

To offer sacrifice to God is a great thing. But to show mercy to a fellow human being is an even greater thing, and is harder. After offering a sacrifice we feel good; we have done something, chalked up some merit. To show mercy is not easy, especially when the person involved deserves to be punished, and when it is in our power to punish him.

One thing helps: the conviction that we ourselves stand in daily need of God's mercy. Blessed are the merciful; they shall have mercy shown them.

PRAYER OF THE FAITHFUL

President: Opening our hearts to the God whose desire is for mercy, not sacrifice, let us pray.

Response: Lord, graciously hear us.

Reader(s): For the Church: that it may show the compassionate face of Christ to sinners. [Pause] Lord, hear us.

For all government leaders: that they may be willing to heal old wounds and divisions. [Pause] Lord, hear us.

For all the rejects and outcasts of our society: that the followers of Christ may show special care and concern for them. [Pause] Lord, hear us.

For each other: that the consciousness of our own sins may make us more understanding in our dealings with others. [Pause] Lord, hear us.

For our own special needs. [Longer pause] Lord, hear us.

President: Heavenly Father, our source of life and holiness, you know our weakness. May we reach out with joy to grasp your hand and walk more readily in your ways. We ask this through Christ our Lord.

REFLECTION   **Gandhi and the untouchables**

In India the untouchables did not belong to any caste.
They were barred from the temples.
In the cities they lived in the slums,
and did only the most menial jobs.
In the country they were forbidden to use the wells.
Yet it was precisely the untouchables
whom the great Mahatma Gandhi befriended.
He ate and drank with them,
and played with their children.
He once said: 'I do not want to be reborn.
But if that should happen,
I would like to find myself among the untouchables
in order to share the suffering they are subjected to.
In this way, I would have the chance to liberate them
and myself from their miserable condition.'

Eleventh Sunday of the Year
HE HAD COMPASSION ON THEM

INTRODUCTION AND CONFITEOR

Jesus had compassion on the people who came to him in their many needs. He has compassion on us too. Therefore, let us turn to him with confidence now, laying our needs before him. [Pause]

Lord Jesus, you were sent to heal the contrite. Lord, have mercy.

Lord, you came to call sinners to repentance. Christ, have mercy.

Lord, you plead for us at the right hand of the Father. Lord, have mercy.

HEADINGS FOR READINGS

First Reading (Ex 19:2-6). God has shown his love for the Israelites by choosing them to be his very own people. They must respond in kind.

Second Reading (Rom 5:6-11). God showed his great love for us by the fact that Christ died for us while we were still sinners.

Gospel (Mt 9:36-10:8). Here we see the compassion Jesus had for the ordinary people in their sufferings.

SCRIPTURE NOTE

There is a clear theme running through all three readings today: God takes the initiative in our regard. God took the initiative in forming a covenant with the Israelites (First Reading). God took the initiative in loving us because Christ died for us while we were still sinners (Second Reading). And Jesus took the initiative in reaching out to the people (Gospel).

HOMILY 1   **Choosing the twelve Apostles**

Jesus had many disciples. From the ranks of these he picked out twelve leaders. He called them apostles. The names of the twelve are given in today's Gospel. Who were these men and what qualifications did they have?

Today companies screen people for management positions. And Church authorities also screen people for positions of leadership. Candidates are not admitted to the priesthood without first undergoing psychological tests. Let us imagine that the twelve apostles were sent by Jesus to a firm of consultants for similar tests. The following report, marked 'Private and Confidential', was sent back to him.

Dear Sir,

Thank you for submitting the résumés of the twelve men you have picked for management positions in your new organisation. All of them have now taken our battery of tests. We have run the results through our computer, and also arranged personal interviews for each of them with our psychologists and vocational aptitude consultants. The results of all the tests are included, and we advise that you study each of them carefully.

It is the opinion of the staff that most of your nominees are lacking in background, education and vocational aptitude for the type of enterprise you are undertaking. Besides, they do not have the team concept. We have found ample evidence of jealousy and rivalry among them. Therefore, we would recommend that you continue your search for persons of experience and proven ability.

Simon Peter is emotionally unstable and given to fits of temper – definitely not the man you would want to head your organisation. Andrew has absolutely no qualities of leadership. He is just a follower. The two brothers, James and John, are too hot-headed. Besides, they place personal interest above company loyalty. Thomas demonstrates a questioning attitude that would undermine morale. Matthew, the tax-collector, is undoubtedly a man of ability, but would project the wrong image for an organisation such as yours. James, son of Alphaeus, and Thaddaeus have radical leanings. Hence, their unsuitability.

There is one of the candidates, however, who shows great potential. He is a man of ability and resourcefulness, good with people, has a keen business mind, and has contacts in high places. He is highly motivated, ambitious and responsible. That man is Judas Iscariot. We recommend him as your controller and right-hand man.

We wish you every success in your new venture.

Sincerely yours,

Jordan Management Consultants.

Those assessors had a point. The apostles had some obvious faults and weaknesses. But so what? After all, they weren't angels, but imperfect human beings. Jesus didn't work with perfect material; he worked with ordinary material.

The twelve men Jesus chose were just ordinary people. They came from ordinary walks of life – a number of them were fishermen. They had no special qualifications. Far from being perfect, they possessed the same human faults and failings we find in ourselves.

Peter blew hot and cold. At times he was as solid as a rock. But at other times he was more like a piece of jelly. Yet, in spite of everything, his heart was sound. And at the end of the day, it's the heart that matters.

James and John were so hot-tempered that once they wanted Jesus to call down fire and brimstone on a Samaritan village that refused to accept him. They were also full of personal ambition, and wanted to have the top places in Jesus' kingdom, thus causing dissension among the others.

Matthew was a member of a hated class – he was a tax collector for the occupying Romans. Simon belonged to a band of people called the Zealots whose aim was to get the Romans out of Palestine. Today Simon would be called a terrorist. Thomas earned himself a nick-name. He became known as the Doubter.

Then of course there was Judas, who not only proved a failure, but actually betrayed him. God did not predestine Judas to play the role of traitor. Judas became a traitor through the choices he made. He wasn't a demon. He was made from human material that might have become something very different.

Anyway, there we have the twelve. But Jesus saw good in each one of them, even in Judas. It shows that one doesn't have to be perfect or possess all the talents in order to be called by Christ.

Choice is a privilege and an honour, but it is also a responsibility. The Israelites were chosen to be a light to the nations. And the apostles too were chosen for a task – to help Christ with the harvest.

And through baptism we too are chosen. Though the harvest is immense, there is no need to be discouraged. We can't do everything, but we can do something.

HOMILY 2   **Christ of the Gospels**

In his famous novel, *The Brothers Karamazov*, the Russian writer, Dostoevsky, gives a moving portrayal of Christ. The action takes place in Seville during the Inquisition. Christ came to visit his people in their sufferings. Only the day before, a hundred heretics had been burned at the stake by order of the cardinal, the Grand Inquisitor.

Though Jesus came without fuss, the people recognised him at once. They crowded around him. He walked among them with an expression of gentleness on his face. He reached out his hands and blessed them. Many were healed of their diseases just by touching his robe.

He stopped at the steps of the cathedral as an open coffin with the body of a little girl in it was being carried out. A hush fell over the crowd. Then a whisper arose: 'He will raise the child'. And he did. However, no sooner had he done so than the Grand Inquisitor arrived in the square. When he saw what had happened he had the stranger arrested and thrown into jail.

That night he visited the prisoner in his cell. 'Is it really you?' he asked him. Receiving no reply he said, 'You have no need to say anything. You have said it all before. I don't know if you really are he. All I know is that tomorrow you will burn at the stake as the worst of all heretics, and the people who today kissed your feet, tomorrow will be throwing sticks on your fire. Do you realise that?'

He waited for some reply but none came. Then the stranger approached him, and with great gentleness, embraced him. That was his answer. For a moment the old man was confused. But he soon recovered. He went to the cell door, opened it, and said to him, 'Go, and come back no more – never, never!' And he let him out, and he disappeared into the dark streets and lanes of the sleeping city.

We can forget what Christ was like. The Church can forget. It can put its doctrines and dogmas, its rules and regulations, before people. Individuals can put their private devotions before Christian living. Today there is an increasing preoccupation with revelations and apparitions. Yet today there is also a hunger for the Christ of the Gospels.

We need to remind ourselves of what Christ was like by going back to the Gospels. The Gospel of today's Mass gives us a beautiful picture of the compassionate Christ in action.

The religious leaders had nothing to offer the ordinary people in their sufferings – neither guidance, nor comfort, nor strength. In fact, they didn't care about them. But Jesus was completely different. When he looked at the ordinary people, he didn't see a crowd but a collection of individuals, each with problems and worries, joys and sorrows. And far from despising them, he had compassion on them, precisely because they were wounded and in need.

He gave himself to them first of all. But then knowing how great the harvest was, he decided to summon helpers. From his followers he chose twelve to be his friends and companions in a special way. He named them apostles – people who are sent. They were from different backgrounds, and none of them was trained. Each had his own character, foibles, weaknesses and strengths. There were tensions and rivalries among them.

Jesus loved them and they loved him in return. He trained them. Not, however, in a formal way, but by living with them, walking with them, being a model for them. They learned to do things as he did them. Then he sent them out to others. They knew what their mission was: they were to be agents of his compassion to others, especially to the poor and the suffering.

Today Jesus depends on us. In order to become an apostle of the Lord it is not necessary to be an exceptional person, much less a saint (at least not to begin with). All one needs is willingness and an open heart.

HOMILY 3   **Loved in our sins**

Philip is a very loveable man. Now in his sixties, he is amiable, good humoured, kind and generous. If you watch him at the annual re-union of his extended family, you can see all this. He doesn't draw attention to himself. He is just a wonderful presence. Smiling and laughing, talking and mixing, he puts people at ease. He attracts people to him. His one and only aim seems to be that of helping others. He has no thought for himself.

But he wasn't always like that. A few years ago he was almost the exact opposite. His presence at the annual family reunion was an embarrassment, especially to his wife and children. Why? Because he was an active alcoholic then. He was drunk from early in the day. He seemed to be interested in nobody but himself. He was incapable of helping anyone. People avoided him, or talked with him as little as possible. To make matters worse, he could be nasty when he was drunk.

It's easy to love him now that he has given up drinking and turned his life around. In fact, you can't help but love him. But it wasn't easy to love him in the old days when he was still drinking. In truth, it was almost impossible. Yet all through the dark years of his drinking his wife and family continued to love him. It was their love and concern for him that eventually enabled him to face his problem and go and look for help. It was their love that brought him around.

In today's Second Reading St Paul says that it is not easy to die even for a good person. How difficult then to die for a bad person. He goes on to say that the real proof that God loves us is the fact that Christ, his Son, died for us while we were still sinners.

To be loved in one's goodness is no big deal. It's no more than one deserves. But to be loved in one's badness, as Philip was, is a wonderful experience.

If we are sinners – and which of us is not a sinner? – then Christ loves us not less but more. It doesn't do us much good to be loved for being perfect. We need to be accepted and loved precisely as sinners.

The task of a Christian is not to win the love of God, but to respond to it. And the best kind of response is to love others in their faults and in their sins.

The best way to show our thanks to God for the love he has shown us in Christ is to share that love with others. Christ chose the apostles and sent them out to others. He now wants us to reach out to others in whatever way we can. Our task is a simple one: we are to be agents of his compassion to others.

PRAYER OF THE FAITHFUL

President: The prayer we now make expresses our trust in the merciful love of God who is faithful from age to age.

Response: Lord, graciously hear us.

Reader(s): For Christians: that they may not be content merely to pray for the relief of suffering in the world, but do something about it. [Pause] Lord, hear us.

For our political and civil leaders: that they may show special concern for those suffering hardship and deprivation. [Pause] Lord, hear us.

For the sick and all those undergoing serious operations. [Pause] Lord, hear us.

For each other: that when we feel lonely and unloved, we may remember that in Christ we have a compassionate Brother and Friend. [Pause] Lord, hear us.

For all here present: that, having experienced Christ's compassion, we may be willing to show compassion to others. [Pause] Lord, hear us.

For our own special needs. [Longer pause] Lord, hear us.

President: Heavenly Father, you sent your Son into our world to help us build a more just and humane world. In working for such a world, we will enhance our own dignity and that of others. We make all our prayers through Christ our Lord.

REFLECTION   **Compassion**

> The person in misery does not need
> a look that judges and criticises,
> but a comforting presence.
> Jesus looked at the ordinary people,
> and seeing how needy they were,
> he had compassion on them
> and began to minister to them.
> Compassion means that I suffer with you;
> I accept into my heart the misery in yours;
> I become one with you in your pain.
> I may not be able to relieve that pain,
> but by understanding it and sharing it,
> I make it possible for you to bear it.
> Lord, give us warm and generous hearts
> so that we may be agents of your compassion to others.

Twelfth Sunday of the Year
WITNESSING IN SPITE OF FEAR

INTRODUCTION AND CONFITEOR

Jesus asks us to be his witnesses in the world. However, we often lack the courage to witness openly to our faith. But Jesus says to us what he said to his first disciples, *'Do not be afraid.'* So let us bring our fears to him, and ask his help in overcoming them. [Pause]

Lord, you give us strength when we are weak. Lord, have mercy.

Lord, you give us courage when we are afraid. Christ, have mercy.

Lord, you give us new heart when we fail. Lord, have mercy.

HEADINGS FOR READINGS

First Reading (Jer 20:10-13). The knowledge that God was with him enabled Jeremiah to remain faithful to his difficult task as a prophet.

Second Reading (Rom 5:12-15). St Paul draws a contrast between Christ and Adam: sin came into the world through Adam; abundant grace came through Jesus Christ.

Gospel (Mt 10:26-33). Christ exhorts his disciples to open and fearless witness to the Gospel, assuring them of God's special care in all their trials.

HOMILY 1   **Do not be afraid**

When Jesus sent the apostles out to proclaim his teaching openly and to witness to him before the world, he knew that they were fearful. And they had good reason to be fearful, knowing that they would have to face hardship and persecution. So, not once but three times he said to them, 'Do not be afraid.'

It is normal and natural that courage will sometimes fail us and that we will be afraid. All those who have accomplished great things have known fear at one time or another. We think of the prophet Jeremiah (First Reading), of Martin Luther King, and of Jesus himself in the garden of Gethsemane.

Fear is not necessarily a bad thing. Fear sometimes has a protective function, warning us of the presence of danger. In this case, fear is a grace. Nevertheless, fear can be a handicap. It can paralyse a person. It can turn a person into a coward.

Once upon a time there was a mouse that had a crippling fear of cats. A magician took pity on it and turned it into a cat. But then it became afraid of dogs. So the magician turned it into a dog. Then it became afraid of panthers. So the magician turned it into a panther. Then it became afraid of hunters. At this point the magician gave up. He turned it back into a mouse saying, 'Nothing I do for you is going to be of any help because you have the heart of a mouse.'

Jesus knew that the apostles were afraid. He understood their fears and took them seriously. When he said to them, Do not be afraid, he was addressing their fears and trying to allay them. He was trying to give them courage. He was trying to move them beyond fear, knowing that fear could make them so timid as to be unable to fulfil their mission.

How did he suggest they might overcome their fears? Basically through trust in God and reliance on God. He urged them to have complete trust in God, who lovingly watches over the life and death of even the smallest and least valuable of his creatures – the sparrows. Jesus assured them that God knew every detail of their lives, and would support them in every crisis.

The prophet Jeremiah lived out his vocation during a time of great turmoil, which saw the defeat of Israel and the destruction of Jerusalem and the temple. He lived with constant threats to his life. Yet, in spite of everything, he remained faithful to his calling. What was it that enabled him to overcome his fears and remain faithful to his mission? It was the conviction that God was on his side: 'The Lord is at my side, a mighty hero.'

The Lord is at our sides too. And while at times we will grow fearful, we mustn't allow our fears to cripple us. To live a Christian life requires courage. But then any meaningful living requires courage. What is needed in life is not so much heroism as ordinary courage.

Courage is the most important of all the virtues, because without courage you can't practise any other virtue with constancy. Faith is a great source of courage. As people of faith, we believe that God will give us the strength to cope with whatever comes.

The greatest freedom of all is freedom from fear. Unless we can overcome our fears, we cannot live a dignified human life. Nevertheless, fear and courage are not mutually exclusive. They can and do coexist. Courage is not never being afraid. It is being afraid, and overcoming it, or carrying on in spite of it.

To be a disciple of Jesus, the heart of a mouse will not suffice. One needs a brave heart. May the Lord give each of us a brave heart.

HOMILY 2   **Someone to watch over us**

When Jesus sent the apostles out to be his witnesses in the world, he knew that they would be putting their lives in danger. He knew that as a consequence they were afraid. He understood their fears, and tried to allay them. He told them not to be afraid of human beings who can kill the body but can do no more. They should fear God who can condemn a person to an even worse fate – to eternal damnation.

There is such a thing as a holy fear of God. The Bible says, 'Fear of God is the beginning of wisdom.' It means the fear of displeasing God, the fear of losing God, the fear of eternal damnation. These can be powerful motivating forces. Fear sometimes has a protective function, warning us of the presence of danger. In this case, fear is a grace.

But Jesus is not telling us that we should base our relationship with God on fear. Rather, he is urging us to base it on trust. He says, 'Can you not buy two sparrows for a penny? And yet not one sparrow falls to the ground without your Father knowing … So do not be afraid; you are worth more than many sparrows.'

What Jesus is doing is trying to move us from fear to trust. Fear creates suspicion, distance, defensiveness and insecurity. Trust leads to closeness, intimacy, and a sense of safety. Good religion makes a person fearless. Bad religion increases one's fears.

When Jesus says, 'Not one sparrow falls to the ground without your Father knowing,' he wants us to know how far-reaching and all-embracing is the knowledge and care of God. Everything that happens to any of his creatures, even the most insignificant of them, is seen by God and is important to him – yes, even the fall of a single sparrow. The fact that he doesn't prevent this fall, doesn't mean that he is indifferent to it. God is never indifferent about the fate of any of his creatures.

If then God is concerned about the sparrows, we can be sure that he is concerned about us who are his children. Still, we have no guarantee that nothing bad will ever happen to us. However, we believe that even should death come, God will take care of us.

Faith is not a comforting illusion that all is well. Rather, it means to know that life is full of risk, full of insecurity, and yet to rejoice in it – that is the essence of faith.

Nowadays, thanks to the security camera, we are often being watched, watched by a cold, dispassionate eye intent only on catching us in wrong-doing. The feeling that someone is watching you is not a pleasant feeling. But the feeling that someone is watching over you is a lovely feeling.

God is not watching us. God is watching over us. The conviction that God is watching over us gives us comfort, strength and hope especially in times of difficulty and danger. In the end only God can allay our deepest fears.

HOMILY 3 **Witnessing in spite of fear**

In the Gospel Jesus calls for witnesses, that is, people who are not afraid to be seen to be followers of his out there in the midst of a sceptical and sometimes hostile world. Fear is one of the things that keeps Christians from a bold and generous witnessing to the Gospel. Three times Jesus said to the apostles, 'Do not be afraid.'

Fortunately, there are always those in the Church who, by the grace of God, are able to overcome fear and witness to the Gospel in the most difficult and dangerous circumstances.

Oscar Romero is an outstanding example. When he was made Archbishop of San Salvador in 1977 he was a conservative. But he soon changed when he saw what was happening. Every Sunday he preached at the cathedral. His homilies so electrified the country that national affairs halted when he spoke from the altar. He made public the unspeakable crimes being committed, many by agents of the government.

He was under constant threat of death. Some of his best friends were murdered. And still he would not be silenced. Nor would he go into hiding or exile. 'At the first sight of danger the shepherd cannot run and leave the sheep to fend for themselves. I will stay with my people,' he said. He was shot dead in March 1980 while saying Mass.

According to Romero it didn't take courage. All it took was the understanding that his enemies dealt in fear, and that if he was not afraid of them, they would have no power over him. They might be able to kill his body, but they could not and would not kill his soul.

There is also the story of the priest, who during the genocide in Rwanda (1994) sheltered Tutsis in his house. When a mob arrived at his door and ordered him to release them, he refused to do so. They shot him and took the people away.

Even though we may not aspire to such heights of heroism, people like these are an inspiration to us. The words of Christ surely apply to them: 'If anyone declares himself for me before men, I will declare myself for him before my Father in heaven'.

Every place needs Christian witnesses. Christ says, 'Witness to me before men'. It's in the world we have to stand up and be counted. It's not good enough to be secret disciples of Christ. We have to give public witness to our Christian faith.

In some countries to witness to Christ is to place one's life in danger. But in most countries this is not the case. But the latter countries too need witnesses, because faith and Christian values are being eroded. It may be even harder to witness in the latter countries. What we are likely to face is not so much hostility or opposition, but something which is even harder – a deadly indifference. To witness in this case requires a special kind of courage. It means overcoming our fear of what people will think of us or say about us, and the fear of what it will cost us in terms of letting go of our ego.

When Jesus said to his apostles, 'Do not be afraid,' he wasn't saying that they should never feel afraid. He knew that at times they would be afraid. The issue was what fear might do to them. It might paralyse them, or make them so timid as to be unable to fulfil their mission. What Jesus was doing was encouraging them so that they might be able to move beyond fear.

How were they to overcome their fear? He urged them to have complete trust in God, who lovingly watches over the life and death of even the smallest and least valuable of his creatures – the sparrows.

PRAYER OF THE FAITHFUL

President: To the God whose love is kind and whose help never fails, we raise our hearts in prayer.

Response: Lord, hear our prayer.

Reader(s): For all Christians: that their lives may bear witness to the faith they profess with their lips. [Pause] Let us pray to the Lord.

For government leaders: that they may protect the rights of all their citizens, especially those of the weaker ones. [Pause] Let us pray to the Lord.

For all those who are suffering because of their faith or because of their stand for truth and justice. [Pause] Let us pray to the Lord.

For all gathered here: that Christ may deliver us from fear and cowardice. [Pause] Let us pray to the Lord.

For our own special needs. [Longer pause] Let us pray to the Lord.

President: Heavenly Father, grant us in all our tasks your help, in all our doubts your guidance, in all our weaknesses your strength, in all our dangers your protection, and in all our sorrows your consolation. We make our prayer through Christ our Lord.

REFLECTION   **A Celtic Prayer**

> I rise today
> with God's strength to direct me,
> God's wisdom to guide me,
> God's eyes to look before me,
> God's ear to hear me,
> God's word to speak for me,
> God's hand to uphold me,
> God's pathway before me,
> God's shield to protect me,
> God's host to save me –
> from temptations,
> from one man or many
> that seek to destroy me. Amen.

Thirteenth Sunday of the Year
HOSPITALITY

INTRODUCTION AND CONFITEOR

We are in God's house. God is the host, we are the guests. We should feel welcome and at home here. God accepts us, therefore we should accept one another. [Pause]

Lord, you came to heal the wounds of sin and division. Lord, have mercy.

Lord, you came to help us to see one another, not as strangers, but as brothers and sisters in God's family. Christ, have mercy.

Lord, you help us to make room in our hearts for the lost, the lonely, and the rejected. Lord, have mercy.

HEADINGS FOR READINGS

First Reading (2 Kgs 4:8-11.14-16). A beautiful act of hospitality is rewarded by God.

Second Reading (Rom 6:3-4.8-11). Through baptism we are united to the death and resurrection of Christ.

Gospel (Mt 10:37-42). This stresses the sacrifices involved in being missionaries of Jesus, and also the greatness of even the smallest act of hospitality offered to those missionaries.

SCRIPTURE NOTE

The Gospel contains the conclusion of Matthew's missionary discourse. Jesus instructs his apostles on the sacrifices involved, and the priorities they must embrace, in being his envoys to the world. He tells them that they must be ready, if need be, to sacrifice the dearest things in life. In certain (rare) circumstances they might have to choose between him and their own relatives.

The Gospel also stresses the profound dignity and implications of even the smallest act of hospitality to Christ's envoys. To receive a person's envoy is to receive the person himself. The First Reading echoes what the Gospel says about the importance of showing hospitality towards the envoy of God.

HOMILY 1   **The cross: following in his footsteps**

'Anyone who does not take up his cross and follow in my footsteps is not worthy of me.'

Each of us has a cross to carry. There is no need to make one, or to look for one. The cross we have is hard enough for us. But are we willing to take it up, to accept it as our cross?

Jesus took up his cross. What we have to do is take up our cross. Our cross is made not of wood but of our burdens – worries, problems, illnesses, conflict within the family ... the list is endless. Perhaps there is no big cross, only a multiplicity of little crosses. However, enough drops eventually fill the cup to overflowing.

The cross we carry may not even be visible to others. It may not be an outward thing but an inward thing, such as depression or grief. These are heavy crosses though we cannot weigh them on a scales.

The most painful cross of all, however, is the one in which we have no choice. For example, the cross of living with a difficult person. It is a lot easier to chose a cross for oneself than to accept the one that comes, so to speak, in the line of duty.

Over and above these crosses, which come to everyone, are the crosses which come to us because we are disciples of Christ. The most common reasons for giving up the practice of the faith are not intellectual but moral. People know that to follow Christ would subvert their plans, which are often mercenary and vain-glorious, and would mean saying no to themselves in certain things.

Following Christ involves a dying to self. This process of dying to self begins at Baptism. St Paul compares Baptism to death: 'In baptism we were buried with Christ'. At Baptism we let go of the old life of sin, and became a new creature able to live in the freedom of the children of God. This is, of course, a lifelong process which we can embark on, and persevere in, only with the grace of Christ.

But the purpose of this death is resurrection. The death of the old, sin-ridden self results in the birth of the new self, modelled on Christ. The person who selfishly grasps at personal fulfilment will only see it slip through his fingers, while the one who sacrifices himself for Jesus (and others) will find true fulfilment.

Christ did not choose the way of ease or evasion. He chose the way of self-sacrifice and suffering. It wasn't that he was in love with suffering. No. It was because he chose the way of love. And love inevitably results in suffering. But then love is the only thing that makes suffering bearable and fruitful.

We are saved not by Christ's suffering but by his love. And It was through his suffering that he attained to glory. If we suffer with him on earth we will be crowned with him in heaven.

The road of suffering is a narrow and difficult one. It is a great comfort for us to now that Christ, the innocent and sinless One, has gone down this road before us, and gone down it to the end. This road is not the same since he travelled it. A bright light illuminates it. And it does not end at Calvary but at Easter.

HOMILY 2   Hospitality

One of the nicest things in life is to meet an open, friendly, warm, hospitable person. Hospitality is a hallmark of a true follower of Christ.

At long last winter ended and spring came. All along the street the people rejoiced. They drew back their curtains and opened up their windows. Fresh air, sunlight, and warmth poured into their homes. 'Thank God for spring! Thank God for the sunshine!' they exclaimed.

Just then a beggar man appeared at the end of the street. He was quickly spotted through the open windows. One by one, down the length of the street, the windows were quickly closed, the curtains silently drawn, and the locks put back on the doors. The beggar man knocked on every door on the street, but not one door opened to him.

Forlornly he left the street and headed for somewhere else. No sooner had he disappeared than the curtains were pulled back again, and the windows and doors opened up once more. And again the sunshine and fresh air poured in, and all the people rejoiced.

Strange how our homes are always open to receive God's sunshine and fresh air, but not always open to receive a child of God, especially when he comes in poverty.

Christ urges us to be hospitable. Nowadays hospitality is a very different matter from what it was in the old days when nobody locked their doors. Sadly, those days are gone. Today is the day of locks, bolts, chains, peep holes, alarm systems, dogs … Yet today there is more need than ever for hospitality and friendliness. In the world today there is a lot of loneliness and there are lots of strangers, aliens, and displaced people.

Hospitality to a friend is no big deal. There is no risk involved, and there is every likelihood that the favour will be returned. But hospitality to a stranger is a great thing. You don't owe anything to a stranger, and there is a risk involved.

But Christ calls us to welcome the strangers in our midst. To be hospitable does not mean making them like us. It means accepting them as they are. This enables them to shed their strangeness, and become members of the community.

If Christians get into ghettos where they secure themselves and their property against those they consider as socially inferior to them, what hope is there for the world? Christ calls us to reach out. And the rewards are enormous. He said that even a trivial act of kindness, like giving a cup of cold water, would not go unrewarded. But there are earthly rewards too, and very great ones – the growth of understanding, friendliness, and cooperation, things our neighbourhoods are crying out for.

This is the kind of spring we ourselves can cause to visit our homes and streets, a spring which will banish from our midst the winter of mistrust, fear, and hostility. For the followers of Christ, hospitality is not an optional extra. It is at the very heart of the Gospel. And the ultimate motivation is clear: to welcome the stranger is to welcome Christ himself.

Hospitality is not so much about open doors as about open hearts. There is a risk in having an open heart. One can get hurt. But to open one's heart is to begin to live. To close it is to begin to die.

HOMILY 3 **A cup of cold water**

Jesus said, 'If anyone gives you so much as a cup of cold water, he will most definitely not lose his reward.' To give a cup of cold water is a very small thing. Yet in the desert it could be the difference between life and death. Which shows that a deed doesn't have to be big in order to mean a lot.

When the Irish writer, Oscar Wilde, was sent to prison (for homosexual activities), it was a terrible humiliation for him. He had made a reputation for himself as a fine writer and was regarded as a celebrity as well.

As Wilde was being brought by two policemen from prison to court, a noisy, hostile crowd had gathered. But then a friend of his appeared, who made a simple gesture of friendship and respect that silenced the crowd.

As Wilde passed by, handcuffed and with bowed head, this man raised his hat to him. It was a very small thing, yet it meant a great deal to Wilde at the time. Reflecting on that simple gesture Wilde later wrote:

> Men have gone to heaven for smaller things than that. I do not know to the present moment whether my friend is aware that I was even conscious of his action. It is not a thing for which one can render formal thanks in formal words. I store it in the treasure-house of my heart. I keep it there as a secret debt that I can never possibly repay.
>
> It is embalmed and kept sweet by the myrrh of many tears. When wisdom has been profitless to me, and philosophy barren, and the proverbs and phrases of those who sought to give me consolation as dust and ashes in my mouth, the memory of that lowly silent act of love has unsealed for me all the wells of pity, made the desert blossom like a rose, and brought me out of the bitterness of lonely exile into harmony with the wounded, broken and great heart of the world. (*De Profundis*)

The spirit in which a deed is done, the person to whom it is done, and the circumstances, can magnify a small deed. It's not how much we do that matters, but how much love we put into it.

Few of us are given the chance to perform great deeds. But the chance to give a cup of water can come our way several times in the course of a day. The 'cup of cold water' is a symbol of the small kind deed. Little deeds may not look much, but they can bring peace.

An Australian priest visiting Ireland went into Dublin. That evening he was asked how he found Dublin. He replied, 'Dublin must be one of the few cities in the world where people will hold a door open for you, or will say "Sorry" if they accidentally bump into you, or "Excuse me" if they have to squeeze past you,' was his reply.

The things he referred to were very small in themselves. Yet the accumulation of those little things led him to conclude that Dublin is basically a friendly place. Little flowers may appear to have no scent on their own. But put a bunch of them together and they can fill a room with fragrance.

Deeds don't have to be big in order to be of help and comfort to the person for whom they are done. They just have to have a certain quality. What is this quality? It is warmth. All deeds which come from the heart have this warmth.

PRAYER OF THE FAITHFUL

President: God's love lasts for ever; God's truth is firmly established as the heavens; with trust we pray.

Response: Lord, hear us in your love.

That Christians may give an example to the world by the way they accept the stranger into their midst. [Pause] We pray in faith.

That government leaders may be generous towards refugees and displaced people. [Pause] We pray in faith.

That the homeless may be rescued and find care. [Pause] We pray in faith.

That we may try to give each person we meet some small sign of recognition and hospitality. [Pause] We pray in faith.

That our own special needs may gain God's favour and blessing. [Longer pause] We pray in faith.

President: Lord God whose Son declared that when we welcome another person, we welcome him, grant that the door of our heart always be open. We ask this through the same Christ our Lord.

REFLECTION   **The circle around my life**

Much of our lives is spent in keeping people out.
We have private houses, private clubs, and so on.
Of course there are times when we need to be alone.
Yet there is a sense in which our size as human beings
can be measured by the circles we draw to take other people in: the
    smaller the circle, the smaller the person.
A strong person isn't afraid of people who are different.
A wise person welcomes them.
By shutting other people out we deny ourselves
the riches of other people's experience.
We starve our minds, and harden our hearts.
In the beginning God gave the earth its shape.
He made it round. He included everybody.
So should we. (*Anon.*)

Fourteenth Sunday of the Year
COME TO ME, ALL YOU WHO LABOUR ...

INTRODUCTION AND CONFITEOR

At times all of us find life burdensome. But Jesus invites us to bring our burdens to him and he will give us rest. Let us come to him now in a spirit of love and trust. [Pause]

One of the burdens the Lord relieves us of is the burden of our sins. So let us confess them with humility and confidence.

I confess to almighty God ...

HEADINGS FOR READINGS

First Reading (Zech 9:9-10). The messianic king is portrayed, not as a proud warrior, but as a humble and gentle champion of peace for all peoples.

Second Reading (Rom 8:9.11-13). St Paul contrasts life 'in the spirit' with life 'in the flesh'.

Gospel (Mt 11:25-30). Jesus reveals the Father to those who are 'little', and lightens the burdens of those who are humble.

SCRIPTURE NOTE

The prophet Zechariah foretells the coming of the messianic king who will put an end to war and to establish peace. It was as such a Messiah that Jesus entered Jerusalem before his passion. Matthew sees Jesus as fulfilling this prophecy. Jesus lightens the burdens of the poor and brings peace to the humble. His life is based on his unique relationship with the Father, a relationship which he wants to share with his disciples.

HOMILY 1   **Jesus reveals the Father**

It gives us joy to know an important person. However, to know often simply means to know facts about the person. But to know another person in this way is to have a very shallow knowledge of that person.

To really know means to have a relationship with the person, a relationship based on trust and love. And also to know that we too are known and loved by the person.

In his biography of George Washington, Richard Brookhiser says:

George Washington is with us every day, on our dollar bills and quarters. He looks down on us from Mount Rushmore. In the national capital that bears his name he has the most prominent memorial. More schools, streets and cities bear his name than that of any other American, and historians rank him among the greatest Presidents America has had.

However, the omnipresence of Washington does not translate into familiarity. He is in our textbooks and our wallets, but not in our hearts. The fault is partly Washington's, since he tended to distance himself from the people.

Some see God as distant and remote, not really concerned about us and our sufferings. Worse still, others see God as a judge, or a spy ready to pounce and punish.

Jesus knows the Father and is known by the Father. This fills him with joy. Because Jesus knows the Father he is able to reveal him to others, especially to those who, like children, are open and receptive. Jesus revealed God as a loving, compassionate, forgiving Father. A God who is passionately interested in us. A God whose concern is not to judge and condemn, but to heal and to save.

Many of the so-called wise people rejected Jesus, but the simple people accepted him. The intellectuals had little use for him, but the humble accepted him. Intellectual pride is a dangerous thing. Simple people are often nearer to God than clever people.

Jesus said, 'I bless you, Father, for hiding these things from the learned and the clever and revealing them to mere children.'

Jesus is not condemning intellectual power, but intellectual pride. It is not cleverness that shuts God out; it is pride. And it is not stupidity that enables God to come in; it is humility.

Because of the coming of Jesus we no longer see God as someone remote. We see him as someone who is very close to us, who knows each of us and is concerned about each of us, because we are his children. He is the God especially of the weak, the poor, the overburdened.

When faith is a matter of the head alone, it becomes a cold, intellectual thing. The result is that God remains outside us, a distant, aloof figure. But faith is not just a matter of the head. It is more a matter of the heart. When faith is rooted in the heart, God is seen as close and loving. Then faith becomes a warm relationship with God.

To know God in this way, and to have a close and loving relationship with him, should be a cause of great joy to us. God is like a spring within us from which we can drink and refresh ourselves.

HOMILY 2   **Strength in weakness**

The First Reading pictures a king coming humbly to Zion, riding on a donkey. He is a messenger of peace. This prophecy was fulfilled on Palm Sunday when Jesus rode into Jerusalem, unarmed and defenceless.

Though Jesus carried no weapons, he was not weak. He was strong. He had power over the human heart as he showed when he changed the hearts of people like Mary Magdalen and Zacchaeus. Stalin could make people tremble before him but could not change their hearts.

Jesus says to us, 'Learn of me for I am gentle and humble of heart, and you will find rest for your souls'. Humility and gentleness don't seem to make much sense in the world of today.

Take gentleness. There is a belief that if you want to get on in life, you have to be hard, because if you're gentle, people will walk all over you. Gentleness tends to be equated with timidity, passivity, and weakness.

Gentleness is not a form of weakness. It is a form of strength. Nothing is so strong as gentleness and noting so gentle as real strength. By 'gentle' we don't mean a timid little person who wouldn't say boo to a goose. It takes a strong, self-confident person to be gentle.

Gentleness is one of the most necessary qualities in life. Think of the gentleness required in the hands of a mother or a surgeon. Deep down we all pine for gentleness, and we can't open up and grow without it. 'A gentle person treads lightly, listens carefully, looks tenderly, and touches with reverence.' (Henri Nouwen). A gentle person knows that healing and growth result from nurturing not forcing.

The lust for power is rooted in weakness rather than strength. Only the weak measure their worth by the number of people they can dominate. Weaklings puff themselves up and try to act strong; tough people hide their vulnerabilities.

There was no harshness in Jesus. His approach was very gentle. He didn't force himself on people. He didn't try to control them or to impose his will on them. He respected their freedom. The people with greatest influence over others have no need to control those they influence.

And take humility. In today's competitive world you are told to project yourself if you want to go places. Humility is seen as weakness. Humility is not a form of weakness. It is a from of strength. Humility is the foundation on which to build the house of the spirit. Humility does not involve self-depreciation. Humility is the grateful recognition of our goodness, but acknowledging that this goodness is a gift from God.

To the gentle and humble Jesus promises peace of soul. It is because we know so little about being gentle with one another, that we have so much trouble in our homes and in the world. We want to dominate others. It is because we know so little about humility, that we have so little peace within ourselves and with others. Proud and arrogant people do not bring peace. They spread confusion and unrest by projecting onto others their own anger and frustrations. Humble people disarm others and bring out the best in them.

Those who are proud and insensitive make life burdensome for themselves and for others. Those who are gentle and humble make life less burdensome for themselves and others.

St Seraphim says, 'Acquire inner peace, and a multitude of people will find salvation near you'.

HOMILY 3   **Lightening burdens**

'Come to me, all you who labour and are overburdened, and I will give you rest.' These are among the loveliest words in the Gospel.

Life can be very burdensome for some people. There are all kinds of burdens – worry, responsibility, disappointments, hurts, bitterness, guilt, illness, unemployment, a difficult relationship, addiction …

Today those who do menial jobs are poorly paid and generally taken for granted. They are valued, not for themselves, but only for the service they provide. They are noticed only when they are missing.

The Irish writer, John McGahern, tells of an incident which happened when he was writer in residence at Trinity College, Dublin. A woman came in one day a week to clean his room. In less than an hour she'd have everything shining and in its proper place. She was a charming woman and often they talked as she cleaned. She told him how she waited each morning for the private bus at six o'clock that took the cleaners to Trinity, and that she was able to be home in time to cook the family dinner.

Of the professor who occupied the room before McGahern she said, 'I cleaned his room for fourteen years, and he never once spoke to me. I used to say "Good morning" at first, but after a while I didn't say anything. They say he's one of the cleverest men in the whole university, but I say he has the manners of a bowsie.'

How a little sensitivity, or a word of appreciation, would help to make a heavy burden light. It makes the world of difference when people are recognised, and treated with kindness and respect.

The Scribes and Pharisees lived a privileged existence. They had no understanding of what life was like for the ordinary people. With their emphasis on the exact observance of the Law, and their multiplication of rules and regulations, they placed an impossible burden on the people. They had little sympathy for those who found this burden too much to bear.

During the years he spent at Nazareth, Jesus lived among the ordinary people. For many of those years he lived the life of a working man. He knew at first-hand the struggles, difficulties and frustrations ordinary people had to endure. He was aware of the heavy burdens life placed on their shoulders.

Consequently, he felt for the ordinary people and wanted to lighten their burdens. People came to him from all quarters with their burdens of sickness and misery. All of them had their burdens lightened as a result of meeting him. His mere presence could bring peace to an anguished soul.

Regarding his own burden he said, 'My yoke is easy and my burden is light.' How could he, who took on himself the burdens of so many, say that? Because he carried his burden with love. Only love can make a heavy burden seem light. A woman who is deprived of food for a day can barely last out till the end of it. But a mother who gives up food for a day so that her children may have something to eat, hardly notices it.

Some of our burdens may be baggage which we could and should let go of. There is a Zen story about an old man going on a spiritual journey with a heavy bag on his back. On his deathbed he passes on the bag to his disciple. When the disciple opens the bag he finds that it is empty. Yet he wonders why it weighed so much. And the old man says, 'It is the weight of everything in my life that I did not need to carry.'

Religion should not make life more burdensome. If Jesus placed any burden on us at all, it was that of loving one another. But if we have love, that is no burden at all. He doesn't take our burdens from us, but gives us the strength to carry them. While faith makes all things possible, love makes all things easy.

A STORY

It is said that old people are not lonely because they have no one to share their burden. They are lonely because they have only their own burden to bear. Perhaps the same is true of others.

An eighty-five-year-old woman was being interviewed on her birthday. 'What advice would you have for people your age?' the reporter asked.

'Well,' said the old woman, 'at our age it is very important to keep using all our potential; otherwise it dries up. It is important to be with people, and, if it is at all possible, to earn one's living through service. That's what keeps us alive and well.'

'May I ask what exactly you do for a living at your age?'

'I look after an old lady in my neighbourhood,' she replied.

The strong should share the burdens of the weak. However, we shouldn't burden ourselves beyond the limit of grace, humanity and survival. Anyone of us can bear the burdens of only a few.

PRAYER OF THE FAITHFUL 1

President: As people in whom the Spirit of God has made his home, let us pray.

Response: Lord, teach us your ways.

Reader(s): For the Church: that it may lighten the burdens of its members by giving them encouragement and support. [Pause] We pray to the Lord.

For the disciples of Jesus: that they may cultivate the virtues of gentleness and humility. [Pause] We pray to the Lord.

For government leaders: that they may lighten the burdens of the poor and the disadvantaged. [Pause] We pray to the Lord.

For all those who are bothered by troubles and anxieties: that they may find peace of mind. [Pause] We pray to the Lord.

For each other: that we may be compassionate and helpful towards those who are finding life difficult. [Pause] We pray to the Lord.

For our own special needs. [Longer pause] We pray to the Lord.

President: God of love and mercy, grant us in all our tasks your help, in all our doubts your guidance, in all our weaknesses your strength, in all our sorrows your consolation, and in all our dangers your protection. We ask this through Christ our Lord.

PRAYER OF THE FAITHFUL 2

President: Let us pray to the God who is faithful in all his works and compassionate to all his creatures.

Response: Lord, hear our prayer.

Reader{s): For those who are burdened with the responsibility of office.

For those who are burdened with hardship.

For those who are burdened with anxiety.

For those who are burdened with loneliness.

For those who are burdened with a handicap.

For those who are burdened with failure.

For those who are burdened with bitterness.

For those who are burdened with guilt.

For those who are burdened with grief.

For those who are burdened with illness.

For those who are burdened with old age and infirmity.

For those who are burdened with the feeling that they are a burden to others.

For our own special needs.

President: God of love and mercy, grant us in all our tasks your help, in all our doubts your guidance, in all our weaknesses your strength, in all our sorrows your consolation, and in all our dangers your protection. We ask this through Christ our Lord.

REFLECTION   **Come to me**

The Lord said to me, 'Come to me.' But I said, 'I'm not worthy.'

'Come to me,' he repeated. And I said, 'I'm afraid.'

'Come to me.' 'I'm too proud.'

'Come to me.' 'But I've no appointment.'

'Come to me.' 'But I can't afford the time right now.'

'Come to me.' With that I fell silent.

Then he said,

'Come … sit down … take the load off your feet.

'Sit here as in the shade of a tree.

'Refresh yourself as at a running stream.

'Here you will find rest. Here you will find peace.

'And your yoke will become easy, and your burden light.'

Fifteenth Sunday of the Year
THE SOWER

INTRODUCTION AND CONFITEOR

God speaks his word to us in many ways. Jesus compared the word of God to a seed, a seed which can make our lives fruitful. However, if a seed is to produce a harvest it must be planted in good soil. What kind of soil do we offer God's word? [Pause]

If our lives are barren it can only mean that we have not allowed God's word to take root in our hearts. But God doesn't given up on us.

Lord Jesus, you continue to sow the seed of your word in our minds and hearts. Lord, have mercy.

You wait patiently for us to accept your word. Christ, have mercy.

When we accept your word and act on it, you make our lives fruitful. Lord, have mercy.

HEADINGS FOR READINGS

First Reading (Is 55:10-11). God cares for the earth by sending rain to make it fruitful. He cares for us by sending us his word.

Second Reading (Rom 8:18-23). The glory which awaits us in the next life far outweighs anything we could suffer in this life.

Gospel (Mt 13:1-23). Jesus compares the word of God to a seed falling into the ground. *(Shorter form recommended.)*

SCRIPTURE NOTE

On the face of it, it might seem from today's Gospel that Jesus taught in parables in order to prevent his hearers from understanding. But such a purpose is completely alien to the character of Jesus. Jesus used parables as an effective way of teaching. Those who were open to him received more. Those who had closed their minds against him received less. The fault lay not with Jesus but with the receiver.

The early Church adapted the parables to the new situation in which they found themselves. The shorter form is most likely the original form of the parable. The explanation reflects the missionary experience of the early Church. It accounts for the relative failure of the message of Jesus. The shallow mind, the hard heart, worldly preoccupations, persecution – these are precisely the obstacles that have frustrated the growth of faith.

As the First Reading suggests, the rain always produces positive results; eventually somewhere the earth responds and becomes fruitful. So God persists with his word until he gets a response.

HOMILY 1   **He taught them in parables**

The Gospels are littered with parables. This was Jesus' favourite method of teaching. Among the rabbis at the time of Jesus there was an attitude almost of reverence towards the parable. So when Jesus adopted this method of teaching he was following a tradition. But why teach in parables?

Once there was a famous rabbi who loved to illustrate a truth by means of a story. One day his students asked him why he adopted this approach. He replied thus: 'The best way to answer your question is through a story.

'There was a time when Truth went around naked and unadorned. But the people shied away from him, and gave him no welcome. So Truth wandered through the land, rebuffed and unwanted.

'One day, very disconsolate, he met Story strolling along happily dressed in a multi-coloured robe.

'"Truth, why are you so sad?" Story asked.

'"I'm sad because I am so old and ugly that everybody avoids me," Truth replied.

'"Nonsense!" laughed Story. "That is not why people avoid you. Here, borrow my robe, and see what happens."

'So Truth donned Story's multi-coloured robe, and lo, everywhere he went, he was welcomed.'

And the rabbi concluded, 'The fact is, people are unable to face the naked Truth; they much prefer the Truth disguised.'

Sometimes the truth can be so painful that we are not able to take it straight. We have to dress it up. We have to adorn it. A story makes a bitter truth more palatable.

A story has another great advantage. Just as a penny candle can help a searcher to find a gold coin or a priceless pearl, so a short parable can contain a great truth and enable us to penetrate to the heart of that truth.

What is Jesus saying to us in his short parable of the sower?

The word of God is to the human heart what a seed is to the earth. Just as soil is barren without seed, so our lives are barren without the word of God. The Word of God is a pure and lasting fount of spiritual life.

The Church has always venerated the Sacred Scriptures as it venerated the Body of Christ in Holy Communion. In the Eucharist it offers us from the one table the Word of God and the Body of Christ.

Through his word God is continually calling us to a better and more fruitful life. Happy those who make the voice of God the most important voice in their lives. God doesn't speak to us like a dictator to his subjects. He speaks to us as a Father speaks to his children. His word is as gentle, as weak, as defenceless as a seed falling into the soil. Yet that word is more effective than the word of the most powerful dictator – it can change people's hearts.

God doesn't speak to us only in the Sacred Scriptures. He also speaks to us through the events of our lives. But it is the words of scripture that help us to interpret what God is saying to us in those events. We will not be judged by results but only by the efforts we have made.

Life is only a kind of sowing time, the harvest is not here. *(Van Gogh)*

HOMILY 2   **Importance of the word**

How many words were spoken to us when we were young. How many seeds were dropped into the soil of our minds and hearts during the springtime of our lives. Those words came from our parents and from many others. We heard words of greeting and welcome, words of encouragement and affirmation, words of advice and guidance, words of correction and chastisement, words of warning and caution, words of comfort and consolation.

At the time we may not have appreciated those words, but we needed to hear them. Only God knows how many of those words took root in our lives. But one thing is clear: our lives would be immeasurably poorer without the sowing of all those words.

As adults we still need the sowing of the word. Pity those people who hear nothing but words of criticism and blame. Pity those who have to survive on a diet of silence. But happy those who hear words of encouragement, love and peace.

But human words, no matter how necessary, will never fully nourish us. We need the word of God. The word of God gives us guidance in times of doubt, reassurance in times of difficulty, comfort in times of sorrow, correction in times of foolishness, challenge in times of laziness and sloth, warning in times of danger, and hope in times of despair.

God's word is never a negative word. It is a word spoken in love. Just as food nourishes the body, so the word of God nourishes the mind, the heart, and the spirit. God speaks to us in the most hidden parts of our being.

But there are many other voices vying for our attention. In fact, every day we are subjected to a veritable blizzard of words. There has never been so much talk on radio and television. How then can we hear or even recognise God's quiet word in the midst of this din? We can do so only by creating a little bit of stillness and quietness within us.

It's not enough merely to remember the word; we have to do it. One of the ways of telling a false diamond from a true one is by means of the light. In the case of a false diamond, the light goes straight through the stone. In the case of a true one, the light remains inside it, bringing it to life and setting it on fire.

With some people, the word of God goes in and comes straight back out. They are mere hearers of the word. But those who 'keep the word', that is, who act on it, are transformed by it.

HOMILY 3   **The word is like a seed**

A seed is a marvellous thing – it can make barren ground fruitful. But a seed is an extremely weak and vulnerable thing. It depends entirely on the kind of soil in which it is sown. If the soil is lacking, the seed will come to nothing; if the soil is good, it will produce a rich harvest.

So it is with a word. A word is a powerful thing. It can comfort, inspire, teach, correct, challenge, change a life … or it can come to nothing. It is completely dependent on the attitude of the one who hears it.

Some seed fell on a hard path where it had no chance of putting down roots. Exposed to full view, it was eaten up by the birds.

So it is with words that are spoken to people with closed minds . Prejudice closes a person's mind. So does pride – the case of the person who thinks he knows it all. So does fear – fear of new truth, or fear of hearing a disturbing truth. Then some people seem to be unteachable. Trying to get through to them is like knocking your head against a wall. There are none so deaf as those who will not hear.

Some fell on stony ground. It took root quickly, but soon withered away because of lack of soil and moisture.

Some hear the word and receive it with enthusiasm, but when the carrying out of it becomes difficult, their enthusiasm wanes and they quickly abandon it. The lives of some people are littered with things started but never finished.

Some seed fell into ground where weeds and thorns lay in wait. It got off to a good start. But then the weeds appeared, and the seed got smothered.

People may receive the word of God, but there are so many other interests in their lives that the most important thing gets crowded out. People are too busy to pray. People are so involved in their careers that they have no time or energy left for the things of the spirit.

Finally some seed fell on good soil, where it put down deep roots, found nourishment and produced a harvest. So there are people who hear the word, understand it, and then act on it. Their lives are enriched by it.

God's word comforts, guides, inspires and challenges us in turn. It is like precious seed. The sower sowed the seed haphazardly: on the path, on the rocks, among the thorns, and on good ground. You might say that he was wasteful and foolish. But there is another way of looking at this. He was extremely generous, even prodigal with the seed. He wanted to give every part of the field a chance to produce something.

God keeps on sowing his word in our hearts even though he knows that much of what he sows will be eaten by the birds, or fall on rocks or among thorns.

In nature the seed has only a short growing season in the early part of the year. Not so with that seed which is the word of God. Growth can come at any stage in a person's life.

Some grains of wheat were found in the tomb of one of the kings of ancient Egypt. Someone planted and watered them. To the amazement of everyone, the grains came to life and began to grow, after five thousand years lying in a tomb.

The seed of God's word, once dropped into the human heart, never dies. It's never too late to act on the word of God.

A word is dead when it is said, some say.
I say it just begins to live that day. *(Emily Dickinson)*

A STORY

Amadeus was a famous violin teacher. He knew his music and had a knack of being able to bring out the best in his pupils. Once four pupils were sent to him. He saw that each of them had talent and this excited him. It was a great opportunity for them.

The first was Mary. She had only just started her music lessons when her friends began to pester her. They would come knocking at her door, begging her to come out to play. After a while she gave in, and that was the end of her music lessons. Amadeus was sorry to see her go.

The second was John. The idea to take music lessons hadn't come from him but from his parents. His heart wasn't in it. Still, for a while, it was exciting to hear the sound of the violin. But soon the novelty wore off. It was just too much hard work. He gave it up. And Amadeus was sorry to see him go.

The third pupil was James. He was multi-talented. He particularly liked athletics and football but was anxious to cultivate all his interests. For a while he succeeded. But eventually something had to suffer. It was the music lessons. First he began to fall behind, then to neglect them, and finally he dropped them altogether. Amadeus was sad to see another of his pupils drop out.

The fourth was Anne. She was by no means the best of the four, but she really wanted to succeed. Right from the start, she put her heart and soul into it. Even so, there were times when practising got boring, and she would have preferred to be out playing with her friends. But she stuck to her lessons, and in the end graduated with first class honours. Amadeus was delighted for her.

The word of God comes to us as a friend. It is a sign of God's love for us. Through his word God calls us to a fuller and more fruitful life. Its purpose is to enrich us, and a great enrichment does result when a person hears the word and acts on it. If we refuse to receive the word, or if we receive it but don't act on it, we are the losers.

PRAYER OF THE FAITHFUL

President: Let us pray that the word of God may take root in our hearts and bear fruit in our lives.

Response: Lord, hear our prayer.

Reader(s): For the Church: that it may continue to proclaim the word of God to the world. [Pause] Let us pray to the Lord.

For world leaders: that they may seek the help and guidance of God in all their deliberations. [Pause] Let us pray to the Lord.

For those who are building their lives on values that are contrary to those of the Gospel. [Pause] Let us pray to the Lord.

For each other: that we may take care of the life of the Spirit within us, and not allow it to be choked by materialism and worldly concerns. [Pause] Let us pray to the Lord.

For our own needs. [Longer pause] Let us pray to the Lord.

President: Lord, grant that what we have said with our lips, we may believe with our hearts, and practise with our lives. We ask this through Christ our Lord.

REFLECTION   **Receiving the word**

The word of God is to the human heart
what a seed is to the earth.
However, just as a seed needs soil,
so the word needs a receptive heart.
The earth responds to the rain and sun
so that even the desert blooms.
But the arid human heart has the power to resist
so that it remains barren.
Lord, soften our hearts with your grace,
open them with your gentle love,
so that the precious seed of your word
may take root in our hearts,
and bear fruit in our lives.

Sixteenth Sunday of the Year
WEEDS AMONG THE WHEAT

INTRODUCTION AND CONFITEOR

We go to church, not because we are saints, but because we are sinners, sinners who know that we are sinners, but who are willing to strive for something better. And God is patient with us, and lenient in his judgements. [Pause]

Lord, you are good and forgiving, full of love to all who call on you. Lord, have mercy.

Lord, you are merciful and gracious, slow to anger, abounding in kindness and fidelity. Christ, have mercy.

Lord, show us your way to walk in your truth. Lord, have mercy.

HEADINGS FOR READINGS

First Reading (Wis 12:13.16-19). God has both the knowledge and the power to root out evil people if he so desired. But this reading talks about his leniency, and how we ought to imitate it.

Second Reading (Rom 8:26-27). The Holy Spirit helps us to pray when we can't find the words to express what is on our minds.

Gospel (Mt 13:24-43). The Church, and indeed the world, is like a field in which wheat and weeds grow side by side until they are separated at the harvest time. *(Short form recommended. The parable of the mustard seed recurs in Year B, Eleventh Sunday, and is dealt with there.)*

SCRIPTURE NOTE

Christ's parable originally addressed the problem of sinners in the Kingdom of God. The Pharisees believed that the Kingdom was for saints only; sinners therefore should be ruthlessly weeded out. But Christ didn't agree, as this parable shows. The main point of the parable is clear: up to the last judgement, the Kingdom will be a mixed bag of good and evil.

Later the parable was applied to the problem of sinners in the Church. Like the Kingdom, the Church is also a mixed bag. It must not play God by trying to purify itself completely through purges and inquisitions. The definitive separation must be left to the last judgement. In the meantime the Church must be patient; it must preach repentance and practice leniency. Mercy and leniency are an expression not of weakness but of strength.

HOMILY 1   **Saints and sinners in the Church**

There have always been two views of the Church – one exclusive, the other inclusive. The exclusive view holds that the Church is for good people, for the fully committed. In the inclusive view, the Church must be open to all, to the hot, the cold and the lukewarm, to saints and sinners.

For some, the presence of sinners in the Church is a cause of scandal. If they had their way, only saints would be admitted. (The emergence of paedophiles among the clergy has thrown the Church into turmoil in recent times.)

The issue of sinners in the Church was a big one for the early Church too. So how did they approach it? Some were for weeding sinners out. But others turned to the example of Jesus for guidance.

First of all, they had his practice to guide them. Not only did he not exclude sinners, he welcomed them. He declared that he had come, not to call the just, but sinners to repentance. Then they had his teaching to guide them. The parable about the field in which wheat and weeds grow together until the harvest was a response to this very question.

Human beings are complex. They can't be divided into the good and the bad, as though they were two completely separate classes of people. There is no line you can draw which would neatly separate the good from the bad. Any such line would go right through each human heart, for there is good and evil in every heart.

All of us are a mixture of good and bad. The people we call 'good' may have terrible things in them – mad moods of recklessness, assertion, jealousy, sin. And so-called 'bad' people may have in them sorrow, repentance, pity, sacrifice.

So what should we do? As far as ourselves are concerned, the best thing we can do is take a good look into our own field. If we find some weeds there, as no doubt we will, there is no law against trying to rid ourselves of them. If we try to do so, we will discover what a painful process this is.

As far as others are concerned, we should try to act towards them as Jesus acted. Isn't it strange that he who had no trace of weed in him could be so understanding towards those who failed to measure up? Why didn't he weed out Judas? And why didn't he weed out Peter? He saw the weeds in Peter's life, but he saw the wheat too. He knew that with encouragement the wheat would prevail. And it did.

The Church can do no better than imitate its Founder. It has to be big enough and loving enough to hold sinners in the fold. If it did not do so, it would not be the Church of Christ.

The suggestion to root out the weeds would seem to make a lot of sense, and indeed it has often been tried. Many governments have tried it in fighting terrorists. Though attractive, it is not a Christian solution, or even a humane one.

A Church that admitted only saints would make about as much sense as a hospital that admitted only people who are well, or a repair shop that accepted only things that are whole. The Church is not a museum for saints, but a school for sinners.

The Church is a temple with a hundred gates, and pilgrims enter from every angle. Through every door, and from all kinds of paths, we enter the house of God on a Sunday morning. Ours is not a Church for those who feel good, but for those who know they are not.

God is a lot more tolerant than we are. Today's First Reading says of God, 'You are lenient to all … mild in your judgement … you govern with great lenience.'

While we distinguish clearly between good and evil, we must aim at being as understanding and tolerant as God is. The time for judgement is not yet. The Kingdom of God is still at the growing stage. Now is the time for conversion. People can change. We can change.

HOMILY 2   **Weeds among the wheat**

The farmer in Jesus' story planted good seed in his field and expected a bumper harvest. Soon a host of sturdy green shoots sprang up, covering the field from end to end. It looked as if his expectations would be fulfilled.

But then one morning he discovered weeds growing among the young shoots of wheat. Not just an odd weed here and there, but weeds everywhere. He got a terrible shock. He was bitterly disappointed. When he looked at the field now, all he could see were the weeds. The wheat seemed to have disappeared.

Sooner or later the weeds appear in our field – a friend betrays us, a partner disappoints us or proves unfaithful … We are shocked and hurt at the appearance of evil. The badness of bad people we expect, and can forearm ourselves against it. But the badness of good people takes us by surprise, and hurts all the more. For a while at least, we tend to see everything as bad – we become very negative.

What could the farmer do? The obvious answer was to pull the weeds up. However, this proved impossible. They were growing so close to the stalks of wheat that he could not uproot them without uprooting the wheat as well.

So what did he do? Well, for one thing he calmed down. This enabled him to see things in better perspective. True, there were some weeds in his precious field. But there was wheat there too, wheat that was just as green and vibrant as ever. He would have to be humble and patient. He would have to work hard on the wheat, coaxing and encouraging it in the hope that it would outgrow the weeds.

We mustn't despair. The world is a mixture of light and darkness, good and evil. Wheat and weeds grow side by side in the same person, indeed, in ourselves. But all is not lost – there is good there too. No one understood this better than Jesus. Even in the small garden (the twelve apostles) which he tended carefully for three years, the weeds persisted, yet he didn't write it off.

We have to work on the good. But what about the evil? Evil has to be resisted. But we have to do so in such a way that we not do further evil in the process. Evil can be overcome only by good.

So the farmer set to work. It wasn't easy. But he tried to concentrate on the wheat. This proved a great help. When he looked closely at it he noticed that it was by reaching and straining upwards that it grew. He took heart from this because it meant that by making the wheat struggle harder, the weeds were actually having a beneficial effect on the crop.

Because of the presence of evil we have to struggle. But it is through struggle that we grow. Struggle awakens all that is good and precious within us. Indeed, the presence of evil could even be said to be necessary. Unless we had to make a choice between good and evil no virtue would be possible.

On harvest day the farmer separated the weeds from the wheat. He reaped a fine harvest. Even though it fell short of the hundred per cent he had hoped for, the quality was excellent. And for some strange reason, he got more satisfaction from reaping that harvest than from any other. There is more joy when the victory is hard-won.

The parable is both realistic and optimistic. In the end good triumphs. Truth and goodness are invincible.

HOMILY 3   **Flawed goodness**

We have a tendency to divide people into two categories: saints and sinners. However, this division is quite unreal. People are not so easily categorised. Human beings are complex, and we find things that are at odds with one another coexisting in the same human being.

Many people were inspired by the story of Oskar Schindler, the German industrialist, who saved over a thousand Polish Jews from the concentration camps. One of the people he saved said of him, 'He was our father, our mother, our only hope. He never let us down.' Yet many who saw the film *Schindler's List* were surprised, if not quite put off, by his vices. He was a man endowed with all the human vices. Hence, he constitutes something of a moral puzzle.

Schindler certainly was no saint. In fact, he was riddled with contradictions. Unfaithful to his wife, he certainly knew how to enjoy the so-called good life – cigars, drink, women … He was a Catholic, but in name only. He was also a member of the Nazi party, and his avowed aim was to end the war with 'two trunks full of money'. He exploited the Jews as a source of cheap labour.

But there was another and better side to him, and in spite of his lapses, he always returned to that better side. There was basic goodness about him. As the war went on he became appalled at the horrors of 'the final solution'. At considerable personal risk (he was twice arrested by the Nazis), he protected his workers from the death camps, thereby showing that he was undoubtedly a courageous man.

But Schindler was no angel. He was a mere human being, an essentially good human being, even though his goodness was seriously flawed. We wonder what he might have achieved had he not been so divided. And the Nazis, for all the horrific things they did, weren't totally evil either. They were not devils incarnate. They too were human beings, though bad human beings.

Some people don't seem to have any understanding of the divided nature of each human being – of the coexistence in every person of good and evil, strength and weakness, loyalty and betrayal ... As soon as they discover a weakness in someone, they write the person off. Their hero must be perfect. As soon as a flaw or a crack appears, they lose faith in him.

But things are not that simple. Human beings are complex – and that includes each of us. We are an extraordinary mixture of good and bad. Moreover, the roots of good are so entwined with the roots of evil that one can't be pulled up one without pulling up the other.

We must learn to be patient and lenient, towards ourselves in the first place. We must be hospitable towards all that we are. We must acknowledge the dark side of ourselves, without conceding victory to it. We must struggle on in spite of the weeds, confident that with God's help, the good will finally triumph. It is through struggle that we grow, provided we don't throw the towel in.

And we must then be lenient towards others. Even though we see only part of a person's life we tend to rush to judgement. We are two quick to classify people, and once we have classified them as evil, for them there is no redemption. Only God has the right and the knowledge to judge; yet God is patient and tolerant.

By concentrating on people's vices, we become blind to their virtues. We are too eager to voice our criticisms, but reluctant to give a single word of encouragement, and in this way we bar every road to improvement. Therefore, let us not knock others. Let us seek the good in everyone, reveal it, bring it out.

A person will be judged, not by a single act or stage in his life, but by his whole life. That is why judgement can't come until the end. A man may make a great mistake, but by the grace of God redeem himself. Of what else but flawed creatures does God make saints?

Attempts to hide the streakiness of our holy people, though sometimes successful, are always dishonest (*Anthony de Mello*).

PRAYER OF THE FAITHFUL

President: Let us pray to the Lord who is abounding in love and truth.
Response: Lord, hear us in your love.
Reader(s): For all Christians: that they may strive to imitate the compassion and understanding of Christ. [Pause] We pray in faith.

For all those in positions of authority: that they may show wisdom and understanding in the exercise of their authority. [Pause] We pray in faith.

For all those who have been uprooted as a result of bigotry or intolerance. [Pause] We pray in faith.

For prisoners; that they may not see themselves as worthless or evil. [Pause] We pray in faith.

For those who have been the victims of violence: that they may not allow themselves to be poisoned by bitterness. [Pause] We pray in faith.

For all here present: that we may be able to see and develop the good that is in ourselves, and in other people. [Pause] We pray in faith.

For our own special needs. [Longer pause] We pray in faith.

President: Heavenly Father, we are like seeds planted by you in the same field. Together we soak in the sun, together we sway in the wind. Grant that we may help one another to grow towards what you have called us to be. We ask this through Christ our Lord.

REFLECTION 1   **A harvest prayer**

On the day of the harvest the straw is set aside,
the chaff is blown away by the wind,
and the weeds are consigned to the flames.
But the wheat, like sacks of gold, is gathered into the barn.
Lord, on the day of death,
the harvest of my life will be poured out before you,
wheat and chaff and weeds together.
Let your wise hand sift through it;
then keep what is worth keeping,
and with the breath of your kindness, blow the rest away.

REFLECTION 2   **Sow good seed**

In general we reap what we sow.
We can't expect to reap good is we have sown evil.
We must sow peace if we do not want reap conflict.

[247]

We must sow loyalty if we not want to reap betrayal.
We must sow honesty if we do not want to reap deceit.
Even though we have no absolute guarantee
that what we sow will always fall on good ground,
or that someone else may not come along
and sow contrary seed, nevertheless,
if we are careful to sow good seeds
we can, within reason, trust our expectations
because nature has shown
that if what is planted bears fruit at all,
it will yield more of itself.
So, let us sow good seed.

REFLECTION 3   **The divided heart**

Reflecting on the years he spent in labour camps, Alexander Solzhenitsyn has this to say:

> I learnt one great lesson from my years in prison camps.
> I learnt how a person becomes evil and how he becomes good.
> Gradually I came to realise
> that the line which separates good from evil
> passes not between states,
> or between classes, or between political parties,
> but right through every human heart.
> Even in hearts that are overwhelmed by evil,
> one small bridgehead of good is retained.
> And in the best of all hearts,
> there remains an unuprooted small corner of evil.
> (*Gulag Archipelago*, volume 2)

Seventeenth Sunday of the Year
WISDOM

INTRODUCTION AND CONFITEOR

The theme of wisdom dominates today's liturgy. Wisdom is a priceless thing and is something we all need. All of us act foolishly at times. [Pause]

Let us now confess our sins and ask pardon from God and from one another.

I confess to almighty God ...

HEADINGS FOR READINGS

First Reading (1 Kgs 3:5.7-12). Told by God that he could have any gift he wanted, Solomon chose the gift of wisdom.

Second Reading (Rom 8:28-30). Those who love God can turn everything to their spiritual advantage.

Gospel (Mt 13:44-52). What God offers us is so precious that it is worth everything we have.

SCRIPTURE NOTE

The parables of the treasure and the pearl have the same message: The kingdom of heaven is worth investing everything we have to acquire it. But we need the wisdom that comes from God to see this.

The parable of the net has the same message as that of the wheat and the weeds. In its present stage the kingdom contains both good and bad things. Only at the final judgement will they be separated.

HOMILY 1   **The search**

Since the dawn of time people have been looking for treasure. In bygone days they searched in the fields, in the hills, under the sea ... If only they could find gold or diamonds or pearls they would be happy. Today people are still looking for treasure. Except now they look for it in the lottery, the casino, the stock market ... If only they could hit the jackpot, all their troubles would be over.

In one way or another, all of us are treasure-hunters. All of us are looking for something that will make us completely happy. There is nothing wrong with this. If we were happy, then the artist would not be painting, nor would the writer be writing. Christ encourages us in our searching as the two stories in today's Gospel show.

Christ loved searchers. He had sympathy for those who were looking, even if they were looking in the wrong places and for the wrong things. He understood their hunger and thirst. He was able to point them in the right direction. But he could do nothing for the smug and the satisfied.

Christ compared the Kingdom of God to a rare pearl or a priceless treasure. In other words, the Kingdom is worth everything we have. Those who find it are truly fortunate. Even if in the eyes of the world they appear foolish and poor, in the eyes of God they are wise and rich.

The Kingdom of God is a very simple concept. It means to know that one is a child of God, with a divine dignity and an eternal destiny. It means to know the meaning of life, and how to live it.

Our chief task in life is not to be successful or even to be fulfilled. It is to live properly. No one can be happy who misses the main purpose of life. The only question that really matters is how best to live in this world.

Those who find the answer to this question have found the pearl.

The pearl of great price is not an illusion. The parable underlines the unrestrained joy of the one who finds the pearl. When a sense of the presence of God, and a certainty about his love for us, suddenly bursts upon us, that is something wonderful. It brings peace to the heart, joy to the mind, and beauty to life. Happy those who taste this joy even sporadically. But happier still are those for whom it is the reality in which they live.

To taste the joy of the Kingdom involves a letting go of all other things. Not in the sense that we have to give them up entirely – we still need a certain amount of them to live. What we have to do is let go of our dependence on them, of the way we make them the be-all and the end-all of our lives.

Life is unintelligible and unbearable without God. A close relationship with God is a real treasure. It gives us a sense of who we are, and where we're going. Only God can give us what we are looking for. If we find God, we find all.

To have faith is not to have all the answers. It doesn't mean all the work is done for us. The opposite would be nearer the truth. Faith commits us to a life of discovering, searching and yearning.

It's not only in holy places such as churches, or only on religious occasions, that we find God and feel close to him. In Jesus' story it was while the man was going about his daily task (of digging) that he found the treasure. The treasure we look for is hidden in the ground on which we stand.

Those who belong to the kingdom of God will taste real joy even here. But that joy is only a foretaste of what they will experience hereafter, when they will come into full possession of the kingdom.

HOMILY 2   **The pearl of wisdom**

Wisdom is the most precious gift a person can have. It is a real treasure. Without it all other things are useless because we won't know how to use them. On being told that he could have anything he wanted from God, Solomon asked for the gift of wisdom. God was pleased with his request and granted it to him.

However, this doesn't mean that wisdom was handed to him on a plate, so to speak. That does not and cannot happen. Wisdom is not acquired overnight. If acquired at all, it is acquired gradually and often painfully. It is the task of a lifetime. Wisdom is like dew; it comes to us in tiny droplets without our knowing it.

However, there can be experiences which enable us to take a giant step forward. Sometimes it takes some kind of a crisis to teach a person a little wisdom. Then the words of St Paul come true, namely, that in his mercy

God can make all things work for our benefit. (Second Reading)

Once there was a teacher who desired to make progress in his career and to climb the social ladder. He worked very hard. In fact, his work was his life. He put his best hours and his best efforts into it. He had little time to appreciate his family, and even less for the enjoyment of life. It was clear to everyone where his treasure was.

But then he had a heart attack. He was taken to hospital where he lay for days, drifting in and out of consciousness, and not knowing whether he would live or die. During moments of lucidity he saw these shadowy figures by his bedside. One day those figures came into focus and he immediately recognised them. They were his wife and children who visited his faithfully every day and spent hours at his bedside.

In that moment he saw where his true treasure lay – it lay in his family, his home, in the gift of life, and of course in God. He saw how foolish he had been up to now. And he prayed with all his heart: 'Lord, give me back my life, and I'll be happy.' And he resolved that if he got well, he would turn his priorities upside down.

He made a full recovery. The day he walked out of hospital he was deliriously happy. Everything had been given back to him. Through that painful experience he acquired much wisdom. Prior to this, he was completely focused on himself and his career. Now he decided to open himself to others and to work for them. And he was happier than he had ever been in his life.

All of us are searchers and treasure-hunters in the sense that we are looking for happiness. The goal is legitimate, but it may be that (like that teacher) we are looking in the wrong place. Jesus said, 'Where your treasure is, there will your heart be too.' So, if we want to know what our treasure is, all we have to do is ask ourselves where our heart is. What is it that we love, that we pursue with all our hearts? There lies our treasure.

Of course, we may try to have it both ways – to keep friends with God and with mammon. However, what we are looking for cannot be found in material things. Riches bring anxiety; wisdom brings peace of mind.

The wisdom we are talking about here is not the same as worldly wisdom. It is something deeper and very much more precious. It means knowing what is truly important in life. It means being able to see life from God's point of view, and being able to live the way God wants us to live. If we don't have that, then no matter how many possessions we have, or how successful we are, we will not be happy.

Wisdom is not the same thing as knowledge. Knowledge is something we have; wisdom is something we are. Unlike knowledge which is acquired through hard work, wisdom is a gift of God. Through the gift of wisdom God communicates to us the meaning of life, and the grandeur of our destiny, which is to be with God.

Wisdom is the pearl of great price. Once found no one can rob us of it.

HOMILY 3 **God turns everything to our good**

It's not possible to go through life without some painful things happening to us. Some of these things we bring on ourselves (e.g. alcoholism). Others are things we suffer at the hands of others (e.g. betrayal). And others are things that happen through nobody's fault (e.g. an accident).

Wherever these things come from, they may bring us to a stage where we think that there is no redemption. That nothing can be salvaged. That everything has gone down the river and is irretrievably lost. As a result we fall a prey to feelings of hopelessness and self-pity. We begin to doubt ourselves, to doubt life, and even to doubt God.

Well, for anyone who ever felt like that, St Paul has a message. He tells us (Second Reading) that God has a saving plan, a purpose, which everything serves. He can turn everything to the benefit of those who trust in him. He can bring good out of our pain, even out of our sins. This is not to say that God wills bad things to happen to us. No. But when bad things do happen to us, God helps us, not only to pick up the pieces, but to reap a harvest from the wreckage.

There is a story about a king who owned a very valuable diamond. One day an accident happened and the diamond got deeply scratched. The king consulted experts to see if anything could be done to save the diamond. But they told him that even if they were to polish it, they would never be able to repair the wound it had suffered.

So the king locked the diamond in his vault where it lay hidden and useless for years. Then one day a very famous diamond cutter arrived in the capital. At the king's invitation he undertook to examine the diamond to see if anything could be done with it. After examining it carefully he said,

'Your Majesty, I will make the diamond look even more beautiful than it was before the accident.'

On hearing this the other diamond cutters laughed. But the king was delighted, and gave him permission to work on the diamond.

Bringing all his artistry to bear on it, he proceeded to engrave a beautiful rose on the diamond, using the deep scratch as the stem of the rose. When the king and the diamond cutters saw what he had done they were filled with admiration. It wasn't just a clever cover-up. He took the diamond's fault and transformed it into something beautiful.

In the same way, God can help us to transform our worst fault into a virtue, our worst misfortune into our greatest blessing. Our troubles are ultimately for your good, and can be an atonement for our sins. However, in our pride or foolishness, or just in our sense of hurt, we may throw away the thing that can bring us closer to God and help us to grow.

From painful experiences and difficult times we learn that God is faithful to us and can bring good out of anything. If we trust him, and have patience, we will see with our own eyes the truth of what Scripture says: 'God makes all things work together for the good of those who love him.'

And if the difficult times should return, we will remember what we have learned, what God has already done for us, and we will not lose heart. God sees us more clearly and knows us better than anyone else. He sees our wounds and sorrows, the scars we carry in our hearts. He will be good to us in the end, both in this world and in the next.

Life is unintelligible and unbearable without God. A close relationship with God is a real treasure. It gives us a sense of who we are, and where we're going. Only God can give us what we are looking for. If we find God, we find all.

OTHER STORIES

1. There was this poor tailor who lived in Krakow. He was a very pious man. One night he had a dream in which a voice said to him, 'If you go to Prague and dig beneath a certain tree behind the emperor's castle, you will find a great treasure.'

Since the poor man placed great trust in dreams, he set out the very next day for Prague. However, when he got there he found that the castle was guarded. Unable to get across the bridge, he lived under it for a while. While there he became friends with the captain of the guard. One day he shared his story with him. He said,

'I had a dream that if I got into the castle grounds, and went to a certain tree and dug there, I would find a treasure.'

'You're a very foolish man,' said the captain. 'You shouldn't believe that sort of thing. I have dreams myself. Once I had a dream that over in Krakow there lived a poor but wise tailor, not unlike yourself. I dreamt that if I went to his house, and dug behind his stove, I would find a treasure that somebody had buried there a long time ago. Of course, I dismissed it as foolishness.'

The tailor thanked him, went back home, dug behind his own hearth, and found the treasure.

We will never be happy unless we find the treasure that God has hidden in our own field. That is, until we have found the treasure of own worth as his children.

2. The painter, Vincent Van Gogh, suffered a lot from ill health. Consequently he often had to call on the services of doctors. But he scarcely ever had any money to pay the doctors.

On one occasion, after a certain doctor had taken care of him and nursed him back to health, Vincent wanted to show his gratitude in his own way. He painted the doctor's portrait, and made him a present of it. However, the doctor didn't think much of the painting. He accepted it all right but put it in his attic. There it took the place of a broken windowpane, serving the purpose of keeping out the drafts.

The doctor threw away a treasure. Today Van Gogh's paintings are almost beyond price.

In his love for us, God has given each of us a great treasure – the treasure of our divine dignity as his children. Let us be careful lest we throw it away.

PRAYER OF THE FAITHFUL

President: With trust that God's word comes into our lives and gives us light, let us pray.

Response: Lord, that we may see.

Reader(s): For the followers of Christ: that they may never exchange what is lasting and priceless for what is passing and cheap. [Pause] Let us pray to the Lord.

For all government leaders: that they may govern with wisdom so that the world may enjoy justice and peace. [Pause] Let us pray to the Lord.

For all who live only for material things: that they may see the primary importance of the things of the spirit. [Pause] Let us pray to the Lord.

For all gathered here: that we may know the will of God and have the strength to do it. [Pause] Let us pray to the Lord.

For our own special needs. [Longer pause] Let us pray to the Lord.

President: Lord, give us the serenity to accept the things we cannot change; the courage to change the things we can; and the wisdom to know the difference. We ask this through Christ our Lord.

REFLECTION   **At the end of the day**

The Kingdom of Heaven is like a net cast into the sea
which catches all kinds of fish.
When it is full, the fisherman hauls it ashore.
Then he sits down and sorts out the good fish from the bad.
The good he keeps, the worthless he throws away.
In a sense, all of us are fishers.
Each day we cast our net into the sea of life.
And at the end of the day we have a catch,
sometimes small, sometimes large.
May we take time to sift through that catch.
And may you, Lord, give us the wisdom to know
what to keep and what to throw away.

Eighteenth Sunday of the Year
FOOD FOR THE HUNGRY

INTRODUCTION AND CONFITEOR

The people followed Jesus to a lonely place, forgetting everything else in order to listen to his words and to seek healing for their sicknesses. We too have left everything, if only for a while, and have come here to listen to the Lord's words and to be healed by him. [Pause]

Lord, you are kind and full of compassion; slow to anger and abounding in love. Lord, have mercy.

You are close to all who call on you, who call on you from their hearts. Christ, have mercy.

You support all who fall, and raise up all who are bowed down. Lord, have mercy.

HEADINGS FOR READINGS

First Reading (Is 55:1-3). This contains an invitation, addressed to the exiles in Babylon, to come to a banquet. The banquet stands for the life of love and friendship God wishes to share with his people.

Second Reading (Rom 8:35.37-39). No matter what bad times we may have to go through, we remain undaunted, because we are certain that Christ loves us.

Gospel (Mt 14:13-21). Jesus shows his compassion for the people by healing their sick, and giving them food to eat.

SCRIPTURE NOTE

In the miracle of the loaves and fishes, we cannot get back to what actually happened. But we can see what it meant to Matthew and his readers. For them the miracle recalled the Old Testament story of manna in the desert. Jesus is the new Moses who feeds his people in the desert. In this feeding they saw an anticipation of the Eucharist. The gestures and words used are those of the Last Supper, and of the Eucharist: 'He took the bread ... blessed it ... broke it ... and gave it to them.' The Eucharist in turn anticipates the final banquet of the Kingdom.

HOMILY 1   **Miracle of generosity**

Mother Teresa told how she once came across a Hindu family that hadn't eaten for days. She took a small quantity of rice and gave it to the family. What happened next surprised her.

Without a moment's hesitation the mother of the family divided the rice into two. Then she took one half of it to the family next-door, which happened to be Moslem.

Seeing this Mother Teresa said to her, 'How much will you have left over? Aren't there enough of yourselves?'

'But they haven't eaten for days either,' the woman replied.

Generosity such as that makes us humble.

The miracle of the loaves and fishes could be called a miracle of generosity. First of all there is the marvellous generosity of the boy, who, with his gift of five loaves and two fish, made the miracle possible. It was a small thing in itself, but for the little boy it was a big thing because it was all he had. It's easy to give something that we won't really miss. But when the gift is as desperately needed by the giver as by the receiver, that is true giving. That is a sacrifice.

Then there was the marvellous generosity of Jesus. To appreciate this we need to consider the circumstances of the miracle. It's easy to reach out to others when it doesn't cause us much inconvenience. Not so easy when it is sprung on us at an awkward moment. Here a real sacrifice is involved. We have to set aside our plans, and forget about ourselves,

So it was with Jesus. He had just learned that his cousin, John, had been murdered. He needed peace and quiet. That is why he and the apostles crossed to the far side of the lake. But when he stepped out of the boat he found a throng of people waiting for him. He might have got angry and sent them away. Instead he had compassion on them and gave himself completely to them.

Then there was the sheer generosity of his response to the hunger of the people. Not only did he feed them, but he saw to it that each got as much as he wanted, and even so there were twelve full baskets left over.

You can see then why this could be called a miracle of generosity. Generosity is not always about giving things. More often it is about giving of ourselves, of our time, our gifts. Giving things can be easy, but giving of oneself is never easy. Before giving himself as food and drink in the Eucharist, Jesus gave of himself to people in so many other ways.

The story of the feeding of the multitude was treasured by the early Christians. The miracle recalled the Old Testament story of manna in the desert. For them Jesus was the new Moses who feeds his people in the desert. Then they saw in this feeding an anticipation of the Eucharist. It was at the table of the Eucharist that Jesus nourished them.

And it is here that Jesus nourishes us now. Only at God's table can we get the nourishment our hearts are longing for. In the Eucharist we are nourished with the Word of God and the Bread of Life. And having invited us to partake of the banquet of life on earth, God has invited us to partake of the banquet of eternal life in heaven.

As the people went back to their homes at the end of that day they knew that they had experienced the goodness and love of God – that love Paul talks about, a love from which nothing can separate us.

In the Eucharist we taste the love of God. The proof that we have experienced that love will be our willingness to love others. We may be able to give only in small ways and in small amounts. However, from the little boy in the Gospel we see that a small amount can become a big amount when placed in the hands of the Lord.

HOMILY 2 **A modern version of the miracle**

Christ fed five thousand people in the desert. Everyone got as much as they wanted, and still there were twelve baskets of food left over. It was an astonishing display of compassion and generosity on his part. But he couldn't have done it without the five loaves and two fish given him by a young boy, and without the help of the apostles.

Mother Teresa fed nine thousand people every day in Calcutta. But she couldn't have done so without the generosity of many people around the world, and the assistance of her sisters and lay helpers. Here is an example of the kind of generosity which made this daily miracle possible.

One day a young couple came into their house and gave them a large sum of money.

'Where did you get so much money?' Mother Teresa asked.

'We were married two days ago,' they replied. 'We decided not to have a wedding feast, but to give the money to feed the poor instead.'

'Why would you do this?' she asked.

'Because we love each other and wanted to begin our married life with an act of sacrifice,' they relied.

What made their act of generosity all the more amazing was the fact that both of them were high-caste Hindus, who normally will have nothing to do with the poor.

Sometimes a small deed takes on an importance far beyond its actual value. When Jesus told the apostles to give food to the people, they said, 'All we have with us is five loaves and two fish.' On hearing this Jesus might have said, 'That's no good. Forget the whole thing. Send the people home.' But he said no such thing. Instead, he took the five loaves and two fish, and with them fed the people.

There is a tendency today to go in for the big gesture, and to neglect the small gesture Hence, we may be tempted to think that because our contribution is small, it will make no difference. So we excuse ourselves from doing anything. But everything helps. Enough crumbs make a loaf. Besides, our example may trigger a response in others.

Feeding hungry bodies is one of the corporal works of mercy. It is something we could and should be able to do for ourselves. But there is a food which only God can give.

Jesus was concerned about those who were hungry. However, he didn't just feed people's bodies; he nourished their minds, their hearts, and their spirits. The people Jesus fed in that lonely place that day went home fully nourished – in body and in spirit.

The miracle involved a lot more than giving food to people. It was an expression of the care and love of God for his people. The food is a symbol of the life God wants us to have – life here on earth, and eternal life in the hereafter.

The miracle recalled the Old Testament story of manna in the desert. It shows us Jesus as the new Moses who feeds his people in the desert. It is an anticipation of the table of the Eucharist where Jesus nourished the early Christians and nourishes us now. In the Eucharist we taste the love of God. The proof that we have experienced that love will be our willingness to love others.

HOMILY 3 **Nothing can separate us from the love of God**

When bad things happen to us, especially when they are not of our own making, we feel that God no longer loves us, or has even abandoned us.

But St Paul tells us that there is no need for us to feel like that. In one of the most memorable passages in the Bible, he assures us that nothing in the whole of creation can separate us from the love of God. On the contrary, our trials and tribulations can actually bring us closer to God. In and through them we experience his love and care for us.

Paul himself experienced lots of troubles. In his second letter to the Corinthians he enumerates some of these troubles. He was imprisoned. He was whipped, almost to the point of death. Three times he was beaten with sticks. Once he was stoned by a mob and left for dead. Three times he was shipwrecked, and spent a day and a night adrift in the open sea. He travelled thousands of miles on foot, often narrowly escaping death at the hands of robbers or enemies. He knew hunger and thirst, cold and nakedness. To say nothing about the burden of worry and concern he carried because of his love for all the Churches.

Yet he says that he was able to overcome all of these things through the power of God who loved him. When he says that nothing can come between us and the love of God, he is talking out of experience.

Life is unpredictable. We can't depend on human things We can be happy one day and sad the next, healthy one day and sick the next, successful one day and a failure the next. So who is there to hold on to? Who is there to trust at all times? Only God. Only God can give us what we are looking for – the sense of having a love that is trustworthy, something that never changes, something that no one can take from us.

In the Eucharist we taste the goodness of God. In the Eucharist Jesus devised a way of giving himself to us and of nourishing our hungers. Here he nourishes us with the Word of God and the Bread of Life. Here God's care and goodness become tangible.

Only at God's table can we get the nourishment our hearts are longing for. Having invited us to partake of the banquet of life on earth, God has invited us to partake of the banquet of eternal life in heaven. We are children of God. There is an unbreakable bond between us and God.

A STORY

Some commentators say that the real miracle here is not Jesus' ability to multiply loaves and fishes, but his ability to get the people to share what little food they had. If the homilist wishes to pursue that line, then the following story could be useful.

One day a village woman was surprised to find a well-dressed stranger at her door asking for something to eat. 'I'm sorry,' she said, 'But I've nothing in the house right now.'

'Not to worry,' said the amiable stranger. 'I have a soup stone in my bag; if you will let me put it in a pot of boiling water, I'll make the most delicious soup in the world. A large pot, please.'

The woman gave him a pot. He put the stone into it and filled the pot up with water. As he put it on the fire she whispered the secret of the soup stone to a neighbour. Soon all the neighbours had gathered to see the stranger and his soup stone. When the water began to boil, the stranger tasted a spoonful and exclaimed, 'Very tasty! All it needs is some potatoes.'

'I have potatoes at home,' shouted one woman. In a few minutes she was back with a large quantity of sliced potatoes, which were placed in the pot. Then the stranger tasted the brew again. 'Excellent!' he said, adding, 'If we only had some meat, this would become a tasty stew.'

Another housewife rushed home to bring some meat, which the stranger accepted graciously and deposited in the pot. When he tasted the broth again, he rolled his eyes heavenwards and said, 'Delicious! If only we had some vegetables, it would be perfect.'

One of the neighbours rushed off home and returned with a basket of carrots and onions. After these had been put in, the stranger tasted the mixture, and in a voice of command said, 'Salt and sauce.' 'Right here,' said the housewife. Then came another command, 'Bowls for everyone.' People rushed to their homes in search of bowls. Some even brought back bread and fruit.

Then they all sat down to a delicious meal while the stranger handed out large helpings of his incredible soup. Everyone felt strangely happy as they laughed and talked and shared their very first common meal. In the middle of the merriment the stranger slipped quietly away, leaving behind the miraculous soup stone, which they used any time they wanted to make the loveliest soup in the world.

That Jesus could feed all those people with five loaves and two fishes must have seemed as impossible and ridiculous as that the stranger could make soup from a stone.

PRAYER OF THE FAITHFUL

President: Let us pray to the Lord who is just in all his ways and loving in all his deeds.

Response: Give us this day our daily bread.

Reader(s): That Christians may give an example of compassion and generosity to the world. [Pause] We pray to the Lord.

That the Church may continue to nourish the people of God with the banquet of the Eucharist. [Pause] We pray to the Lord.

That the governments of the world may strive to ensure that people everywhere have food to eat. [Pause] We pray to the Lord.

That we may hunger for the food which only God can give us. [Pause] We pray to the Lord.

That mindful of God's generosity to us, we may strive to be generous to others. [Pause] We pray to the Lord.

That we may have confidence that God grants our own special needs. [Longer pause] We pray to the Lord.

President: God of love and mercy, grant your children food for soul and body, so that we may walk steadfastly towards the Promised Land of eternal life where all our hungers will be satisfied. We make this prayer through Christ our Lord.

REFLECTION   **Feeding the hungry**

The multiplication of the loaves happens in our fields
every year between sowing and harvest time.
Like the miracle of Jesus, this miracle too
is brought about by the power of God.
And just as Jesus needed the hands of the apostles
to distribute the bread to the people,
so God now needs human hands to make
this abundance available to the hungry.
In some countries today the problem is over-eating.
In other countries the problem is getting anything to eat at all.
Today we don't need anyone to multiply the loaves for us.
The food is there.
What is not always there is the will to share it.

Nineteenth Sunday of the Year
WALKING ON WATER

INTRODUCTION AND CONFITEOR

In times of difficulty we find it natural to turn to God. But we must learn to turn to God at all times. Let us turn to God now. [Pause]

O Lord, you hear our cries. Lord, have mercy.

Your ears are attentive to the voice of our pleading. Christ, have mercy.

With you is found mercy and fullness of redemption. Lord, have mercy.

HEADINGS FOR READINGS

First Reading (1 Kgs 19:9.11-13). Fleeing for his life, the prophet Elijah takes refuge in a cave where he encounters God.

Second Reading (Rom 9:1-5). St Paul tells us about the sorrow and anguish he suffers because his fellow Jews refused to accept Christ as the Messiah.

Gospel (Mt 14:22-33). When they are caught in high winds and rough seas, Jesus comes to the apostles; he calms their fears, and brings them peace.

SCRIPTURE NOTE

As Matthew relates it, the incident described in today's Gospel is clearly symbolic. The boat represents the Church; the disciples are beaten by the winds and the waves of persecution. Jesus is not with them physically; he is in heaven, praying to the Father. However, in the hour of need he comes to them, and with his presence calms their fears and brings them peace.

The incident of Peter sinking and being saved by Jesus is probably a reference to Peter's failure during the Passion, and his restoration after the resurrection. The writer would have known this, and almost certainly had it in mind when telling this story.

In any case, Peter represents the typical disciple, caught between faith and doubt. Jesus' rebuke, 'Man of little faith! Why did you doubt?' is directed at us, who often start out courageously only to lose heart when faced with a crisis.

The prophet Elijah adopted a very militant, even bloodthirsty, approach in his battle against idolatry. Now on the run for his life, he takes refuge in a cave where he is taught that God's ways are not man's ways. God's approach is as gentle as a breeze.

HOMILY 1 **Calm in the storm**

If taken literally the Gospel story has little or no relevance for us. But it seems that Matthew meant to be taken symbolically. The boat represents the Church; the winds and the waves stand for the persecutions that had been let loose on the early Christians. Jesus is not with them physically; he is in heaven, praying to the Father. However, in their hour of need he makes his presence felt among them, thus calming their fears and bringing them peace. Understood like this, the story has great relevance for us.

Some people think that if you have enough faith life will be all plain sailing for you. But this is not so. Faith doesn't shield us from the hard knocks of life and death.

We see this in the case of the great prophet, Elijah (First Reading). Elijah was undoubtedly a man of faith. But because of his opposition to idolatry, Queen Jezebel wanted to kill him. So he fled to the desert and took refuge in a cave. A beaten and broken man, he just wanted to die. However, in the cave he experienced the presence of God. And strengthened by that experience, he was able to go on.

We see the same thing in the lives of the early Christians. They too were people of faith. Nevertheless, when they encountered persecution, they thought that the Lord had abandoned them, and their faith began to wilt. However, they discovered that even though the Lord was not with them physically, he was with them, and could still help them. Hence, their faith revived, and they were able to face their trials and dangers.

The example of Peter is especially enlightening. The story of Peter sinking and being saved by Jesus is a strange one. Yet it represents something that really did happen to Peter. It is a reference to his failure during the passion, and his restoration after the resurrection.

Initially he is full of faith as he sets out across the water. We remember his brave words at the last supper: 'Lord, I'm ready to die with you if necessary.' But then come doubt and cowardice, and he begins to sink, so that Jesus has to rescue him. Peter represents the typical disciple of the present time, caught between faith and doubt.

It is comforting for us to see that at times the apostles and early Christians were weak and fearful. In other words, they were just like us. At the start of an adventure we may be convinced that we are full of faith. However, as we go along, and difficulties arise, we discover that we have very little faith. It is then that we have to turn to the Lord for help. It's in our weak moments that we experience the strength of God. If we never felt ourselves going under, then we'd never know the rescuing power of God.

Faith doesn't save us from trials and tribulations. What it does is give us strength to face them. The person who has faith has a source of strength and inspiration, especially when trouble strikes. It's not we who keep the faith. It's the faith that keeps us. 'A person with a grain of faith in God never loses hope.' (Gandhi).

The person without faith, on the other hand, has nowhere to turn when trouble strikes. He/she is utterly alone, with neither comfort nor inspiration.

The Gospel story shows us the power of faith. It shows us what Jesus always does for his people, when the wind is contrary and they are in danger of being overwhelmed by the storms of life. To those with faith, Jesus is not a ghost from the past. He is the Son of God, who is present with us, and whose grace upholds us when things are too much for us.

HOMILY 2   **Upheld by his power**

Taken in a literal sense, the story of Peter attempting to walk on water may not be relevant for us. But taken symbolically (which seems to be how Matthew intends it to be taken) it has great relevance for us. 'Walking on water' is a symbol of something that is impossible to unaided human beings. There can be many situations in which we feel weak and powerless.

At some time or other, every disciple of Jesus is faced with very trying circumstances, very difficult decisions, very great sorrows, very powerful temptations. At those times it is as if we are being asked to 'walk on water'. Here are some examples of the kind of things the modern Christian might have to cope with.

John is a young person living away from home. It is Sunday morning. He is in a warm bed and it is cold outside. Should he leave that bed and go to Mass? He knows that he will have to face the laughter of his mates as they take their 'liturgy of the word' straight out of the tabloids. Will John be able to obey the gentle voice of Christ calling him to walk across the water of cynicism to go to church and listen to the Word of God?

Mary is a single girl who has become pregnant. She is heading into the middle of a storm of protest from her parents and gossip from her neighbours as soon as the news breaks. Then she is offered a way out – a quiet abortion. No one will ever know. But then she hears the gentle voice of Christ saying that abortion is wrong. Will she have the courage to listen to that voice?

Eileen is a young mother with three children. Suddenly her husband leaves her for another woman. She feels hurt and betrayed, lonely and angry. Then she hears the voice of Christ inviting her to trust. Will she have the courage to walk on those troubled waters, relying only on the word of Christ?

Gerry is a policeman. A drug dealer offers him a large amount of money if he would turn a blind eye to his activities. It's very tempting. But then he hears the voice of Christ saying, 'Do not participate in corruption.' Will he be able to walk across those foul and ugly waters?

Paul is a commercial traveller. He is away from home. One night he meets a very attractive woman. He hasn't been getting on very well of late with his wife. No one will ever know if he is unfaithful to her. Will he have the strength to walk across the waters of fidelity at the call of Christ, who tells him that adultery is wrong?

We could multiply the examples, but I think the point has been made. At some time or other, everyone is faced with very trying circumstances. At those times it is as if the Lord is asking us to 'walk on water'. But at the same time he stretches out his hand to uphold us.

At those times we can draw courage from the example of Peter. Peter represents the typical disciple who is caught between faith and doubt. He set out to obey Jesus, but 'as soon as he felt the force of the wind', that is, persecution, his faith failed him. Jesus' rebuke, 'Man of little faith! Why did you doubt?' is directed at us too. Like Peter, we often start out courageously only to lose heart when the going gets tough.

We have to contend not only with an outer struggle (against 'the elements'), but also with an inner struggle (against ourselves). To some extent, the whole life of a Christian is a kind of 'walking on water', in so far as it implies walking in faith, which means relying only on the word of Christ. Many times we are asked to step out on his word. But Christ is not a ghostlike figure from the past. He is the Son of God who lives among us.

One day we will have to leave the earthly 'boat' that has carried us through the stormy waters of this world, and set out across the dark waters of death. If at difficult moments during life we have opted for Christ, then at death it will come naturally to us to reach out and take his hand, so that he may haul us onto the shores of eternity.

HOMILY 3   **Whisper in the storm**

You could say that basically there are just two forms of verbal communication, all other forms being modifications of these two. The first is loud and harsh. It consists of the shout. Many put their faith in this method. It is generally used for giving commands. You hear it a lot on parade grounds and football touchlines. It is widely used in radio and TV commercials.

While the shout has its uses, it is often counter-productive. Loud sounds can deafen. They force us to close our ears, or to switch off altogether, as in the case of some commercials. Besides, we don't like it when people shout at us. It usually means that we are being given no choice in the matter. 'Come here!' 'Stand up straight!' 'Get out!' We feel under threat, and our spontaneous reaction is to defend ourselves.

The second method is soft and gentle. It consists of the whisper. Sometimes a whisper can be more effective than a shout. It is very personal, very individual. If you want to get someone's attention, whisper. When someone whispers to us, we have to strain our ears. A whisper disarms us because we don't feel under threat. It doesn't break down the door and force itself on us. It respects our freedom. By adopting such a gentle approach we know the person wishes us well. Thus we are more open to what he or she has to say. In certain cases the whisper is the only approach. For example, what other way can one convey a message of love and peace?

But a whisper is a very fragile thing. We have to really concentrate to hear it. It can easily be ignored, and it doesn't take much to drown it out.

God's voice is more like a whisper than a shout. In fact, God's voice is the quietest, gentlest voice of all. God's voice is a voice of love. God did not make himself heard to Elijah in the sound of the mighty wind or the earthquake, but in the whisper of a gentle breeze. God speaks to us in the most hidden parts of our being and in the promptings of our conscience.

Since we live in a very noisy world, if we want to hear the voice of God we need to create some stillness and quietness. (Elijah had to go to a cave to hear it.). Many other voices clamour for our attention, voices that are loud, strident and seductive. But the voice that presents the greatest threat to the gentle voice of God is the voice that comes from within ourselves – the strident voice of our outraged self-esteem.

Yet, for those who know how to listen, the God's gentle voice can make itself heard even in the midst of a storm. Over the roar of wind and the waves, the apostles heard the gentle voice of Jesus saying to them, 'Courage! It is I! Do not be afraid.'

To live by faith means to trust in God and to rely on his power. God won't carry us, but he will uphold us if we let go. We have to take the risk, only then can God help us. Modern life with its emphasis on security, and its distrust of the unknown, doesn't make faith easy. It fact, it makes it seem foolish.

We are God's children. There is an unbreakable bond between us and God. With this conviction our prayer should produce a kind of lightness in us that makes it possible for us to walk over the waves of danger.

PRAYER OF THE FAITHFUL

President: When we pray we trust God to let us see his kindness and to grant us his salvation.

Response: Lord, save us.

Reader(s): For Christians: that they may have the courage to live by the word of Christ. [Pause] We pray to the Lord.

For those in positions of responsibility: that they may have the strength to do the right thing in times of difficulty. [Pause] We pray to the Lord.

For those who are finding life difficult, and whose faith is weak. [Pause] We pray to the Lord.

For those who have no faith. [Pause] We pray to the Lord.

For ourselves: that we may have a sense of Christ's presence with us at all times, but especially in times of trial. [Pause] We pray to the Lord.

For our own special needs. [Longer pause] We pray to the Lord.

President: Heavenly Father, the hand of your loving kindness gently yet powerfully guides all the moments of our lives. Strengthen our little faith, so that we may walk with confidence over the waves of danger towards your Kingdom. We ask this through the Christ our Lord.

PRAYER/REFLECTION   **Courage! Do not be afraid**

Like Peter we too have often set out confidently
across the waters of life.
However, as soon as the winds of trouble rise against us,
and the waves of adversity begin to buffet us,
we lose our nerve and begin to sink.
Lord, when our faith falters, as it often does,
may we hear your gentle voice saying to us,
'Courage! Do not be afraid.'
In that moment, Lord,
may your divine power uphold us,
calm our fears, steady our nerves,
and enable us to steer our little boat
to a place of safety and peace,
beyond the wind and the waves.

Twentieth Sunday of the Year
THE CANAANITE WOMAN

INTRODUCTION AND CONFITEOR

In today's Gospel we meet a pagan woman who had the most extraordinary faith in Jesus, a faith that was rewarded with the cure of her sick daughter. During this mass let us with faith bring our needs and concerns to God, whose children we are. [Pause]

Lord Jesus, you are gracious and you bless us. Lord, have mercy.

You let your face shed its light upon us. Christ, have mercy.

You guide the nations on earth. Lord, have mercy.

HEADINGS FOR READINGS

First Reading (Is 56:1.6-7). God's house is open to all those who worship with sincerity.

Second Reading (Rom 11:13-15.29-32). God never takes back his gifts. Those who return to him are sure of obtaining mercy.

Gospel (Mt 15:21-28). The story of a pagan woman who had extraordinary faith in Christ, and how that faith was rewarded.

SCRIPTURE NOTE

The theme of the First Reading and the Gospel is that of inclusiveness. At the time Isaiah was writing there were lots of foreigners in Israel. The question arose as to whether or not the benefits of salvation should be extended to them. Isaiah gave a clear and positive answer: ' "My house shall be called a house of prayer for all the peoples," says the Lord.'

The early Church faced a similar problem with regard to the Gentiles. Matthew sees Jesus as having broken down the barrier between Jew and Gentile. Even though his own mission was restricted to Israel, Jesus did reach out to individual Gentiles such as the Canaanite woman. Hence, after the resurrection of Jesus, the early Church extended its mission to the Gentiles.

HOMILY 1   **Tough faith**

Love is the greatest power in the world. To be possessed with love is to be filled with a power which will not be denied. It's amazing what people can do, and will do, when they are motivated by love. We see this especially in the case of a mother.

A mother will do anything, brave anything, suffer anything, endure anything, for the sake of her child.

> In all my years in the prison service I have not met five prisoners who have not had a good relationship with their mothers. The mothers never fail to visit and they never fail to take responsibility. We see them every day, mothers with maybe more than one drug addict in the family, queuing to visit the son in jail, living out their lives with no resources, no support, nothing.
>
> It is unbelievable, considering the amount of pressure that mothers come under and the amount of torture they have to go through because their children get into trouble and into crime. (John Lonergan, Governor of Mountjoy Prison, Dublin)

Once, during a particularly severe winter in the Arctic, all but two people in a certain camp died of starvation. The two survivors were an Eskimo woman and her baby.

The woman began a desperate search for some means of obtaining food. Eventually she found a small fish-hook. It was a simple matter to rig a line, but she had no bait, and no hope of getting bait. Without a moment's hesitation she took a knife and cut a piece of flesh from her thigh. Using this as bait she caught a fish. She fed her child and herself, saving the fish gut for bait. She lived on fish until spring when she walked out of the camp and found some other people.

It was no coincidence that the only adult to survive in that camp was a mother. What kept the mother alive was her concern for her child. There seems no limit to what a mother will go through for the sake of her child. A mother doesn't give up easily.

We see another wonderful example of this in today's Gospel story. There we see the unshakeable determination of a mother. She just refused to be put off or to give up. How delighted she must have been when Jesus finally answered her prayer. It meant that all her trouble, all her begging, all her embarrassment, had not been in vain.

She is an example to us of perseverance, courage and love. But she is also an example of faith. Jesus said to her, 'Woman you have great faith. Let our wish be granted.'

She is a model of what could be called tough faith. Sometimes you hear people say, 'Ah, it's easy for you; you've great faith.' But it's not like that at all. Faith doesn't always make things easy. In fact, the opposite is more likely to be the case. It's because we have faith that we refuse to give up. Faith impels us to persevere, to struggle on, often with no guarantee of a happy outcome.

Faith is not a magic wand. It calls forth from us humility, courage, perseverance, and above all love. A mother never gives up. Neither does a person with faith. Faith and love are inseparably connected. Love is the expression of our faith.

HOMILY 2   **The cry of the poor**

The Gospel story is a strange one, and yet it is one that all of us are familiar with. It involves an encounter with a beggar. True, the Canaanite woman was not begging for money. But she was begging, begging for a favour. At one time or another all of us have been approached by a beggar, either at our doorstep or on a public street. One wonders how Jesus would deal with these kind of situations.

Jesus had withdrawn with his apostles to the region of Tyre and Sidon, which was Gentile country. It seems that he had gone there for a break. However, no sooner had he arrived there, than he was accosted by a pagan woman who pestered him to cure her sick daughter.

How do we react when we encounter someone begging? I think it would be fair to say that few of us come out of such an encounter with credit. Generally we refuse to help the person. We justify our refusal to help by telling ourselves that we haven't the time, that we can't help everyone, that it is better not to give them anything because in giving we are only encouraging a begging mentality.

However, we can draw some comfort from the Gospel story. The apostles reaction was not unlike our own. For them the Canaanite woman was a nuisance. They just wanted Jesus to get rid of her, and as quickly as possible.

Indeed, Jesus' own reaction surprises us. At first he ignored her. Then he refused her and tried to put her off. However, she was a very determined lady and refused to take No for an answer. Finally, he granted her request.

What it comes down to is this: we are afraid of the cry of the poor. An encounter with a beggar can be a disturbing experience. It can stir up unpleasant things inside us. It tends to arouse within us conflicting feelings of pity, discomfort, anger, and guilt. We hate what we discover about ourselves. And unless we are careful we may direct that hate at the poor unfortunate person who has dared to approach us.

An encounter with a poor person can be a humbling experience because it makes us aware of our own poverty. We realise that while the beggar is materially poor, we are poor in a different sense. We are poor in compassion, poor in our willingness to help another person, poor in our capacity to love.

Nevertheless, even though an encounter with a poor person may disturb us, it can also be fruitful. Through the poor we discover our own weakness and woundedness, which we are good at concealing. This means that we do not have to wear a mask and pretend to be what we are not. It thus results in a deep inner liberation. It puts us in touch with our true selves.

The encounter can also awaken and reveal the heart. It can awaken within us feelings of tenderness and compassion, kindness and communion. It shows us that it is possible to be more, to love more, and to give of ourselves more. It can change us. It calls us forth. It calls us to humanity. Thus it can lead to a new beginning.

And it reminds us that before God all of us are poor. The priest says the prayers of the Mass with outstretched hands. To pray like this is to acknowledge that before God we are poor, and stand in daily need of his mercy and love. Therefore we hold up our empty hands to God as a beggar holds out an empty bowl to passersby. We are saying in effect, 'Lord, before you I am as poor as a beggar.'

HOMILY 3   **The last shall be first**

The woman who came to Jesus was a pagan. To make matters worse, she was a member of a tribe that had been ancestral enemies of the Jews. Yet she had more faith in him than his own people. They wouldn't believe in him unless they saw signs and wonders. Indeed, they saw signs and wonders, and still refused to believe.

Once upon a time a group of people gathered outside the gates of heaven. They were good-living, respectable, God-fearing people – the solid element, the very backbone of society. Down on earth they had moved in the same business and social circles. As they stood around waiting for St Peter to open the gates, they exchanged friendly greetings: 'Thank God you made it, John!' 'Good to see you, Mary!' and so on.

St Peter had already greeted them and right now was fumbling with the keys of the gate. They were amazed that there had been no judgement – not that they were complaining! Now that they were sure of getting in, they were eager to occupy their reserved places in the front rows.

Suddenly there was commotion, and a voice was raised, 'Well, look who's coming! If it isn't old Mr Jacob.' Jacob was a Jewish businessman who back on earth had a reputation for meanness. Next a gypsy woman, who had a number of convictions for shoplifting, arrived. Then, to their horror, they saw a woman approaching who had been a street girl. She was followed by a young man who had spent time behind bars.

These late arrivals, feeling the hostility of the first group, gathered in a little group by themselves. Then a man turned to them and said, 'What makes you people think you're going to get into heaven? Surely not your own merits?'

'Certainly not,' came the surprising reply. 'We are hoping to get in through the mercy and goodness of God. And, if I may ask, what makes you people think you're going to get in?'

'A good life, of course,' came the confident reply.

Time was beginning to drag for the first group. They started to complain to one another: 'It's not fair that people like these should get in. There's no justice.' And they worked themselves up into a fury. But then the Lord himself arrived. Turning towards the first group he said,

'I understand you have been wondering why there has been no judgement.'

'Yes,' they cried out. 'We want a judgement. We want justice.'

'But the judgement has already taken place,' the Lord answered.

'What do you mean?' they asked in surprise.

'You've judged yourselves,' said he. 'By judging these people, you have judged yourselves.'

They were flabbergasted, and began to complain bitterly: 'It's not fair. We tried to live a good life. But these others lived bad lives.'

'Yes, they have done evil things,' the Lord answered, 'but they have repented, and I am merciful. I do not find any signs of repentance among you, however. You've had an abundance of the good things of life, but they've had to get by on crumbs.

'Take that businessman. He was no saint, but he worked hard for his family, and in quiet ways did many charitable deeds. And that gypsy woman. She was the mother of eleven children. Her husband was an alcoholic. Many would have thrown the towel in. But she showed great courage and faith, without a crumb of support from the community.

'And that Mary Magdalen. At heart she was a kind woman. When she got married she was expecting a feast of love. Instead she got beating after beating from her husband. The dog got better treatment than she did. And this young prisoner. He grew up in an environment in which he had to make do with crumbs by way of facilities and opportunities. He couldn't get a job. And of course, once he got a record, even the crumbs were denied him.

'Yet I find more faith, more courage, more humility, and more love among them than among you who sat down at the banquet table.'

Having said this, the Lord opened the gates, and the second group followed him inside, radiant with smiles.

There are no reserved places at the banquet of the Kingdom. We must try to do our best, but not count on anything we may do except on the mercy and goodness of God.

The Canaanite woman had to face all kinds of obstacles in order to obtain a cure for her daughter. She had to overcome her pride in order to beg. As a Gentile she knew she wasn't welcome among Jews. She had to overcome, firstly the apparent indifference of Jesus, and then a 'put-down' and a rejection.

But she was not put off. Why not? Because she wasn't seeking something for herself. Unselfishness enables us to put up with almost anything. It enables us to transcend ourselves.

She is an amazing person. Yet most mothers (and fathers too) would do, and many have done, the same kind of thing, with no guarantee of a happy outcome. A mother never gives up.

That poor Canaanite woman is held up to us as an example of faith, courage and love.

PRAYER OF THE FAITHFUL

President: We join in prayer to the God who shows mercy to all humankind.

Response: May the Son of God, have pity on us.

Reader(s): For all Christians: that they may try to imitate the faith and courage of the Canaanite woman. [Pause] Let us pray.

For government leaders: that in their planning they may not forget the poor and disadvantaged members of society. [Pause] Let us pray.

For those who have to get by on crumbs from life's copious banquet. [Pause] Let us pray.

For all parents, but especially those who have a sick or problem child. [Pause] Let us pray.

For all gathered here: that we may be grateful for all the good things we enjoy, and be generous in sharing them with others. [Pause] Let us pray.

For our own special needs. [Longer pause] Let us pray.

President: God our Father, we are your children. Help us to hunger for a life of goodness and holiness. We ask this through the same Christ our Lord.

REFLECTION **An Irish wish**

> God be good to you in all your days,
> God be kind to you in all your ways.
> God give strength to you when crosses lean,
> God send light to you, the clouds between.
> God give peace to you in times of strife,
> God bless everything that fills your life.
> God send joy to you when grief is o'er,
> God make way for you at Heaven's door. (*Brian O'Higgins*)

Twenty-first Sunday of the Year
PETER'S PROFESSION OF FAITH

INTRODUCTION AND CONFITEOR

Christ chose Peter to be the chief shepherd of his flock. Though Peter had strengths he also had weaknesses. We too have weaknesses. When those weaknesses cause us to fall, Christ forgives us and helps us go forward again. [Pause]

Lord, you strengthen us when we are weak. Lord, have mercy.

Lord, you raise us up when we fall. Christ, have mercy.

Lord, you guide us in time of doubt. Lord, have mercy.

HEADINGS FOR READINGS

First Reading (Is 22:19-23). Here we read about one man being dismissed from high office, and the keys of authority are passed to another. The New Testament applies this text to Jesus.

Second Reading (Rom 11:33-36). This is a hymn of praise to the wisdom of God, which is far too deep for us to fathom.

Gospel (Mt 16:13-20). This contains Peter's declaration of faith in Jesus, and Jesus' promise to make him the rock on which he will build his Church.

SCRIPTURE NOTE

Jesus rejects the inadequate ways in which others understand his role, and demands that his disciples speak for themselves. Peter replies with what no doubt was a solemn confessional formula of Matthew's Church. Then Jesus reciprocates by conferring a new title on Peter. He will be the foundation-stone of the new people of God.

The story shows that the primacy of Peter was not something that was invented by the Church later on. It went right back to the beginning, yes, to the mind and will of Jesus himself. The failures of popes throughout history do not contradict Jesus' promise that the gates of hell would not prevail against the Church. Peter himself failed the Lord. In giving authority to the man who denied him, Jesus wanted to show that he was establishing his Church not on human strength, but on his own love and faithfulness. The Church's true foundation is Christ himself. The pope is his servant, not his substitute.

HOMILY 1 **The formation of a leader**

The Gospel story shows that the primacy of Peter was not something that was invented by the Church later on. It went right back to the beginning, yes, to the mind and will of Christ himself.

Peter is one of the most interesting characters in the Gospel. It's clear that he had leadership qualities. But it's also clear that he had glaring weaknesses. In the Gospels we see his ups and downs. Sometimes he is very brave; other times he is very cowardly. Sometimes he is like a rock; other times he is more like a piece of jelly. He is almost too human. Certainly not our idea of a saint, or even the ideal person to be the head of Christ's Church.

But it's very interesting to see how Jesus dealt with him. How he helped him to grow into the man who was ready to lay down his life for him, and who eventually did. This growth was a gradual thing, and there were some regressions. But this is how growth happens. To live is to change, and to be perfect is to have changed often.

Let us take a closer look at the relationship between Jesus and Peter. It will help us to grow as human beings and as disciples of Jesus. And it will show us how best to help those we love to grow.

It all began when Jesus called him. Obviously Jesus saw potential in him. We all need someone to believe in us. It's hard to believe in ourselves if no one else believes in us.

Peter didn't think he deserved that call. He said, 'Lord, depart from me, for I am a sinful man'. Jesus did not deny that Peter was a sinner, but he challenged him to grow. We need to be challenged. Demands have to be made on us. Not to demand anything from someone is to condemn that person to sterility.

Jesus involved him in his work. He made him a partner in it, not a mere messenger boy. Responsibility helps people to grow.

He asked him to declare his loyalty. Once when large numbers of people were leaving him, Jesus turned to Peter and said, 'Will you also go?' This forced Peter to look into his own heart, and to stand on his own two feet. This helps growth.

When Peter made his great declaration of faith: 'You are the Christ, the Son of the living God', Jesus praised him and promised him further responsibility. We all need recognition for work well done. We all need affirmation. This encourages further generosity.

Jesus corrected him. When Peter drew his sword in the garden of Gethsemane Jesus said to him, 'Put away your sword'. It takes courage on the part of the tutor to point out mistakes. And to learn from one's mistakes is an essential part of growth.

Jesus once told him off. Thus when Peter wanted to prevent him from going to Jerusalem, Jesus said, 'Get behind me, Satan, you are more of a hindrance to me than a help'. At times the tutor may have to reprove. But there is an art in doing it.

Jesus confronted him with his failure to stay awake in the garden: 'Can you not watch even one hour with me?' It doesn't help to let someone away with sloppiness and shoddiness.

He even threatened to cut him off over the feet-washing incident. We have to be stern at times and refuse to compromise on matters of principle.

He understood that when Peter denied him, he did so more out of weakness than out of malice. He forgave him and gave him the chance to be begin again. We all need someone who can understand our weakness, and who doesn't write us off when we don't produce the goods right away.

But Jesus never spoilt Peter. That would be to ruin his chance of growing.

The thread which runs right through their relationship was love. Peter knew that Jesus loved him. Love is the climate in which people can grow. This was the rock in Peter's life.

We can imagine that Peter made a very good leader. A leader has to be aware of his own weakness. The experience of denying Jesus rid Peter of pride and blind reliance on his own resources. At the same time it enabled him to understand the weakness of others.

Peter's story is our story too. We too blow hot and cold. Sometimes we are strong, and other times we are weak. Without a warm relationship with Christ, we are only on the fringes of Christianity. We are like someone talking about love compared with someone who is in love.

HOMILY 2   **Giving our own answers**

In today's Gospel we have an early example of an opinion poll. And it was Jesus himself who conducted it. Even though it was a very limited one, it concerned a central issue: the identity of Jesus.

Today we have a glut of polls. One thing polls show us is the variety and often contradictory views people can have about any particular issue or individual. The poll in the Gospel bears this out. We see that the people came up with a variety of answers to the crucial question as to who Jesus was.

The question Jesus raised with the apostles was not a trick one or a trivial one. It was a very serious question. It is a question that resounds through the entire Gospel. It is the main question of the Gospel. It concerns the identity of Jesus. Everything hinges on this. He didn't pluck this question out of the air. It was a question that obviously was on the lips of everyone: 'Who is this man Jesus?'

Having heard what others were saying, Jesus turned to the Twelve and asked, 'And you, who do you say that I am?' No doubt he already knew what they thought. Still, he gave them the opportunity to express it themselves. We can only marvel at how Jesus said nothing to Simon, but waited for the Father to speak to him first.

It is important for us to come up with our own answers. To be able to state our own beliefs and values as Christians. It is no longer sufficient to repeat the official answers. We have to make the faith our own. A second-hand faith is a poor faith.

In the past everything about the faith was dictated to us. We were not only given the answers but the questions too. No one ever asked us, 'What do you think?' We weren't even given a chance to discuss, not to mind question anything. As a result we might have been able to give the right answers, but if pressed as to why we believed a particular truth, or what it meant for us, we were often at a loss.

Today there may be a danger of going too far in the other direction. To hear some people talk, you would think that there are no objective truths or values. It's what I think, what I feel, what I want, that matters. But one's own view can be wrong. Jesus praised Peter, not because he had his own answer, but because he had the right answer.

However, we will see that Peter didn't fully understand what he had said. While he recognised Jesus as the Messiah, he didn't know that Jesus would be a suffering Messiah. This was something he had yet to learn, and learn the hard way.

We must grow in our understanding of the faith. The important thing is to believe out of personal conviction. The more of such people we have in the Church, the more it is founded on rock.

The crucial question for each of us: Who is Christ for me? Is he the Son of the living God for me? And if so, how does this belief affect the way I live?

HOMILY 3   **The real Peter**

The Gospel story shows that the primacy of Peter was not something that was invented by the Church later on. It went right back to the beginning, yes, to the mind and will of Christ himself. His position as the leader of the Twelve is shown in many details in the Gospels. For instance, he is presented as the spokesman of the Twelve, and whenever the twelve apostles are listed his name is always first.

Yet the Gospels do not spare Peter, but clearly show the high and low points in his life. No doubt the lowest point was when he denied Jesus. The incident related in today's Gospel (his great profession of faith in Jesus) was almost certainly his finest moment.

Jesus might have tempered this moment with a touch of reality, in case Peter might get a swelled head. Instead, he praised and blessed Peter, and promised to bestow responsibility and authority on him.

There was a solid, even rocklike side to Peter's character. He was always the one to come forward. It's obvious that he had leadership qualities which Jesus recognised.

But there was another side to his character, a weaker and darker side, of which he was not yet aware. But he would find out about it in time. It would prove to be a very humbling and bitter experience for him. It is important that those in positions of leadership be aware of their weaknesses. People who act as if they are infallible make a lot of mistakes and hurt a lot of people.

It's important to remember that the Peter who said, 'You are the Christ, the Son of the living God,' was the same Peter who later said, 'I do not know this man.' If it was a different Peter, that would explain everything. But it was the exact same Peter. We might be inclined to say, 'Ah, but the first Peter was the true or real Peter.' But this would be a mistake. There was only one Peter.

What does this tell us? That there was division within Peter, just as there is division within each of us. Just as Peter was capable of being courageous at one moment and cowardly at another, so are we.

Each of us has high and low moments. We must not let our low moments get us down, and we must draw encouragement from our high moments. While we must not forget our weak side, we must try to act out of our strong side. The Lord smiles on us in our good moments, and upholds us in our low moments.

The low moments of others should not cause us to put them down or write them off. Their good moments should help us to see their potential, and to affirm and encourage them. In general we are eager to voice our criticisms, but reluctant to give a single word of encouragement, and in this way we bar every road to improvement.

A remark I read somewhere: 'I used to find the worst thing about others and tear them down. Now I try to find something good to say about them and thus build them up.' In considering what people are not, we overlook what they are. Better to appreciate what a person has than brood over what he hasn't.

Peter had his faults, but those faults were very obvious. But so too were his strengths: his generosity, his enthusiasm, his leadership. Jesus saw that, in spite of everything, his heart was sound.

We must try to seek the good in everyone, and to reveal it and bring it out, as Jesus did in the case of Peter.

PRAYER OF THE FAITHFUL

President: With trust we pray to the God whose love is eternal and who heeds the words of our mouths.

Response: Lord, hear us in your love.

Reader(s): For the Pope, the successor of Peter: that he may be a worthy representative of Christ on earth. [Pause] We pray in faith.

For all leaders: that they may learn from their mistakes and failures. [Pause] We pray in faith.

For parents, teachers, and all those working with the young: that they may help them to grow by showing them patient love and understanding. [Pause] We pray in faith.

For ourselves: that we may recognise Christ, not only as our Lord and Saviour, but as a Friend who loves us with a rocklike love. [Pause] We pray in faith.

For our own special needs. [Longer pause] We pray in faith.

President: Lord, three things we ask: to see you more clearly, to love you more dearly, and to follow you more nearly, day by day. We make all our prayers Christ our Lord.

REFLECTION   **Peter**

Peter has been called a stumbling saint.
He is a great consolation to us because courage fails us all.
All of us are mere mortals,
who are inconstant in our beliefs.
We must learn to forgive ourselves
momentary weaknesses and failures.
We need to surmount these things
and see the world in less rigid terms.
We must not judge ourselves or others

by momentary inconsistencies,
but rather by commitment given over a long time.
Jesus was well aware of Peter's faults,
but he saw that, in spite of everything,
his heart was sound.
Which meant he had the ability to love.
And in the long run love is what counts.

Twenty-second Sunday of the Year
THE COST OF DISCIPLESHIP

INTRODUCTION AND CONFITEOR

To follow Christ is inevitably to suffer. But there are great rewards too. However, we are weak and cowardly. Without God we can do nothing. Let us turn to God now, asking pardon for our failures and strength in our weakness. [Pause]

I confess to almighty God ...

HEADINGS FOR READINGS

First Reading (Jer 20:7-9). Even though speaking God's message to the people has brought Jeremiah nothing but insults, he is unable to remain silent.

Second Reading (Rom 12:1-2). St Paul urges the Romans not to live like the people around them.

Gospel (Mt 16:21-27). Jesus foretells his suffering and death, and tells his disciples that they too must be prepared to suffer.

SCRIPTURE NOTE

In the First Reading we see Jeremiah's faithfulness to his God-given mission, and what that faithfulness cost him. In the Gospel we see the faithfulness of Jesus, and the kind of faithfulness that is demanded of those who would follow him.

Peter gladly received the revelation of Jesus as Messiah and Son of God. But he rejected out of hand the revelation of a suffering Messiah. In this he represents the typical Christian, caught between faith and doubt, for whom the cross is a stumbling block.

HOMILY 1 **Trying to lure him from his destiny**

'Get behind me, satan!' These are strong words. What had Peter done to deserve such a stern reprimand?

Nelson Mandela tells us that when he was struggling to establish himself as a young lawyer in Johannesburg he was friendly with a businessman by the name of Hans Muller, a man who saw the world through the prism of supply and demand. One day Muller pointed out the window, and said, 'Look out there, Nelson. Do you see those men and women scurrying up and down the street? What is it that they are pursuing? What it is it that they are working for so feverishly? I'll tell you: all of them, without exception, are after wealth and money. Because wealth and money equal happiness. That is what you must struggle for: money, and nothing but money. Once you have enough money, there is nothing else you will want in life.'

The advice was well-meant. But that only made it all the more dangerous. Mandela was an intelligent man. If he had taken Muller's advice he could have done very well for himself. Luckily for South Africa, he didn't. Instead of looking after Number One, Mandela decided to dedicate himself to serving his country.

This incident helps us to understand today's Gospel. A short time prior to this Peter had recognised Jesus as the Messiah. Now, according to popular expectation, the Messiah would be a great military leader – another King David who would restore Israel to its former military greatness. No doubt this is the kind of thing Peter had in mind.

But this wasn't Jesus' idea of the Messiah. He told the apostles that the Messiah would suffer and be put to death. That was what God wanted. Not that God wanted the suffering of his Son, but that he wanted to show us the depth of his love for us in and through the faithfulness and love of his Son, a faithfulness and love which cost him his life.

The notion of a suffering Messiah was entirely foreign and completely unacceptable to Peter. So, out of concern for Jesus, he tried to stop him. But no doubt he was thinking of himself too. Being a disciple of a suffering Messiah was not a role to be relished.

Thus Peter had become a stumbling block to Jesus. And even though Peter had a very important role to play in his plans, Jesus was prepared to lose his friendship rather than allow him to deflect him from his destiny.

Jeremiah didn't know what he was letting himself in for when he agreed to become God's prophet. When Mandela decided to dedicate his life to his country he didn't know that it would mean spending twenty-seven years of his life in prison. But when Jesus set out on the road to Jerusalem he did know the full consequences of the decision he had made. This makes his sacrifice all the greater.

However, when the hour came for him to drink the cup of suffering and death, he didn't find it easy. On the contrary, he underwent a terrible agony, and asked the Father to remove the chalice from him. Nevertheless, he remained faithful.

Jeremiah underwent a similar struggle. He was so overwhelmed by the demands of his task that he wanted to pack it all in. His cry will find an echo in the heart of anyone who serves God in a difficult situation. It is never easy to bear witness in the face of indifference and hostility. Only a profound conviction of vocation can hold one to the task. But it is comforting for us to know that even a Jeremiah could contemplate opting out.

This is a struggle which we all experience in some shape or form. There are things which we don't like doing, but which we know we have to do if we want to be faithful to our responsibilities and obligations. Sacrifice is not an easy road. But it is in this way that our best self takes shape. This is how one becomes a person of character and integrity. And paradoxically this is also the road to happiness. Our happiness does not lie in doing our own thing, or what we feel like doing, but in doing what we have to do.

The only thing that makes sacrifice easy is love. Love enables us to turn the cross from a stumbling block into a stepping stone. What Jesus did was an expression of his love for us and for his heavenly Father.

The road to Jerusalem brought Jesus to Calvary. But it didn't end there. It led to Easter. Jesus supports all those who follow him down the narrow road of sacrifice, and shares his Easter victory with them.

HOMILY 2   **The cost of discipleship**

Jesus said to his disciples, 'Unless you take up your cross and follow me you cannot be my disciple.' The word 'cross' has been softened, so that the saying of Jesus has lost its force. The cross doesn't mean your arthritis, your indigestion, that difficult relationship, at least not in the first place. These are things which come to us in spite of ourselves. The 'cross' in the New Testament means that suffering which comes into our lives because of the choices we have made for the Kingdom. In that sense it is always something we choose.

An illustration – Nelson Mandela spent twenty-seven years in prison, or ten thousand days (approximately). Before that he was on the run for a couple of years. Of the time he was on the run he wrote later:

> It wasn't easy for me to separate myself from my wife and children, to say good-bye to the good old days when, at the end of a strenuous day at the office, I could look forward to joining my family at the dinner-table, and instead to take up the life of a man hunted continuously by the police, living separated from those who are closest to me, facing continually the hazards of detection and of arrest. This was a life infi-

nitely more difficult than serving a prison sentence. (*Long Walk to Freedom*, 1994, Little, Brown and Company)

What drove him to make such great sacrifices was his love for his country. This was the 'cross' he carried because of his love for his people.

It has been claimed that religion asks too little of people. It is too ready to offer comfort and to console, but has lost the courage to challenge. The result is that for many religion is just a crutch – something to lean on in times of weakness and infirmity. But in times of wellbeing they more or less forget about it.

It is true that faith is the best support we can have in times of weakness. But it is a lot more. It should be a positive force in our lives. It is a crutch in times of sadness and weakness, but it should be a pair of wings in times of joy and strength. In other words, it doesn't merely appeal to our weaknesses, but also to our strengths.

The trouble is that religion has become just 'religion', so respectable that its acceptance involves neither risk nor strain. Religion should challenge and stretch one to one's limit and beyond, so that thereafter one has new standards by which to judge oneself.

There is a religion of devotion, and a religion of commitment. A religion of devotion is a religion of comfort, and is often centred on self rather than on others. A religion of commitment is religion of challenge, of risk, of unselfishness.

In the Gospel Jesus asks for commitment from his followers. 'If anyone wants to be a follower of mine, he must renounce himself and take up his cross and follow me … anyone who loses his life for my sake will find it.' For the committed Christian, suffering is not a likelihood; it is a certainty.

Being a disciple is a serious business. Yet this doesn't mean that suffering is something Christians should seek. Jesus did not seek suffering; Gethsemane makes that clear. But suffering will inevitably be part of Christian life as it was part of Jesus' life.

But our following of Christ can be in small steps. God is patient. His challenge is invitation. What does following Christ mean in practice? It means faithfulness to one's way of life, concern for others in whatever manner, the caring gesture, the kind word – these add up. The Lord does not overlook the painful decision, the unspoken sorrow, the secret suffering. There can be much heroism in ordinary life. There are many more saints that those whom we honour as such.

HOMILY 3   **Saving one's soul**

'What good will it do you, even if you gain the whole world, if you lose your soul?' These are good words to recall when we are faced with important and difficult choices. Here is a modern example.

The scene: a prison for political prisoners near Moscow (during the era of Stalin). Ivan, a prisoner and an expert in physics and optics, sat facing the prison governor and an army general. Ivan knew at once that they wanted something from him.

'Would you like a remission?' they asked him.

'What do I have to do?' he asked.

'We'd like to transfer you to another prison to take charge of an important project. If you agree, you will be free in six months'.

'What is the project?'

'We want you to perfect a camera that works in the dark, and another miniature one that can be fitted to the jamb of a door, and which works when the door is opened. We know you can do this.'

Ivan was perhaps the only person in the whole of Russia who could produce a blueprint for these devices. After seventeen years in prison the idea of going home appealed to him. Here surely was the answer to his wife Natasha's prayer. All he had to do was invent a device that would put a few unsuspecting fools behind bars in his place, and he would be free.

'Could I not go on working on television sets as I am at present?' he asked.

'You mean you refuse?' said the general.

Ivan thought: Who would ever thank him? Were those people out there worth saving? Natasha was his lifelong companion. She had waited for him for seventeen years.

'I couldn't do it,' he said at last.

'But you're just the man for the job,' said the general. 'We'll give you time to make up your mind.'

'I won't do it. Putting people in prison because of the way they think is not my line. That's my final answer.'

Ivan knew what his 'no' meant. A few days later he was on a train to Siberia to work in a copper mine where starvation rations, and probable death awaited him. No fate on earth could be worse. Yet he was at peace with himself.

We are filled with admiration for Ivan. There are many more saints that those whom we honour as such. Wouldn't it be ironic if people like Ivan (who was not a Christian) were producing the goods and paying the price, while we the followers of Christ were living the 'good life'?

It has been claimed that religion asks too little of people, that it is too ready to offer comfort and to console, but has lost the courage to challenge. Being a disciple of Jesus is a serious business. Few of us will ever be faced with a decision as tough as that of Ivan. Our following of Jesus is more likely to consist of being faithful in the low-key events and decisions that add up to heroism in ordinary life.

We get opportunities to die to self in little ways every day – to die to our pride, to our selfishness, to our lust for pleasures and power. We have to die so that the real self can be born.

Ivan's sacrifice brought him a great benefit – deep peace of mind. Jesus talked about losing life, but he also talked about gaining life. This death to self is, in fact, the entrance to a higher life. It is death for the sake of life.

PRAYER OF THE FAITHFUL

President: As we lift up our hearts in prayer, we trust in the strength and the glory of the God whose right hand holds us fast.

Response: Lord, graciously hear us.

Reader(s): For all Christians: that in setting goals for their lives they may be guided by the values of the Gospel. [Pause]. Lord, hear us.

For the Pope and the bishops: that by word and example they may encourage the faithful to live the Gospel. [Pause]. Lord, hear us.

For those who are suffering for their belief in Christ: that they may remain steadfast. [Pause]. Lord, hear us.

For each other: that we may unite all our sufferings to those of Christ. [Pause] Lord, hear us.

For our own special needs. [Longer pause] Lord, hear us.

President: Lord, teach us to serve you as you deserve: to give and not to count the cost, to fight and not to heed the wounds, to toil and not to seek for rest, to labour and not to ask for any reward except that of knowing that we do your will. We ask this through you, Christ our Lord.

REFLECTION   **Gaining and losing**

There is a way of losing by gaining.
You can win an argument but lose a friend.
Though competition and promotion
I may advance in my profession,
but in terms of relationships I am impoverished.
My energies are so focused on efficiency and success
that I haven't time to grow emotionally
and to develop my capacity for relationships.
In one's drive to attain power,
a person may sacrifice friendship and loyalty,
so much so that one ends up alone.
Lord, let me never forget your haunting words:
'What good will it do you to gain the whole world
if you lose your soul?'

Twenty-third Sunday of the Year
ON FRATERNAL CORRECTION

INTRODUCTION AND CONFITEOR

Jesus says, 'Where two or three meet in my name, I will be there with them' – words we hear in today's Gospel. We are meeting in the Lord's name. Indeed, we are meeting at his command. Hence, we are confident that he is with us. Let us begin the Mass by making ourselves present to him. [Pause]

Christ binds us together as a community.

Lord, you are the vine, we are the branches. Lord, have mercy.

You let us see God's work in the world. Christ, have mercy.

You unite us to yourself and make our lives fruitful. Lord, have mercy.

HEADINGS FOR READINGS

First Reading (Ezek 33:7-9). The appointed leaders bear the responsibility to point out to wrong-doers the error of their ways and to try to get them to reform.

Second Reading (Rom 13:8-10). If we truly loved our neighbours we would not harm them in any way.

Gospel (Mt 18:15-20). We hear about the duty a Christian to correct an erring brother or sister. But there is a proper way of doing it.

SCRIPTURE NOTE

The question in today's Gospel is not forgiveness (dealt with later), but the sin of one member of the community. Every effort is to be made to bring the erring person to repentance: first in private, then before a few, finally before the whole community. If he is still unrepentant, he must be excommunicated. The decision of the Church will be honoured by God, since God inspired them in making that decision. The harsh phrase 'treat him as a pagan or a tax collector' reflects the strict Jewish Christianity of Matthew's Church.

The First Reading talks about the grave responsibility leaders of the community have to try to correct the erring.

HOMILY 1   **Harden not your hearts**

'O that today you would listen to his voice! Harden not your hearts.' (Responsorial Psalm).

When you go to the Middle East or to Africa you see what the absence of rain means. Without rain even the best ground turns into a desert. Sometimes when the rain eventually comes, the ground is so hard that it can't penetrate, and so it runs away causing flash-flooding.

So it is with the human heart when it becomes hard. Hard-heartedness gives one a measure of invulnerability in so far as one can't feel and therefore can't be hurt. Nevertheless, hard-heartedness is a sad and pitiable state. To adopt a hard-hearted attitude is to maim oneself.

A hard heart can't feel, can't respond, can't love. A hard heart can't experience sorrow, but neither can it experience joy. A hard heart is a closed heart, so it can't receive. A hard heart is a barren heart. A hard heart is the most serious handicap of all. From a spiritual point of view it is one of the worst things that can happen to anyone. It's bad to harden one's heart even against one person. We may have very good reasons for doing so, but we do ourselves serious damage spiritually.

A soft heart, on the other hand, is a blessing. True, it makes one vulnerable; the soft-hearted are easily hurt. But a soft heart can also be touched, moved, and warmed. It can receive. It can be saddened but it can also be deliriously happy. It can respond. It can burst into life like a garden in springtime.

Jesus came not just to purify our hearts, but to soften them, to open them, to sow the seed of God's word in them; to turn them from wastelands into fertile ground. He enabled many to experience what the Russians call 'the melting of the heart'.

The Irish writer, Oscar Wilde, was sent to prison for having sexual relations with a young man. It was a terrible humiliation for someone who was as well-known as he was. The bigger the boulder, and the higher up the mountain it has stood, the more damage it does to itself and to other stones when it falls. So it was with Wilde. Imprisonment was a calamity for himself, and a cause of great sadness to his friends.

What was it about prison that he feared most? 'The most terrible thing is not that it might break one's heart – hearts are made to be broken – but that it might turn one's heart to stone.'

'O that today you would listen to his voice! Harden not your hearts.' These words are addressed to us in today's liturgy. God is calling us from the error of our ways into a closer relationship with him and with one another. Today provides us with an opportunity to heed them.

To harden our hearts against one another is bad enough. But to harden our hearts against God would be the ultimate calamity. It would mean that God himself could not get through to us.

But when we heed the voice of God everything changes. Softened by the rain of God's grace, and warmed by the sun of his love, the human heart can be turned from a desert into a garden.

HOMILY 2   **Seeking to be reconciled**

The Gospel raises a very practical issue: how to act when someone close to you is treating you badly. Obviously these kind of problems occurred even in the first Christian community. Today's Gospel gives us a way of tackling a problem like this. First of all, however, let us take a look at the usual way the injured party goes about solving the problem.

We begin by keeping it to ourselves. It may be that we are ashamed or simply unable to talk about it to anyone. So we pretend that everything is normal. Meanwhile we brood over the injury. This tends to magnify it. We become sullen and sour and depressed, and may cut the offender off as a kind of revenge.

Eventually, unable to keep it to ourselves, we begin to tell others about it – friends, neighbours, relatives. Sometimes total strangers are brought into it. We bring them in, not as advisers, but as people who will corroborate our reading of the situation and who will sympathise with us. The last person to hear about the hurt is often the person who is causing it.

Today's Gospel shows that there is another approach. We should confront the person who is causing the hurt. Indeed, we have a duty to do so. Failure to do so shows a lack of love for the person. Confrontation takes courage and involves risk. But sometimes a little honest talking may clear the air. The person may not be aware of the extent of the hurt he is causing. He may see the light at once, and you have won him over.

The confrontation should not be done in anger or annoyance. Nor should it be done out of a desire to get even. It must be done out of concern for him too, not just out of a desire to appease one's own wounded pride. Also, before we do it, we should examine our own conscience to see if maybe we are not partly to blame.

The highest point we can attain in a confrontation is when we get the other person to see what he had done wrong and to condemn it himself. If he repents, forgiveness must be warm and without limits or conditions.

If he refuses to see the light, what then? We should seek advice. We should get one or two wise people and enlist their help to face him. The rabbis had a very wise saying: 'Judge not alone, for none may judge alone but God'.

If even then we fail, we should go to the community. Community need not necessarily mean the Church. It could mean family, or some other group of concerned and responsible people. The whole aim of the exercise is not to score points against one's brother, but to help him to amend his ways, and to be reconciled with him. To seek reconciliation is, according to Christ, more important even than offering sacrifice to God. (Mt 5:23-24)

If at the end of the day, reconciliation proves to be impossible, then the

[286]

verdict you (and the community) come to will be ratified by God.

But reconciliation can happen and it leads to great growth for both parties. Reconciliation is hard, but for that reason it should not be left untried. Needless to say, the Christian will pray about it. Prayer disposes one to follow Christ's approach.

HOMILY 3   **How to change a person**

Jesus says, 'If your brother does something wrong, go and have it out with him alone' He doesn't say, 'Put up with it, suffer it, endure it.' He says, 'Go and confront him with his wrong-doing.'

If someone is doing us a wrong, we have a duty to point it out to him or her. It is a special duty for those in positions of authority (see First Reading). People put up with all kinds of abuse for the sake of a phoney peace. They may think that this is the will of God for them.

However, there is an art in confronting a person. If we adopt a harsh approach with someone, all we do is cause him to harden his heart. In that case, not only is nothing achieved, but further harm is done. Whereas if we adopt a gentler approach, we may soften his heart, help him to see the error of his ways, and so enable him to change.

In his autobiography, *Long Walk to Freedom* (1994), Nelson Mandela describes his long years of imprisonment on Robben Island. He tells how one day he was called to the main office. General Steyn was visiting the island and wanted to know from Mandela if the prisoners had any complaints. Badenhorst, the officer in command on the island, was also present. Now Badenhorst was feared and hated by the prisoners.

In a calm, but forceful and truthful manner, Mandela informed the visitor about the chief complaints of the prisoners. But he did so without bitterness or recriminations. The general duly took note of what he had to say, which amounted to a damning indictment of Badenhorst's regime. The following day Badenhorst went to Mandela and said, 'I'm leaving the island. I just want to wish you people good luck.'

The remark left Mandela dumbfounded.

Later he said, 'I was amazed. He spoke these words like a human being, and showed a side of himself we had never seen before. I thanked him for his good wishes, and wished him luck in his own endeavours.'

Mandela says that he thought about this incident for a long time afterwards. Badenhorst had perhaps been the most callous and barbaric commanding officer they had had on the island. But that incident revealed that there was another side to his nature, a side that had been obscured but that still existed.

And Mandela concludes, 'It was a useful reminder that all men, even the most seemingly cold-blooded, have a core of decency, and that if their hearts are touched, they are capable of changing. Ultimately, Badenhorst was not evil; his inhumanity had been foisted upon him by an inhuman system. He behaved like a brute because he was rewarded for brutish behaviour.'

To confront another person is a difficult thing and calls for courage and wisdom. If we do it in anger and in a vengeful frame of mind, in all probability it will be counter-productive. We have to do it not just out of concern for ourselves and the hurt caused to our pride, but out of concern for the other person. It is a way of showing love for him. (See Second Reading.)

We don't show love for someone if we allow him to do wrong to us. By hurting us he is also damaging himself. It is in his interest too that he desist from what he is doing. Besides, to watch someone doing wrong, and not try to stop him, is to bear part of the responsibility for the wrong he is doing.

We are responsible for one another, but the duty to speak out falls most heavily on the leaders in the community. But it is the duty of every Christian. We should not remain silent when silence can be taken to mean that we approve of what is happening. In that case we share responsible for the evil. Ezekiel was called to be a watcher for the house of Israel. He speaks to them, not out of arrogance, but out of genuine humility and care for them.

If we confront the offender in the right spirit, and he is genuine, he will want to put it right. If not, he won't be able to plead ignorance, saying, 'Why didn't you tell me?' The object is not to score a victory over our brother, but to win him over, to be reconciled with him. Perhaps the person is not aware that he is doing wrong.

In the response to the psalm we repeated the words: 'O that today you would listen to his voice. Harden not your hearts.' God is continually calling us from the error of our ways into a closer relationship with him and with one another.

PRAYER OF THE FAITHFUL

President: Meeting in Christ's name, we are full of trust that the God of grace will grant what we ask.

Response: Lord, hear our prayer.

Reader(s): For all Christians: that they may give an example of the art of reconciliation. [Pause] We pray to the Lord.

For all those in positions of leadership: that they may be willing to take the first step in seeking reconciliation. [Pause] We pray to the Lord.

For those who have been deeply hurt by other people, and who are resentful and bitter. [Pause] We pray to the Lord.

For those who are hurting others by their behaviour: that they may truly repent. [Pause] We pray to the Lord.

For grace to be able to forgive those who have offended us. [Pause] We pray to the Lord.

For our own special needs. [Longer pause] We pray to the Lord.

President: Lord, grant that what we have said with our lips, we may believe in our hearts, and practise in our lives. Through Christ our Lord.

REFLECTION   **Harden not your heart**

'O that today you would listen to his voice.
Harden not your hearts.'
From a spiritual point of view, hardness of heart
is one of the worst things that can happen to anyone.
To adopt a hard-hearted attitude is to maim oneself.
A hard heart can't feel, can't respond, can't love.
A hard heart can't experience joy.
A hard heart is a closed heart.
A hard heart is a barren heart.
A soft heart, on the other hand, is a blessing.
A soft heart can receive and can respond.
It can be saddened but it can also be deliriously happy.
Softened by the rain of God's grace,
and warmed by the sun of his love,
the human heart can be turned from a desert into a garden.

Twenty-fourth Sunday of the Year
FORGIVENESS

INTRODUCTION AND CONFITEOR

In the Gospel, Jesus makes it clear that if we want God to forgive us, we must forgive others. We all know how hard it can be to forgive. At the same time we know how lovely it is to be forgiven.

We always begin Mass by asking forgiveness for our sins. As we do so we should also ask for the grace to able to forgive those who have sinned against us. [Pause]

I confess to almighty God ...

HEADINGS FOR READINGS

First Reading (Ecclesus 27:30-28:7). In refusing to forgive those who have sinned against us, we exclude ourselves from receiving God's forgiveness for our own sins.

Second Reading (Rom 14:7-9). The entire existence of a Christian is for

Christ and for others.

Gospel (Mt 18-21-35). We must be willing to extend to others the generous forgiveness God has extended to us.

SCRIPTURE NOTE

Today's Gospel raises the question of sin between brothers and sisters, that is, fellow-Christians. The psalm talks about the greatness of God's forgiveness, (which contrasts with our miserly forgiveness). Anyone who is forgiven has an obligation to forgive. If we cannot bring ourselves to do this, it is an indication that we really haven't experienced God's forgiveness. The position of the servant in Jesus' story was absolutely hopeless. He owed the king so much money that even if he worked forever, he would not be able to repay him. This is our situation before God. We can't win God's forgiveness. All we can do is plead for his mercy.

HOMILY 1   **Importance of forgiveness**

Today's Gospel deals with a subject which concerns us all – forgiveness. None of us can go through life without getting hurt. How do we cope with these hurts? They can provide us with an opportunity to grow, or they can become a stumbling block to human and spiritual development.

Hurts are not easy to deal with. As soon as we get hurt self-pity walks in our front door – which is only natural. But once self-pity is entertained, it produces a legacy of bitterness, resentment, and anger. The memory of wrongs flows inwards where it festers. It poisons our spirit, and destroys our capacity to love. Some people have years of stored hurts inside them.

From time to time the cellar of the mind and heart has to be cleaned out. The cobwebs of self-pity have to be swept away. The cancerous growth of bitterness has to be cut out. Hurt feelings have to be dug up, owned and then let go.

Here is where forgiveness comes in. Though never easy, even from a human point of view it makes great sense. We rid ourselves of the burden of bitterness and resentment. As a result, we experience a sense of freedom, relief, and cleanness. Once again we are able to devote all our energies to loving, which is the only activity that befits a Christian. Forgiveness is first and foremost a healing of our own hearts. It is precisely our hearts that are wounded.

Forgiveness also works wonders for the person who is forgiven. He/she is set free to walk in friendship with God and with the person he/she has offended.

Forgiveness implies an understanding of our own poverty, brokenness, and sin, and therefore our own need of forgiveness. This enables us to forgive with understanding and humility. To forgive in a high-handed way is not a Christian way to forgive. We have to be willing to admit that we may have been at least partly to blame for what happened. It is not good enough to forgive in word. We must forgive, as the Gospel says, from the heart.

It's not a question of forgiving if and when the offender repents – that would be relatively easy. We are expected to forgive even if the offender doesn't repent – this is what makes it so difficult, and why we need God's grace.

Forgiveness clears a path for God to forgive us. The only obstacle we can put in the way of God's forgiveness of our sins is our inability to forgive the sins of others. We all need forgiveness. People who cannot forgive break down the bridge over which they themselves must pass.

Blessed are those who forgive; they shall obtain forgiveness for their own sins.

HOMILY 2   **The process of forgiveness**

Jesus asks us to forgive 'seventy times seven'. Which means forgiveness must be unlimited. There is no point in being glib about forgiveness, or pretending that it is easy. It is never easy. Without the grace of God it is sometimes impossible. When we get hurt, we naturally grow resentful and bitter. Resentment and bitterness are very dangerous things, and we cannot be healed of them unless we forgive.

We all need to forgive because at one time or another we all have been hurt. But what can we do? We must realise that forgiveness cannot be achieved overnight. It is not something that happens in one go. Forgiveness is a process, and like all processes it takes time. There are steps we can take, which, with the grace of God, will lead to forgiveness and healing of the hurt.

We must recognise that a wrong has been done to us. There is no point in pretending it didn't happen.

We must recognise that we have feelings about this – feelings of anger and hurt. These feelings are not sins. In fact, they are natural and healthy.

We should talk about these feelings. If we can't do this with the person who has hurt us, we should do it with someone else.

Then at some point we make a decision to forgive. Forgiveness is an act of the will. But this doesn't mean that feelings of hurt and bitterness will suddenly disappear. The healing of these will take time.

Finally we have to make a decision about our relationship with the person who has hurt us. Here we have three choices: to continue it, break it off for a while, or discontinue it altogether. Reconciliation is not always possible. It takes two to be reconciled.

Unless we forgive others we ourselves will not be forgiven. It is not that God is vindictive. It is just that if we do not forgive others we make it impossible for ourselves to receive God's forgiveness. Imagine two people living in the same room, one of whom closes the blind because he doesn't want the other to enjoy the sunlight. But in so doing he also deprives himself of the sunlight.

It's not a question of forgiving if and when the offender repents. We are expected to forgive even if the offender doesn't repent – that is what makes it so difficult, and why we need God's grace.

We need to pray for the gift of forgiveness. Unless we forgive, we will not be able to let go of bitterness and resentment, and so will not know peace or healing. Forgiveness doesn't mean forgetting. It means remembering and letting go. Forgiveness is a holy task. Only God can help us to accomplish it fully.

HOMILY 3 **Asking for forgiveness**

To forgive someone who has hurt or offended us is never easy. Sometimes it is extremely difficult. Nevertheless, to forgive is to be in a position of strength. We are the injured one. We are doing the giving. We are in control. It makes us feel good. We have something to gain from it.

To ask for forgiveness can be a lot harder. It is to put yourself in a position of weakness, poverty, and humility. Now you are the one who has done wrong. You have to humble yourself to ask another for something, which you may or may not receive. You are not in control. Things are out of your hands.

According to Jewish law, sins committed against God can be absolved by sincere repentance. But for sins committed against fellow human beings we must first seek the forgiveness of those whom we have wronged in order to be in a position to invoke divine mercy. (I don't think the Christian position is much different).

Once in Poland an elderly rabbi boarded a train to travel home to Warsaw. He entered a compartment in which three salesmen were playing cards. In need of a foursome, the salesmen asked the rabbi to join in, but he politely refused, saying he had been busy all day and needed to catch up on his prayers, and that in any case he didn't play cards. They tried to persuade him, but he still refused. At this they got very hostile and started to abuse him. When he still refused, they threw him out of the compartment, so that he had to stand in the corridor for the rest of the journey.

On arriving at Warsaw the rabbi got off the train. So too did the salesmen. The rabbi was met by a large crowd of his followers. On seeing this one of the salesmen asked,

'Who is that man?'

'That's rabbi Solomon, the most revered rabbi in the whole of Poland,' came the answer.

On hearing this the man regretted what he had done. He had no idea who he had offended. So he quickly went up to the rabbi and asked for forgiveness. However, the rabbi refused to forgive him.

The rabbi's followers were taken aback at this. They couldn't figure out how their rabbi, a man renowned for his gentleness and holiness, could refuse to forgive someone. So they asked him,

'When someone who has offended us asks for forgiveness, should we not forgive him?'

'Yes,' the rabbi replied.

'Well then, why didn't you forgive that man?'

'I cannot forgive him. The salesman didn't offend me, the chief rabbi of Warsaw. He offended a common man. Let him go to him and ask for forgiveness.'

In other words, he was asking for forgiveness only because he had offended a famous person. But had it been just an ordinary person that he had offended, he would never have asked for forgiveness.

I wonder if God doesn't sometimes feel like saying something similar to us: 'Why do you tell me that you are sorry for offending your neighbour? Why don't you go to your neighbour, tell him you're sorry, and ask his forgiveness? By that very act you would open the door and my forgiveness would come in.'

Fortunately, in our communities there are many who are willing to forgive others. But, alas, there are very few who are willing to seek forgiveness from others.

OTHER STORIES

1. Once upon a time two prisoners shared the same cell. A dank, dark cell it was. One of them was a strong, crude individual. The other was gentle and timid. The prisoners were handcuffed to one another. The strong man was mean and cruel to the timid man.

One day, while his companion was asleep, the timid man found the key to the cell. He desperately wanted to get away from this horrible cell. But at the same time he had no wish to do any favours to his obnoxious companion. However, he soon realised he could not set himself free unless he also set his companion free.

It is in forgiving that we ourselves are forgiven.

2. According to an ancient legend Christ assembled the eleven apostles in heaven and asked them to celebrate the Last Supper with him. They readily agreed. On their arrival he welcomed them and asked them to take their seats. They were surprised to find that he had set out thirteen seats. Even though everything was ready he refused to start.

He waited and waited until finally Judas came in. On seeing him, Christ rose from his seat and went to meet him. He kissed him and said, 'We have waited for you.'

The story may sound far-fetched. But does it do anything more than echo that other story we find in the Gospel of Luke – the story of how as he hung on the cross, Jesus prayed for his executioners?

By word and example, Christ taught us how to forgive.

3. Even before the six-day war Israel and Jordan have been mutual enemies. But in the summer of 1994 King Hussein of Jordan and the late Prime Minister Rabin of Israel signed a peace accord. They said they did so in order that their children would not need to fight any more.

To prepare the way for the signing of the peace treaty, Israeli foreign minister, Simon Peres, crossed the Dead Sea by helicopter to end nearly half a century of enmity. He was the first high-ranking official from his country openly to visit Jordan.

He said, 'It took us a mere fifteen minutes to ride over. But it took us forty-six years to arrive at this time and this place of peace and promise.'

On signing the treaty Hussein said, 'Out of all the days of my life, I don't believe there is one such as this.'

Peace is a process. So too is reconciliation. They both take time.

PRAYER OF THE FAITHFUL

President: We turn in prayer to the God who forgives all our guilt and crowns us with love and compassion.

Response: Lord, hear our prayer.

Reader(s): For Christians: that they may give an example to the world of the art of forgiveness. [Pause] Let us pray to the Lord.

For all those in authority: that they may forgive with humility and understanding those who fail them. [Pause] Let us pray to the Lord.

For those who have been badly sinned against and who are unable to forgive. [Pause] Let us pray to the Lord.

For all of us gathered here: that we may be able to forgive those who have sinned against us and so be healed of resentment and bitterness. [Pause] Let us pray to the Lord.

For each other: that we may have the humility and courage to seek forgiveness of those we have offended. Pause] Let us pray to the Lord.

For our own special needs. [Longer pause] Let us pray to the Lord.

President: All-powerful God, grant that we who stand always in need of your mercy, and who love to receive it, may be ready to show mercy to others. We ask this through Christ our Lord.

REFLECTION   **Forgiveness**

When we forgive we free ourselves of the burden of bitterness,
and we free the other person of the burden of guilt.
But our forgiveness must come from the heart,
which means it must be true, sincere, and warm.
A cold forgiveness is not much use.
Forgiveness should start now.
Putting it off only deepens the wound,
prolongs bitterness, and postpones happiness.
Life is short, time is fleeting.
Today is the day to forgive.
Lord, deliver us from the poison of bitterness,
and give us the grace to forgive from the heart
those who have offended us.
Then we will know the warmth of your forgiveness.

Twenty-fifth Sunday of the Year
THE WORKERS IN THE VINEYARD

INTRODUCTION AND CONFITEOR

Often we are small and petty in the way we think and act. Fortunately for us there is nothing small or petty about God. His ways are as high above our ways as the heavens are above the earth. Let us ask God for forgiveness for our smallness of heart, while at the same time opening ourselves to the goodness of God. [Pause]

Lord, you are kind and full of compassion, slow to anger, abounding in love. Lord, have mercy.

You are just in all your ways, and loving in all your deeds. Christ, have mercy.

You are close to all who call on you, who call on you from their hearts. Lord, have mercy.

HEADINGS FOR READINGS

First Reading (Is 55:6-9). As high as the heavens are above the earth, so high are God's ways above our ways.

Second Reading (Phil 1:20-24.27). Writing from prison, Paul is thinking of his death, and longing for complete union with Christ.

Gospel (Mt 20:1-16). This is a story about the generosity of God, which soars above human standards.

SCRIPTURE NOTE

The First Reading states, 'God ways are not our ways, God's thoughts are not our thoughts'. Just how vast is the difference between God's ways and our ways, between God's thoughts and our thoughts, is illustrated in the Gospel. God's generosity utterly transcends human generosity.

The parable of the workers in the vineyard was aimed at the Pharisees. These legalistically minded men were critical of Jesus because he befriended sinners and outcasts. In the parable Jesus faces up to his critics, and shows them what God is like: God is generous and full of compassion for the poor and the outcast. In that respect the parable is similar to that of the prodigal son.

HOMILY 1   **An unfair story?**

Many people consider Christ's story an unfair story, because it seems to favour the idler at the expense of the hard worker. In order to understand and appreciate the story we need to know what is going on in it.

Imagine the following scene (which I witnessed myself). A cross-roads on the edge of a shanty town near Cape Town, South Africa. It's mid-morning. Men are gathered at the side of the road. Some are lying down under the trees to escape the blazing sun. But most are standing in the open.

What are they doing there? They are waiting – waiting for some farmer or builder to come along and hire them for the day. Some have been there since sunrise. Indeed I'm told that some of them have been there overnight. And still you will find people who say that these kind of people don't want to work.

They are totally exposed. They are on display. Many eyes scan them – indifferent eyes, curious eyes, hostile eyes. Their value depends on what people want from them. They have no value in themselves. They will settle for the minimum wage. It is already eleven o'clock in the morning. A look of dejection is beginning to settle on their furrowed faces. The day is wearing on. Hope is fading.

For most of these men there will be no eleventh hour reprieve. They will go home to their shacks and their families empty-handed. In this world the first shall be first, and the last shall be last.

The eleventh-hour people in Jesus' story were not idlers. They wanted to work. It was just that nobody had hired them. Imagine how they felt as the day drew to a close. They felt rejected, useless, hopeless.

The idea that any employer would take these people on at the eleventh hour, and pay them a full day's wage, was unthinkable. Yet this is exactly what the owner of the vineyard did. This is the strong point of the parable.

Jesus' audience knew exactly what he was getting at. The vineyard was the Kingdom of God. Those who had been working all day long were the Pharisees and the Jews in general. The eleventh-hour people were sinners and the Gentiles.

Jesus was saying that God was offering the Kingdom to sinners and Gentiles on equal terms with the Jews. The Jews objected vigorously. They didn't think it was fair; they thought they deserved preferential treatment. They assumed that God worked on the merit system. According to this system, you must earn your graces by hard work. And here was Jesus saying that God does not work on the merit system at all.

You would expect that people who have worked hard and risen from poverty to relative wealth would be compassionate towards those who haven't made that journey. Yet the contrary seems to be generally the case. They tend to be rather harsh in their judgement of the poor, and to resent help given to the poor. Their attitude is: I had to work hard in order to make it. Nobody gave me anything for nothing. If I did it, why can't they?

If one is into worthiness, competition, and rewards, this Gospel won't make much sense. Jesus' parable makes little sense from the point of view of strict justice. But which of us would want to be treated by God according to strict justice? Do we not all stand more in need of his mercy and generosity than of his justice? This parable is not about justice; it is about mercy and generosity.

When we come into God's presence let us not parade our entitlements, our rights, our deserts. We can't put God in our debt. Everything comes to us as a gift from God, a gift motivated by his love for us. Let us rejoice that God is generous to a degree that far outstrips human generosity. Let us open our hearts to God's generosity. And having experienced it, let it serve as a model for our dealings with others.

A conversion is required before we can begin to act like God. Not an intellectual conversion, but a conversion of the heart.

HOMILY 2   **The last shall be first**

If one considers Jesus' story unfair, here is another story which may help us to understand the point Jesus was making.

The final of the 3000 metres was in progress. The runners stayed bunched together until halfway round the last lap. Then the eventual winner eased himself into the lead. As he did so another man fell back into last place after a desperate effort to keep up. The other runners were strung out in between.

As the leader, a local man, came into the home straight, the spectators rose to him. When the news was flashed up that he had set a new world record, thunderous applause echoed around the stadium. The cameras followed him as he did a lap of honour. He got a standing ovation as he went around. Bouquets of flowers were thrown in his direction.

Afterwards everybody wanted to clap him on the back and shake his hand. Microphones were thrust in front of him. 'How does it feel to be a champion?' he was asked. Beaming all over he replied, 'Wonderful! Absolutely wonderful!' Already newspapers were queuing up for the exclusive rights to his story, and company executives, cheque books in hand, were doing likewise for the right to use his name to endorse their products.

While all this was going on, the other runners had finished the race. The last man had to really struggle to finish. Then, with head bowed, he departed for the dressing rooms.

A VIP had been invited to perform the prize-giving ceremony. The first three runners home were waiting, all smiles, to take their places on the victory podium. The first sign that something unusual was about to happen was when the VIP said he wanted all the runners present at the ceremony. The runners were duly called, and all was now set.

Then what did he do? He called the man who came in last and gave the gold medal to him. He gave the silver medal to the man who had come second last, and the bronze medal to the man who came third last. There were gasps of astonishment from the crowd, and sighs of embarrassment from the organisers. The mistake was pointed out to him. But he said, 'This is the way I want it.' Then he proceeded to give a warm handshake to each of the other runners right down to the man who came first. When the latter came forward he was very angry.

'This is not fair!' he exclaimed.

'So you think it's not fair?' the VIP replied calmly.

'I do,' said the man. 'I won the race. So I deserve to get the gold medal.'

'Friend,' said the VIP, 'haven't you got enough already?'

'What do you mean?' the man asked.

'You've had the satisfaction of winning the race. You've had the applause of the crowd and the attention of the media. On top of all this, you've had lucrative contracts offered to you. Now consider the man who came last. He finished the race too. And what did he get for his efforts? Nothing. Would it be fairer if you got everything while he got nothing?'

With that the victor was reduced to silence. Still fuming, he turned and went away.

The aim of this story is not to down-play the achievement of the winner but to make a point. It seems wrong that one person should get everything, while another gets nothing. I know this is exactly what happens in our world – the winner takes all.

Some might still say that the story an outrageous one. But is it any more outrageous than Jesus' story about the workers in the vineyard?

What point was Jesus making? The key to understanding the story is contained in the phrase, 'Are you envious because I am generous?' The story is not about justice. It is about generosity, but not ordinary generosity. It's about a generosity unlike anything we've ever known. It is about the generosity of God.

The generosity of God is a great comfort to us. But it is also a great challenge, because we are called to imitate it; to make our ways of dealing with one another more like God's way of dealing with us. A conversion is required before we can begin to act like God. Not an intellectual conversion, but a conversion of the heart.

Which of us would like to be treated by God according to strict justice? Do we not all long for mercy rather than justice? We can't put God in our debt. But we don't need to. God is generous to a degree that far outstrips human generosity. All we have to do is open our hearts to God's generosity. And having experienced it, let it serve as a model for our dealings with others.

HOMILY 3   **What God is like**

Some people think that Jesus' story in an unfair and unjust one. (I've heard this many times). This is a very serious accusation. Injustice is an ugly thing. All of us have some experience of it. Injustice leaves a wound that takes a long time to heal. Jesus' story is not about injustice, because no injustice is done in it.

Nor is his story about justice, though it goes out of its way to state that justice is done. Justice is a great thing. It is one of the things that is stressed again and again in the Bible. But Jesus' story is not about justice.

What then is Jesus' story about? It is about generosity. 'Are you envious because I am generous?' That is the key phrase in the story. The story is about generosity, but not ordinary generosity. It's about a generosity unlike anything we've ever known.

The eleventh-hour workers were not idlers who didn't want to work. They were people no respectable employer would hire. They were the left-overs, the rejects. The idea that any employer would take these people on at the eleventh hour, and pay them a full day's wage, was unthinkable. Yet this is exactly what the owner of the vineyard did. This is the strong point of the parable.

Jesus wasn't talking about human generosity but about the generosity of God. He was illustrating what the First Reading said, 'God's ways are not our ways, God's thoughts are not our thoughts'. God's generosity utterly transcends human generosity.

The parable was aimed at the Pharisees. They were critical of Jesus because he befriended sinners. Jesus gave them his answer in this parable. In it he showed them what God is like: God is generous and full of compassion for the poor and the outcast.

God deals with us in ways that are very different from the ways we normally deal with one another. As high as the heavens are above the earth, so high is God's generosity above our generosity. The goodness of God is a great comfort to us. But it is also a great challenge, because we are called to imitate it; to make our ways of dealing with one another more like God's way of dealing with us.

A conversion is required before we can begin to act like God. Not an intellectual conversion, but a conversion of the heart.

One man who grasped this was Pope John XXIII, who launched the Second Vatican Council. He has rightly been called a genius. In what sense? He was a genius of the heart. His genius consisted in his generosity, his largeness of heart.

Faith is a call which above all is addressed to the heart. In essence it consists of a relationship of love with the God who first loved us. It is with the heart that we best grasp God. St John says: 'Everyone who loves is born of God and knows God.'

Once God has touched our hearts, and warmed them with his love, we will begin to love in our turn. And then we will truly know what God is like. God is love.

PRAYER OF THE FAITHFUL

President: We call out in prayer to the God who will take pity on us, and whose greatness cannot be measured.

Response: Lord, hear us in your love.

Reader(s): For Christians: that they may prove themselves faithful workers in the Lord's vineyard. [Pause] Let us pray in faith.

For those who hold public office: that they may prove worthy of their stewardship. [Pause] Let us pray in faith.

For the disabled and the sick. [Pause] Let us pray in faith.

For those who cannot find work, and for those who are retired. [Pause] Let us pray in faith.

For all gathered here: that we may serve God out of love, and that our love may be reflected in our dealings with others. [Pause] Let us pray in faith.

For the God's blessing on our own personal needs. [Longer pause] Let us pray in faith.

President: Lord, give us work till our lives are ended, and give us life till our work is done. We ask this through Christ our Lord.

PRAYER/REFLECTION

'My thoughts are not your thoughts,
nor are my ways your ways.
As high as the heavens are above the earth,
so high are my ways above your ways,
my thoughts above your thoughts,' says the Lord.
How small our thoughts can be,
and how poor our ways of seeing and judging.
We think miserly thoughts, and act in miserly ways.
Why?
Because we have small minds and small hearts.
Lord, open our minds and enlarge our hearts,
so that we think more like you,
and act more like you.
Let us not to begrudge your goodness to others,
knowing that we too are undeserving of your favours,
and stand more in need of your mercy than of your justice.
Amen.

Twenty-sixth Sunday of the Year
THE TWO SONS

INTRODUCTION AND CONFITEOR

We have the freedom to say 'Yes' or 'No' to God. But this means we are responsible for our actions. We sometimes abuse our freedom, but God in his goodness calls us to repentance. We are called to repentance now. [Pause]

Lord, you make us know your ways, and teach us your paths. Lord, have mercy.

You show the path to those who stray and you guide the humble in the right path. Christ, have mercy.

You remember your mercy and the love you have shown from of old. Lord, have mercy.

HEADINGS FOR READINGS

First Reading (Ezek 18:25-28). Each of us is responsible for his or her own conduct, and will be judged accordingly.

Second Reading (Phil 2:1-5). Self-seeking and rivalry have no place in the Christian community. We must imitate the humility of Christ.

Gospel (Mt 2:28-32). Actions speak louder than words.

SCRIPTURE NOTE

The parable of the two sons was addressed to the chief priests and elders of the people. Its purpose was to defend Jesus' invitation of sinners and outcasts to the Kingdom, in the face of the sneers of the religious establishment. The parable outraged the religious people.

The first son represents sinners. Like him they originally chose to go their own way but then repented and took God's way, and so gained entry into the Kingdom. The second son represents the chief priests and elders. Like him they promised to work for God but failed to do so, and so have excluded themselves from the Kingdom. Repentance is a necessary disposition for entry into the Kingdom. The theme of sin and repentance is also dealt with in the First Reading.

The parable also echoes a favourite theme of Matthew: the split in the religious person between saying and doing. Hence, its relevance for 'religious' people in every age.

HOMILY 1   **Giving one's word**

One of the greatest things we can give another person is our word. In fact, there are those who believe that our word is the only thing we have to give. But it's easy to give our word. It doesn't cost anything there and then. The cost comes later, if and when we honour our word.

Some people are very generous with their word. They will promise you the sun, moon and stars. But you can't rely on them. They don't really mean it. Their word is worthless. Their promises dissolve like salt in water. How painful it is to deal with such people. There is not one of us who has not experienced the pain of being let down by someone who failed to keep his/her word.

But there are others who are slow to give their word. They don't make promises easily. But when they do make a promise, you can rely on them to honour it. Their promise is like a chain around their leg. How lovely it is to deal with such people.

When the father in Jesus' story asked his two sons to go and work in the vineyard, one of the sons said an immediate and definite 'yes'. He gave his solemn word that he would go. But he didn't keep his word. He didn't go.

The other son also gave his word. He said he wouldn't go. However, later he changed his mind and went.

Jesus was not holding either son up as an ideal. Yet we can learn from both. The son who said he would go but didn't is meant to act as a warning to us. We call ourselves Christians but outsiders sometimes accuse us of being hypocrites because our lives do not bear witness to the faith we profess with our lips. Sin does not necessarily imply doing something wrong. The greatest sin is not to do good: the sin of inactivity, of doing nothing.

And we can learn from the son who said 'No' but later changed his mind. To change one's mind is generally regarded as a fault and a weakness. But this is not always the case. It takes humility to admit one's mistake, and courage to put it right.

The second son, because he finally obeyed his father, is a lot better than the first. The ideal son, however, would be the son who immediately and willingly carried out his father's wishes. That is what we should aim at. Jesus is the ideal Son. As St Paul says, 'He emptied himself and became obedient to the point of death, death on a cross. Therefore, God exalted him.' (Second Reading)

The parable teaches us that promises can never take the place of performance, and fine words can never be a substitute for fine deeds.

Faithfulness is one of the greatest and most necessary things in life. But faithfulness is costly. It is not an easy road. It demands unselfishness and a spirit of sacrifice. But even here on earth it brings great rewards in terms of growth, serenity, and joy.

There are no such rewards for the unfaithful. There is no happiness at the end of the day for the one who gives his word but fails to honour it. But there is great joy for one who gives his word and honours it.

It is said that a person is as good as his word. If that is so, then the question I must ask myself is: How good is my word?

The person who makes a vow or a promise makes an appointment with himself at some distant time or place.

HOMILY 2   **The difference between saying and doing**

There are two words which we use very frequently, often several times in the course of a day. They are two very small words but are very important ones. Sometimes an awful lot hangs on them. It is no exaggeration to say that our lives could be summed up in terms of these two words. What are these two words? They are the words 'Yes' and 'No'.

Of course, it's not the words in themselves but the spirit in which they are said that makes the difference. They can be said glibly and without sincerity, or they can be said thoughtfully and with great sincerity. But that's only the beginning. At the end of the day what matters is whether or not they are acted on.

In Jesus' story, when the father asked his sons to go and work in his vineyard, the first son said an immediate and definite 'No. I will not go.' We don't know why he refused to go. Maybe he thought, 'Why does it always have to be me? Let someone else go for a change.' Maybe he had other plans for that day. Or maybe he was just plain lazy.

However, it was early morning when he said that 'No'. A lot can happen between morning and evening. At some point during the course of the day, the word 'Yes' began to sound inside him – at first faintly, then more loudly. A struggle ensued between it and the initial 'No'. Eventually the 'Yes' won the struggle, and he went to work in the vineyard. Of course by this time some of the day was lost. Even so, the father would have been happy to see that he changed his mind.

Now let us consider the second son. He said an immediate and definite 'Yes' to his father: 'Certainly, sir'. But in fact he didn't go. We wonder why not. Maybe he genuinely intended to go but forgot. Maybe he postponed it, and then found it wasn't worth his while. Or maybe he said, 'They'll manage without me.'

At any rate, the day wore on, and the 'Yes' he had said so loudly and clearly in the morning got fainter and fainter. By evening it had turned into a clear and definite 'No'. His case is worse than that of the first son. He had given his word. His father would have been counting on him, and would feel let down when he discovered that he didn't go.

There is part of both of those sons in each of us. Part of the second son because our performance doesn't always match our promises; we sometimes give our word but don't always keep it. And there is part of the first son in us too because we are capable of turning a 'No' into a 'Yes'.

We can learn from both of the sons. All of us have said some important 'Yeses' that we need to see through. (Marriage is an obvious one.) And we have said 'Nos' that should and could be turned into 'Yeses', lest we become known and remembered, not for what we did, but for what we didn't do, for the promises we made but didn't keep.

It's easy to say 'Yes' in the morning of life. In the morning we don't really know what is involved in the task to which we are committing ourselves when we say 'Yes'. But as the day of life goes by this is gradually revealed to us. Then we may have second thoughts. We may begin to entertain doubts. Hence, our 'Yes' can easily turn into a 'No.' If we want to turn our promises into fulfilment we have to go on saying 'Yes'.

The opposite can also happen. We may say 'No' to something or someone in the morning. But during the day we may see things differently, and turn that 'No' into a 'Yes'. A person may make a great mistake, and then redeem himself, and, by the grace of God, atone for it by making the rest of his life a lovely thing.

Many of the greatest saints in the history of the Church were sinners who initially said 'No' to God, and who later changed their minds and said 'Yes'. St Augustine is perhaps the most obvious example, but there are many others. A person will be judged, not by a single act or stage in his life, but by his whole life.

God has given us the freedom to say 'Yes' or 'No' – our 'Yes' would have no value unless we were free to say 'No'. However, we may say

'Yes' to God with our words, and 'No' to God with our deeds. We profess to believe, but fail to translate our belief into active obedience. Words are no substitute for deeds.

We must, therefore, constantly examine ourselves. We must try to turn our promises into fulfilment, and our words into deeds. Every day we can turn one of yesterday's 'Nos' into one of today's 'Yeses'.

HOMILY 3   **Personal responsibility**

At the time of the prophet Ezekiel, there was a belief that the child was punished for the sins of the parent. There was a popular saying, 'Parents eat sour grapes, and their children's teeth are set on edge.' But the prophet didn't agree with this. He stated clearly and unequivocally that each individual is responsible for his or her actions, and he or she alone will have to answer for them.

He pointed out that we can t hide behind the goodness or evil of others; each of us stands before God in his own goodness and in his own badness, and is judged accordingly.

What Ezekiel was talking about is the principle of personal responsibility. It is wrong to blame the past for everything. All of us must look into our own hearts, and we will see plenty to blame. But repentance will win us pardon and life.

There is a tendency today to take responsibility away from the individual. The whole thrust of modern psychoanalysis seems to be that someone else is to blame – one's companions, one's parents, one's environment, and so on.

We are, of course, influenced by our upbringing and environment. Still, there must come a time when we stop blaming others, and accept responsibility for our actions. We have to say, 'The buck stops with me.' My own sins are my own, and I and no one else will have to answer before God for them. It's refreshing to hear someone say, 'I am to blame. I am responsible.' But how seldom we hear that.

Unless we accept responsibility for our sins, we will see no need to repent of them. If we do accept responsibility for them, we will want to do something about them, and God will help us. If we confess our sins we have nothing to fear but the mercy of God.

Jesus' story of the two sons is very relevant here. One son gave his word that he would go and work in his father's vineyard, but in actual fact he didn't go. He probably said to himself: 'They'll get on without me'. Here we have a total abdication of personal responsibility.

The other son at first refused to go. However, later in the day he reflected on his decision, saw that it was wrong, and decided to put it right. Here you have an example of someone who took responsibility for his life.

But even this son is not held up as a model. True, he had a conversion. But it seems to have been just a change of mind. There is no suggestion that he had a change of heart. A change of mind is a good thing, but a change of heart is a deeper and better thing.

A change of mind may lead to a change of some aspect of a person's behaviour. But a change of heart leads to a complete change of life. A change of heart is conversion at the deepest possible level. A change of mind is usually brought about by fear or self-interest. A change of heart is brought about by love.

All us are called to conversion, because conversion is a necessary disposition for entry into the Kingdom. But the conversion which above all Jesus sought to bring about in people was a change of heart. And he succeeded in bringing it about in the most unlikely of people. Many sinners heeded his call to conversion of heart, changed their lives, and made their way into the Kingdom. But many religious people stubbornly resisted his call to conversion of heart, refused to change their lives, and so excluded themselves from the Kingdom.

We need the Lord to touch our hearts with his love and compassion. People are essentially good. But this goodness has to be awakened and called forth if we are to enter the Lord's Kingdom, which is a Kingdom of love.

PRAYER OF THE FAITHFUL

President: When we pray we are confident that God will remember his mercy and the love he has shown from of old.

Response: Lord, hear our prayer.

Reader(s): For Christians: that they may show forth in their lives the faith they profess with their lips. [Pause] Let us pray to the Lord.

For all who hold public office: that they may be faithful in carrying out their responsibilities. [Pause] Let us pray to the Lord.

For those who have been the victims of broken promises. [Pause] Let us pray to the Lord.

For ourselves: that we may never allow words to take the place of deeds. [Pause] Let us pray to the Lord.

For our own special needs. [Longer pause] Let us pray to the Lord.

President: Lord, grant that what we have said with our lips, we may believe with our hearts, and practise with our lives. We make this prayer through Christ our Lord.

REFLECTION   **The three sons**

A father had three sons. One day he said to them,
'Go and work in the vineyard today.'

The first said, 'Sure, Dad.' But he didn't go.
The second said, 'I won't go.' However, later in the day
he changed his mind and went grudgingly.
The third said, 'Sure, Dad.'
And he went immediately and willingly.
Which of the sons will feel closest to the father
at the end of the day?
The third, of course.
The more we do the will of God out of love,
the more we will appreciate his love for us.
Lord, save us from the darkness of broken promises,
and help us to walk in the light of faithfulness.

Twenty-seventh Sunday of the Year
THE FRUITLESS VINEYARD

INTRODUCTION AND CONFITEOR

The Old Testament tells us that God cared for his people as a good gardener cares for his vineyard, yet they failed to produce the desired fruits. We are the new people of God, the vineyard planted and cared for by Christ. God looks to us to produce the fruits of justice, holiness, and peace. This is a great privilege and a great challenge too. [Pause]

Sadly, we often fail God. Let us confess our sins, especially those of omission.

I confess to almighty God ...

HEADINGS FOR READINGS

First Reading (Is 5:1-7). Israel is compared to a well cared for vineyard which fails to produce fruit.

Second Reading (Phil 4:6-9). St Paul warns the converts at Philippi against anxiety, and advises them as to how they should live in order to enjoy the peace of God.

Gospel (Mt 21:33-43). The parable of the wicked vine-dressers tells of God's goodness to his people, and of their failure to respond in kind.

SCRIPTURE NOTE

History is littered with stories of good tenants and wicked landlords. In the Gospel we have a story of wicked tenants and a good landlord. The parable is an allegory of God's dealings with his people. The landowner is God. The vineyard is Israel. The wicked tenants are the people of Israel, but more especially the religious leaders who had been given charge of the vineyard by God. The servants are the prophets sent by God and so often rejected and killed. The son is Jesus himself whom they killed.

Like the parable of the two sons, this parable was directed at the chief priests and elders. It was meant as a warning, but it went unheeded. The tenants came to a bad end, Jerusalem was destroyed, and the Gentiles replaced the Jews as God's people. All this would have been clear to Matthew's readers.

HOMILY 1   **The stone rejected by the builders**

'The stone which the builders rejected has become the cornerstone; this was the Lord's doing, and it is a marvel in our eyes.'

South Africa is a country blessed by God in a great many ways. It is a large country, has a good climate, and is rich in agricultural land and minerals, especially gold and diamonds. But the country which should have been a haven for all the peoples of Southern Africa became instead a haven for a privileged white minority.

Many people tried in vain to change South Africa's iniquitous apartheid system. Finally Nelson Mandela appeared on the scene. He too tried to bring about reforms. But like reformers before him, he was rejected. Worse, he was hounded by the government, and ended up spending twenty-seven years in prison. However, he not only survived prison, but came out of it with the respect of his enemies and of the entire world.

Furthermore, he came out without bitterness. In fact, he came out smiling, and immediately sought reconciliation with the leaders of the regime that kept him in prison all those years. But even greater things were to follow. The man once rejected was to become the President of a new multi-racial South Africa. The stone which the builders rejected became the cornerstone of a new and better building.

Mandela's is a marvellous story, one of the great stories of the century. What makes it so great is the fact that in it good finally triumphs over evil. Make no mistake about it, what was done to Mandela (and to others before him) was evil. He did not deserve to be treated like that. His only crime was to seek justice for his brothers and sisters. But in the end, good came out of this evil. A new, free society emerged. Mandela's story helps us to understanding Jesus' story of the vine-dressers.

God had bestowed on his people the sort of love and care which a dedicated vine dresser bestows on a vineyard. But the vineyard failed to produce the fruits of right living. God sent messenger after messenger in the persons of the prophets. But far from listening to them, the people abused some of them and killed others. Finally he sent the Son and Heir – Jesus. But the tenants killed him in the hope of taking over the vineyard themselves.

What the tenants did was ugly and sinful. Yet God did not abandon or destroy the vineyard. He handed it over to others, who would produce the fruits. Thus a new building came into being – the new people of God. Jesus, the one they rejected and killed, is the cornerstone of this new building (the Church).

God never retaliated, never returned evil for evil. He was not vindictive in taking the vineyard from the Jews and giving it to the Gentiles. The tenants brought it on themselves. God never gave up on his people. Just as the rain ensures that the earth becomes fruitful, so God persists until he gets a response.

The parable shows us that there is only one way to overcome evil, and that is with good. What happens in the story is both nasty and ugly. However, while there is much evil in the story, evil does not have the last say. In the end good triumphs.

No one can say that Jesus didn't live in the real world. He did. He experienced its ugliness himself. But he didn't answer it with more ugliness. He triumphed over evil by good. He has become a model for all those who suffer unjustly in the cause of right. And he challenges us, his followers, the tenants of the new vineyard (the Church), to produce the fruits of justice, love and peace. It's a great privilege and a great challenge too.

HOMILY 2   **The way to peace**

St Paul urges the Philippians not to be anxious. He tells them, 'There is no need to worry.' This may seem an unreal piece of advice. There is no way to avoid all worry. Good and sincere people are naturally worried about many things. It is part of the burden they carry precisely because they are people who care, who care about loved ones, and many other things.

But Paul is not talking about normal concerns. He is talking about anxiety. Nothing is more debilitating or fruitless than anxiety. Of itself it does nothing to solve our problems. Rather, the opposite is the case. By dissipating our energy, anxiety weakens us and makes it more difficult for us to find a solution to our problems.

The root of anxiety is lack of trust – lack of trust in oneself, in others, and especially in God. Hence, the first piece of advice Paul gives the Philippians is to pray. They must learn to commit their cares to the Lord: 'If there is anything you need, pray for it.'

He is not suggesting that prayer should take the place of action. Nor is he implying that their prayers will always be answered. What, then, does prayer do? Prayer implies a willingness to do what we can, and then to leave things in the hands of God. To accept what happens then as his will, even though we may not understand it.

Then Paul tells his readers to think positively. People who are over-anxious tend to think very negatively. They imagine the worst scenario. This is disastrous. We must concentrate on the good, not on the bad.

Many people devour the newspapers every day. It's hard to read the newspapers these days without coming away depressed, so full are they of bad news. Instead of filling our minds with all kinds of trash, Paul says, 'Fill your minds with everything that is true, everything that is noble, everything that is good and pure, everything that we love and honour, everything that can be thought virtuous and worthy of praise.' The power of positive thinking is well known.

However, it is not just a question of thinking nice thoughts. We must try to do these things. Thoughts alone will not suffice. We must pursue goodness in our actions. Paul says, 'Keep doing the things you have learned from me.'

In Jesus' parable of the vineyard a lot of ugly things happen. But evil does not have the last say. In the end good triumphs. This shows us that there is only one way to overcome evil, and that is with good. Jesus didn't answer evil with more evil. He triumphed over evil by good.

If we do what we can, and put our trust in God, then Paul assures us that 'the peace of God, which is so much greater than we can understand will guard your hearts and minds in Christ Jesus.'

Peace comes, not from having an easy and tranquil life. We can have peace even in the midst of struggle and turmoil provided we are on the side of right. Then the God of peace will be with us.

HOMILY 3   **Ingratitude**

Peter and Anne raised four children but are now alone. They feel disappointed and sad. Anne tells us why.

'We did everything we could for those children. We wanted them to have the things we didn't have. We bought a house. Peter had to do a lot of overtime to be able to keep up with the mortgage repayments. Times were hard. Life was a constant struggle. Still, those children never lacked anything.

'Many's the night I didn't get a wink of sleep because of them. They had a lot of illnesses when they were young but, thank God, in time they grew out of them. Though we saw some of our neighbours going regularly to the pub, we hardly ever went out. We saw others going abroad for their holidays, but we could never afford to do that. But we gladly sacrificed these things for the sake of the children.

'We sent them to good schools. They never lacked money for books or school outings. They were always well dressed. We taught them good values. We taught them their religion, and we tried to give them good example. And just look at how they have repaid us. They say that good example rubs off on the children. Well, in our case, it didn't.

'John (the oldest) quit university and went into the pub business. He works hard, and by all accounts is doing well. He now owns three pubs. But money has become his god. Though he sends us a couple of bottles at Christmas, we hardly ever see him.

'Anne, a teacher, married a fellow with a big job. They don't believe in having children. They rarely come to see us, though we get cards from them from exotic places.

'Peter has three children and seemed to be a happily married. But then he suddenly left his wife, and went to live with a young girl. He never shows up.

'Paul, our baby, is still unmarried. He's touring the world like a hippie. Doesn't believe in working or settling down. Last word we got from him he was somewhere in Australia.

'None of them go to Church. Now what more could we have done for them? Do we deserve to be treated like this?'

Thereis great heart-break for religious parents who see their children abandoning the faith and/or adopting a lifestyle which they regard as immoral. How hard it is to go on loving them in spite of it all. Even when we do favours out of the goodness of our heart, we expect a return, and are hurt when it doesn't come. It's only natural. We feel taken for granted or even used.

What hurts Anne and Peter most is not the ingratitude of their children, but rather the way their children have turned out. They are sad for themselves, yes, but they are even sadder for their children. How frustrating and painful it is to give life to something and then give up control of it.

Today's readings seem to suggest that even God sometimes feels like this. The words of the First Reading, 'What more could I have done for my vineyard that I have not done?' is a cry from the heart. In spite of all the love he showed his people, Israel, all he got in return was utter ingratitude.

The people of Israel had been treated in a privileged manner by God. But privilege brings responsibility. They failed God. Yet God is not disappointed for his own sake. Rather he is disappointed because his people have squandered the blessings he wanted them to enjoy. Sadly, the vineyard is destined to become a wilderness.

What sort of fruits did God expect from his people? God looked for peace from his people, and got war; for true worship, and got idolatry; for justice in their dealings with one another, and got injustice, corruption, and exploitation of the poor and the weak; for goodness, and got evil; for caring and sharing, and got greed and acquisitiveness; for temperance, and got excessive eating and drinking; for community, and got exclusiveness and snobbery; for humility, and got pride; for wise and godly living, and got a pagan lifestyle.

This to some extent is our story too. God wants us to make use of the gifts and opportunities he has given us so that we can grow as his children. But often we fail to respond to his love. And yet, God doesn't write us off, but gives us chance after chance.

We fail not just as individuals but as Church. The Christian community is the vineyard Christ planted and tended with such care that he gave his life for it. He looks to us his followers, the tenants of his vineyard, to produce the fruits of justice, love and peace. It's a great privilege and a great challenge too.

A STORY

It is very hard to go on loving those who are ungrateful and unresponsive, those who take everything and give back nothing.

Once there was a woman who lived in a vinegar bottle. One day a kind magician passed by and heard her complaining, 'It's a shame that I have to live like this. I ought to live in a cottage with a thatched roof and roses growing up the walls.'

The magician took pity on her and granted her wish. She was very pleased but forgot to thank him. A year later as he was passing the cottage he heard her complaining, 'It's a shame that I have to live in a small isolated cottage like this. I ought to live in a house, among other houses, with lace curtains on the windows and a brass knocker on the door.'

The magician took pity on her and granted her wish. She was delighted but forgot to thank him. Another year went by. Then one day as he went past her house he heard her say, 'It's a shame that I have to live among such common people. I ought to live in a great mansion in the country, with a big garden and servants to answer the doorbell.'

Again the magician took pity on her and granted her request. She was very pleased, but again forgot to thank him. A few years went by, and the magician decided to call on her to see how she was doing. She said, 'It's a shame that I'm living all alone. I ought to be a duchess, driving my own coach and waited on like a queen.'

Once again the magician granted her request. And she was very pleased, but forgot to thank him. When he visited her a year later she said, 'It's a shame that I'm a mere duchess and have to courtesy to the queen. Why can't I be a queen myself, and sit on a throne, with a golden crown on my head?'

The magician granted her request. She was delighted but failed to thank him. Years passed and the magician said, 'I'll go and see how the old lady is doing. Surely she must be satisfied now?' But she said, 'It's a shame that I'm queen in a wretched little country like this. Why couldn't I be queen in a great country?'

The magician told her that he would grant her request in the morning. That night she went to bed, full of proud thoughts. However, when she woke up next morning she was back in her vinegar bottle. In a sense, she had never left it.

She reminds us of God's people who, no matter what God did for them, refused to produce the fruits, not so much of gratitude but of good living.

PRAYER OF THE FAITHFUL

President: We turn to the God of hosts, that he may visit us and protect us and let us face shine upon us as we call on his name.

Response: Lord, graciously hear us.

Reader(s): For the Christian community, the vineyard of Christ: that it may produce the fruits of justice, love and peace. [Pause] Lord, hear us.

For all believers: that they may realise that life is a gift from God, and use it wisely. [Pause] Lord, hear us.

For all those in positions of leadership: that they may be faithful in carrying out their duties. [Pause] Lord, hear us.

For all victims of ingratitude. [Pause] Lord, hear us.

For all gathered here: that we may be able to respond to God's love by loving others. [Pause] Lord, hear us.

For the blessing of God on our own special needs and concerns. [Longer pause] Lord, hear us.

President: Lord, watch over your Church with unfailing compassion, and since left to ourselves we are prone to evil, by your grace turn us away for all that is wrong, and direct us into the way of what is right. We make this prayer through Christ our Lord.

SIGN OF PEACE

Lord Jesus Christ, you said to your disciples: 'I am the vine, you are the branches. Separated from me you can do nothing; but united with me you will bear much fruit'. Strengthen the bonds that unite us with you and with one another, so that we may enjoy the peace and unity of your kingdom where you live for ever and ever.

PRAYER / REFLECTION   **Planted by God**

Lord, you planted me on this earth.
You fenced me around with the love of family and friends.
Their care towered over me.
In the shelter of this tower I grew in safety and peace.
I put out early blossoms; I filled up with leaves.
People had great hopes for me.
You had great hopes for me.

But now the year of my life is passing.
The harvest is approaching.
What fruit have I to show?
What if, after all this care,
I had nothing to offer but sour grapes?
May you, Lord, have mercy on me,
and with your patient urging
help me to produce the fruits of love.

Twenty-eighth Sunday of the Year
THE WEDDING FEAST

INTRODUCTION AND CONFITEOR

We are gathered here to participate in the banquet of the Eucharist. We are here because God, in his love, has invited us, and we have accepted his invitation. Let us try to bring a spirit of thankfulness and joy to our celebration. [Pause]

Lord, you invite us to a banquet of truth and life. Lord, have mercy.
You invite us to a banquet of holiness and grace. Christ, have mercy.
You invite us to a banquet of justice, love and peace. Lord, have mercy.

HEADINGS FOR READINGS

First Reading (Is 25:6-10). The image of a banquet describes the blessings God wishes to bestow, not only on Israel, but on all nations.

Second Reading (Phil 4:12-14.19-20). Paul thanks the Philippians for their support but says that his real strength comes form the Lord.

Gospel (Mt 22:1-14). Isaiah's promise is fulfilled in Jesus: through him all God's people are invited to the banquet feast of the Kingdom.

SCRIPTURE NOTE

Isaiah uses the image of a banquet to describe the fullness of life that God wants to bestow, not just on Israel, but on all the peoples of the earth. Jesus uses the same image in his parable. In its original, simpler form, the parable made the point that those to whom the invitation was first sent (the Jews) rejected it, and their place has been taken by others (the Gentiles). The details about the sending of troops and the burning of the city, were added later. They refer to the destruction of Jerusalem in 70 A.D., which was seen as a consequence of the refusal of the Jewish leaders to listen to Jesus.

The incident concerning the wedding garment seems to have belonged to a separate parable. It introduces contradictory elements into the story, and is perhaps best omitted. However, if used, keep the following in mind. Courtesy demanded that any guest at a wedding should have the proper wedding garment. One man came without it, symbolising a life that has undergone no basic change, a life that has not produced the fruits of repentance. The new guests (Christians) will suffer the same fate as Israel if they don't produce the fruits of good works.

HOMILY 1   **The good is the enemy of the best**

A royal wedding feast was (and still is) a wonderful event, and to be invited to it was a marvellous privilege. The question arises: Why would people refuse something as wonderful as that? The following story may help to answer this question.

Tom was doing his spring ploughing when the king's messenger appeared unexpectedly in his field, bearing some wonderful news.

'You are invited to the royal banquet,' the messenger said.

On hearing this Tom began to glow like a full moon. In a flash, his humdrum life was transformed. 'When exactly is the banquet?' he asked.

'Tonight,' the messenger replied, adding, 'I'll be back in about an hour for your answer. I must have a clear yes or no.' With that he departed.

The banquet was to be held that very night! This changed things. He looked back over the work he had done. It was going well. Then he looked ahead at what remained to be done. With luck he could finish it today. It would be a great relief to have it over with. The weather was ideal. But would it last? Then he considered the oxen. They were new to the job. He was still breaking them in. This was something which should not be interrupted.

At that moment he looked up and what did he see? He saw the royal messenger going into his neighbour's field. So that man was being invited too! Suppose, as was quite likely, he was placed next to him at table? That would be intolerable. All of a sudden the banquet began to lose some of its appeal.

Then there was the tedious business of getting washed and changed. And what clothes would he wear? Even his best suit was hardly good enough for a royal banquet, and he would hate to look shabby in the presence of the king and all the other guests.

Thus, one by one, the clouds of doubt began to gather, and what only a short while ago had been a blue and radiant sky, now turned murky and dark. Tom began to have second thoughts. Then third thoughts. It would be nice to finish the ploughing today. It was necessary to complete the breaking in of the oxen.

'Ah,' he sighed, 'if only the banquet was tomorrow night, and I had the ploughing done, I wouldn't think twice about accepting the invitation.'

By the time the messenger came back his mind was made up.

'Well,' said the messenger, 'are you going?'

'I have to finish this piece of ploughing,' Tom began. 'I have to finish breaking in the oxen. Besides, I ... ' But the messenger was in a hurry and interrupted him:

'Just tell me whether it is yes or no.'

'I'm afraid it will have to be no,' said Tom. He was about to resume his litany of excuses, but the messenger was already out of earshot.

Notice that the things which kept Tom from accepting the invitation were not bad things, but good things. And in Jesus 'story, the things which kept the invited guests from accepting the invitation were, for the most part, not bad things, but perfectly reasonable things: the cares of work and business. We have more to fear from the good than the bad. The bad is more likely to repel us, whereas the good attracts us.

It is not when the path is strewn with difficulties that we may fail to reach our goal. Rather it is when it is easy and full of attractions. In the latter case we are tempted to dally, are easily side-tracked, and so may forget our goal.

Those who are well-fed have no need of a banquet. Those who are materially secure may experience no need of God or spiritual things. It is the poor who are likely to be rich in faith. Everything comes as a blessing to them.

Jesus says, 'Woe to you who are full now, for you will go hungry. But blessed are you who are hungry now, for you will be filled.' A sense of something missing can be a blessing. A spiritual hunger and thirst are God's ways of inviting us to his banquet.

What is the banquet? The banquet stands for the fullness of life to which God is calling us. It is a call to intimacy with God, and to a deeper and more authentic personal life. But it is also a call to community with others. The invitation challenges us to abandon our isolationism, our exclusivism, our self-sufficiency, and to be willing to share with others, to associate with others, and to collaborate with others. And, of course, in the final analysis, it is a call to eternal life in the hereafter.

Just as parents want the best for their children, so God wants the best for us who are his children. And only God knows what is truly best for us.

HOMILY 2   **Ways of responding**

Let us suppose that you are giving a party. When you have fixed the date, you draw up a list of the people you wish to invite. Then you send out the invitations with RSVP emblazoned on them, and wait for the responses to come back. Basically you can expect three kinds of responses.

Some accept your invitation. Every acceptance makes you feel happy. Of course there can be degrees of acceptance. Some may accept half-heartedly; they are coming only because they feel in some way obliged to come. But others may accept with enthusiasm; they feel honoured and grateful for having been invited.

Others refuse your invitation. Every refusal disappoints you, perhaps even hurts you, but at least you know where you stand with these people. There can also be degrees of refusal. In some cases it may that people would like to come but can't because they have a prior engagement on the date in question. But in other cases people are just not interested; it's not that they can't come, but that they won't come.

There is a third way of responding to the invitation – by not responding at all. Yes, that too is a response. You wait and wait for a reply but none comes. This is worst kind of response of all. It's worse than a refusal. When people refuse the invitation, you know where you stand with them. But here you don't. You are left wondering what's going on. Have you inadvertently done something to offend the invited ones? You don't know, and you probably never will know. If you were to contact them, they would probably say, 'Oh, I meant to reply, but . . .' I meant to! What an empty feeling this leaves you with.

God doesn't compel us. He invites us. A command can't be so easily ignored, but an invitation can. Advertisers can't compel us to buy a certain product, but they resort to all kinds of gimmicks to try to persuade and cajole us into buying it. God doesn't act like that. He has too much respect for our freedom.

Often we don't know what we really want, or even what is good for us. What we are seeking, and what deep down we really value and desire, are not always the same thing. Perhaps we are so busy, our lives are so full, that even God has difficulty in breaking through to us.

Only God knows what is truly best for us. And just as parents want the best for their children, so God wants the best for us, who are his children.

What is God calling us to? God is calling us to a deeper and more authentic life here on earth. He is calling us into intimacy with himself. He is calling us into community with others. And at death he will call us into eternal life.

To ignore God's invitation altogether is the worst form of refusal. It implies indifference. Indifferent people are the hardest to convert.

HOMILY 3   **The banquet**

Jesus' story might seem a bit far-fetched. Who would be so crazy as to turn down an invitation to a royal wedding? But people can be very foolish. There is a streak in us that not only refuses the good, but can't even recognise it. God is continually calling us, as individuals and a community, to a deeper and more authentic life. But, alas, this precious invitation is like the seed that fell among the thorns. It gets choked. A brief look at our lives will show how this happens.

There is that letter I know I should write, but just now I'm not in the mood.

There is that sick person I know I should visit, but right now my favourite programme is on television.

I know I need to pray, but I just don't seem to be able to find time for it.

I know I should make an effort to get to Mass on time (or just to get to Mass at all), but something always gets in the way.

I know I should be more charitable towards X, but I just can't summon up the will to make the effort.

I know that dishonesty is wrong, but I tell myself that everybody does it, and what I do is minor compared to what others are up to.

I know I don't do my job as well as I should, but why should I break my back when others aren't pulling their weight?

I know I drink too much, but I'm under a lot of pressure these days.

I know I should spend more time with my children, but I need that overtime money.

One could go on. Each of us, if we got down to it, could draw up quite a long list of things which we know, in our heart of hearts, we should do, or should not do, but which we refuse to look at. And we have no shortage of excuses. They spring up to our defence like over-enthusiastic security guards.

The excuses that kept the invited guests from attending the wedding feast, weren't all bad. In fact, in most cases they were perfectly good ones: one man wanted to attend to his land; another to his business; and so on. But this is precisely what makes them so dangerous. We don't see them as posing a threat.

The greatest danger facing us is not that we might abandon God and turn to evil, but rather that we might just ignore his invitation. To ignore God's invitation altogether is the worst form of refusal. It implies indifference. Indifferent people are the hardest to convert.

We are invited not merely as individuals but as a community. It is the banquet of the new People of God, namely, the Christian community. The invitation challenges us to give up our isolationism, our exclusivism, our self-sufficiency. To accept means to admit our need and willingness to receive from others, to share with others, to associate with others, and to collaborate with others.

We don't have to earn our place at the banquet. We are invited. It seems so simple to come to an unearned banquet. However, for class-conscious people, that can be difficult.

ANOTHER STORY

Excuses, excuses, excuses! We have excuses for not doing what we know we should do. And we have excuses for doing what we know we shouldn't do. Some of these excuses are reasonable, some shabby. But all are effective.

Once there was a tailor who mended the clothes of everybody in town, yet he himself went about with his coat in tatters. And to the embarrassment of everyone he appeared like that in church on Sundays.

One Sunday a friend said to him, 'It's a disgrace that you, a respectable tailor, should go around in a tattered coat. Shame on you for coming here dressed like that.'

'But what can I do? I'm a poor man and I have to work all week long to make a living,' the tailor replied. 'Where am I going to find the time to mend my own clothes?'

'Look,' said the friend. 'Here's £20. Think of me as one of your customers. I'm paying you to mend your own coat.'

'I'll agree to that,' cried the tailor as he took the money.

However, when he came to church on the following Sunday the friend noticed that once again he was dressed in his old tattered coat. Extremely annoyed, the friend said to him,

'Now there is no excuse for this kind of behaviour. Didn't I give you £20 last Sunday to mend your coat? Yet I can see that you never even touched it.'

'What can I do?' said the tailor apologetically. 'When I went home last Sunday I examined my coat, and I realised that I'd be losing money on the job if I did it for £20.'

A man like that will always find an excuse.

PRAYER OF THE FAITHFUL

President: As we meet in God's house, we trust that God's goodness shall follow all those for whom we pray.

Response: Lord, hear our prayer.

Reader(s): For the Christian community: that it may strive to provide a feast of faith, hope and love for all of God's children, but especially the poor. [Pause] Let us pray to the Lord.

For all government leaders: that they may be untiring in their efforts to provide all their people with a feast of freedom, justice and peace. [Pause] Let us pray to the Lord.

For all those who through poverty, illness, or oppression are locked out of life's banquet. [Pause] Let us pray to the Lord.

For this congregation: that we may experience a hunger and thirst for goodness of life. [Pause] Let us pray to the Lord.

For opportunities to bring our own special needs into the presence of God. [Longer pause] Let us pray to the Lord.

President: Lord, may we love you in all things and above all things, and reach the joy you have prepared for us, which is beyond all our imagining. We ask this through Christ our Lord.

REFLECTION   **God's call**

God's call comes to us in many ways
and at many different levels.
However, his call is not so much a voice
as a tug at our hearts, which we feel
at quiet and reflective moments in our lives.
He is calling us to a deeper and more authentic life.
He is calling us into intimacy with himself.
He is calling us into community with others.
And at death he will call us into eternal life.
To accept means to admit our need.
Jesus said, 'Woe to you who are full now,
for you will go hungry.
But blessed are you who are hungry now,
for you will be filled.'
A sense of something missing in our lives
is not a curse but a blessing.
A spiritual hunger
is God's way of inviting us to his banquet.

Twenty-ninth Sunday of the Year
GOD AND CAESAR

INTRODUCTION AND CONFITEOR

We give God something that we do not give to any earthly ruler. That thing is worship. And this is precisely why we are gathered here – to worship God, Creator of the universe and Lord of all. Sadly, in practice we don't always put God first in our lives. [Pause]

Even though God is all-powerful, he exercises his power by showing mercy to sinners.

Lord, you are kind and full of compassion; slow to anger, abounding in love. Lord, have mercy.

Lord, you are faithful in all your words, and loving in all your deeds. Christ, have mercy.

Lord, you support the weak, and raise up the fallen. Lord, have mercy.

HEADINGS FOR READINGS

First Reading (Is 45:1.4-6). The return of the people from exile – a return made possible by King Cyrus – is seen as a sign of God's love for his people, Israel, and of his lordship over all peoples.

Second Reading (1 Thess 1:1-5). Here we see Paul's concern for the Christians at Thessalonika.

Gospel (Mt 22:15-21). This is the story of an effort by the enemies of Jesus to trap him into saying something incriminating.

SCRIPTURE NOTE

The question put to Jesus was a test question to see whether he would declare himself on the side of those who opposed paying taxes to the Romans (e.g. the Pharisees), or on the side of those who collaborated with the Romans (e.g. the Herodians). If he said Yes, he would lose the esteem of the people, and would be regarded as a traitor to the Jewish cause and the Jewish religion. If he said No, he could be denounced as fomenting rebellion against Rome. In his answer Jesus recognises that the State has a role, but its power is limited and does not supplant God.

HOMILY 1   **Dual citizenship**

The question as to whether or not it was lawful to pay taxes to Caesar was a serious one, and it really put Jesus in a spot. If he said it was lawful, he would be regarded as a traitor to the Jewish cause and the Jewish religion. If he said it was unlawful, he could be denounced as fomenting rebellion against Rome.

In his answer Jesus implied that there need not be conflict between the demands of the State and those of God. The State has a role, but its power is limited and does not supplant God. From this principle Christians deduced that they could accommodate loyalty to the State.

Today you can find people who enjoy dual citizenship – they are citizens of two countries. Every Christian has dual citizenship.

Christians are citizens of the country in which they happen to be living or in which they were born. To it they owe many benefits. To its forces of law and order they owe the fact that they are able to live in peace and security. To its public services they owe transport, water, light, etc. In a welfare state they also owe their education, medical care, unemployment benefits, and so on, to it.

All of these benefits mean they are under obligation to the State. The legitimate State has rights, and Christians will respect those rights. They must respect its laws and rulers. They must be responsible citizens, and, as far as they are able, must play their part in making the country a good place for all its citizens. Failure to be a good citizen is a failure in Christian duty. To cheat the State is to cheat one's fellow citizens, and to cheat one's fellow citizens is the cheat God.

But Christians are also citizens of the Kingdom of Heaven. To it they owe certain other privileges, and to it they also have obligations. In many cases the two responsibilities do not clash. But at times they may. And when they do, Christians will spontaneously know which comes first.

However, it may not always be that simple. What Jesus gave us was only a principle. He didn't give a detailed theory of political obligations or a blue-print for Church-State relations. Christians would have to work out the implications of it. In practice it is not always easy to say this is for Caesar and that for God. Life is a unity. It can't be split into two clearly defined parts – the secular part and the religious part.

However, history shows unequivocally that separation of Church and State is absolutely essential. But when Jesus said, 'Give to Caesar what belongs to Caesar' his assumption was that Caesar's claim would be just. He wasn't giving Caesar a blank cheque.

Christians can sometimes be faced with a real dilemma – how to be a Christian in a secular world where the laws may often be unchristian. However, true Christians will strive to be good citizens of their country, and at the same time good citizens of the Kingdom of Heaven. They will fail neither in their duty to God nor to their fellow men and women.

But as Christians our first and deepest loyalty is to God. To God alone we render worship, but in other things we gladly acknowledge and serve the secular powers, praying that they will rule wisely and justly.

HOMILY 2 **The Christian and politics**

The question posed to Jesus was an attempt to draw him into the world of politics. Politics has a very bad name today. Politicians are frequently caricatured and laughed at. Hence, Christians tend to opt out of the affairs of the world, and to leave to others dangerous, daring, and responsible things such as politics, law-making, and business. But when they do this they are leaving these things to others who may not be motivated by Christian values and principles.

Christians should not shirk public office, but see it as a chance to serve their fellow men and women and thereby God. The Pharisees opted out of real life and kept themselves apart. The result was a vain religiosity which had little or nothing to do with life.

Dag Hammarskjold was Secretary-general of the UN. When he died in a plane crash in central Africa in 1961 at the age of fifty-six the world lost a great servant of peace. He was that rare person for whom public service is not simply a career or a means of achieving power, but a religious vocation, a way of being faithful to God. He drew inspiration from the Old Testament prophets. He said, 'Indifference to evil is worse than evil itself, and in a free society, some are guilty, but all are responsible.'

Gandhi is another example of a deeply religious man who involved himself in politics. He said, 'I am in politics because I cannot separate life from belief. Because I believe in God I have to enter politics. Politics is my service of God.'

And Nelson Mandela is yet another example. Mandela tells how when he began to get interested in politics a friend tried to warn him off, saying, 'Politics brings out the worst in people. It is the source of trouble and corruption, and should be avoided at all costs.' Fortunately for South Africa and for the world, Mandela ignored his advice.

It's a great pity that politics is so lowly regarded. Politics plays a vital role in creating the kind of society in which we live. What greater vocation is there than to assume responsibility for national and international affairs – to work for peace and justice in the world, for the betterment of human life for all. 'No life is more satisfactory than that of selfless service to your country or humanity.' (Dag Hammarskjold)

But politics is not an easy profession, and the temptations are great. The chief temptation is to promote one's own good rather than the good of society. It's not easy for a Christian to be involved in politics and in business today. It means he or she is God's servant and Caesar's too.

Jesus' injunction: 'Give to Caesar what belong to Caesar, and to God what belongs to God' is only a principle. We have to work out the implications of it. and in practice it may not always be easy to draw a clear line between the civil sphere and the religious sphere.

The lines of division are not clearly marked. The boundaries are often blurred and areas overlap. Of course, for a believer, in a sense everything is given to God, even what is given to Caesar. But if it is a question of having to choose one against the other, the Christian has only one choice.

What history shows unequivocally is that separation of Church and State is absolutely essential. However, when Jesus said, 'Give to Caesar what belong to Caesar, and to God what belongs to God,' his assumption was that Caesar's claim would be just. He was not giving a blank cheque to Caesar.

A true Christian is at one and the same time a good citizen of his country, and a good citizen of the Kingdom of Heaven. He will fail neither in his duty to God nor to his fellow men and women.

Our first and deepest loyalty is to God. To God alone we render worship, but in other things we gladly acknowledge and serve the secular powers, praying that they will rule wisely and justly.

HOMILY 3   **Allegiance to God comes first**

God and Caesar (or at least those who speak in their names) have always proved hard to reconcile. Each seeks to swallow up the other. On the one hand, you can have a dictatorship in which God and religion are outlawed. On the other hand, you can have a religious fundamentalism which leads to theocracy, and theocracy is the arch-enemy of democracy.

The most important part of a ship is the rudder. Without the rudder it could not be steered. It would simply run amuck. The most precious thing we possess is our conscience. Without a conscience we could not steer the barque of our lives towards the harbour of truth and right. It is easy to sell one's conscience or to hand it over to someone else. But for Christians God must always have the first claim on our conscience.

Franz Jäggerstatter was born in Austria and was brought up a Catholic. He was an ordinary, unremarkable young man who had only an elementary education and who became a casual worker. There was nothing about him to suggest that he had in him the stuff of martyrs.

However, at some stage he suddenly matured. He became very responsible and began to take his religion seriously. He was not, however, fanatical about it. He married a girl by the name of Anna, and they had three children.

By this time the Second World War was raging. At thirty-six Franz was called up to serve in Hitler's army. But he refused to join up. This was tantamount to suicide. Friends tried to talk him into joining up.

'I cannot join,' he said simply.

'Why not?' they asked.

'Because I believe that this war is not a just war. Therefore, it would be wrong for me to join up. It would be against my conscience.'

'But many others have joined up. So why can't you?' they persisted.

'What others do is their business. I have to answer for my own conscience.'

'But where's your loyalty to your people, to your country, to your flag?' they continued.

'I love my people, and I love my country. But there's a higher law – God's law. And God's law tells me that this war is wrong.'

It wasn't that he wanted to die. He had a lot to live for. He was arrested and put in prison. There further efforts were made to get him to change his mind. Even his wife begged him to reconsider his decision. But all to no avail. Franz was beheaded on August 9,1943. He felt he was obeying the words of Christ: 'Give to Caesar what belongs to Caesar, and to God what belongs to God.' Indeed, the memorable words of Thomas More could be applied to him: 'I die the King's good servant, but God's first'.

Today you could say that Caesar's place is taken by the secular State, that is, the State which is not so much against God as without God. It no longer bases its law on God's laws. This can pose serious dilemmas for Christians, especially those in public office. They cannot impose their own moral values and beliefs on others, yet they must not take part in what, from a Christian viewpoint, is morally wrong.

Every Christian living in the modern world is faced with difficult decisions. There are so many little 'Caesars' vying for a piece of our conscience. There is the party, the company, the club. Franz Jäggerstatter shows us that we must give God the first and highest claim on our loyalty. Whatever else we must give to Caesar, let us make sure that we do not give him our conscience.

PRAYER OF THE FAITHFUL

President: Let us pray that we may not be afraid to stand up and be counted in a world that often ignores the values of Christ.

Response: Lord, graciously hear us.

For all Church leaders: that they may not be afraid to speak out, and so provide a voice for truth and justice in the world. [Pause] Lord, hear us.

For our political and civil leaders: that they may respect freedom of religion and freedom of conscience. [Pause] Lord, hear us.

For those who are suffering in the cause of right. [Pause] Lord, hear us.

For all gathered here: that our lives may bear witnesses to the faith we profess with our lips. [Pause] Lord, hear us.

For our own special needs. [Longer pause] Lord, hear us.

President: Lord, grant us in all our tasks your help, in all our dangers your protection, in all our doubts your guidance, and in all our sorrows your consolation. We ask this through Christ our Lord.

REFLECTION   **Life and religion**

Who can separate his faith from his actions,
or his belief from his occupations?
Who can spread his hours before him, saying:
'This for God and this for myself;
this for my soul and this other for my body?'
He who wears his morality but as his best garment
were better naked.
Your daily life is your temple and your religion.
Whenever you enter into it take with you your all.
Take the plough and the forge and the mallet and the lute,
the things you have fashioned in necessity or for delight.
And take with you all men.
And if you would know God ... look about you
and you will see him playing with your children. (Kahlil Gibran, *The Prophet*, William Heinemann)

Thirtieth Sunday of the Year
THE TWO GREAT COMMANDMENTS

INTRODUCTION AND CONFITEOR

Today's Gospel reminds us of the two great commandments: love of God and love of neighbour. Here in a nutshell we have the whole teaching of the Bible. The only real failure for a Christian is the failure to love. Let us reflect for a moment on this. [Pause]

Lord Jesus, you teach us how to love God with all our heart and all our soul. Lord, have mercy.

Lord Jesus, you teach us how to love our neighbour as ourselves. Christ, have mercy.

Lord Jesus, you teach us that these two commandments sum up the whole of religion. Lord, have mercy.

HEADINGS FOR READINGS

First Reading (Ex 22:20-26). God tells the Israelites that there must be no discrimination against or exploitation of the weak members of their society.

Second Reading (1 Thess 1:5-10) Paul encourages the Thessalonians by telling them that their exemplary lives have become known far and wide.

Gospel (Mt 22:34-40). Jesus tells us that the whole of religion can be summed up in two commandments of love.

SCRIPTURE NOTE

By rabbinical count, 'the Law' consisted of some 613 commandments. The question as to which commandment was the greatest was one frequently discussed among the rabbis. Jesus was asked to name one, but responded by naming two. That is because, for him, the second followed directly and necessarily from the first. Love of neighbour arises out of love of God. Both commandments are found in the Old Testament. What is new is not the fact that Jesus brought these two commandments together, but that he made them of equal importance.

HOMILY 1   The total Gospel

Jesus was asked to name the greatest commandment, and responded by naming two, both found in the Old Testament. Jesus brought them together and made them of equal importance. Hence, we must not separate them. However, in practice we often do.

In the time of the desert monks there was an abbot by the name of

Moses who had a great reputation for holiness. Easter was approaching, so the monks met to see what they should do to prepare for it. They decided to fast the entire length of Holy Week. Having come to the decision, each monk went off to his cell, there to fast and pray.

However, about the middle of the week, two wandering monks came to visit the cell of Abbot Moses. Seeing that they were starving, he cooked a little vegetable stew for them. To make them feel at ease he took a little of it himself.

Meanwhile the other monks had seen the smoke rising from their abbot's cell. It could mean only one thing – he had lit a fire to cook some food. In other words, he had broken the solemn fast. They were shocked, and in the eyes of many of them, he fell from his pinnacle of sanctity. In a body they went over to confront him.

Seeing judgement in their eyes, he asked, 'What crime have I committed that makes you look at me like this?'

'You've broken the solemn fast,' they answered.

'So I have,' he replied. 'I have broken the commandment of men, but in sharing my food with these brothers of ours, I have kept the commandment of God that we should love one another.'

On hearing this, the monks grew silent, and went away humbled but wiser.

There is a terrible sterility about the lives of those who claim to love God, but in reality dispense themselves from all obligations to love other people. Such people have at best got only half of the Gospel.

There are others who go to the opposite extreme. They exhaust themselves in working for a better world, but never think of God or pray to him. Though the latter are on firmer ground, they too have only half of the Gospel – the half believers sometimes throw away.

Christ showed us how to live the total Gospel, that is, how to love God and to love our neighbour as well. He didn't say they were the same thing, but that we can't have one without the other.

HOMILY 2   **Love your neighbour as yourself**

Jesus said, 'You must love your neighbour as yourself.' Only when we accept ourselves as fundamentally good, and begin to love ourselves, will we be able to start loving other people as the Lord commanded.

Those who are filled with self-loathing and self-hatred are not going to be able to love others. They will project these feelings onto others. They will blame and castigate others for what they do not like in themselves.

An old man was sitting on a bench at the edge of town when a stranger approached. 'What are the people in this town like?' the stranger asked.

'What were they like in your last town?' replied the old man.

'They were kind, generous, and would do anything for you if you were in trouble.'

'Well, I think you will find them much the same in this town.'

Some time later a second stranger approached the old man and asked the same question: 'What are the people in this town like?'

And the old man replied: 'What were they like in the town you have come from?'

'It was a terrible place,' came the answer. 'To tell you the truth, I was glad to get out of it. The people there were mean, unkind, and nobody would lift a finger to help you if you were in trouble.'

'I'm afraid,' said the old man, 'you'll find them much the same in this town.'

The main point of this story is: We see other people not as they are but as we are. If we see people in a bad light, it is a sign that we are ill at ease with ourselves. A man who is not at peace with himself spreads a contagion of conflict around him.

Unless we love ourselves we cannot love others properly. So to begin with we must love ourselves. But if we love ourselves in the wrong way, then we become incapable of loving anyone else. Few love themselves in such a way as to be able to love others properly.

There is an idea that love of self is wrong, even sinful. There is, of course, a form of self-love which is wrong. We call it selfishness or egoism. But there is a form of self-love which is healthy and good, and without which we cannot really love others.

You can't fly without wings. You can't grow without roots. We can't offer warmth to others if our own fireplace is cold and empty. We can only love with the amount of love that is in us. Whether we are conscious of it or not, we do love others precisely as we love ourselves.

It's very important, then, to have a healthy love and respect for ourselves. This is where love starts, but of course it is not meant to end there. All true love of self overflows in the form of love of others and of God.

It's easy to love certain people because they are loveable. But not so easy to love others, who are clearly and obviously flawed. But that is the real test of love. Where there is no love, sow love, and you will reap love. Where there is no love, put love, and you will find love.

HOMILY 3   **Remember that you were once strangers**

We are often told to forget painful experiences. But how can we learn from them if we forget them? Memory of suffering can be used in a positive or negative way. It can be used to say, 'We know what suffering is like, therefore we have no excuse for allowing it to be inflicted on others.' Or it can be used to say, 'We have suffered, therefore, we have a right to inflict suffering.'

They say that compassion is not learned without suffering.

Yet suffering doesn't always help people to grow in compassion. Suffering can harden people, so that they end up inflicting on others the cruelties inflicted on them. And so the cycle goes on.

The time of the exile and enslavement in Egypt was undoubtedly the darkest time in the history of God's people. It took them a long time to escape from there, and even longer to put it behind them. And yet they are told not to forget it but to remember it (First Reading). Why?

Because now things have changed for the better for them. They have a homeland of their own. They have a king of their own and an army of their own. However, there are many foreigners among them, as well as their own poor, especially orphans and widows. These people are very vulnerable.

Only once in the Old Testament do we find the commandment: 'You shall love your neighbour as yourself' (Lev 19:18). But in no fewer than thirty-seven places we find the commandment to love the stranger. The 'stranger' stands for refugees, exiles, foreigners, that is, anyone in an alien country in which he or she has no civil rights.

The Jews were reminded continually that they themselves were once strangers and exiles in Egypt, depending on the kindness of others. Now that they are settled, they have a duty to be kind to the stranger in their midst.

God commanded his people to remember so that history would not repeat itself. He wanted them never to forget the experience of being a minority without power in Egypt. They must not oppress the stranger, because they were once strangers themselves. They must plead the cause of the underprivileged, because they were once underprivileged themselves. Having felt the pain of injustice and oppression themselves, they must never inflict that pain on others.

The saying of God, 'I will kill you by the sword,' sounds shocking. However, it is not to be taken literally. God does not act like this. What the prophet wants to convey is just how abominable it is in God's eyes when we mistreat anyone, especially the defenceless. As a people who have experienced God's love in a very special way, they must now show that love to others. To seek to be attached to God while treating others unjustly would be a contradiction in terms.

It's easy to forget where we have come from. There are signs that this is happening to American Catholics. Many of them seem to have forgotten that not so long ago they were strangers in a strange land, where they were subjected to economic and social discrimination. Increasingly they vote for candidates who spread rancour against the poor and the foreigner. In so doing they encourage people with twisted minds to take the next step – violent action against the stranger and outsider.

The health of a society can be measured by the way it treats such people. It's not good enough to give them charity. What they need is justice. If you say you love someone, then treat him justly. Charity is no substitute for real loving. 'Charity is the opium of the wealthy.' (Chinua Achebe, Nigerian writer)

PRAYER OF THE FAITHFUL

President: We join our hearts and our voices in prayer to the God who is our rock, our mighty help, our stronghold.

Response: Lord, hear us in your love.

Reader(s): For all Christians: that they may live out in their lives the two commandments of love. [Pause] We pray in faith.

For political leaders: that they may show special concern for the weaker members of society. [Pause] We pray in faith.

For the world in which we live: that love and peace may prevail over hatred and violence. [Pause] We pray in faith.

For refugees, strangers and aliens: that they may find hospitality. [Pause] We pray in faith.

For all gathered here: that we may love ourselves in such a way that it enables us to love others and to love God. [Pause] We pray in faith.

For our own special needs. [Longer pause] We pray in faith.

President: All-loving God, your Son summed up all your law in two commandments: that we should love you and love one another. He himself lived these two commandments to the full. Help us to follow his example. We ask this through the same Christ our Lord.

REFLECTION **The total Gospel**

To separate the two great commandments
is a tragedy and goes clean contrary to the Gospel.
Yet unfortunately this often happens.
Those who have faith often have no love,
and those who love often have no faith.
Thus the Gospel has been torn in two.
Jesus spoke of two great commandments.
The first – that we should love God.
The second – that we should love our neighbour.
He didn't say that they were the same thing,
but that they are like two sides of the one coin.
If we want the total Gospel we must have both.
He himself showed us how to do this.

Thirty-first Sunday of the Year
ATTACK ON THE SCRIBES AND PHARISEES

INTRODUCTION AND CONFITEOR

Jesus had some harsh criticism to make of the Scribes and Pharisees. He called them hypocrites, because they didn't practise what they preached. Which of us can truthfully say that our deeds match our words? Therefore, to some extent, all of us are hypocrites. But each time we come to celebrate the Eucharist we are called by God to a life of truth and genuine goodness. [Pause]

Let us confess our sins humbly to God and to one another.

I confess to almighty God …

HEADINGS FOR READINGS

First Reading (Mal 1:14-2:2.8-10). The prophet berates the priests of his day for failing to live up to their calling.

Second Reading (1 Thess 2:7-9.13). Paul reminds the Thessalonians of his love and care for them, and how hard he worked to bring them the Good News.

Gospel (Mt 23:1-12). Jesus launches a strong attack on the Scribes and Pharisees, but what he says is important for us too.

SCRIPTURE NOTE

Malachi attacks the laxity and carelessness that have set in regarding morality and worship. He specifically takes the priests to task, berating them for not living up to their calling, and thus being responsible for the erosion of faith among the people.

In the Gospel we see how strong Jesus was in his criticism of those who use religion to gain spiritual power, and who do not live what is at the heart of religion: love and compassion, justice and faith.

Matthew applies it to Christian leaders, who are in danger of repeating the mistakes of the Pharisees.

The message is as relevant now as it was back then. Religious office-holders are still reluctant to let go of ostentatious dress, places of honour, titles and so on, which are clearly contrary to the spirit of the Gospel.

HOMILY 1   **All words but no deeds**

At the root of innumerable wrongs in our world is the discrepancy between word and deed. It is the weakness of churches, parties, and individuals. It gives people and institutions split personalities. This was the chief fault Christ found with the Pharisees: 'They do not practise what they preach.'

The rose is one of the most beautiful flowers of all. However, it requires a lot of careful tending if it is to be seen at its best. In the part of the world I then lived in, we were lucky to have an expert on roses. Damien was his name. His fame had spread far and wide. Proof of this could be seen in the fact that he was in constant demand.

He travelled the length and breadth of the country giving talks on roses and how to grow them. He spoke not only with great knowledge of his subject but also with great love of it. Thanks to his talks, many people filled their gardens with exquisite roses.

As I am keenly interested in roses, there was a time when I followed Damien around, lapping up every word that fell from his lips. One of the very first things I heard him say was, 'No garden can truly be called a garden if it does not possess at least one rose.' I also heard him say, 'If you wish to have good roses be prepared for a lot of hard work. If you are afraid of thorns then leave roses alone.'

One day I shook hands with him after one of his talks, congratulating him on the excellence of it. As I did so I was conscious of one thing. This was the hand of a master rose grower. Naturally I expected his hand to be hard and coarse. Yet to my surprise I found it to be smooth and soft. I looked at it. It didn't bear the slightest mark of a rose thorn.

The following evening I found out why those hands were so well-preserved. I visited the expert in his own home. To my astonishment I found that his garden – that little plot of ground which had been given to him alone to till – was not only bereft of the humblest specimen of rose, but also overgrown with weeds.

The sad thing was: the master rose-grower did not practise what he preached. And he himself was the chief loser. His own garden, which could have been filled with beautiful roses, was overgrown with weeds. We should never recommend something unless we can provide a little sample of it.

If we practise what we preach, if we live by our beliefs, we ourselves will be the first to benefit. But we will also set a good example for others. People whose religion begins and ends with worship and ritual practices are like soldiers forever manoeuvring, but never getting into action, or footballers forever training but never playing a competitive game.

Like beautiful flowers full of colour but without scent, so are the well-chosen words of the person who does not act accordingly.

What great prophets have said is forgotten, but what heroes and saints have done is still remembered. There can be no happiness for us, as long as the things we believe in are different from the things we do.

Do not say things. What you are stands over you all the while and thunders so loudly that I cannot hear what you say to the contrary. (*Ralph Waldo Emerson*)

Neglecting the interior

Today there is great emphasis on appearances. The image is everything. People put on a front, but deep down they are not like that at all. You can't go by appearances.

The castle stands on an elevation overlooking beautiful woods and lakes. It dominates the surrounding countryside. Though it hasn't been lived in for the best part of a century, it still seems to be in good shape – from the outside at least. Not a stone appears to be missing. Its stout walls, turrets, towers, buttresses all are intact and give it an impressive appearance.

But just step inside the castle and you see a completely different picture. Inside it is a complete shambles. There are heaps of fallen masonry and plaster everywhere. The main roof is missing and so are most of the ceilings and floors. Of course, there isn't a stick of furniture to be found in it. The big fireplaces are cold and empty. The building is little more than a shell. How deceptive appearances can be.

So it was with the Scribes and Pharisees. On the outside they appeared to be good and holy people. But inside they were anything but.

This is a danger that faces all of us. Each of us has two selves – an outer self and an inner self. The outer self is the public self – the one that is seen by others. The inner one is the private self – the one seen only by ourselves. The outer self is the shell; the inner self is the kernel. Too often the nuts with the biggest shells are empty.

Why do we feel the need to pretend, or to impress others? Because most of us get our self-worth from what others think of us. Hence, in our need for approval, acceptance, and status, we may promote the outer self at the expense of the inner self. But of what use is the appearance without the reality, the image without the substance?

We cannot achieve either happiness or holiness as long as we pretend to be what we are not. The moment we try to be what we are not, we become a fictitious personality, an unreal presence. Many religious people are not saints because they never succeed in being themselves.

When people concentrate on inner goodness they don't have to shout about it, or even want to. They know with a quiet certainty that they have something which no one can take from them, something which makes them feel worthwhile, no matter what others may think of them. They have self-esteem and self-respect.

Christ was able to see beneath the appearances, behind the masks. He saw the inner person. Thus he looked at the Scribes and Pharisees and saw a pious exterior. But on looking deeper he saw, sadly, that beneath the religious pomp and show, they were hollow inside. On the other hand, it gave him great joy when he found a genuine person. He gladly put up with Peter because he knew that in spite of his obvious faults his heart was sound.

We have to try to be true to ourselves, otherwise we are false. When we are false, the outward appearance ceases to be an expression, a revelation of the soul, but instead becomes a shell to hide the soul. Our greatest task is to try to conform our lives with our convictions, and thus to make peace between our inner and outer selves.

In some so-called primitive societies outer beauty is believed to be the result of good inner moral character. This means that if we take care of the inner self, the outer self will take care of itself.

HOMILY 3   **Looking into the mirror**

There is a story about a Jewish man who survived the concentration camps. The night after his liberation, he went to stay in a nearby house. There he found about thirty other survivors gathered in one room. Seeing a mirror on the wall, he went over to it. He was anxious to see what he looked like. But in the same mirror he saw the reflections of some of the other people as well. There were many faces in the mirror. And he couldn't tell which face belonged to him. He had to make faces and gestures, in order to be able to distinguish himself from the group.

And when he did distinguish his own face, he got a terrible shock. Because the person he saw in the mirror was one he had never seen before. He was so changed that the person in the mirror didn't bear any resemblance to the person he had seen before the war. A strange story, but a true one.

Jesus' harshest words were directed, not at sinners, but at religious people such as the Scribes and Pharisees. Right from the beginning of his ministry the latter had dogged him. He had been very patient with them. He had reasoned with them, but to no avail. Eventually he was forced to expose them.

How did he do this? In a manner of speaking, he did it by holding up a mirror in front of them so that for the first time in their lives they might be able to see their true image. It was a image that few of them would have recognised as their own. If they did, they would have got a terrible shock.

The picture Jesus painted of them was not a pretty one. In fact, we are filled with loathing when we contemplate their religious pomp and show, together with the horrible inconsistencies of their lives.

What were the main faults Jesus found in them? They didn't practise what they preached. The made things impossible for ordinary people by multiplying rules, and demanding exact observance of these rules, without offering the slightest help to those who found them burdensome. They sought their own glory, rather than the glory of God. They were full of themselves, and were interested only in themselves. And the most damning thing of all – they lacked charity and compassion in their dealings with others.

Jesus shattered their complacent belief in their own goodness and virtue. He showed them up for what they really were – men bursting with vanity, and full of pride. Everything they did had one aim – to build up the castle of their own supposed goodness and excellence.

Yet the Scribes and Pharisees were not a uniquely evil group of people. They were just human. They could be any group of people any time and anywhere. The picture Jesus painted of them is a mirror into which we too are invited to look. If we do look into it, we will see our own face there, for we have some if not all of their faults.

Do we not sometimes consider ourselves better than others? Do we not lay down the law for others? Do we not demand sacrifices of others which we don't demand of ourselves? Do we not like to be noticed, to be admired, and to take the best seat – if we can get it? A uniform or special dress can be a great help in this regard. Are we too not lacking in charity, compassion, a sense of justice and a spirit of service?

The real tragedy of the Scribes and Pharisees wasn't the fact that they had faults, but that they were blind to their faults. Yet many of them were sincere and pious people. But what good is piety if it doesn't make us more humble, more loving, and more compassionate? Piety is no substitute for goodness.

We don't have to put on an outward show, or pretend to be what we are not. All we have to do is try to be true to what we are – God's sons and daughters.

PRAYER OF THE FAITHFUL

President: Let us pray to the God who is devoted and protective towards us.

Response: Lord, graciously hear us.

Reader(s): For Christians: that they may not be content with the appearance of goodness but seek the real thing. [Pause] Lord, hear us.

For the leaders of the Church: that they may practise in their own lives what they preach to others. [Pause] Lord, hear us.

For all who hold public office: that they may not seek their own glory but to be of service to others. [Pause] Lord, hear us.

For all those who are overburdened, and who have no one to help them. [Pause] Lord, hear us.

For each other: that the practice of our religion may help us to grow in love and compassion. [Pause] Lord, hear us.

For our own special needs. [Longer pause] Lord, hear us.

President: Lord, grant that what we have said with our lips, we may believe with our hearts, and practise with our lives. We make this prayer through Christ our Lord.

REFLECTION   **Being genuine**

A peacock's feathers are very colourful;
they are worn more for show than for warmth.
The Pharisees wore their virtue for show;
they wanted to be seen and praised by others.
They were more concerned with *appearing* good
than with really *being* good.
Today there is great emphasis on appearances.
The image is more important than the reality.
We may deceive others but we cannot deceive God.
But then it would be foolish even to try.
We don't have to put on an outward show,
or pretend to be what we are not.
All we have to do is try to be true
to what we are – God's sons and daughters.
Lord, help us to shun all falsity and pretence,
and to live a life of genuine goodness.
Then our deeds will flow from what we are,
as naturally as good fruit from a good tree.

Thirty-second Sunday of the Year
PARABLE OF THE LAMPS

INTRODUCTION AND CONFITEOR

Every Christian is meant to be lamp-carrier – a bearer of the light of Christ to a darkened world. But like the foolish bridesmaids we read about in today's Gospel, we sometimes allow the precious light of Christ to grow dim, or even to go out altogether. [Pause]

Through a spirit of prayer and watchfulness, Christ will help us to keep his light burning brightly.

Lord Jesus, you call us to keep the lamp of faith burning brightly. Lord, have mercy.

You call us to keep the lamp of hope burning brightly. Christ, have mercy.

You call us to keep the lamp of love burning brightly. Lord, have mercy.

HEADINGS FOR READINGS

First Reading (Wis 6:12-16). This sings the praise of wisdom, which can be found by all those who seek it.

Second Reading (1 Thess 4:13-18). St Paul consoles his converts at Thessalonika who are worried about the fate of their loved ones who have die before the return of the Lord.

Gospel (Mt 25:1-13). A story which urges us to stay awake because we do not know the day nor the hour of the Lord's coming.

SCRIPTURE NOTE

The First Reading eulogises wisdom. We see this wisdom exemplified in the five wise bridesmaids in the Gospel parable.

Whereas Paul expects the second coming of Christ to happen soon, Matthew has accepted that the parousia may be delayed. The point of the parable is this: since the disciples do not know the day nor the hour of the Lord's coming, they must be prepared so that when he comes they can enter his kingdom. To be prepared means to be a doer rather than a mere hearer of the word.

HOMILY 1   **Waiting for the Beloved**

The other night I found myself walking towards the gate of heaven. On the way there I ran into some figures in the dark who were crying. 'Why are you crying?' I asked. 'We're crying because the Lord refused to let us in. He said he didn't know us,' they replied. I arrived at the gate to find it locked. So with some hesitation and no little trepidation I rang the bell, knowing that it was the Lord himself who would answer.

As I stood there waiting, a terrifying question arose in my mind: Will he know me ? Of course he'll know me! Ah, yes, but will he recognise me as a disciple of his? That's the question. And it's one I can't do anything about now. It's too late to change anything. I dreaded the thought that I might find myself excluded, an outsider, alone.

What's he going to look for? I asked myself. Then I thought of the parable of the lamps. He will look for a lamp that is burning brightly. What have I done with my lamp? 'Oh, good, I still have it,' I exclaimed. But when I looked at it I found to my horror that it had gone out.

However, at that moment I woke up to find that it was only a dream. What a relief! It was just a warning that the Lord in his goodness had given me to wake me up, to shake me out of my sloth and carelessness.

Wouldn't it be terrible to arrive at heaven's door, to knock and then to have the Lord come out and say to you, 'I do not know you.' And you find yourself outside alone in the dark, while inside all is light, joy, community, and celebration.

What lamp are we talking about? Essentially it is the lamp of love. Love, in order to be genuine, doesn't have to be extraordinary. What we need is to love without getting tired or cynical.

How does a lamp burn? Through a continuous input of small drops of oil. If the drops of oil cease, the lamp will go out. What are these drops of oil in our lamps? They are the small things of daily life: faithfulness, punctuality, small words of kindness, a thought for others, our way of being silent, of looking, of speaking, and of acting. These are the drops of love that keep our religious life burning like a lively flame.

Jesus shared our life, our loneliness, our anguish, our death. He is not far away from us. He is very close to us. We can touch, serve, and love him every day of our lives. With the oil of prayer and good works we must keep the lamp of faith burning, and he will recognise us. We won't be judged on a momentary lapse, but on our life as a whole.

Since we do not know the day nor the hour of the Lord's coming, we must be prepared so that when he comes they can enter his kingdom. To be prepared means to be a doer rather than a mere hearer of the word.

All that Jesus says to us in this parable is meant as a warning. This warning is a sign of his love for us. It tells us that every moment should be beautiful. That the soul should always be ready for the coming of the Bridegroom, always waiting for the voice of the Beloved.

HOMILY 2   **The lamp of wisdom**

Wisdom is one of the great themes of the Bible. And it is easy to see why. Without wisdom we are like travellers in the dark. With wisdom we have an unfailing lamp for our steps. But if acquired at all, wisdom is acquired slowly and often painfully. To meet someone who has gleaned wisdom along the path of life is a great joy, a great encouragement, and a great inspiration.

Michael is a prisoner in his mid forties. He is serving a sentence for a very serious crime. (He killed his wife.) Though he looks serious, he is by no means dour or downcast. He is a reflective, intelligent man. He has already served eight years, and is hoping to be released in three or four years time.

Once he was asked, 'If on your arrival in prison, someone had offered you a drug that would have put you to sleep for the entire duration of your sentence, would you have taken it?'

'I certainly would,' he replied. 'Not only that, I'd have asked for a double dose to make absolutely sure that I didn't wake up. But I wouldn't take it now.'

'Why not?'

'Because I've learned a lot about myself inside here. And I've changed too. I'm now a humbler and I hope a wiser man.'

One can see why initially he would have taken the drug. He was embarrassed and ashamed at what he had done and wanted the ground to swallow him. But now he realised that to take the drug would have been to waste the whole experience. Like the foolish bridesmaids, he would have slept his life away. Sleep would have shortened his sentence and made it easier to bear. But he realised it was not something to be skimmed over lightly and painlessly. It had to be lived out slowly and deliberately, step by step, day by day.

It helped that Michael was a believer who attended church regularly. During all those dark years he never lost faith in God. He said, 'Without that faith I would have lost hope, and without hope I would have given up.'

Many prisoners squander their years in prison. They come out worse not better than they went in. There is no awareness, no reflection in their lives. Therefore, they learn nothing as they go along. By the grace of God, Michael had acquired wisdom. Even a little wisdom can save us a lot of worrying and fretting.

Wisdom is the highest virtue. Through wisdom God communicates to us the meaning of life, and the grandeur of our destiny, which is to be with God, a greater good than life itself. Unlike knowledge, which is acquired through hard work, wisdom is a gift of God and is found by those who desire and seek it.

In Christ's story we are not talking about a momentary lapse of memory on the part of the foolish bridesmaids – forgetting to bring along extra oil for their lamps. What we are dealing with are two contrasting attitudes towards the wedding feast. For the wise maids it was the chance of a lifetime, a never-to-be-repeated opportunity to meet the Bridegroom. For the foolish ones it was more like a bit of fun, a bit of a lark.

We can understand a prisoner wanting to sleep his life away, but not the bridesmaids waiting for the Bridegroom to come so that they could accompany him to the wedding feast. Since they didn't know exactly when he would come, they had to wait in readiness. Yet five of them couldn't do that and found themselves locked outside.

We are like those waiting bridesmaids. We are not dealing with a once-off wedding feast. We are dealing with something infinitely more precious – entrance into the Kingdom of heaven. As a beacon guides a ship to port, this vision should guide our way on earth.

HOMILY 3   **A hopeful grieving**

While the Gospel is talking about rejoicing, the Second Reading is talking about grieving. Both are part of life and can be very close to each other. Today I may be attending a wedding, tomorrow a funeral.

The early Christians believed that Jesus would return soon and take them all to heaven. This made it difficult for them to accept the death of some of their members before Jesus returned in glory. In the Second Reading we heard Paul reassuring the Thessalonians. He tells them that as surely as God raised Jesus from the dead, Jesus will raise those who have died, and present them to God in the final showing of his Kingdom.

But meanwhile they are grieving. What should be their attitude to grief? He didn't tell the Thessalonians that they should not grieve. What he said to them was: 'Do not grieve like those who have no hope.' Grief is not an easy thing to handle. You still find people who directly or indirectly discourage it.

Vincent had recently lost his wife, and was now living on his own. He was still in the early stages of a very deep grief. Her death left not only a great void in his life, but a great silence too.

To their credit, his grown children visited him regularly. However, they made sure not to bring up the one subject he desperately wanted and needed to talk about, namely, the death of his wife. They said they didn't want to upset him. So they acted as if nothing had happened, and expected him to do the same. Even though they meant well, they were not helping him. He had to do his grief-work. That grief was all the greater for not being shared.

Grief follows the loss of a loved one as surely and naturally as night follows day. Grief is one of the strongest emotions we will ever experience. Many people have a problem about expressing grief, and may try to suppress it. To suppress grief is dangerous, and can result in serious emotional problems.

To live fruitfully after the death of a loved one, people need to go through a period of mourning. The way to deal with grief is not to run away from it, or pretend it isn't there, but to face it and work through it with as much honesty and courage as one can.

Those who do this will emerge enriched as persons. Grief has a great purgative value. God cannot fill the soul until it is emptied of trivial concerns. And a great grief is a tremendous bonfire in which all the trash of life is consumed.

Faith should not be used as a barrier against grief. Sometimes people say about someone who does not grieve, 'What great faith he (she) has!' But even Christ grieved. To grieve over the loss of a loved one is a good and necessary thing.

While faith doesn't do away with the necessity of grieving, it is a wonderful comfort and support at a time of death. Paul says, 'We believe that Jesus Christ died and rose again, and that it will be the same for those who have died in Christ … Comfort one another with these thoughts.' Faith doesn't dispense us from grieving. What it does do is enable us to grieve with hope.

There's no escaping the work of grief, and there can be no economising in that work. If we suppress it now it will burst out later, when there's another death to mourn or another anniversary.

We mustn't be afraid to cry, to let ourselves go. It's part of the healing. We have tears in our eyes but hope in our hearts. If we do the work of grief, we will wake up one morning, liberated and full of energy for life.

The wedding feast to which Jesus invites us will be all the more joyful for those who have walked through the dark valley of grief, and emerged with the lamp of love still burning brightly.

A STORY

The Kingdom of Heaven is like ten young people who wanted to hear a very popular pop group that was due to arrived in town. Five of them were foolish and five were wise. When the tickets went on sale the five wise ones queued up all night and duly secured their tickets. But the five foolish ones didn't bother to queue up for them. On the night of the concert they went along nevertheless, thinking that they would be able to buy tickets at the door, or that she would meet someone who would get them in. Alas, when they got there, all the tickets were gone, and they were turned away at the door. They went away with a sad and empty feeling.

Most of us know that feeling. It's not a pleasant feeling. Still, we get over it. Usually what's at stake is not all that important – a football match, or a concert, or some such thing. Life goes on, we survive and soon forget about it.

But in Jesus' story what is at stake is nothing less than our eternal salvation.

PRAYER OF THE FAITHFUL

President: With hope in our hearts we pray for light and wisdom.
Response: Lord, hear our prayer.
Reader(s): For the Church: that through an effective preaching of the Gospel it may provide a lamp of hope for a world darkened by despair. [Pause] We pray to the Lord.

For all political leaders: that they may be watchful and responsible, and so provide a lamp of peace for a world darkened by war. [Pause] We pray to the Lord.

For those who grieve the loss of a loved one: that they may know the comfort of God. [Pause] We pray to the Lord.

For those who have nothing to wait for, nothing to hope for. [Pause] We pray to the Lord.

For this congregation: that through the practice of prayer and good works we may wait in joyful hope for the coming of our Saviour, Jesus Christ. [Pause] We pray to the Lord.

For our own special needs. [Longer pause] We pray to the Lord.

President: God of mercy, you continue to love us even when we live foolishly and forget who we are and where we are going. Help us to grow in wisdom and love, as we travel towards the wedding feast of your Kingdom. We ask this through Christ our Lord.

REFLECTION   **Waiting for his coming**

> The foolish have no oil in their lamps.
> They burn themselves out
> through a life of self-seeking
> and dedication to worldly cares and vanities.
> They do not even think of the Lord,
> much less wait for his coming.
> The wise, on the other hand, have oil in their lamps.
> They are detached from themselves
> and from the cares of the world,
> and are full of charity.
> They are waiting for the Lord,
> and desire nothing else but his coming.
> Let us keep our minds alight with faith,
> our souls alight with hope,
> and our hearts alight with love,
> as we wait in joyful hope
> for the coming of our Saviour, Jesus Christ.

Thirty-third Sunday of the Year
THE RESPONSIBILITY OF TALENT

INTRODUCTION AND CONFITEOR

Of all the people gathered here this morning no two of us are alike. God has given each of us special gifts (talents). If used well, these gifts will enrich our own lives and the lives of others. But which of us can say that we have made full use of the gifts of grace and nature that God has given us? Have we not at times left them unused, or, worse, misused them? [Pause]

So let us confess our sins to God who is generous with his forgiveness. I confess to almighty God …

HEADINGS FOR READINGS

First Reading (Prov 31:10-13.19-20.30-31). By today's standards the woman at the centre of this reading would hardly be called a talented person. Yet she is held up as a model.

Second Reading (1 Thess 5:1-6). Since they don't know exactly when the Lord will return, Paul urges the disciples to be always ready lest they be caught unawares.

Gospel (Mt 25:14-30). The parable of the talents tells us how best to await the Lord's return.

SCRIPTURE NOTE

Paul believed that the second coming of Christ was imminent. Hence, he urges the Thessalonians to be watchful. However, Matthew has accepted that the *parousia* would be delayed. Even so, he too spoke about the necessity of being watchful. In the parable of the talents he spells out what this watchfulness consists in: it consists in carrying out the Lord's instructions to the best of one's God-given ability. The First Reading sets before us the example of a woman who uses her talents to live an industrious and virtuous life.

HOMILY 1   **What have I made of myself?**

Once a re-union took place of the past pupils of a famous school run by a religious order. An elderly priest, who had come back to be present at the reunion, found himself surrounded by a host of former pupils most of whom he hadn't met since they left the school many years previously. It was obvious from the way they flocked to him that he enjoyed great respect among them.

He received them with graciousness. Then, without the slightest prompting from him, they began to pour out their stories. One was an architect who had built a number of public buildings, including two churches. Another was a university professor who had written several learned books. Another was the head of a business company which had branches in over a dozen countries. Another was a highly successful farmer. Another was a monsignor in the Church. Another was the principal of a very prestigious school.

The old priest listened with pleasure to the impressive litany of successes and achievements. There didn't seem to be a single failure or loser among them. If there were any such people among the ranks of his past pupils, it was obvious that they hadn't shown up at the reunion.

As they told their stories he said little, contenting himself with nodding his head and smiling. When they had finished he complimented them on their achievements. Then, looking at them with affection, he said,

'And now, tell me what you have made of yourselves?'

A long silence followed. They were reluctant to talk about themselves. It seems that they were so absorbed in their careers that they had neglected their personal lives. Their energies were so focused on efficiency and success that they didn't have the time to grow emotionally, with the result that in terms of relationships many of them were impoverished.

The painter, Picasso, said, 'It's not what an artist does that matters, but what he is.' Though Picasso's pictures are now worth millions, he wasn't as successful in his personal life. In fact, his personal life was something of a disaster area, especially his relationships with women.

People may have done great things in their public lives but failed in their private lives. Most people who are successful at their careers leave their personal lives a long way behind. Indeed, their successes are often achieved at the expense of their personal lives.

In the Gospel Christ talks about three people who were given different talents. He commends the first two because they used their talents. And he censures the third because he buried his talent.

When Christ talks about talents, we must not think he means a musical talent or a footballing talent. Such talents are important, and all credit to those who possess them, develop them, and use them. But they are outrageously over-valued and over-rewarded in our times. Christ's parable goes a lot deeper. Ultimately the only thing that matters is what we make of ourselves.

However, we are mistaken if we think it is about making something of oneself in a materialistic sense, though this is not ruled out. The woman spoken about in the First Reading could hardly be described as being either successful or famous. Yet she is held up as a model. Why? Because of the kind of person she is … industrious, caring, wise, and virtuous. She possesses something more valuable than wealth or beauty. She possesses a loving heart. She has put her talents at the service of her family, her neighbours, and the poor. Hence, she has the respect of the entire community.

Life is God's gift to us. What we do with life is our gift to God.

HOMILY 2   **Wasted talent**

I don't believe there is any such thing as a born footballer, or writer, or painter. But Paul came very close to being an exception. He was a star footballer. Of course he had to work at it. But everybody agreed that he was a natural. He knew he was better than any of the kids around him.

It came as no surprise when at fifteen he was snapped up by a top professional club. He didn't have long to wait for his big chance. He had only just celebrated his sixteenth birthday when he found himself selected for the first team. He made an immediate impact. Almost overnight he shot from obscurity to fame.

From there on it was one success after another. Within two years he was the club's leading scorer. By now he was also playing for his country. Everywhere football was talked about his name was mentioned. To the fans he was a hero. To the media he was a celebrity.

He revelled in his success. A few years ago he was a poor kid playing in the back streets of a provincial town. Now he was rich and famous. He married a beautiful model, drove a Mercedes, and was the envy of every schoolboy who played football.

However, things soon started to go wrong. There were rumours that he was drinking heavily. The rumours proved to be well founded. His football began to suffer. His personal life began to disintegrate. His wife suddenly left him, claiming that he was selfish and immature.

Sadly, Paul's glittering career came to a premature end. And he was remembered as much for the manner in which he squandered a rare talent as for what he achieved with it.

It is dangerous when a talent springs up overnight. Far better that it should grow up quietly and almost unnoticed, like a seed grows into a tree. When a talent grows up like that, a kind of wholeness results.

Some people who start with great promise fail. Others who start with a little talent succeed. Why is this? Because the qualities that help a person to succeed are less those of talent than of character – faith, patience, readiness to learn, and ability to work hard. Many people are born with great natural ability, but do not have the self-discipline and patience to build on their endowment. Talent is a responsibility, and in some cases it can be as much a burden as a gift.

Talented people can easily become inflated by their talent. They may forget that all talents are gifts from God. We are merely the custodians of those gifts.

Talent is important but character is even more important. Talent is formed in quiet; character in the midst of the world. Of what use is it to develop my talent if I leave myself undeveloped?

HOMILY 3   **The need for self-expression**

A talent has first of all to be discovered and recognised. It has been said that our true birthplace is the place in which we awaken to our gifts and talents. Often it takes an outsider to recognise the talent.

Just as the sun helps to bring to birth the fragrant flowers that lie hidden in the soil of the fields, so there are people who find their fulfilment in helping to unfold the talents God has deposited in others. Perhaps these are the most talented people of all.

The Russian writer, Dostoevsky, was only twenty when he wrote his first book, entitled *Poor Folk*. The foremost critic of the day was a man by the name of Belinsky. When Belinsky read the manuscript of the young Dostoevsky he said, 'You have a brought a terrible truth to our attention. You have a great gift. Take good care of this gift, and then you will become a great writer.'

Dostoevsky was intoxicated by the words of the famous critic. Many years later he wrote, 'That was the happiest moment of my entire life.'

Why was that moment so important for Dostoevsky? Because he was just awakening to his talent as a writer. He was still very unsure of himself, and therefore very vulnerable. Recognition by Belinsky confirmed him in his belief in his own talent. It did more. It launched him on his way. He spent the rest of his life expressing himself through his writings.

One of our greatest needs is the need to express ourselves. Unless we express ourselves we cannot realise or fulfil ourselves. Expression is as necessary for us as leaf and blossom are for a tree. The poet and artist, Kahlil Gibran, put it like this: 'There is a great loneliness in almost everyone – a great hunger to express oneself.' And the painter Van Gogh said, 'Between what I perceive and what I express there is a wall; I have spent my life trying to break down that wall.'

To express oneself is the way to make oneself whole, and therefore holy. How many of us could say that we have developed our full potential as human beings? Of course, there are many ways in which people can express themselves. Nevertheless, a lot of talent goes unexpressed. When this happens, the possessor of the talent is the greatest loser. Some people drift through life, and die having realised only a fraction of their potential.

Expression is the opposite to repression. To repress is to bottle up, to stifle, to smother, to suppress. Repression inevitably gives rise to depression. To express is to articulate, to reveal, to bring out … Expression may involve pain but it ultimately leads to joy.

It is by living that we discover our talents, and it is by using them that they grow. Every talent has to be developed. Sometimes a lot of hard work, discipline, and patience are required if a talent is to bear its full fruit. We see this in the example of the first two servants in Jesus' story.

We see the opposite of it in the case of the third servant. It wasn't the harshness of his master that prevented him from using his talent – that was merely an excuse. Nor was it lack of opportunity. He himself was to blame, through a combination of laziness, cowardice, and selfishness.

Life is God's gift to us. What we do with life is our gift to God.

A STORY

Once upon a time there was a wealthy miser who melted down his hoard of gold into a single lump which he then secretly buried in his garden. Every day he went to look at it, and would spend hours gloating over it.

Then one of his servants discovered his secret, and came by night and stole the gold. When the miser discovered that his treasure had been stolen, he was heart-broken.

But a friend said to him, 'Don't take it so badly. Just put a brick in the hole, and take a look at it every day. You won't be any worse off than before, for even when you had the gold you never used it.'

All of us bury some talent which we refuse to use either for our own benefit of for the benefit of others. And what is buried is of no earthly use to anyone.

PRAYER OF THE FAITHFUL

President: God wants us to use the gifts he has given us so that we may live full lives here and enjoy eternal life hereafter.

Response: Lord, graciously hear us.

Reader(s): For the Church: that it may help its members to develop and use all the talents that God has given them. [Pause] Lord, hear us.

For all leaders: that may allow their subordinates the opportunities to develop their talents. [Pause] Lord, hear us.

For all those who through laziness, carelessness, or simply lack of opportunity, have failed to make use of their talents. [Pause] Lord, hear us.

For each other: that, instead of envying others who are more talented than we are, we may strive to use our own particular talents to the full. [Pause] Lord, hear us.

For God's blessing on our own special needs. [Longer pause] Lord, hear us.

President: Heavenly Father, help us to use well the gifts of grace and nature which you have given us so that one day we may merit to hear those happy words: 'Well done, good and faithful servants'. We ask this through Christ our Lord.

REFLECTION   **The cost of talent**

I have not the fine audacity of men
Who have mastered the pen
Or the purse.
The complexes of many slaves are in my verse.
When I straighten my shoulders to look at the world boldly
I see talent coldly
Damning me to stooped attrition.
Mine was a beggar's mission
To dreams of beauty I should have been born blind.
I should have been content to walk behind
Watching the reflection of God's delight:

A second-hand teller of the story
A second-hand glory.
It was not right
That my mind should have echoed life's overtones
That I should have seen a flower
Petalled in mighty power. (From *The Complete Poems of Patrick Kavanagh,*
   1984, Goldsmith Press)

Thirty-fourth Sunday of the Year
CHRIST THE KING

INTRODUCTION AND CONFITEOR

Today we celebrate the feast of Christ our King. When we think of a king
we think of someone who is very remote from his people and who lords
it over them. But Christ is not like that. He lives among us, and came not
to rule but to serve. The best way to show our loyalty to him is by serving
one another. [Pause]

   Lord Jesus, you say to us: 'Follow me and share with one another'.
Lord, have mercy.

   You say to us: 'Follow me and forgive one another'. Christ, have mercy.

   You say to us: 'Follow me and love one another'. Lord have mercy.

HEADINGS FOR READINGS

   First Reading (Ezek 34:11-12.15-17). God is portrayed, not so much as a
judge of his people, but as someone who cares for them as a good shepherd cares for his sheep.

   Second Reading (1 Cor 15:20-26.28). At the end of time Christ will reign
as universal King, having overcome all hostile forces, including death.

   Gospel (Mt 25:31-46). We don't know exactly how the last judgement
will happen, but they we do know what the followers of Jesus will be judged
on.

SCRIPTURE NOTE

In Matthew's scene of the Last Judgement, Christ is portrayed as a stern
King and Judge. But this image shouldn't be over-emphasised. Ezekiel
(First Reading) has a gentler image – that of a good shepherd who, while
caring for all the sheep in his flock, shows particular care for the weak
and wounded ones. This was the image Christ himself used to describe
his person and his mission. And his followers show that they truly belong to his kingdom by their service of 'the little ones'.

Paul says that at the end of time Christ will triumph over all evil, the last evil being death.

HOMILY 1   **Serving the King**

People's basic material needs have to be taken care of before any kind of higher life is possible. But in many countries these needs have been taken care of. Does this mean then that the words of Christ about feeding the hungry or clothing the naked are no longer relevant? No indeed.

In Mother Teresa's memorable words: 'The worst disease in the world today is the feeling of being unwanted, and the greatest evil is lack of love. What the poor need even more than food, clothes, and shelter, is to be wanted.' Hence, the words of Christ are as relevant today as ever. We might put them as follows.

The King will say to those on his left:

'Depart from me, for I was hungry, not for food but for a smile, and all I got from you was sour looks. I was hungry for a word of encouragement, but all you did was criticise me. I was hungry for a word of appreciation, but you didn't give me so much as a crumb.

'I was thirsty, not for drink, but for a word of recognition, but all you did was nag and give out to me. I was thirsty for a sign of friendship, but you ignored me. I was thirsty for a little companionship, but you never gave me a drop.

'I was a stranger, and you refused to have anything to do with me. I was a child and you forbade your children to play with me because my clothes were dirty. I was a neighbour, and you wouldn't allow me into your club because I wasn't in your class.

'I was naked, not because I lacked clothes, but because I lacked self-worth, and you refused to cover me. I was stripped of self-confidence, and you made me feel the chill wind of disapproval. I was naked from the loss of my good name through a story that wasn't true, and you refused to clothe me with the garment of truth.

'I was sick, not in body, but with doubt and worry, and you never even noticed. I was wounded by failure and disappointment, and you couldn't care less. I was sunk in depression, desperately needing the medicine of hope, and all you did was blame me.

'I was a prisoner, but not behind iron bars. I was a prisoner of nerves, and you shunned me. I was a prisoner of loneliness, and you gave me the cold shoulder. I was a prisoner of guilt, and you could have set me free by forgiving me, but you let me languish there to punish me.

'I was homeless, not for want of a home made of bricks and mortar, but for the want of tenderness and affection, and you left me out in the cold. I was homeless for the want of sympathy and understanding, and you treated me as if I was a block of wood. I was homeless for want of love and acceptance, and you locked me out of your heart.'

Then the King will say to those on his right hand:

'Come, you who have been blessed by my Father. For I was hungry for a smile, and you gave it to me. I was hungry for a word of encouragement, and you praised me. I was hungry for a word of appreciation, and you thanked me.

'I was thirsty for a word of recognition, and you took notice of me. I was thirsty for a sign of friendship, and you wrote me a letter. I was thirsty for a little companionship, and you stopped to chat with me.

'I was a stranger, and you made me feel welcome. I was a young a person from a bad area, and you gave me a job. I was socially inferior to you, but by your acceptance you built me up.

'I was naked for the want of self-esteem, and you covered me with self-worth. I was stripped of self-confidence, and you dressed me in the cloak of confidence. I was naked from the loss of my good name through a story that wasn't true, and you clothed me in the garment of truth.

'I was sick with doubt and worry, and with your cheerful attitude you lightened my burden. I was wounded by failure and disappointment, and by your supportive attitude you healed me. I was in a pit of depression, and by your patient attitude you gave me hope.

'I was a prisoner of nerves, and through your attitude of calm you set me free. I was a prisoner of loneliness, and through your friendship you released me. I was a prisoner of guilt, and through your forgiveness you broke the chains of my guilt.

'I was homeless for want of tenderness and affection, and you embraced me. I was homeless for want of sympathy and understanding, and you listened to me. I was homeless from want of love and acceptance, and you took me into your heart.' (Pause).

There are lots of things we could do if we were more aware and more sensitive. It's not so much a question of giving things, but of giving of ourselves – of our time, our energy, and our love. Thus we will serve Christ and help to build his Kingdom.

In the evening of our lives we will be judged on love.

HOMILY 2   **Messengers of the King**

Oscar Wilde wrote a beautiful story called *The Happy Prince*. During his life on earth the prince had lived a very sheltered life. When he died the people erected a statue of him in the main square of the capital city. The statue was covered all over with leaves of gold. It had two sapphires for eyes, and a large red ruby on the handle of the sword.

One cold evening, a little swallow, on its way south, landed at the base of the statue. As he was resting there, a few drops of water fell on him. He looked up and saw that the Happy Prince was crying.

'Why are you crying?' the swallow asked.

'When I was alive I saw no suffering,' said the Prince. 'But from my perch up here I see that there is a lot of unhappiness in the world. I'd like to help but I can't because my feet are fastened to the pedestal. I need a messenger. Would you be my messenger?'

'But I have to go to Egypt,' the swallow answered.

'Please stay this night with me.'

'Very well, then. What can I do for you?'

'In a room there is a mother tending a sick child. She has no money to pay for a doctor. Take the ruby from my sword and give it to her.'

The swallow removed the ruby with his beak, and bore it away to the woman and she rejoiced. The doctor came and her child recovered. The swallow came back and slept soundly. Next day the prince asked him to stay another night. Then he asked him to take out one of the sapphires, and give it to a little match girl down in the square. She had sold no matches that day and was afraid she would be beaten when she got home. Once again the swallow did as he was asked.

As he was running these errands of mercy, the swallow's own eyes were opened. He saw how much poverty and suffering there was in the city. Then he was glad to stay with the prince and be his messenger. One by one, at the Prince's urging, he stripped off the leaves of gold and gave them away to the poor and the needy.

Finally he arrived back one evening. But by now the statue was bare, having been stripped of all its ornaments. The night was very cold. Next morning the little swallow was found dead at the base of the statue. The prince had given away all his riches, but he could not have done so without his faithful messenger, the little swallow.

Christ, our King, gave himself totally while he lived on earth. Even as he died he was still giving to those who were receptive. And from his lofty perch in heaven he surveys the plight of God's children on earth. But his feet are fastened, his hands tied, and his tongue silent. He needs messengers. He needs us. He has no hands but ours, no feet but ours, no tongue but ours. And it is his riches, not our own, that we are called on to dispense – his love, his forgiveness, his mercy, his good news ...

What is involved is helping in simple things, things which are available to everyone – giving a hungry person something to eat, or a thirsty person something to drink, welcoming a stranger, or visiting someone who is sick or in prison ...

To do things such as these one doesn't have to be either wealthy or talented. All one needs is a warm and willing heart. Every one can do something – yes, even a little 'swallow'.

HOMILY 3 **Lord, if only we knew it was you**

The fact that in Jesus God became human, and lived among us, meant he ran the risk of not being recognised for what he really was. We have no problem recognising Christ in church. But when we meet him out on the streets, where he is sometimes sunk in poverty and sorrow, we are reluctant even to bid him the time of day.

Nelson Mandela was still a young man when he became leader of the banned African National Congress (ANC). At a certain stage in the struggle he was forced to go underground. During that time he used many different disguises. In general he remained as unkempt as possible. He knew that by being so disguised he ran the risk of not being recognised even by his own. And this often happened.

Once he was to attend a meeting in a distant part of Johannesburg. A priest had arranged with friends of his to put him up for the night. However, when Mandela arrived at the house, the elderly lady who answered the doorbell took one look at him and exclaimed, 'We don't want your kind here!' And she shut the door in his face. Later when she found out who it was that she had turned away she was horrified and said to him, 'If only I knew it was you, I'd have given you the best room in the house.' Mandela didn't allow incidents like this to deter him.

Yet, in spite of his many disguises, there were friends who still managed to recognise him. For instance, one day he was posing as a chauffeur in Johannesburg. Wearing a long dust-coat and cap, he was waiting on a corner to be picked up when he saw an African policeman striding deliberately towards him. He looked around to see if he had a place to run, but then the policeman smiled at him, surreptitiously gave him the thumbs-up ANC salute, and was gone. Incidents like this happened many times, and Mandela was reassured to know that he had the loyalty of many Africans.

We could say that Jesus too goes about in many different disguises. How then are his friends to recognise him? It is comparatively easy. He always poses as a person in need – in need either of food, or drink, or lodgings, or welcome, or a visit …

'If only I had known it was you,' said the woman to Mandela. We hear the same words in today's Gospel: 'Lord, if only we had known it was you, we'd never have treated you like that. But we thought it was only some common person who was not worthy of our help.' But Jesus said that his disciples would be judged precisely by their response to such people – the poor, the lowly, the unimportant.

It's easy to be kind to the important – there is or will be a return in some shape or form. But it's quite another matter to be kind to those from whom we can expect nothing in return, perhaps not even thanks.

The uncaring are full of excuses. The genuinely caring on the other hand are almost apologetic about their goodness. 'Lord, when did we see you hungry and feed you … ' They are embarrassed if you praise them. They don't want any big deal made of it. Charity is never so lovely as when one has lost consciousness that one is practising charity.

In the judgement scene, people are condemned, not for sins of commission but for sins of omission. We may think we are good simply because we don't do any harm to anyone. But what about the good we fail to do? The sin of omission is one of the worst sins in the world.

From a Christian point of view, there is only one real failure in life – failure to love. We have to concentrate on doing good, rather than on merely avoiding evil. Let us not wait for big opportunities. Let us avail of the little opportunities that come our way every day – opportunities to be friendly, to be helpful, to be considerate, to be obliging …

Thus we may be spared the ache of loneliness and sadness which good people often experience late in life at the realisation of having left undone what they ought to have done.

OTHER STORIES

1. There was a queue of people outside the gates of heaven. Each person was asked the question: 'Why do you think you should be admitted?'

The first person in the queue, a very religious man, said, 'I studied the Bible every day.' 'Very good,' said the Lord. 'However, we'll have to carry out an investigation to see why you studied the Bible. So please step aside for a moment.'

The second was a very pious woman who said, 'Lord, I said my prayers every day without fail.' 'Very good,' the Lord answered. 'However, we'll have to see if your motives were pure. So step aside for a moment.'

Then an innkeeper approached. He just said, 'Lord, on earth I wasn't a very religious man, but my door was always open to the homeless, and I never refused food to anyone who was hungry.' 'Very good,' said the Lord. 'In your case no investigation is needed. Go right in.'

It has been said that if you do a good deed, but have an ulterior motive, it would be better not to do it at all. The only exception is charity. Even though it is not as good as doing it with a pure motive, it is still a good deed, and benefits the other person, no matter what your motive.

2. In the year 1880 in Paris a rather poorly dressed priest showed up at a presbytery looking for a night's lodgings. He had come all the way from Turin, in Italy, and was trying to raise funds to build a church. The visitor's name was John Bosco, but this meant nothing to the resident priest, so he put him in the attic. Many years later when John Bosco was declared a saint by the Church, the priest said, 'Had I known it was John Bosco, I would not have put him in the attic; I would have given him the best room in the house.'

We never know exactly who it is we are meeting in the person of our neighbour. But this is not important. What is important is that we see in that person a needy human being, and that we do our best to meet his need. For those with faith, behind the face, no matter how strange, the face of Christ lies hidden.

PRAYER OF THE FAITHFUL

President: Let us pray that we may be found worthy to be counted as true followers of Christ the King.

Response: Thy kingdom come.

Reader(s): For Christians: that they may give an example to the world of loving service to the poor. [Pause] We pray to the Lord.

For our government leaders: that they may work for a fair distribution of the wealth of the country. [Pause] We pray to the Lord.

For the members of the Society of St Vincent de Paul and all those who work for the poor: that they may take courage from the words of Christ. [Pause] We pray to the Lord.

For all gathered here: that the words of Jesus, 'Whatever you do to the least of my brothers and sisters you do to me', may influence our dealings with others. [Pause] We pray to the Lord.

For our own special needs. [Longer pause] We pray to the Lord.

President: God of love and mercy, your Son so loved the world that he gave his life for us. May we have the courage to practise that same love. We ask this through Christ our Lord.

REFLECTION   **The greatest evil in the world**

Mother Teresa said:
'Many today are starving for ordinary bread.
But there is another kind of hunger –
the hunger to be wanted, to be loved, to be recognised.
Nakedness too is not just the want of clothes,
but also about loss of dignity, purity, and self-respect.
And homelessness is not just want of a house;
there is the homelessness of being rejected,
of being unwanted in a throwaway society.
The biggest disease in the world today
is the feeling of being unwanted and uncared for.
The greatest evil in the world is lack of love,
the terrible indifference towards one's neighbour.'
Lord, warm our cold hearts with your grace,
so that we your disciples may produce the fruits of love.

SOLEMNITIES

'A Saint and His World'

St Patrick and Croagh Patrick

PATRICK PYE

17 March: Saint Patrick

Today we think of the great gift St Patrick brought to Ireland – the Good News of the Gospel. He left behind him a document called his *Confession*. From this we draw inspiration to live the faith Patrick brought us.

We see his humility when he says: 'I was like a stone lying in the mud, but God, in his mercy, pulled me out and placed me at the very top of the wall.'

We see his faith when he says: 'My faith grew stronger, and in the course of a single day I would say as many as a hundred prayers.'

We see too how he had to endure sacrifices for he tells us: 'In preaching the Gospel to the Irish, I endured many persecutions.'

Lord Jesus, you help us to walk in humility. Lord, have mercy.

You help us to nourish our faith with daily prayer. Christ, have mercy.

You help us to make sacrifices in living the Gospel. Lord, have mercy.

HEADINGS FOR READINGS

First Reading (Jer 1:4-9). This tells of the call of the prophet Jeremiah. Patrick had a lot in common with Jeremiah.

Second Reading (Acts 13:46-49). Paul decides to preach the Gospel to the Gentiles who receive it with enthusiasm. Patrick's preaching to the Irish met with a similar reception.

Gospel (Lk 10:1-12.17-20). The sending out of missionaries to preach the Gospel has its origin in Christ's sending out of his disciples to preach the Gospel to their contemporaries.

HOMILY

This homily is a brief commentary on the scripture readings for the feast of St Patrick, and points to their relevance for us.

First Reading: Jeremiah had a very strong sense of vocation and received that vocation at a young age. He protested his unworthiness and inadequacy for the work to which God was calling him. He lived out his vocation during a time of great turmoil, which saw the defeat of Israel and the destruction of Jerusalem and the Temple. He lived with constant threats to his life. Yet, in spite of everything, he remained faithful to his calling. What enabled him to remain faithful was the conviction that God was with him: 'Do not be afraid of them, for I am with you to protect you.'

St Patrick had much in common with Jeremiah. Like Jeremiah he had a strong sense of vocation and received that vocation at a young age. He too had a sense of unworthiness and inadequacy. In living out his vocation he had to face much opposition and numerous dangers. And he knew where his strength came from. In his *Confession* he says, 'I give thanks to God, who kept me faithful.'

Patrick's life of struggle and fidelity is a source of courage and inspiration to us. The Church (in Ireland) has been going through difficult times. It's not easy to remain faithful. St Patrick shows us where our strength lies – it lies in God, whose help comes to us especially through prayer and the sacraments.

Second Reading: This highlights a radical new departure for the early Christian missionaries – the decision to reach out to the Gentiles. Up to that the Christian movement was almost wholly Jewish. The Gentiles embraced the Gospel with joy and gratitude.

Patrick's decision to preach the Gospel to the Irish shows a similar boldness and courage. And the joy and gratitude with which the Gentiles received the preaching of Paul and Barnabas is seen again in the reception given by the Irish to the preaching of Patrick.

The Gospel is not a burden. It is a source of liberation and joy. Joy is one of the great signs of the presence of God. We cannot truly live without joy, without celebration. This is one of the things religion can give: the gift of delight in existence. Such delight is a source of immense energy.

Gospel: Jesus sent the disciples out. Christianity is never something to be kept to ourselves. It always involves an out-reach to others. This was only a temporary mission, limited to the surrounding Jewish towns and villages. The final commissioning, in which they were sent to the whole world, was still in the future.

The missionaries' main task was to preach the message. But they had to expect that some would refuse it. If their preaching was rejected they were to react only with a symbolic gesture – shaking the dust from their feet. Its purpose was to make the people think again about what was being offered them and the consequences of their refusal.

Patrick's mission to Ireland was an extension of the mission Christ gave to his apostles. And, right from the earliest times, the Irish have always sought to spread the Gospel they received. Thousands of missionaries have gone out from this small country to all parts of the world.

The Gospel still needs to be preached, and it needs those who accept it. It's a great challenge to us all to be active, not passive followers, not only to be receivers but also to be givers.

As Christians we have a positive role to play in the world. We have something to offer, something the world desperately needs, even though it may not always welcome it. We should not be shy or apologetic about our role. A certain boldness and courage are called for.

There is a religion of devotion, and a religion of commitment. A religion of devotion is a religion of comfort, and is often centred on self rather than on others. A religion of commitment is a religion of challenge, of risk, of unselfishness. A good life is a strong and effective witness, and in itself is a proclamation of the Gospel.

PRAYER OF THE FAITHFUL

President: With St Patrick to intercede for us, let us pray to God for our own needs, the needs of our country and of the Church.

Response: Lord, graciously hear us.

Reader(s): For all Christians: that the faith they profess with their lips may bear fruit in their lives. [Pause] Lord, hear us.

For our civil, political and religious leaders: that they may lead by word and example. [Pause] Lord, hear us.

For a true and last peace in our country. [Pause] Lord, hear us.

For the spiritual and temporal well-being of our exiles who are scattered all over the world. [Pause] Lord, hear us.

For our missionaries and aid-workers: that God may sustain them in their generosity. [Pause] Lord, hear us.

For ourselves: that we may realise the great treasure we have in the Christian faith and experience joy in living it. [Pause] Lord, hear us.

For all those who passed on the faith to us, often at great cost, and who are now deceased: that God may reward their faithfulness. [Pause] Lord, hear us.

President; May the power of God preserve us; the wisdom of God instruct us; the hand of God protect us; the way of God direct us; and the shield of God defend us. We ask this through Christ our Lord.

REFLECTION   **A simple life but close to God**

It is a simple life we lived here,
but nobody could say that it was comfortable.
I was often in the grip of sorrow,
but when the need was greatest,
God would lay his merciful eye on me,
and the clouds of sorrow would be gone without a trace.
There are people who think this island is a lonely place,
but the peace of God is here.
We helped each other,
and lived in the shelter of each other.
But now my life is spent like a candle,
and my hope is rising every day
that I'll be called into the eternal kingdom.

May God guide me on this long road
I have not travelled before.
I think that everything is folly except for loving God.

> (Peig Sayers, reflecting on her life on the Great Blasket Island, from
> *An Old Woman Remembers*, translated by Seamus Ennis, Oxford University Press)

---

15 August: The Assumption of Mary
THE GLORIFICATION OF MARY

INTRODUCTION AND CONFITEOR

Today we celebrate the glorification of Mary. She who shared intimately in the joyful and sorrowful mysteries of Jesus' earthly life, now shares his glory in heaven. We too are called to share in the glory of Jesus. Mary, our mother, will help us in moments of discouragement and failure. [Pause]

Let us confess our sins to God, asking Mary and all the saints to intercede for us.

I confess to almighty God …

HEADINGS FOR READINGS

Vigil Mass
First Reading (1 Chron 15:3-4.15-16; 16:1-2). This shows the reverence with which the ark of the Old Testament was regarded. Mary is seen as the ark of the New Covenant.

Second Reading (1 Cor 15:54-57). This celebrates Christ's victory over death, a victory in which Mary shares fully.

Gospel (Lk 11:27-28). Mary is blessed not only because she is the mother of Jesus, but also because she heard the word of God and obeyed it.

Day Mass
First Reading (Rev 11:19;12:1-6.10). This describes the battle between God and Satan, with the ultimate triumph of God. Mary and her Child were at the heart of that battle.

Second Reading (1 Cor 15:20-26). Christ is the new Adam who undoes the harm done by the old Adam. (The Church sees Mary as the new Eve who by her obedience to God undoes the harm done by the old Eve.)

Gospel (Lk 1:39-56). This tells of Mary's visit to Elizabeth, and contains her hymn of praise to God for his goodness to her and to his chosen people.

HOMILY 1   **Homily for vigil Mass**

This homily is based directly on the vigil readings. It shows why these particular readings were chosen for this feast, and the relevance they have for our lives.

First Reading: It's hard to exaggerate the importance of the ark for the Israelites. Built according to divine instructions, it contained among other things the two tablets on which were written the Ten Commandments. Carried around from place to place, it was seen as assuring God's presence with his people. It was carried before them into battle, and led them as they crossed over the Jordan into the Promised Land. When David established Jerusalem as the political capital of the united tribes, he built a tent for it there. Note the joy the ark causes, and the respect and reverence with which the people treat it.

Mary is called the 'Ark of the New Covenant' because she bore within her, not words etched in stone, but the Living Word of God – Jesus. Through her the Lord not only came among us, but actually became one of us.

We also should have a sense of the presence of God with us and within us. St Paul says, 'Your bodies are temples of the Holy Spirit.' This should be a cause of great joy for us.

Second Reading: In this short but powerful text Paul celebrates Christ's victory over death. Like a snake that has lost its venom, death has lost its sting and cannot destroy us. It is sin that gives death its sting, because sin can cause eternal death. But Christ has defeated the power of sin, and so has taken the sting out of death.

It is a most appropriate text for this feast. Through his resurrection Christ overcame death, not just for himself, but for all of us. Mary is the first one to share in Christ's victory. And she shares in it fully, that is, body and soul. We too hope to share in Christ's victory, but later. And to share in it in body and in soul.

Gospel: You often hear it said, 'It's not what you are, but who you are in this world that matters'. In other words, what matters is to have the right connections. This is more or less what the woman in the crowd was saying to Mary. But Jesus turned it around. He said that Mary was blessed, not simply because she was his mother, but because she heard the word of God and did it. Which means she was doubly blessed.

And we will be blessed too if, like Mary, we hear the word of God and do it. Mary will help us to hear God's word and to do it. Then we will have a spiritual kinship with Jesus, which is closer and more important than a blood relationship.

HOMILY 2   **Sharing his glory**

Just as on the feast of the Ascension we celebrate the crowing of Jesus, so on the feast of the Assumption we celebrate the crowning of Mary, his mother. We owe our salvation to Jesus, but (under God) we owe Jesus to Mary.

A story is told how once the Comache Indians were praying for rain: 'O great Spirit, tell us what we have done wrong that has made you angry with us. Tell us what we must do so that you will send rain once more and restore life to our land.' They prayed thus for three days but no rain came. The children and the old people began to die.

Then the elders of the tribe went into the hills to listen to the wind which carried the voice of God. When they returned, they said to the people: 'The drought has been caused by the our selfishness. For years we have taken from the earth but given nothing back. We must all make a burnt offering to God of our most valued possession. We must scatter the ashes over the land. Then the rain will come, and life will return to the earth.'

The people thanked God for the message. But when they went home and looked at their most valued possession they hesitated, and began to make excuses. Instead of sacrificing their most valued possession they sacrificed something else in its place.

Now there was a little girl called Miriam who had a blue warrior doll which she treasured above everything else. Since she was the last child left alive, she realised that a sacrifice was being asked of her too. So one night she crept out of the camp. Taking the doll with her together with a lighted stick, she made her way to the top of the hill.

There she set fire to the doll. With tears in her eyes she watched it turn into ashes. Then she gathered the ashes into her hand and threw them into the air so that the wind scattered them over the land. Then she fell asleep right there on the hilltop.

When she awoke next morning, she looked out over the land. As far as she could see, the ground was covered with blue flowers. The people were delighted when they saw what had happened. They got the message at once. Feeling ashamed at their selfishness, each got out the treasure they had been guarding so carefully, sacrificed it, and scattered the ashes over the land. Once again they began to pray to God, and this time God answered. Soon a gentle rain started to fall. On seeing it, they embraced little Miriam who had shamed them into doing what God had asked of them.

This little story helps us to understand the role of Mary, and to appreciate why the Church honours her on this day. It was through the sacrifice of her Son, that God's forgiveness, peace, and love rained down on our earth and brought life to us. Mary played a vital role in that sacrifice.

She consented to bring him into the world. She loved him tenderly and valued him above every other possession. But when the salvation of her people demanded that he be sacrificed, she stayed at his side, even though sorrow pierced her heart like a sharp sword.

Today we honour her crowning in heaven, which means that she shares the fullness of Christ's glory. It is a day for joy and celebration. She will shame us into being more generous in following her Son, and in sacrificing what we hold dear so as to bring life to others.

Mary is blessed because she is the mother of Jesus. But she is more blessed still because, like little Miriam, she heard the word of God and obeyed it. She will help us to obey that word too, and so follow Jesus along the road that leads to glory.

HOMILY 3   **True self-esteem**

Elizabeth said to Mary, 'Of all women you are the most blessed.' Great praise indeed. It might have gone to Mary's head. But what happened? She denied it? No, not at all. She accepted it graciously, but attributed everything to God and his goodness to her: 'My soul proclaims the greatness of the Lord … the Almighty has done great things for me.'

We may have been taught that humility involves self-depreciation. Humility is the opposite to that. It is the grateful recognition of our goodness, but acknowledging that this goodness is a gift from God.

Today in psychology and in therapy great emphasis is placed on self-esteem. The unhappiest state of all is to have low self-esteem. And the happiest state of all is to have high self-esteem. The important thing, we are told, is to feel good about ourselves, to like ourselves, to be able to say 'I'm okay.'

This approach is good – up to a point. Self-esteem is a good thing. It is important to have a good self-image, but this self-image must be founded on truth, otherwise we are building on sand.

We have every reason to have high self-esteem. Each of us can say: 'I have a great worth, a great dignity. God made me in his own image, and he sustains and loves me as his child.' Therefore, we have every right to feel good about ourselves. But, like Mary we know that we owe everything to God. Therefore we shouldn't hesitate to make our own Mary's beautiful and joyful prayer: 'My soul proclaims the greatness of the Lord … the Almighty has done great things for me.'

However, this is not the whole truth about us. We also have a dark side which makes us prone to evil, and from which we need to be saved. Psychology won't save us. Often it won't even admit that we need to be saved. Only God can save us. We mustn't be afraid to look at the dark side of ourselves.

False self-esteem makes us preoccupied with ourselves, and therefore makes us self-centred. True self-esteem, on the other hand, helps us to forget ourselves, and makes us more loving, more capable of reaching out to others. We see this realised in Mary.

After hearing the wonderful words of praise from Elizabeth, she might have gone back home immediately and basked in the sunshine of self-approval, expecting others to wait on her. Instead she stayed on with her aged relative for three months to help her through her pregnancy.

Today we celebrate the glorification of Mary. Since she shared the life, passion, and death of Jesus on earth, it is fitting that she should share his glory in heaven. But we mustn't think that everything was easy for her. The opposite would be nearer the truth. She too had to live her life in the darkness of faith. For her there were no short-cuts. She had not only to hear the word of God but to do it.

We are called to share in the glory of Jesus. Mary, who is our spiritual mother, will help us in moments of discouragement and failure. Just because she is in heaven doesn't mean that she can't help us on earth. It is precisely because of where she is now, with God, that she can help us.

PRAYER OF THE FAITHFUL

President: Let us pray to the God who comes to the help of his people and who is mindful of his promise of mercy.

Response: Lord, hear our prayer.

Reader(s): For Christians: that Mary may inspire in them a greater generosity in following Christ. [Pause] Let us pray to the Lord.

For all the human family: that all of God's children may share in the fruits of Christ's redemption. [Pause] Let us pray to the Lord.

For government leaders: that they may work to narrow the gap between rich and poor. [Pause] Let us pray to the Lord.

For all those who are poor, humble, and lowly: that God may give them a sense of their great dignity as his children. [Pause] Let us pray to the Lord.

For all gathered here: that we may learn from Mary how to serve others with a generous heart and a joyful spirit. [Pause] Let us pray to the Lord.

For our own needs. [Longer pause] Let us pray to the Lord.

President: God of goodness and love, in offering you these petitions, we pray that your mercy may reach from age to age as you come to the help of your people. We ask this through Christ our Lord.

REFLECTION   **Singing God's praises**

Mary was a humble person.
Humble people care nothing for acclaim.

They receive praise and honour the way a clean window
receives the light of the sun.
The brighter and more intense the light is,
the less you see of the glass.
It retains nothing of the light for itself
but lets it all shine through.
Mary attributed everything to God:
'The Almighty has done great things for me;
holy is his name.'
Mary will help us to be humble,
open and trusting before God.
Then God will enrich us,
and we too will sing his praises.

---

1 November: All Saints

INTRODUCTION AND CONFITEOR

What great prophets have said may be forgotten, but what heroes and saints have done is still remembered. Today we honour all the saints, but especially the unknown and unrecognised ones. Saintly people remind us that we too are called to holiness. As does this lovely feast. [Pause]

Lord, you make us holy by helping us to be gentle and merciful in our dealings with others. Lord, have mercy.

Lord, you make us holy by helping us to be pure of heart and makers of peace. Christ, have mercy.

Lord, you make us holy by awakening within us a hunger for what is good and true and right. Lord, have mercy.

HEADINGS FOR READINGS

First Reading (Rev 7:2-4.9-14). Here we have a vision of the victorious followers of Christ rejoicing in his presence in the heavenly Kingdom.

Second Reading (1 Jn 3:1-3). In his love for us, God has made us his children, and destined us one day to see him as he is. We should live a life that is consistent with this great hope.

Gospel (Mt 5:1-12). Jesus talks about the qualities he wishes to see in his disciples, qualities that are exemplified in the lives of the saints.

HOMILY 1   **Trail blazers**

To visit the great national parks of America is an unforgettable experience. But to explore one of them is better still. There you will find carefully laid out trails for hikers and walkers. On those trails you will find lots of markers. In difficult uphill or downhill parts you will find steps cut out in the rocks. In marshy places you will find stepping-stones laid out. And in dangerous parts you will see warning signs posted.

Thanks to these well-made and well-worn trails, even amateurs can make their way safely through deep forest and rugged mountain terrain. As you travel these trails you marvel at the hard work that went into the making of them. And one thing becomes abundantly clear: without those trails the ordinary hiker would be completely lost.

The saints have done something similar for us. They have laid out paths for us. They have put down markers on those paths. They have travelled the way ahead of us, a great host of them. They have shown us what ordinary human beings like us can achieve when they avail of the grace of God. They have set us an example of determination, dedication, and sacrifice.

Christians have always turned to the example of the saints. Some saints went straight to the goal. Others fell, stumbled, blundered, before finally getting it right. But all have expanded the possibilities of human love and courage.

Such examples are not confined to the roll of official saints. All around us (even in our own times) there are men and women whose stories guide and goad us on our journey – people in whom the two great commandments, love of God and love of neighbour, have been joined to an extraordinary degree.

We draw encouragement and inspiration from these men and women who have gone before us and blazed a trail for us. Each one has made the path that bit easier for the rest of us. And when we experience weariness and a sense of failure and futility, it's as if they are saying to us, 'We are with you. Don't give up.'

However, there is a tendency to put the saints on such an exalted pedestal that we feel justified in excusing ourselves from imitating them. In this case devotion to the saints becomes more of a hindrance than a help.

The saints serve as models for us precisely because they were sinners like us. They are reminders to us of what life is about. They inspire us, guide us, encourage us and give us hope. And, of course, they also intercede for us.

But they can't do it in our place. Nor will they provide us with shortcuts and ways of evading the hard slog and the narrow road. We must not expect others to do for us what we cannot discipline ourselves to do. We ourselves have to walk the path. We have to make the journey. The saints help us to dare that journey.

HOMILY 2   **How not to imitate the saints**

Today in popular psychology (and indeed in spirituality) great emphasis is put on finding oneself. This is important but there is something even more important, namely, being oneself, or better, becoming oneself. Society is no help. It tells us in so many ways that we can most be ourselves by acting and looking like someone else. *(The two stories which follow make the same point. One of them is enough to use at a time).*

1. Once there was a young man by the name of Simon, who wished to live a holy life. He decided to model himself on Francis of Assisi. He was deadly serious about it. He had only one goal in life – to turn himself into a copy of St Francis.

Years went by. There was no doubt but that outwardly at least he had made progress. His friends jokingly referred to him as a St Francis lookalike. Yet he wasn't happy. In his unhappiness he went to consult a wise old monk by the name of Barnabas. Barnabas listened patiently as Simon poured out his story.

When he had finished Barnabas said, 'You have chosen a good model. An excellent model. But a model is not a mould into which we pour ourselves. A model is a spur to help us to be true to what is within us, to what is given to us and only to us. Simon, you have been living outside yourself. You have been playing a part written for another.

'The most important task in life is to become ourselves. Unless we become ourselves, no growth, no happiness, no holiness is possible. But when we become ourselves, then everything about us becomes real and true. Francis of Assisi became a saint, not by becoming someone else, but by becoming his true and full self.

'Simon, when you come before the Lord on the day of judgement, he won't ask you, "Why didn't you become Francis of Assisi?" He will ask you, "Why didn't you become what Simon was intended to be?"'

2. When the legendary Bill Shankley retired as manager of Liverpool Football Club, Bob Paisley was appointed to succeed him. Realising that it would be a hard act to follow, the soft- spoken, retiring Paisley at first refused the job. Finally, after a lot of persuasion, he agreed to accept it.

It truly was an onerous job to take over from someone who was as successful as Bill Shankley. Liverpool not only prided itself on success on the football field, but on possessing a special approach off it. The manager, the players, the ladies who made the tea – all felt part of a great family. That's how the club was run.

Right from the outset there was enormous pressure on Paisley to be another Bill Shankley. But he resisted the temptation. Instead, he brought his own style to the job. He managed to continue the traditions of the club, while remaining the unique individual he was. And he went on to become even more successful than Shankley.

When he retired he was asked what the key to his success was. He replied, 'There is no way you can imitate someone else and be great. You've got to be yourself.' Wise words.

Both Shankley and Paisley were very successful men. And that both achieved greatness is beyond dispute. But achieving greatness as a human being may have little in common with conventional success.

Many religious people are not saints because they never succeed in being themselves. To be a saint one doesn't have to be an ascetic, or even serious and solemn. But one has to be oneself.

Saints help us to do this, even the little ones. They cause the vision of a higher and purer life to rise up before us. They inspire us to try to win back our finer, kinder and healthier selves.

They provide us with a mirror. Looking at them, we see what we could be. In them we see human beings at their brightest and best. They are examples, teachers, friends, and advocates.

Whatever our path in life, what really matters is that we should be ourselves, our unique selves, but the best that we can be – the kind of people God intended us to be. Not to refuse life, or to try to be someone else, but to grow from the seed of life within each of us. This is the journey home.

HOMILY 3   **Being the genuine article**

Anyone who knows anything about the beauty of wood will tell you that tropical woods such as mahogany and teak should never be painted. Tropical woods are beautiful as they are in their natural state. It would be a sin to cover them up with paint or anything else – a total waste of time, effort and money. If anything is added it should serve one purpose and one purpose only – to bring out the natural beauty of the wood.

Yet sometimes one finds them painted, presumably with the aim of making them more attractive. Even when this is done tastefully and imaginatively, harm rather than good is done. The finished object comes across as false, or at least unreal. And while it may be pretty, it is not authentic. Tropical woods are best left as they are. They are far more interesting and impressive in their natural state.

Beautiful wood is God's gift. To paint over it is akin to desecration. The role of the cabinet-maker is to enhance the beauty inherent in the wood, not to obscure it with paint.

There is a tendency to do something similar with the saints. To so polish up the image that their humanity disappears. They cease to be human beings. But if they cease to be human, they become unreal and unbelievable.

The saints didn't become saints by putting on a false or artificial self. The role of spirituality is not to cover-up. Its purpose is to bring out what is inside us. Grace builds on nature. It doesn't destroy nature, but brings it to its fullest development.

Even the little saints cause the vision of a higher and a purer life to rise up before us. They inspire us to try to win back our finer, kinder and healthier selves. They expand the possibilities of human love and courage.

Piety is no substitute for goodness. Perhaps there can be goodness without holiness. But I'm quite sure that there is no holiness without goodness. Since we are made in God's image, all of us have the capacity for goodness. The saints show us how to express this goodness.

Our real goal is not to strive for happiness but for goodness. If we strive for goodness, happiness will follow. There are good people who ache with loneliness and a feeling of sadness for having left undone what they ought to have done. This is the sadness we all feel at times – the sadness of not being saints.

PRAYER OF THE FAITHFUL

President: We seek blessings from the Lord to whom belongs the earth and its fullness, the world and all its peoples.

Response: Lord, hear our prayer.

Reader(s): For the Church: that its members may realise that holiness is the most important thing in life. [Pause] We pray to the Lord.

For our leaders: that the saints may inspire them to be wise and prudent in the exercise of their responsibilities. [Pause] We pray to the Lord.

For all those who are suffering persecution because of their faith in Christ. [Pause] We pray to the Lord.

For each other: that our devotion to the saints may bring us closer to Christ, the model of true holiness. [Pause] We pray to the Lord.

For our own special needs. [Longer pause] We pray to the Lord.

President: Heavenly Father, with the saints to inspire and guide us, may we seek after holiness, and thus live lives that are worthy of our Christian dignity. We ask this through Christ our Lord.

REFLECTION   **Windows**

Saints are like windows.
Through them the light of God's wisdom
streams into the world,
banishing the darkness,
and brightening the road for uncertain travellers.
Through them the warmth of God's love

radiates through the world,
banishing the coldness,
and warming the hearts
of even the most forlorn of his creatures.
And through them we catch a glimpse of another world,
a world that lies not just beyond the walls of our earthly home,
but even beyond the stars.

8 December: The Immaculate Conception

INTRODUCTION AND CONFITEOR

A woman had a dream that she died and came before the judgement seat of God. Holding out her hands she said to God: 'You see, Lord, I've done nothing wrong. My hands are clean.' And God said: 'Yes, but they are empty.'

Mary's greatness does not consist in the fact that she did no wrong, but rather in the fact that she said 'yes' to God. The Christian is not content with avoiding sin but is intent on doing good. [Pause]

Let us now confess our sins of commission and omission.

I confess to almighty God ...

HEADINGS FOR READINGS

First Reading (Gen 3:9-15.20). This deals with the origin and consequences of sin, and with God's promise of salvation.

Second Reading (Eph 1:3-6.11-12). Through Christ, God has adopted us as his children, and called us to holiness.

Gospel (Lk 1:26-38). In the story of the Annunciation, we see Mary's obedience to God, which opens the way for the coming of the Saviour.

HOMILY 1   **Reflecting on the readings**

This homily is based directly on the readings. It shows why these particular readings were chosen for this feast, and the relevance they have for our lives.

First Reading: This tells part of story of the fall of Adam and Eve, a story which deals with the origin and consequences of sin. God gave Adam and Eve the freedom to choose good or evil, to obey or disobey. But they chose evil. To choose evil is to abuse freedom. Sin consists in disobedience to God.

Their sin had very serious consequences. First of all, it damaged their relationship with God. Before their sin they enjoyed a beautiful closeness to God. We have the image of them walking with God in the cool of the evening. But after their sin, that closeness is no more. Now they are trying to hide from God. Sin damages our relationship with God.

Then they damaged their relationship with one another. Before their sin they enjoyed harmony with one another. After it a breakdown occurs between them, and they start to blame one another for what happened. Sin damages our relationships too.

All of this came as a result of their sin, and as a punishment for it. But it wasn't God who punished them. They brought it on themselves. It is not God who changed but they. We are not punished *for* our sins, but *by* our sins.

And like children who have done wrong, Adam and Eve tried to hide rather than face the consequences of what they had done. But God came looking for them and confronted them about it. He did this out of love for them. God confronts us too when we do wrong through the still, small voice of conscience, or through the voice of others.

But the story has a hopeful ending because it includes a promise of salvation. And this is the main reason why this reading is used on this feast.

Second Reading: This reminds us that God, in his graciousness, has an eternal plan of salvation for humankind. Through Christ, God has adopted us as his children, and called us to holiness.

Gospel: This shows that God's promise of salvation was fulfilled in Jesus. And Mary had a vital part to play in that. By her 'yes' to God, she opened the way for the God's Saviour to come into the world.

Christ is the new Adam. Unlike the first Adam, he obeyed God and conquered Satan. Through his death and resurrection he undid the first Adam's sin and its evil effects. In the Immaculate Conception, he conquered sin first of all in his own mother.

And Mary is the new Eve. With her perfect obedience, she cancelled out the disobedience of the first Eve, when she said, 'Let it be done to me according to your word.' In this way she became a model for believers. She is the 'handmaid of the Lord'. This is how she is portrayed in the Gospel.

In Christ we have become God's adopted children. As his children we are called to holiness. All holiness comes through Christ.

Mary attained holiness by obedience to God. She keeps the vocation of holiness before us, and serves as a model for us. She is blessed, not simply because she was the mother of Jesus, but because she heard the word of God and did it.

And we will be blessed too if, like Mary, we hear the word of God and do it. Mary will help us to do this. Then we too will be responding to the call of holiness.

HOMILY 2   **Mary's true greatness**

When we say that Mary was conceived without sin, we are not saying something negative about Mary, but something very positive. An illustration may help.

Snow-white and Lily-white were two spotless sheets of art paper. One day as they stood admiring each other's whiteness they saw an artist approaching, carrying a palette, paints, and brushes. Should they or shouldn't they allow him to touch them?

Snow-white : No way is he going to touch me. I don't trust him. Look at those rough brushes, and all those evil-smelling paints he has! No, this art business is not for me. I was created pure, and that's the way I'll remain. I would rather be burnt and reduced to white ashes than allow any stain to touch me or darkness to spoil me.

Lily-white: But what if he's a really good artist? In that case you could become something beautiful.

Snow-white : What do you mean? I'm already beautiful.

Lily-white: But if he painted something on you, you might turn into a masterpiece. Then you would become very valuable, and millions would come to see and admire you.

Snow-white : Ah yes, but suppose he's no good, then I'd be ruined. And then you know what would happen to me? I'd be thrown into a refuse bin with all the other junk. Even if he does know how to paint, who can say that he will paint something good on me? What if he were to paint something evil? Then I'd be the bearer of ugliness, and people would despise and hate me. I'll have nothing to do with him. It's too big a risk.

Lily-white: But if you remain as you are people won't find anything to admire in you. Surely even a poor painting would be preferable to being as you are now – empty.

Snow-white : I still say it's too risky. I'd rather preserve my purity. My name is Snow-white . Snow-white is what I am, and that is what I will remain.

Lily-white: Well, I intend to take the risk. I'm going to say 'yes' to the artist.

It proved to be a risk well worth taking for Lily-white. The artist knew his job, and painted a picture of stunning beauty on her. As for Snow-white , she stayed just as she was – spotlessly clean, but quite empty.

There is a tendency to see Mary in the role of Snow-white . But this is a mistake. She is more like Lily-white. She entrusted herself to the paint and brushes of the Supreme Artist, God, who in her and through her, produced his masterpiece – Jesus Christ.

Mary of course was not a passive sheet of paper in God's hands. She was a free human being. She had first of all to give her consent, then to cooperate actively at every stage. It wasn't easy or free of risks. There were plenty of black smudges and ugly stains (tears, hardship, suffering), which didn't make sense at the time, and which caused her pain and anguish. But then there were also splashes of colour (joy, meaning, hope, love) which brought happiness to her and confirmed her faith.

Even though it took a long time for any clear pattern to emerge, she still continued to confirm the first 'yes' she said to the Artist. In the end it was well worth it, both for her and for us. She became the faithful and loving mother of God's Son. And thanks to her, we have a Saviour and a Brother.

Mary keeps the vocation of holiness before us, and serves as a model for us. She attained holiness by obedience to God. She is blessed, not simply because she was the mother of Jesus, but because she heard the word of God and did it.

HOMILY 3   **Images of Mary**

Many people have a completely unreal image of Mary. It's as if she never got her hands dirty, never made mistakes, never experienced doubt or fear, never had to struggle against evil, and so on. Because of this we find it hard to see how she could serve as a model for us. Donald Nicholl would have included himself in this category until something happened to him.

Donald Nicholl was an English Catholic, and a very good one. He died in 1997. As a lecturer, he spend most of his life in universities. From 1981 to 1985 he was Rector of the Ecumenical Institute at Tantur, near Jerusalem. The experience of being in the Holy Land served as an eye-opener to him in many ways, but one in particular. It changed his image of Mary forever.

In his book, *The Testing of Hearts*, he tells us that prior to going to the Holy Land his image of Mary was derived from famous paintings, poems, and music. His image was that of 'some dreamy, ethereal young lady, untouched by human toil'. But after meeting the peasant women of Galilee he formed a very different image of Mary. He says:

> The image which now comes spontaneously to mind is of a woman with strong hands, sinewy through much work; of a face whose skin is rough from exposure to the sun and wind; of feet that are broad-spread through climbing the hills around Nazareth barefoot; but above all, of eyes that are steady, and a mouth that is firm, through enduring the sorrows of the refugee, the poor, and the oppressed.

Mary didn't live a sheltered life. She was a woman of the world, and a strong woman. Strength is not the same as power. One could enjoy great power and yet be very weak. And one might have no power at all and yet be very strong.

Women have a different kind of strength to men. Their strength is less obvious, less showy, and is allied to apparent fragility. It is longer-lasting. It is marked by grit, shrewdness, patience, courage, and steely determination. This kind of strength may often go unnoticed. Indeed, it may even be seen as weakness. But nothing could be further from the truth.

Mary possessed this kind of strength. Like most mothers, she had remarkable powers of endurance and survival, overcame disappointment and distress, was dogged but not insensitive, and seemed always capable of renewing herself, no matter what misfortune hit her.

We honour her sinlessness on this feast. But this must not be seen as something negative. It is something positive. Mary was a loving, caring and compassionate person. That is where her holiness lay. And that is where our holiness must lie too, because we too are called to holiness. There can be no holiness without goodness.

Mary is a model not just for mothers but for all Christians. She understands all those who struggle with the demands of ordinary, decent, human living in a world that sometimes makes little sense. And she understands, and is especially supportive of, those who try to be faithful followers of her Son, Jesus.

PRAYER OF THE FAITHFUL

President: On this feast we honour the greatness of Mary, the Mother of Christ. At the same time we ask God to help us to imitate her holiness.

Response: Lord, hear our prayer.

Reader(s): For all Christians: that they may accept the word of God in faith and obey it as Mary did. [Pause] Let us pray to the Lord.

For the human family: that in spite of all evidence to the contrary, the world may believe that goodness and love are more natural to us than evil and hate. [Pause] Let us pray to the Lord.

For those who find life difficult: that Mary, who endured poverty and hardship, may give them hope. [Pause] Let us pray to the Lord.

For the suffering and the dying: that Mary, who stood at the foot of the cross, may comfort them. [Pause] Let us pray to the Lord.

For those who grieve: that Mary, who endured the burial of her Son, may console them. [Pause] Let us pray to the Lord.

For each other: that no matter what happens to us in life, we may never lose sight of the fact that we are in the hands of a loving and caring God. [Pause] Let us pray to the Lord.

For our own special needs. [Longer pause] Let us pray to the Lord.

President: God our Father, Mary has left us an example to follow. Liv-

ing in a sinful world, she shared the pain of the world but not its wicked-
ness, and so became a worthy mother for your Son, who lives and reigns
with you and the Holy Spirit, one God, for ever and ever.

REFLECTION   **Mary, friend to the poor**

Mary experienced uncertainty and insecurity
when she said 'yes' to the angel.
She knew what oppression was when she couldn't
find a room in which to give birth to Jesus.
She lived as a refugee in a strange land.
She knew the pain of having a child
who does not follow the accepted path.
She knew the loneliness of the widow,
and the agony of seeing her only Son executed.
She is the friend of all the poor
and oppressed women of our times.
She gives hope to those who struggle for justice,
and challenges us all to live a simpler life,
a life of unconditional trust in God.